Complicity in the Third Reich

Ordinary Germans, Perpetrators and Post-War Justice

Other Books by Andrew Elsby

Britain and the World: Case Studies in British Foreign Policy Decision-Making 1939–1968

Chamberlain and Appeasement

The Burghers of Ceylon

Complicity in the Third Reich
Ordinary Germans, Perpetrators
and Post-War Justice

Andrew Elsby

_____cHp_____
CentreHouse Press

CentreHouse Press
centrehousepress.co.uk | borsadellaposta@centrehousepress.co.uk

Cover image Shutterstock / Adolf Martinez Soler

British Library Cataloguing in Publication Data
A catalogue record for this book is available from
the British Library

ISBN 978-1-902086-29-3

CONTENTS

General Introduction

This book is a trilogy of work on German complicity in the objectives and activities of the Nazi regime. It attempts to establish the nature and extent of the complicity of ordinary Germans in all their various roles and to indicate the commonality between the decisive causal influence on their behaviour in the Third Reich and that which informs and has informed human behaviour in all cultures, societies and time periods. The argument presented here is that the primary and decisive influence on the behaviour of ordinary Germans and Nazi perpetrators was pursuit of personal interest to optimise personal material, social and psychological outcomes by conformity to the dictates of the Nazi regime, and that conformity to optimise personal outcomes is the decisive causal influence on all human behaviour, regardless of culture, society and time.

The case is that it was this drive for personal optimisation that informed the reaction of all Germans to the Nazi regime and its totalitarian control, and not underlying long-term cultural characteristics peculiar to the German people or some presumed effectiveness of Nazi ideological propaganda vilifying Jews and portraying them as enemies of the German race and state and associated with an ideological enemy in the form of Bolshevism and partisans in the total war of the eastern front. It is further argued that this human optimisation of personal outcomes is derived from evolutionary natural selection of traits that enhance chances of survival to reproduction age in competitive circumstances of scarcity and natural hierarchies, and that it takes the form either of dominance, possible only for the few, and conformity, the optimal survival strategy for the many.

The case is also that human optimisation of personal outcomes in the Third Reich was achieved in different ways (as in all normal life), with some aspiring to privilege, enhanced status and power over others, and so opportunistic, competitive and exhibiting zeal and slavish orthodoxy, and other people conforming more minimally by doing no more than meeting role requirements at work and otherwise attending to the private sphere in ways that did not take advantage of the misfortune of others, in this case Jews. It is acknowledged that it is impossible to establish how many ordinary Germans exhibited aspiration and opportunism relative to those whose conformity was more minimal and defensive, but both optimised outcomes for people of different personalities and therefore different aspirations to maximise or to preserve status, or to be left alone.

The first book addresses the controversy over the nature and extent of complicity of ordinary Germans. It claims that ordinary Germans were indifferent to what happened to the Jews and conformed either minimally or opportunistically to the dictates of the Nazi regime to avoid repressive state sanctions for non-compliance with such dictates and to optimise perceived personal outcomes. Goldhagen's alternative explanation, that ordinary Germans' complicity is explained by the existence of eliminationist antisemitism in German culture even prior to the accession to power of the Nazis, is rejected on grounds of lack of evidence for it, and there is reference to the context for the reaction of ordinary Germans to the Third Reich in extensive evidence of the prevalence, in fact the ubiquity, of conformity in all cultures and societies, not least the Soviet Union under Stalin. There is consideration of the complicity of German women in the objectives of the Nazi regime and whether or not there was a gender difference in complicity, but the conclusion is that the evidence indicates no difference in primary motive, just in social roles and so in extent of direct involvement in Nazi perpetrator behaviour. The argument here and in the two other books in this trilogy is that the primacy of human optimisation of outcomes does not change and that what differentiates behavioural outcomes is circumstance and context.

The second book considers in some detail the notorious case of Adolf Eichmann, the SS officer responsible for arranging the transportation of Jews to extermination centres, and addresses the perspectives of Arendt, Stangneth and Cesarani in the context of the evidence on Eichmann's behaviour during the war, personality, attitude to superiors and responsibility, and tendency to present an optimal self to audiences. The book attempts to establish the decisive causal influence on Eichmann's perpetrator behaviour and argues that Eichmann was aware of the consequences of his role in transporting Jews to extermination camps, contrary to Arendt's view, and that he was motivated by careerism in his desire for enhanced SS rank and identity and for approbation from superiors and peers in the SS, rather than by ideological eliminationist antisemitism, contrary to the views of Stangneth and Cesarani. The argument is that Eichmann was the sort of personality found in the careerist middle to upper echelons of organisations in the state and private sectors of states in all time periods, someone aspiring and compliant, the ideal functionary.

The third book deals with the issue of post-war justice and addresses its nature, the influences on it, including that of the emerging Cold War, and the influence of modern western liberal humanitarianism on judgements made of the adequacy of post-war justice. The argument is that ordinary Germans in the British, American and French zones of post-war Germany exhibited the same lack of interest in the Jews that had characterised their attitude towards Jews in the war, and a similar exclusive concentration on their own outcomes, an orientation enhanced by the post-war devastation and widespread poverty and deprivation in western Germany, and that there was an appreciation amongst western leaders that a robust West German state was needed to combat the spread of communism that was taking hold all over central and eastern Europe and threatening to do so in France and Italy, both with significant communist parties.

The argument is that the Nuremberg trials initiated by the Americans after the end of the International Military Tribunal that tried the major Nazi war criminals resulted in some convictions but that those sentenced to prison had their sentences reduced under an amnesty that reflected Cold War considerations and the fact that the most reliable German anti-communists would be former Nazis and would be needed to support the new West German state in security, judicial and other positions in the apparatus of an anti-communist state, for under the Nazi regime so many Germans were involved in the Nazi state apparatus given its totalitarian nature, and their administrative experience would have been needed in any West German government.

There is also an argument against Fulbrook's view that, because the great majority of Nazi perpetrators were not even prosecuted, post-war justice was inadequate, for one legitimate question is the extent of human agency and responsibility in a totalitarian society at war and another is the issue of motivation and criminal intent, for the motivation of Nazi perpetrators was to optimise their own outcomes by compliance with the dictates of the state and so similar to the motivation that characterises ordinary people's behaviour in all societies, and the characteristic Nazi perpetrator defence of obedience to orders from the Nazi hierarchy, when set in the experiential context of the Führerprinzip that legitimised any order from Hitler and dictated compliance with it, does seem to have psychological validity.

There is also rejection of the view of Douglas, who claims that it was legitimate that post-war courts should serve as means of disseminating information regarding the extermination of the Jews and of permitting Jewish survivors a forum for recounting their own terrible experiences, for courts cannot serve educative and therapeutic functions and deliver justice for the defendant that would meet the criminal standard of proof beyond all reasonable doubt. The argument here is that modern western liberal humanitarian judgements regarding the nature and adequacy of post-war justice reflect conformity to a narrative of liberal humanitarian consideration for victims and that this narrative disregards the experiential context of Nazi perpetrators and the primary motivation of human behaviour, optimisation of perceived personal outcomes, in all contexts.

The general discussion of post-war justice and the role of the courts and their legitimacy is followed by consideration of a number of specific cases. These begin with the Einsatzgruppen trial of Einsatzgruppen, Einsatzkommando and Sonderkommando commanders whose units murdered Jews in great numbers behind the German lines in the Soviet Union from June 1941. The legitimacy of the justice meted out to Einsatzgruppen, Einsatzkommando and Sonderkommando commanders is addressed and the case for reference to the experiential context of the SS and the war in the east is considered.

The Einsatzgruppen trial was conducted by the US military, but the trial of Rudolf Höss, the commandant of Auschwitz, was in Warsaw, Poland, and the rather different nature of the defendant and his defence is discussed. Höss appears to have had no careerist aspirations but does seem to have had faith in the legitimacy of any order from Himmler, including Himmler's direction to him to become commandant at Auschwitz and to exterminate Jews in great numbers there, evidence that indicates a susceptibility in Höss to leadership figures, a desire to believe in something he did not have to question, and a need for the approbation of Himmler indicated by Höss's meticulous attention to the efficiency of Auschwitz in its extermination of Jews. The case is indicative of the different rewards to different personalities of careers in the Nazi and SS hierarchy.

The individual cases conclude with a discussion of Gitta Sereny's assessments of

Franz Stangl, commandant at the extermination camps at Sobibor and Treblinka, and Albert Speer, the Nazi armaments minister, who devised a devious defence that facilitated his evading the gallows at Nuremberg. The effect of Sereny's western liberal humanitarian perspective, her journalistic, psychoanalytic and impressionistic approach, and her moralising conceit on her appraisals of Stangl and Speer is discussed.

Ordinary Germans

Popular complicity on the part of ordinary Germans in Nazi Germany over the extermination of the Jews – reflective of peculiarly German cultural characteristics or of a universal human attribute of conformity to optimise personal outcomes?

Chapter One
Introduction

The extent of the complicity of the German population as a whole in the genocidal criminality of the Nazi regime has been debated by historians. The Nazi regime did of course engage in perpetrator behaviour in relation to a number of groups in addition to the extermination of the Jews of Europe, including Soviet POWs, whose losses have been estimated to be as many as 2.2 million by February 1942,[1] and those perceived to be Bolsheviks, partisans or Soviet commissars in Operation Barbarossa, the invasion of the Soviet Union in June 1941. And before that there was the systematic destruction of the Polish leadership following the invasion of Poland in September 1939 and the persecution of the Jews and incarceration of nonconformist minority groups and political dissenters such as trade unionists, socialists and communists in Nazi Germany itself. The concentration here shall be on the passive and active complicity of the German public in the activities of the Nazi state in general terms and the Holocaust in particular.

The argument here is that the repressive nature of the Nazi state and its use of concentration camps for political dissenters from very early on in the Nazi period resulted in either passive conformity, that is, the German public's turning away from anything political to exclusive attention to meeting the requirements of role at work and to the private sphere in order to optimise personal outcomes in a context of persecution of Jews, of other minority groups and of dissenters by the Nazi state, or more active complicity to take advantage of the opportunities proffered by the totalitarian state.

The argument is that the reaction of ordinary Germans reflected a human attribute not related to German cultural characteristics or to Nazi ideology, that German complicity resulted from unreflective or deliberate pursuit of personal interest regardless of the cost to other people, an exclusive attention to optimising personal outcomes and relative indifference to the effect on others of doing so. For some ordinary Germans the reaction to the dictates of the Nazi regime was passive or defensive, with minimal compliance to meet role requirements to avoid the formal sanctions of a totalitarian state, whereas others were opportunistic, exceeding the requirements of their roles or engaged in voluntary involvement of some sort with the agents of a totalitarian state in order to maximise positive personal outcomes.

The careerists of the upper echelons of the SS, including the educated Einsatzgruppen leaders and SS functionaries like Eichmann, were in the more opportunistic part of the ordinary German population of the Third Reich in their active conformity to the ideology and objectives of the Nazi state and unquestioning compliance with role requirements regardless of their nature, to optimise their outcomes in terms of career, status and identity as part of an elite. This was dictated by their aspirational nature and the context of a Nazi state characterised by colossal bureaucratisation and its corollary, that a great deal of employment at all levels was for the Nazi state apparatus, from the Wannsee attendees whose seniority in their posts permitted them to represent various parts of the Nazi state when the decision to exterminate the Jews was being discussed and approved, to the SS camp guards some of whom did no more than meet the appalling requirements of their roles in the camps and others of whom, it seems a small minority, exceeded them in brutality for reasons such as sadistic pleasure. There was also the reality that even private businesses were, in the totalitarianism of the Nazi regime, engaged in work for the Nazi state and so implicated in its objectives.

The point here is that all these ordinary Germans, whether in state employment or employed by private businesses, were to some extent complicit in the activities of the Nazi state, and were differentiated from each other only by aspiration and opportunism and so by different degrees of conformity to the dictates of the Nazi state. The only exceptions to this general degree of complicity and its variations depending on motive were the sadistic camp guards who constituted a tiny minority of ordinary Germans. The other indication is that passive complicity could involve nothing more than the peripheral complicity that almost all Germans had given the bureaucratisation of the Nazi state, for that meant that a the great majority of ordinary Germans found themselves working for the Nazi state or in businesses controlled by the Nazi state, with direct involvement in perpetrator behaviour where the requirements of role meant participation in the extermination of Jews, for instance. The difference with the Einsatzgruppen commanders was their aspirational motive for accepting command of units that exterminated Jews, for they could have chosen other work of less prestige in the SS, because their educational, class and ideological background in right-wing politics in German universities meant that they had more choice than other ordinary Germans and that they would not have expected sanctions for declining Einsatzgruppen command roles apart from possible loss of SS rank, career and peer group regard. The difference between passive and active complicity is then one of motive, perception and personal circumstance in the Third Reich.

The case here is that pursuit of personal interest at the expense of others is a universal human attribute rather than a peculiarly German characteristic and that it exerts a dominant influence on almost all human behaviour in all circumstances and societies, with culture and ideology not being decisive for behaviour except for very small minorities of zealots or others of abnormal psychological attributes who may derive some psychological reward from membership of extreme groups and their convictions and practices, as seems to have been so with the early Nazis. Even in their case though the psychological rewards they derived from Nazi Party membership indicate optimisation of personal outcomes for them. The other very small minority would be those who engage in resistance to conformity predicated upon principle or personality in all societies. The actual nature of responses would be expected to vary with political and social context, as the contrast between majority responses in Nazi Germany, the Stalinist Soviet Union and the modern liberal west indicates, because very different behaviour would be optimal in terms of personal outcomes in the different societies.

Notes

[1] See Kay, Alex J., Rutherford, Jeff, and Stahel, David (eds.), *Nazi Policy on the Eastern Front, 1941: Total War, Genocide and Radicalization*, University of Rochester Press, 2012, p. 4. Estimates of Soviet POW losses range from 2 million to 3.3 to 3.5 million.

Chapter Two

The historical controversy – the views of Gellately, Evans, Goldhagen, Kershaw, Kulka, Bankier and Browning (including Browning's reference to the social psychological experiments of Milgram and Zimbardo) on the Third Reich, and the views of Fitzpatrick and Fulbrook on the historical context of other totalitarian regimes

The issue of German popular complicity in the criminality of the Third Reich and in particular the Holocaust may be contextualised by reference to a more general controversy over the extent of popular support for the Nazi regime in general.

Gellately characterises Nazi ideas as a combination of 'radical nationalism, a variety of socialism, and passionate antisemitism', and a 'quest for Germany's reawakening and the pursuit of "living space"', none of which, Gellately claims, was 'new or particularly original to Germany in 1918 or 1919'. For Gellately the attraction of the Nazi Party for ordinary Germans was not Hitler's charisma but the fact that the Nazis' ideas were already part of 'Germany's political culture', and he emphasises the centrality of the Volksgemeinschaft or 'community of the people', socialism and antisemitism (for the Jews were excluded from the 'community of the people') to Nazism. Nationalism was enhanced by the punitive terms of the Treaty of Versailles with its war guilt clause, reparations and loss of historically German territory, and the Weimar Republic was associated with its acceptance and was characterised by economic problems and political extremism from the nationalist and militaristic Freikorps and the communists in a context of there being no legitimacy from tradition for liberal democracy in Germany. Gellately claims that the result was popular desire for 'some kind of authoritarian dictatorship'. He does acknowledge the causal influence on the assumption of power by the Nazi Party in Germany of the Great Depression that started in 1929 but emphasises the consonance between German political attitudes before the Nazis assumed power and Nazi political attitudes.

Even so, in 1928 the Nazi share of the vote was a mere 2.6 per cent, whereas in 1930 it was 18.25 per cent, a reflection of the adverse economic consequences of the depression, and in 1932, after extensive experience of the effects of the depression in Germany, where it was exacerbated by the US loans taken out to make reparations payments and facilitate economy recovery, it was 37.27 per cent, indicating the decisive causal influence of economic factors on the Nazis' electoral success. Gellately does not appear to differentiate between the causal influence of traditional German nationalism, socialism, militarism and antisemitism on the Nazis' enhanced political fortunes or to assess their influence relative to economic factors. Nor does he seem to address the difference between an acknowledged cultural antisemitism not uncommon in interwar central Europe and the eliminationist antisemitism that the Holocaust represented and that Goldhagen has claimed was characteristic of ordinary Germans prior to Nazi propaganda and power. Gellately does not then present evidence that contradicts the case that the attitude of ordinary Germans to the Jews was indifference to what happened to them in Germany or the occupied territories of eastern and western Europe. Gellately refers to an incidence of 'race defilement' cases involving relationships between Jews and Germans being brought in the summer of 1935, before the Nuremberg Laws of September 1935, but one cannot infer that these were indicative of the prevalence of such antisemitic attitudes amongst ordinary Germans, for there is the difficulty of inferring incidence from instances, and other motives were also plausible. These possible motives included political ingratiation with a totalitarian Nazi state that had passed antisemitic laws from 1933, when the Nazi Party assumed power, the settling of personal scores, and some German public envy of Jewish affluence and success.[1] Gellately does himself, in his work on Gestapo records (see below), refer to a multiplicity of motives in voluntary denunciations to the Gestapo and notes that antisemitism as a motive was in fact rare.

Evans refers to a controversy between two views of the Third Reich. The earlier view was that the behaviour of ordinary Germans was a response to Nazi totalitarianism and the threat of repression from a totalitarian Nazi state apparatus, an argument of coercion rather than popular consent. The more recent view has been that the Third Reich was characterised by popular consent rather than coercion and that there was a prevalence of voluntarism on the part of ordinary Germans under Nazi rule, that 'only a small minority ever feared being arrested by the Gestapo' and that 'the Third Reich was not a dictatorship maintained by force' but rather 'a popular regime, sustained by the enthusiasm of the vast majority for its achievement, early on, of material prosperity and social equality' and a 'broad consensus' rather than imposed by totalitarian terror. The claim here is that the Third Reich was a 'dictatorship by consent'.[2]

Evans challenges this view, arguing that the Nazi acquisition of power was not 'legal' but characterised by opportunism, and that Nazi terror was not directed solely against small minorities of Germans and approved by the majority, for the victims of Nazi stormtrooper violence as soon as the Nazis assumed power included communists and social democrats, which would have had, though Evans does not allude to it, a demonstration effect on those who voted for them. Evans concludes that Nazi terror was perpetrated against a majority of Germans, for the working class, including communists, social democrats, trades unionists, and Catholics, who collaborated with the Nazis, together represented a majority of the German population in the Third Reich.

Evans acknowledges that the German middle class and peasantry had a preference for authoritarian solutions to the threat of communism but points out that Nazi violence extended even to the Nationalist Party, the conservative coalition, and the SA (in 1934). This violence does seem to be intended to be exemplary, and would have had a deterrent effect on the population of ordinary Germans. Evans then addresses the argument that the Gestapo was too small in its numbers to have controlled and repressed the population of ordinary Germans, but does not refer to the possibility of a public perception that arrest would ensue for any dissent even if the objective risk was minimal. He does note that the Gestapo and concentration camp were not the 'only agents of control and repression' and refers to the judicial system that existed in Germany before Nazi rule and to the new repressive laws that eliminated civil liberties and criminalised any behaviour the Nazi state disliked. These were accompanied by Special Courts and the People's Court and other punitive sanctions such as loss of job, reassignment to work that constituted punishment through labour, propaganda that vilified dissenters, control over the granting of educational qualifications, block warders in communities and Labour Front officials at work, compulsory joining of the Hitler Youth from 1939, and denunciation not just to the Gestapo, all of which combined to produce a society characterised by surveillance, control, repression and state violence in which individuals were atomised and alienated from each other into caution and silence in a climate of fear. Evans concludes by observing that evidence of continued popular support for the Nazi regime reflects voter intimidation and the treason law that forbade criticism of Hitler, that there was popular belief that ballots were numbered so voters could be identified, that votes cannot therefore be regarded as an accurate reflection of the attitudes of German voters, and that most Germans appeared to be mixed in their responses to surveys, approving of some but not other Nazi policies.[3]

It does seem possible to reconcile the view that claims popular consent to the Nazi regime and Evans' critique of that view by reference to the different effects of Nazi rule on different classes. For the German middle classes Nazi rule and the bureaucratised Nazi state apparatus may have offered career opportunities, not least for members of the lower middle class who had been disadvantaged by the inflation that eroded their savings in the 1920s and by the unemployment that followed the Wall Street Crash in 1929. These members of the German middle classes may also have been natural supporters of the Nazi Party because of its antipathy for communism and its having eradicated the threat of communism in Germany and would have constituted those who were part of the popular consent to Nazi rule (as would the peasantry, also concerned over the threat of communism given the history of Stalinism and collectivisation in the Ukraine in the early 1930s). But Evans' critique of Gellately's concentration on the German middle class is indicative of the need to address the entire German population when generalisations are made regarding the attitude of ordinary Germans to Nazi rule and of a need to include the extreme violence of the Nazi state and its repression of communists, social democrats and trades unionists, who as Evans notes constituted a majority of ordinary Germans in the Third Reich. In both cases, that of the German middle class and that of the working classes in Nazi Germany, the evidence indicates that ordinary Germans either endorsed the Nazi regime because they believed they benefited from its opportunities and its protection against communism or because they were apprehensive of the repressive violence of the Nazi state and wished to avoid it, both instances of personal optimisation of perceived outcomes.

This controversy over coercion and popular consent on the part of ordinary Germans in the Third Reich does not of course establish, regardless of which view is taken, that ordinary Germans endorsed eliminationist antisemitism, not least as much of the evidence of popular consent relates to the acquisition of power by the Nazis and the earlier period of Nazi rule, and to material advantages under Hitler rather than to any approval of his antisemitism. Nor does it indicate the motives for endorsement of or actual involvement in the extermination of the Jews on the part of ordinary Germans. What Evans does indicate is the climate of fear, repression and state control experienced by ordinary Germans in the Third Reich and the existence of a compelling motive for conformity and so passive complicity in the criminality of the Third Reich.

Even so, Goldhagen, addressing the complicity of ordinary Germans in the Holocaust, claims that eliminationist antisemitism was part of German culture rather than imposed on the German population by Nazi totalitarianism and propaganda, and that, far from persuading the German public of the need to rid Germany and Europe of Jews, the Nazi regime unleashed an existing German eliminationist antisemitism by disinhibiting it. Goldhagen uses 'thick description' to identify the 'phenomenology' of German perpetrators of genocide and to bring 'humanity' to German perpetrators by alluding to 'actors' capacity to know and to judge' and to 'understand and have views about the significance and morality of their actions', and refers to the decisive influence on 'ordinary Germans' of a 'pervasive anti-Semitism endemic to German culture'. Goldhagen rejects alternative explanations of the Holocaust such as disenchantment with the Weimar Republic and the appeal of Nazism, prejudice inspired by 'economic hardship', 'the coercive means of a totalitarian state', 'social psychological pressure' and 'invariable psychological propensities'.[4] The latter are said to refer to an imputed German propensity for following of orders or the pursuit of personal interest, though that disregards the reality that conformity in the interests of the self is precisely what the great majority of people do in all societies at all times.

Goldhagen's claim that 'eliminationist antisemitism' was characteristic of ordinary Germans even before the effect of Nazi propaganda, so that the Nazis merely unleashed a pent-up desire in the German public to exterminate Jews, has been widely discredited by historians whose expertise has been in the issue of German public opinion.[5]

There are some differences between these historians but all dismiss the claim by Goldhagen that ordinary Germans wanted the Jews exterminated. Browning addresses the claim by Lucy Dawidowicz in 1975 that 'generations of anti-Semitism' in Germany resulted in a situation in which, of the various appeals of the Nazi Party, 'its racial doctrine was the most attractive', not its political or economic policies, a claim that tends to support Goldhagen's reference to German antisemitism, though it does not mention eliminationist antisemitism by name. Dawidowicz claims that the 'insecurities' in Germany in the interwar years resulted in popular 'irrationality' and 'delusions', and that a 'psychosis damaged a whole people' in interwar Germany. Browning notes that three major scholars of public opinion in interwar and wartime Germany, Ian Kershaw, Otto Dov Kulka and David Bankier, dispute Dawidowicz's view, that Kershaw claims that antisemitism was not even the most salient concern of those who joined the Nazi Party early on and that Kershaw notes that Hitler in his speeches avoided references to antisemitism during the period of his attempting to obtain political power by democratic means and even up to 1939, concluding that antisemitism could not be accorded a 'decisive role in bringing Hitler to power'.

For the years of the Nazi regime before the war there is agreement between Kershaw, Kulka and Bankier that the German public endorsed legal measures against the Jews but reproved disorder and violence against Jews of the sort witnessed in the Kristallnacht destruction of Jewish synagogues and property in 1938. There is a difference of view as to the motives of the German public in their disapproval of Nazi violence against Jews, with Kulka and Bankier indicating concern for order for pragmatic reasons and Kershaw's not discounting 'moral concerns'. Even so there is agreement that a 'gulf had opened up between the Jewish minority and the general population'. Ordinary Germans were becoming more '"apathetic", "passive", and "indifferent"' to what happened to the Jews. Referring to the wartime period, Browning notes that Kulka and Bankier claim 'a more specific awareness of the Final Solution' than Kershaw.[6]

Browning quotes Kershaw's reference to 'a general retreat into the private sphere as the basis for widespread indifference and apathy toward Nazi Jewish policy', but this sentence is difficult to understand. For a 'retreat into the private sphere' could not have caused 'indifference and apathy'. On the contrary, it is more plausible that indifference to the Jews was a result of ordinary Germans' sense of Jewish 'otherness' and of their exclusive concern to optimise their own outcomes under a totalitarian regime that was violent in its antisemitism and in time of war, which dictated conformity to role requirements at work and otherwise turning to the private sphere, which is consistent with the references by Evans to Nazi totalitarian repression and control in the Third Reich.

Browning also quotes Kershaw's reference to the 'depersonalisation of the Jew' in Nazi propaganda and his claim that 'the "Jewish question" was of no more than minimal interest to the vast majority of Germans in the war years' and that 'popular opinion, largely indifferent and infused with latent anti-Jewish feeling' 'provided the climate within which spiralling Nazi aggression toward the Jews could take place unchallenged. But it did not provide the radicalization in the first place.' The latter statement differentiates Kershaw's view from that of Goldhagen. The reference to Nazi propaganda in Kershaw is difficult to understand in terms of what he is claiming influenced the attitudes of ordinary Germans. Any attribution of ordinary Germans' indifference to the Jews to Nazi propaganda is controversial and conjectural, for in a context of totalitarian control and fear of state reprisals for anything of which it did not approve it is not possible to identify which characteristic of the context was the decisive influence on ordinary Germans' attitudes, Nazi propaganda or the desire to avoid state sanctions and live a quiet life by behaviour that elicited no criticism at work and attention to the private sphere. The evidence of

Bankier that popular endorsement of Nazi propaganda was contingent upon ordinary Germans' views of what was optimal given the war situation does tend to challenge the view that Nazi propaganda was the decisive influence and does indicate that ordinary Germans did what they conceived would be best for them.

Browning quotes Kulka's observation that wartime SD reports were characterised by an 'almost total absence of any reference to the existence, persecution and extermination of the Jews – a kind of national conspiracy of silence', and that Kulka's claim of an 'abysmal indifference' to what happened to the Jews on the part of the German public is drawn from 'few reactions'. Browning notes that Kulka sees greater 'internalization of Nazi antisemitism' and acceptance of some kind of 'elimination of the Jewish Question' on the part of ordinary Germans and so prefers the term 'passive' or 'objective complicity' in reference to a 'general passivity of the population in the face of the persecution of the Jews'.

Browning also notes Bankier's view that ordinary Germans differentiated between 'an acceptable discrimination' and 'the unacceptable horror of genocide', that there was a sense of 'guilt and shame among Germans, widespread denial and repression', that 'the more the news of mass murder filtered through, the less the public wanted to be involved in the final solution of the Jewish question', and that there was 'a growing fear concerning the consequences of impending defeat and a commensurate rejection of the regime's antisemitic propaganda'.[7] There is here a claim of coexistence of rather dissonant experiences among ordinary Germans, for 'guilt and shame' would have precluded experience of 'denial and repression', and there is an indication of the contingency of the persuasiveness of Nazi propaganda in the reference to its being abandoned when the threat of post-war reprisals became salient. It also indicates the primary role of pursuit of personal interest for ordinary Germans, who wished to dissociate themselves from the Holocaust as wartime defeat seemed imminent. The implication is that there was little genuine belief in the propaganda at any time and mere expression of acceptance of Nazi propaganda under Nazi rule.

Bankier's observation of a change in popular German attitudes with the imminence of wartime defeat is indicative of the most plausible sequence of the attitudes of ordinary Germans. The sequence began with popular support for the Nazi regime when Hitler became Chancellor in January 1933, when the Nazi Party was the most popular political party in Germany, and for the remainder of the interwar period as Nazi economic and foreign policies appealed to the German electorate because of German economic recovery from the Depression and Hitler's success in violating the Treaty of Versailles and in annexing Austria and then the Sudetenland in a recovery of German national power and autonomy, albeit with a context of immediate and known brutal repression of all forms and sources of dissent, not least socialists, communists, trades unionists and social democrats, who were incarcerated in concentration camps and compelled to labour there.

In an indication of the parochial concerns that appear to have dominated ordinary Germans' perceptions of life in the interwar and wartime periods, Herbert refers to evidence that in 1951 half of the citizens of the Federal Republic of Germany remembered the 1933 to 1939 years as the best ones for Germany. Herbert comments that 'for a large part of the population the image of National Socialism was characterised not by terror, mass murder and war but by reduction of unemployment, economic boom, tranquility and order'. He also refers to a 1949 survey that corroborates this view, indicating popular concentration on guaranteed work and no 'disarray' in political life, and to an oral history project in 1960 conducted with former blue- and white-collar workers at a Krupps plant that indicates primary concern over lack of continuous employment before 1932, and regarding work, 'economic advancement', family and leisure time but no interest in politics.[8]

There ensued the early wartime period of continued genuine popular support for Hitler and the Nazis with the German military victories in Poland, Norway, Denmark, the Netherlands, Belgium and France, and over the Red Army in the invasion of the Soviet Union in the summer and autumn of 1941, followed by more victories there in 1942. Thereafter, beginning with the German defeat at Stalingrad and the loss in the ensuing battle of Kursk on the eastern front, the context for ordinary Germans changed, for the deteriorating position on the eastern front was accompanied by increased bombing of German cities that caused terrible destruction and loss of German lives, and the following year there was the July 1944 bomb plot. The Nazi regime's reaction was far greater repression in Nazi Germany, culminating in the resort to summary execution for any hint of defeatism in the final months and weeks of the war. Ordinary Germans may have been shielded from any immediacy of appreciation of the extermination of Jews, which took place in the camps of Poland, Sobibor, Treblinka, Majdanek, Chelmno and Auschwitz, rather than in Germany itself. However, with the increasing numbers of slave labourers in Germany, as the war went on, and the more compelling became the shortage of German labour, with more German men sent to fight in the war, the more the German public witnessed the condition of the slave labourers, given the location of the sites of their employment – labourers who were Jews or Eastern European from the occupied territories of the east and regarded as dispensable. In all these periods the German public conformed, initially because the regime had brought German success, and thereafter, as witnesses to the condition of slave labourers in Germany, because they were focused on the maintenance of their own standard of living and on avoidance of the greater repression of the Nazi state apparatus.

Kershaw claims that 'apathy and "moral indifference" to the treatment and fate of the Jews was the most widespread attitude of all' in the German population, and points to a low salience of the 'Jewish Question' for ordinary Germans, contrasting 'the centrality of antisemitism in Hitler's world view and the apathy towards the "Jewish Question" of the bulk of the population'. Kershaw claims that such indifference to the fate of the Jews, which was of 'no more than minimal interest to the vast majority of Germans during the years of Nazi annihilation of the Jews', was accompanied by a turning away to the private sphere by ordinary Germans.[9]

Even with differences of emphasis, all the historians referred to here do reject the claim of eliminationist antisemitism in ordinary Germans. What does seem to be indicated is the influence of motivation on cognition, in the form of ordinary Germans' inattention to what was happening to the Jews, an instance of people tending to 'know' what they find expedient to know and not to 'know' what would be inexpedient for them to know, and selective attention to other matters.

In other evidence that challenges Goldhagen's claim of eliminationist antisemitism in the German population as a whole even before the effect of Nazi propaganda, the Nazi Party was not elected as the largest party in the Reichstag on a platform that was overtly antisemitic in nature, which indicates Nazi understanding that the German public was at the time less interested in antisemitism than the Depression of the early 1930s and its unemployment. The Nazi Party platform that brought it to power does seem to indicate that the German public at the time was not seen as being motivated by an eliminationist antisemitism that Goldhagen claims preceded Nazi propaganda, and though it does not preclude German public indifference to Jews who seem to have been regarded as 'other' in Germany that is of course not what Goldhagen claims.

Gordon refers to the view of several historians that Hitler's major speeches between 1930 and 1932 refrained from reference to the Jews and to antisemitism, that Hitler 'toned down his antisemitism to win votes after 1928', and that in the 1928 and 1930 elections antisemitism was not a 'major theme'. Nazi posters did link Jews to 'socialists, Weimar leaders, Versailles, the Young Plan, unemployment, corruption and profiteering', and some historians have claimed that antisemitic propaganda increased between 1928 and 1933 under the influence of Goebbels. Even so, Gordon's conclusion is that Hitler's electoral success is not to be attributed to the appeal of his antisemitism, and that the German general public did not know of Hitler's intentions towards the Jews because the Nazis adjusted their message to different audiences, including refraining from antisemitic references in some cases.[10]

Reference to other countries in interwar Europe also challenges the Goldhagen thesis that the Nazi regime simply released a German eliminationist antisemitism that existed before the Nazis came to power. For Germany was at one time significantly less antisemitic than other nations in Europe, especially to the east. There was a sense of Jewish 'otherness' in many nations in Europe in the late nineteenth and early twentieth centuries, and whilst there does seem to have been popular German endorsement of a sense that something should be done to curb excessive Jewish influence in Germany it does not follow that ordinary Germans endorsed eliminationist antisemitism, unless the term endorsement refers also to turning away from the plight of Jews under the Nazis. That would of course be to distort the meaning of the term, and in fact one reason Goldhagen's 'Hitler's Willing Executioners' has been dismissed by academic historians has been its conflation of different forms of antisemitism and eliminationist antisemitism.

Though Goldhagen does contribute to the literature on the Holocaust by pointing out that it involved the active complicity of very significant numbers of ordinary Germans in the persecution, ghettoisation and extermination of the Jews of Europe, it does not follow that the reason for such widespread complicity on the part of ordinary Germans was the long-standing historical eliminationist antisemitism in the general German public that Goldhagen claims, for passive or active compliance with the dictates of a totalitarian regime is exactly what would be expected without eliminationist antisemitism, just on grounds of preservation of the circumstances of life or their enhancement.

Goldhagen's claim is in fact more than would be necessary to attribute responsibility for the Holocaust to the German people as a whole, because popular German endorsement of a policy of eliminationist antisemitism was not a necessary condition to its prosecution by the Nazi regime. All that was needed was what seems to have occurred, a general reaction of acquiescence or indifference in the form of turning away from the fate of the Jews of Germany and elsewhere in Europe occupied by the Nazis and conformity to role requirements for those involved in the Nazi bureaucracy, the military and the SS. Though there is evidence that the Jews were perceived to have a quality of 'otherness' because of Nazi propaganda vilifying Jews in a context of a longer term culture of Jewish 'otherness' in Germany, the case being made here is that cultural or ideological antipathy for Jews in Germany was facilitative rather than decisive as far as the reactions of ordinary Germans were concerned. The argument is that neither was in fact a necessary condition for German popular complicity, for that took place to optimise personal outcomes by avoiding political matters, turning away to the private sphere, and meeting role requirements. Goldhagen has elaborated upon his book 'Hitler's Willing Executioners' in an exchange with Josef Joffe. In this exchange he explains that his approach began with identification of a majority view in the 1930s that 'the Jews and Jewish power had somehow to be eliminated from German society', that it continued with an appreciation of the numbers of ordinary Germans voluntarily involved in the Holocaust and their varied social backgrounds, and that it culminated in an inferred hypothesis that ordinary Germans murdered Jews because of their antisemitism. He then claims to have considered and rejected all the other possible explanations (referred to above) on the basis of a systematic appreciation of the evidence, and to have inferred that Germans in general would have acted to eliminate the Jews had they been in positions in which that was possible.

There are some difficulties with Goldhagen's claims. To begin with he does not specify when in the 1930s he is claiming that there was a general feeling that the Jews had to be dealt with (before or after the Nazis assumed power) or just what the 'elimination' of 'the Jews and Jewish power' meant. It could have meant their emigration from the Reich, the first option considered to remove Jews from Nazi territory. The critical failing in Goldhagen seems to be that he dismisses the possibility that ordinary Germans committed genocide or were complicit in it just to optimise their outcomes in terms of maximising rewards and minimising adverse consequences for them. Though Goldhagen does withdraw the claim that eliminationist antisemitism was a sufficient cause of German perpetrator behaviour and other forms of complicity he does not specify which other factors were necessary. Joffe's criticism of Goldhagen is rather different, claiming that it is not legitimate to infer from the behaviour of a small sample that has common sociological characteristics with the majority that such behaviour would have been characteristic of the total population of the country.[11]

Goldhagen's claim of German cultural eliminationist antisemitism was a reaction to Browning's 'Ordinary Men' with its claim that peer group conformity was the explanation for many ordinary Germans' murdering Jews in great numbers. Browning claimed that many middle aged men in a Reserve Police Battalion from Hamburg with no Nazi background executed 1,500 Jewish elderly people, women and children not long after arrival in Poland, just to avoid peer group disapproval, ostracism and ridicule. In other words a small cost to them had a more compelling influence on their behaviour than being an agent in the murder of helpless Jews even though the men experienced genuine distress at and repugnance for the task. That is of course consistent with the argument here that optimisation of personal outcomes despite the cost to other people was the primary influence on human behaviour in Nazi Germany and is so in all societies at all times.[12]

Browning related his findings to the work on obedience to immoral authority of Stanley Milgram, a social psychologist whose work was a development of the earlier work on conformity by Solomon Asch, who found evidence of normative influence in subjects' conformity to group norms even when the conformity was in contradiction to the evidence of their senses.[13] Milgram's basic experiment was presented to prospective participants as one regarding the effect of punishment on learning, though the 'learners' or 'victims' were in fact confederates of the experimenter, who was the authority figure and who instructed naive participants that incorrect responses by 'learners', who were instructed to make incorrect responses, should be 'punished' by increasing levels of 'electric shock'. 'Learners' had been told to feign pain, distress, to call for the experiment to be halted and to complain of dangerous health conditions that were being put at risk by the experiment. In most variations participants had auditory evidence of the pain, distress, pleas to stop and refusal to continue on the part of the 'learner'. What Milgram found was a quite extraordinary preparedness of ordinary people drawn at random from the normal population of a liberal democratic society with a constitutional and cultural respect for human rights and freedoms to inflict what they believed was severe pain and risk to ensuing health of their 'victims'. For as many as sixty-five per cent were prepared to shock the 'learner' to the maximum level permitted despite increasingly worrying evidence of the welfare of the 'learner', and all participants were prepared to administer shocks beyond levels that resulted in evidence of pain, distress, pleas to stop and risk to health from the 'learner'. And the thirty-five per cent who did at some point before the maximum level of 'shock' decline to continue did not check on the welfare of the 'learner' or 'victim' before leaving the experiment, or insist that the experiment be stopped, indicating that their concern was with their own responsibility rather than with the welfare of the 'learner'.

Milgram explained his evidence by reference to an 'agentic state' in which the participant was the 'agent' of the experimenter and so felt no responsibility for his actions in the experiment. Some of Milgram's own variations on his original experiment do though challenge the existence and influence on behaviour of an 'agentic state', for when participants could instruct someone else to 'administer' the shocks compliance with the experimenter's instruction to continue to administer 'shocks' to 'learners' rose dramatically, with very few declining to continue, and when participants were required to administer the shock directly to the 'learner', not through a system, preparedness declined significantly. That seems to indicate that differences in experienced personal responsibility for administering what participants believed were electric shocks to 'learners' affected their preparedness to obey, which is not what would have happened had they been in an 'agentic state', for that attributed all responsibility to the experimenter. And the distress of participants even as they continued to administer shocks is another indication that they were not in an 'agentic state' when doing so. The more plausible explanation seems to be that Milgram's participants continued to inflict shocks on 'victims' to avoid the embarrassment of having to confront the experimenter and being seen to have failed at a task they had undertaken before the experimenter as an authority figure, that is, to optimise their own outcomes.[14] That is of course consonant with Browning's finding of avoidance of informal peer group sanctions even if the means of doing so was murdering innocent Jews.

Milgram's experiments also indicate a significant incidence of conformity to optimise personal outcomes even when participants were required to administer the 'electric shock' directly to the 'victim' and witness his pain, distress and pleas (thirty per cent were prepared to do so), a contrast with the many perpetrators in bureaucratic Nazi Germany who were removed from direct responsibility for the outcomes for their victims, as the difference between the Einsatzgruppen, who murdered Jewish men, women and children mostly by shooting, and Eichmann, a 'desk murderer' who arranged for the transportation of Jews to extermination centres, indicates.

Browning also related his findings to the work of Philip Zimbardo, who found alarmingly high rates of conformity to role requirements in his Stanford Prison Experiment, which became notorious for its having to be discontinued before it was scheduled to end, because of the effect of role on the behaviour of those in the role of 'warders' and their effect on those in the role of 'prisoner'. Browning noted that his research revealed exactly the same percentages of avid and minimal conformity to role requirements and resistance to role requirements as those Zimbardo had found. Though the initial indication was that the role of warder and the prison setting had had an autonomous effect on warder behaviour, an ensuing assessment of Zimbardo's experiment found that Zimbardo had identified with the 'warders' and instructed 'warders' to mistreat prisoners, to create a sense of 'powerlessness' in them. Haslam, Reicher and Van Bavel have claimed that the Stanford Prison Experiment is an example of 'identity leadership' on the part of Zimbardo and 'engaged followership' on the part of warders, but produce no direct evidence of warder acceptance of the legitimacy of the experiment and the legitimising of warder brutality in the cause of understanding prisoner mistreatment in the real world. What is indicated is directive leadership from Zimbardo as prison superintendent and a respected university professor and Jaffe, the Warden, both of whom gave instructions as to the desired behaviour of warders, including mistreatment of prisoners, evidence indicating that 'warders', who were students, were trying to impress a respected university professor in their role or to avoid the embarrassment of having to confront and defy him or being seen to have failed at the task they had undertaken, in other words pursuing their own interests at the expense of those of 'prisoners'.[15]

An oblique indication of the extent of active rather than passive conformity in Nazi Germany, and the motives behind it, is to be found in the work of Gellately on Gestapo files that have survived and that are indicative of the nature of Gestapo work in general, for Gellately found evidence that the Gestapo spent much of its time dealing with denunciations from German citizens. Such denunciations exceeded the more minimal turning away to the private sphere and complying with role requirements at work in a passive form of compliance, for they were entirely voluntary and many

were anonymous, 'written for selfish interests' such as 'revenge', with the great majority of denunciations being for 'instrumental' reasons such as 'informing on a rival or
someone involved in a social dispute', or 'a certain hatred'. Noting that 'evidence of
affective motivation, especially over antisemitism, is rare', Gellately concludes that
'denouncers took advantage of the state's means of coercion for selfish purposes', like
populations 'in other 'totalitarian regimes', with 'the terror system not simply feared
and avoided, but used and manipulated' by a German citizenry that took advantage
of 'the new opportunities that opened up and were not merely passive, dependent,
or powerless'. Gellately's evidence is of ordinary Germans' opportunism at the expense of other ordinary Germans or Jews.[16]

Gellately does not refer to the incidence of voluntary denunciation relative to the total
adult German population under Nazi rule, and there is an issue regarding the extent of
inculcation of fear and apprehension of arrest amongst the German public by the
existence of the Gestapo, the numbers in which were far less than would have been
necessary to impose the sort of control it is claimed to have achieved through its
reputation and the consequence of a climate of fear amongst ordinary Germans. For only
fifteen per cent of Gestapo investigations were begun by the Gestapo itself, with twenty-
six per cent resulting from denunciations from ordinary Germans. This does not of
course indicate the incidence of voluntary and active rather than passive German public
complicity but if the Gestapo's reputation resulted in very little defiance of the Nazi state
because of fear of arrest and passive complicity by the majority of Germans,
denunciation may have been uncommon relative to the population of ordinary
Germans, the great majority of whom conformed, so the twenty-six per cent of Gestapo
investigations derived from denunciations from the German public could have been a
very low number relative to the numbers of ordinary Germans. Passive rather than active
complicity could then have been the response of the majority of ordinary Germans to the
Nazi state, and would be the more plausible inference given that the population of
ordinary Germans was so much greater than the numbers of Gestapo officers.[17] The
incidence of voluntary denunciation to the Gestapo by ordinary Germans in the Third
Reich and the reasons for it are of course related to the wider issue of the extent of
popular German endorsement of the Nazi regime and the reasons for such popular
endorsement. For evidence of popular approval of the Nazi regime could reflect genuine
public endorsement of Nazi government because of the benefits it accorded the majority
of Germans who were perceived to be Aryan or because of fear of the repressive nature
of the Nazi state and endorsement under duress and fear of arrest and incarceration in a
concentration camp, both of which are pragmatic and optimising motives, or could
reflect cultural, ideological or eliminationist antisemitism. The attitude of the great
majority of ordinary Germans does seem to have been indifference to the Jews and what
happened to them and exclusive concentration on optimisation of personal outcomes
that included acceptance of the benefits of the Nazi state through opportunism and
careerism, and avoidance of the known sanctions for non-conformity to the dictates of
the Nazi state. This is of course the same human optimisation of personal outcomes upon
which all societies are predicated, not least those of the modern liberal democracies with
their incentives, inequality and hierarchies.

Other evidence of ordinary Germans' complicity having been a reflection of the decisive influence of their pursuit of their own interests may be found in a number of inferences. For instance, if the German population was, as Goldhagen claims, characterised by eliminationist antisemitism even prior to any effect from Nazi propaganda, why was there no manifestation of this sentiment before the Nazi regime, with its reputation for repressive violence and incarceration of dissenters, as incentivised ordinary Germans' avoidance of dissent? Why was ordinary Germans' eliminationist antisemitism not 'unleashed' by the adverse circumstances of the post-World War One period, with the national disgrace of the German defeat and loss of historically German territory, disarmament and colossal reparations, the resulting hyperinflation, the threat of communism and a Weimar Republic that had no legitimacy for many ordinary Germans who had no experience of liberal democracy or respect for the ethos? Why was there no apparent diminution in preparedness for complicity with a lack of Nazi ideological indoctrination, as was so with Browning's 'Ordinary Men'? If Nazi propaganda was so effective why was there popular disapproval of the Nazi destruction of Jewish synagogues and property in Kristallnacht in 1938? Why is the evidence of German conformity and so complicity so similar to the conformity that holds together all societies, even without totalitarian control over information in the form of state propaganda and without the threat of state repression and violence? The most plausible inference appears to be that the passive and active complicity of ordinary Germans reflected the reality that human behaviour is decisively influenced by the drive to optimise personal outcomes. The German public's sense of Jewish 'otherness', derived from German cultural antisemitism or Nazi propaganda, does seem in this context to have been facilitative rather than a necessary condition to complicity, for it does seem that even without Nazi ideological indoctrination in antisemitism and German cultural antisemitism compliance with the Nazi state's totalitarian control with its known repressive measures would have been the norm for ordinary Germans. This is of course counterfactual and so cannot be proved by direct evidence, but may be inferred from the contextual evidence presented here.

Fitzpatrick addresses the incidence of denunciation under Stalin, which she claims took place for a number of reasons. She cites tradition, in the form of appeal to a higher authority to correct injustices committed by the lower echelons of the state, a practice inherited from the Tsarist period. She refers to optimisation of personal outcomes as a motive for denunciation. And she points to ideological reasons in denunciations by communists of other communists alleged to have betrayed the Bolshevik revolution, though she does note that such denunciations could have been a means of safeguarding the interests of the self, in that not denouncing someone for having made an anti-Soviet statement for instance could result in one's own arrest as an accomplice should the statement be reported to the state by someone else.

Though Fitzpatrick does not mention it, there is also the possibility that such 'duty' or 'loyalty' denunciations were intended to demonstrate to the state the communist credentials of the individual concerned to the end of precluding their being suspected of anti-state activity and being arrested in more general terms, that is, that they were a means of the individual's feeling reassured of personal safety in a totalitarian state in which those who were not seen to be for the revolution were suspected of being against it, when there was in fact nothing counterrevolutionary to report. Fitzpatrick does note that 'duty' or 'loyalty' denunciations were far more common in the late 1930s purges, indicating a more pervasive concern for personal outcomes in conditions of enhanced terror, for the alternative explanation, that there was in fact a greater incidence of counterrevolutionary activity, is not plausible for the more repressive late 1930s. Fitzpatrick does not note that traditional denunciations could represent opportunism rather than expression of legitimate grievances, which she seems to infer from their being 'not furtive and mean, but morally indignant', an inference from language that does not seem justified.

Fitzpatrick claims that Nazi Germany had greater reliance on unsolicited denunciations than was so under Stalinism because of the extent of police 'saturation' under Stalinism, and that in the GDR there was even less spontaneous denunciation because of the extent of Stasi penetration into society in the GDR. That seems to indicate that the opportunity for unsolicited denunciation was diminished where totalitarian state penetration into society was greater. As to incidence of denunciations under Stalinism, she notes the popular phrase in answer to the question of who wrote the denunciations, 'everyone, except the people who were too lazy'. The reference to laziness in those who did not denounce people seems to indicate that she is referring to spontaneous or unsolicited denunciations rather than to those extracted by the state under Stalinism, indicating an extraordinary incidence of unsolicited denunciations under Stalin, though that seems to contradict her indication that spontaneous or unsolicited denunciations were diminished under Stalin by state penetration of society. The evidence of Fitzpatrick on denunciations seems to indicate optimisation of personal outcomes by individuals in their adjustment to the opportunities and threats of Stalinist totalitarianism.[18]

The indication is that denunciation is in fact characteristic of totalitarian societies whose people were incentivised to engage in denunciations to take advantage of the state's coercive power against other people or to protect themselves from the totalitarian power of the state. It is worth adding that the evidence on unsolicited denunciations discussed here is of pre-emptive protection of the self or opportunistic taking advantage of the possibilities of totalitarianism. These are distinguished in their being voluntary from denunciations obtained by the totalitarian state, which were also of course a form of optimisation of personal outcomes but in circumstances of prospective loss to the self.

Fulbrook, commenting upon Germans' reactions to the Nazi dictatorship and to the communist regime that succeeded it in the east, in what became the GDR, argues that totalitarian dictatorships and other forms of political regime should be understood not in terms of 'distinctive combinations of terror and obedience, or congruence of interests and commitment to ideology, or social backgrounds and personal motives' but in terms of 'how people adopted and learned how to play new roles; and how they developed the newly appropriate "manners of speaking and acting" required of them under the new circumstances'. Fulbrook seems here to be indicating the primacy of human adaptation to changed reinforcement contingencies in behavioural responses to totalitarianism (and in fact to any political regime), which could only be to optimise personal outcomes through assimilation of new vocabularies and behavioural norms.[19]

For some Germans the perceived optimal response in Nazi Germany was avoidance of political references and attention to work role requirements and the private sphere, a form of passive conformity, and for the more opportunistic voluntary denunciations or obtaining the property of deported Jews were added to such minimal conformity to optimise outcomes.

The broader historical context also indicates that German popular complicity in the genocide of the Jews of Europe is not to be attributed to peculiarly German cultural attributes. For though Germans had committed genocide against the native Herero and Nama peoples of German South West Africa between 1904 and 1908, which would tend to indicate influence from German culture on a unique German predisposition to genocide, there have been many other instances of genocide, including the Armenian genocide that was carried out by the Ottoman government from 1915, the Rwandan massacres of Tutsis under the Hutu government in 1994, the ethnic cleansing of the Balkans in the 1990s and the Cambodian genocide perpetrated by the Khmer Rouge between 1975 and 1979. And the Nazi genocide of the Jews was assisted by Eastern European nationalist paramilitary groups, for nationalist Lithuanians and Ukrainians were violently antisemitic and carried out murders of Jews following the German invasion of their countries. It was also assisted by Soviet POWs whose prospects were bleak if they did not become 'Trawnikis'.

Though finding many other examples of genocide does not of itself refute the Goldhagen thesis that the Nazi Holocaust involving the Jews of Europe reflected a long-standing German cultural eliminationist antisemitism, in that it is possible that each instance of genocide had very different causes, the evidence presented here on ordinary Germans in everyday life and as perpetrators in Nazi Germany and of other totalitarian states does indicate that the Nazi Holocaust is not explained by reference to German cultural eliminationist antisemitism but by a universal human attribute of individual optimisation of outcomes regardless of the cost to other people as the decisive influence on behaviour, for that seems to have obtained both in the ordinary German population in its minimal conformity to the dictates of the Nazi state or more opportunistic behaviour taking advantage of the plight of the Jews and in perpetrator behaviour reflective of aspirational careerism or avoidance of informal sanctions. Other totalitarian states have had similar experiences of popular conformity and opportunism.

Notes

[1] See Gellately, Robert, *Hitler's True Believers: How Ordinary Germans Became Nazis*, Oxford University Press, 2020, pp. 253 and 315–17. See p. 254 for evidence of popular aversion for actual violence against Jews in 1935.

[2] See Evans, Richard J., 'Coercion and Consent in Nazi Germany', Raleigh Lecture on History, 24 May 2006', Proceedings of the British Academy 151, 2007, pp. 53–81.

[3] See ibid.

[4] See Goldhagen, Daniel Jonah, *Hitler's Willing Executioners: Ordinary Germans and the Holocaust*, Knopf Doubleday Publishing Group, 2007, and Crownshaw, R., *The Afterlife of Holocaust Memory in Contemporary Literature and Culture*, Springer, 2016, pp. 132 and 133.

[5] See Eley, Geoff (ed.), *The 'Goldhagen Effect': History, Memory, Nazism – facing the German Past*, University of Michigan Press, 2000, p. 5.

[6] See Browning, Christopher R., 'Ordinary Germans or Ordinary Men? A Reply to the Critics', in Berenbaum, Michael and Peck, Abraham J.(eds.), *The Holocaust and History: The Known, the Unknown, the Disputed, and the Reexamined*, United States Holocaust Memorial Museum, Indiana University Press, 1998, p. 254.

[7] See ibid, pp. 253–55.

[8] See Herbert, Ulrich, 'Good Times, Bad Times: Memories of the Third Reich', in Bessel, Richard (ed.), *Life in the Third Reich*, Oxford University Press, 2001, pp. 97–107.

[9] See Kershaw, Ian, *Hitler, the Germans and the Final Solution*, Yale University Press, 2008, pp. 198 and 229.

[10] See Gordon, Sarah Ann, *Hitler, Germans and the "Jewish Question"*, Princeton University Press, 1984, pp. 68–70.

[11] See '"Hitler's Willing Executioners": An Exchange', Daniel Jonah Goldhagen, reply by Josef Joffe, *The New York Review of Books*, February 6, 1997 issue.

[12] See Browning, Christopher, *Ordinary Men, Reserve Police Battalion 101 and the Final Solution in Poland*, Penguin, London, 2001, pp. 184 and 185.

[13] See Asch, S. E., 'Opinions and Social Pressure', *Scientific American, 193*, 1955.

[14] See Milgram, Stanley, 'Behavioral Study of Obedience', *Journal of Abnormal and Social Psychology, 67 (4), 1963*, pp. 371–78, and Milgram, Stanley, *Obedience to Authority: An Experimental View*, Harper & Row, New York, 1974, p. 148.

[15] See Howarth, Caroline, and Andreouli, Eleni (eds.), *The Social Psychology of Everyday Politics*, Taylor and Francis, 2016, p. 105, Rector, John M., *The Objectification Spectrum: Understanding and Transcending Our Diminishment and Dehumanization Of Others*, Oxford University Press, 2014, p. 169, and Haslam, S. A., and Reicher, S. D., *The Psychology of Tyranny, Scientific American Mind, 16 (7)*, p. 47. See also Haslam, S. Alexander, Reicher, Stephen D., and Van Bavel, Jay J., 'Rethinking the nature of cruelty: The role of identity leadership in the Stanford Prison Experiment', *American Psychologist 2019, Vol. 74, No. 7.*

[16] See Gellately, Robert, *Backing Hitler: Consent and Coercion in Nazi Germany*, Oxford University Press, 2002.

[17] See McDonough, Frank, *The Gestapo: The Myth and Reality of Hitler's Secret Police*, Hachette, 2015.

[18] See Fitzpatrick, Sheila, 'The Practice of Denunciation in Stalinist Russia', The National Council for Soviet and East European Research.

[19] See Fulbrook, Mary, *Dissonant Lives: Generations and Violence through the German Dictatorships*, OUP, 2011, p. 98.

Chapter Three
A psychologist's analysis. The view of Ervin Staub

The preceding chapter addressed the historical controversy over the nature and extent of ordinary Germans' complicity in Nazi crimes against humanity and over what explains popular complicity on the part of ordinary Germans: an eliminationist German cultural antisemitism, Nazi propaganda or conformity to the dictates of a totalitarian state to optimise personal outcomes through opportunism or avoidance of Nazi state sanctions. Gellately, Evans, Kershaw, Kulka and Bankier are all distinguished social historians on the Third Reich, Browning is a Holocaust historian and his references to Milgram and Zimbardo are to the work of famous experimental social psychologists who have attempted to assess obedience to immoral authority and the power of the situation and role on human behaviour respectively. Staub by contrast is a psychologist who has attempted to identify the causal influences that resulted in the criminality of the Nazi regime and who has in doing so addressed the psychology of ordinary Germans and perpetrators (there was in fact no distinction between ordinary Germans and Nazi perpetrators, for Nazi perpetrators were ordinary Germans who found themselves in roles that required them to engage in perpetrator activity against Jews and others).

Staub explains the Holocaust by reference to a series of antecedent circumstances but does not seem to differentiate preconditions for the extermination of the Jews of the occupied territories from facilitating factors for perpetrator behaviour in general. He points to adverse adverse socioeconomic circumstances he refers to as 'difficult life conditions' and claims that they threaten not only the basic need for material sufficiency but also other primary needs, for 'security', for 'a positive identity', for a sense of 'effectiveness' and 'control', for positive connections with others, for some comprehension of reality and for hope for the future. Staub's reference to the German economic and social landscape following the Wall Street Crash of 1929 is hardly controversial, as has been seen. But he goes on to claim that 'since the capacity to control or address life problems and satisfy material needs is limited, the psychological needs become predominant in guiding action,' and continues, 'the pattern of predisposing cultural characteristics intensifies the basic needs and inclines the group toward fulfilling them in ways that turn the group against others.' Staub claims that 'scapegoating and destructive ideologies' 'brought an ideological movement to power' in Germany that ultimately resulted in the Holocaust.[1]

The argument that psychological needs take precedence over material needs that are not met is controversial, and Gordon (referred to above) notes that even as late as October 1930 Hitler claimed he had nothing against 'decent' Jews, 'discountenanced violent anti-Semitism', and avoided reference to 'future measures against Jews'. In 1932 too Hitler omitted antisemitic references, with some evidence that he particularly avoided antisemitic references when addressing members of the upper middle classes. Gordon notes antisemitism's poor 'drawing power among the electorate; consequently, Hitler toned down his anti-Semitism to win votes after 1928'. Gordon does refer to other historians who argue that there was an increase in antisemitism in the publicity of the Nazi Party, if not in Hitler's speeches, between 1929 and 1933 but reconciles the opposing views by reference to the Nazi Party's antisemitism, to the extent to which it was mentioned in Nazi publicity, as an 'abstraction' rather than indicating any specific intentions towards the Jews, so what may be said with certainty is that ordinary Germans' votes for the Nazi Party from 1930 onwards did not reflect any desire for violence against the Jews, let alone for their destruction.[2]

The effect of the Wall Street Crash with its dramatic deterioration in conditions of life for ordinary Germans has been noted above, as has its other effect, enhancing the national popularity of the Nazi Party. This greater Nazi Party appeal to the German electorate was a consequence of its promise to the German public of employment and an enhanced standard of living, an end to the political instability of the Weimar Republic, rejection of the loathed and humiliating constraints of the Treaty of Versailles and affirmation of German national prestige. Germans were in other words understandably attracted to the promise of a dramatic rise in their standard of living and of stable government, and to the idea that they were special in racial terms, not because of Nazi antisemitism.

The necessary and sufficient conditions for the Holocaust seem to have been—

- the Great Depression, which offered the Nazi Party the opportunity to cultivate an appeal to the German electorate it had not had in the 1928 election, when its share of the vote was minuscule;
- the dismal record of political instability of the Weimar Republic;
- the content of the Nazi manifesto with its promise of better living standards and the psychological reward of a nationalistic identity that was prestigious;
- the intransigence of Hitler and misjudgement of him by German Conservatives, who believed they could control him;
- Hitler's own combination of decisive, radical authoritarianism and opportunism in using the Reichstag fire on 27 February 1933, just after his accession to the Chancellorship in January 1933, to accuse the communists of responsibility and to have President von Hindenburg pass the Reichstag Fire Decree, under which civil liberties were abolished and political opponents of the Nazis were subjected to extreme violence;
- Hitler's wanting yet more exclusive power and forming an alliance with nationalists and conservatives, neither apparently concerned by the recent evidence of Hitler's opportunism, against the social democrats for the 5 March 1933 election, which followed SA and SS 'terror, repression and propaganda'

against communists, socialists and social democrats but did not give the Nazi
Party an overall majority yet was sufficient, with the continued support of
nationalists and conservatives, to have the Reichstag pass the Enabling Act of
23 March 1933, which permitted Hitler as Chancellor to pass laws and enforce
them without approval from the Reichstag or the President;

- Hitler's assumption of total power in Germany on the death of von
  Hindenburg and merging the Chancellorship and the Presidency to become
  Führer and the ultimate source of authority and legitimacy in the Third Reich
  after obtaining popular approval in a referendum on 19 August 1934
  characterised by intimidation of voters;
- Hitler's ruthless sacrifice of the SA to secure the support of and in fact an oath
  of personal allegiance from the German Army, in doing so nullifying a final
  threat to his total power;
- Hitler's use of his powers to eradicate liberal rights and democratic
  government, to employ state violence against communists, socialists, trades
  unionists and social democrats, in fact anyone who showed the slightest hint of
  dissent against the Nazi regime, and to incarcerate them in concentration
  camps in which the treatment of those interned was barbaric and included
  forced labour;
- the resulting nature of Nazi society, with ordinary Germans rewarded by the
  ending of the unemployment and destitution of the Great Depression and by
  the rise in German international prestige, but repressed, atomised,
  apprehensive of the state and concentrated on meeting role requirements and
  on the private sphere;
- the nature of the Nazi state apparatus, with every echelon compliant with
  Hitler's every inferred wish under a system that dictated that Hitler's desires
  had the legitimacy of the law, and the competitive Nazi elite the members of
  which attempted to determine Hitler's preferences to enhance their status
  relative to their colleagues;
- and Hitler's violent, radical antisemitism, which resulted initially in
  discrimination and SA violence against Jews in Nazi Germany, a policy of
  Jewish emigration from the Reich, and then, with the inheritance of enormous
  numbers of Jews in the Nazi occupation of western Poland in 1939 and
  invasion and occupation of the rest of Poland and the western Soviet Union in
  1941, in a policy of Jewish ghettoisation, impoverishment that resulted in
  destitution and starvation, and ultimately transportation to extermination
  camps in Poland and shootings of Soviet Jews by the Einsatzgruppen.

The Holocaust did then result from Hitler's ascent to power in Germany, his total
power and legitimacy in the Third Reich, the repressed and apprehensive nature of
ordinary Germans under the Nazi regime, and Hitler's radical antisemitism, and did
not result from the cultural antisemitism of ordinary Germans exacerbated by
deprivation in the Great Depression, as Staub seems to indicate. On the contrary, the
Holocaust was an outcome of the Nazi regime's rewards to ordinary Germans in terms
of standard of living and a sense of racial superiority with German reaffirmations of

power In Europe and of Nazi totalitarian repression of political opposition, for that resulted in popular compliance with the dictates of the Nazi regime to optimise personal outcomes by avoidance of anything political and by exclusive attention to meeting the requirements of role at work and otherwise confining oneself to the private sphere. The Holocaust was in other words a top down, not bottom up phenomenon that emerged in small increments of marginalisation of and discrimination against Jews, their exclusion from ordinary German life in which they had been integrated before the Nazis came to power, their emigration for the fortunate and for the others ghettoisation and finally transportation to extermination centres in Poland.

Ordinary Germans were apprehensive regarding the state sanctions of Nazi totalitarianism but were not simply terrorised into acquiescence by Nazi repression, which admittedly began immediately in early 1933, as soon as Hitler's Chancellorship began, with arrests and internment in concentration camps of communists, socialists, trades unionists and social democrats conducted without secrecy and possibly intended to be exemplary and indicative of the adverse consequences of political opposition to the Nazi government. For as has been indicated the record of the prewar years of Nazi government were ones of economic recovery from the unemployment and deprivation of the Great Depression for the great majority of ordinary Germans, of a better standard of living, government stability unknown in the Weimar Republic and greatly enhanced German international prestige as Hitler defied the terms of the Treaty of Versailles by rearming, the introduction of conscription, the remilitarisation of the demilitarised Rhineland in 1936, the Anschluss with Austria in March 1938, the triumph over the Sudetenland in September of that year, and the occupation of the entirety of Czechoslovakia in March 1939 in violation of the undertakings he had given European leaders at Munich in September 1938. There followed the Blitzkrieg against Poland, the first military victory and one accomplished with astounding speed, and then similar successes against Denmark and Norway in April 1940 and France just months later. For ordinary Germans then, with their attention to their own lives and futures, the Hitler years between 1933 and 1941 had been advantageous, and the casualties of the Nazi regime elicited inattention or indifference from the great majority of Germans, and continued to do so during the war years.

For ordinary Germans' optimisation of their own outcomes resulted in selective attention to what conferred on them some advantage or disadvantage and in disregard for the welfare of others. This situation did not change during the earlier part of the campaign against the Soviet Union in 1941 and most of 1942, for there were more military victories for the Wehrmacht against the Red Army, but after the decisive German defeat by the Red Army at Stalingrad in late 1942 and early 1943 and with British and US bombing of German cities the emphasis may have changed from natural support for a regime and leader that had brought such success to Germany to conformity out of fear as the German population itself began to suffer because of the failure of the Luftwaffe to protect them, the losses especially on the eastern front that began to affect many ordinary Germans, and Goebbels' call for commitment to total war and enhanced sacrifice from the German public in 1943 as the war turned against Germany. And following the July 1944 bomb plot, as has been seen above, the Nazi regime responded by becoming very much more repressive and instituted a policy of extreme violence, including execution, for any departure from desired public behaviour, a policy that was to continue to the end of the war, when any failure to conform or acknowledgement that Germany had lost the war, which had been apparent for several months to any rational observer, resulted in immediate execution at a local level.

There is one other strand of evidence regarding what the German public knew of the Nazi regime that is significant for the degree of its conformity to optimise its outcomes. For labour was central to the idea of the Volksgemeinschaft, the German people's racial community, and to the subordination of the individual to the collective and of the collective to the race and to Hitler as Führer, and forced labour was instituted in the early concentration camps as a form of humiliation of internees even though the work appears to have had no positive output. That was to change with the exigencies of war with a limited population, for compared to the immense reserves of manpower of the Soviet Union the far lower population of Germany became an endemic problem in the military sphere, in which the Red Army generals could afford to engage in warfare that meant far greater losses than those sustained by the Wehrmacht, which did not have the luxury of opting for such tactics and so was at a disadvantage once the initial assault with Blitzkrieg tactics had been endured. The limited German population was also a problem in the production of armaments, the result of which was the use of foreign labour, initially not forced and from Italy, Germany's Axis partner, and thereafter from the occupied territories of the east, from which forced labour became Nazi policy and was so prevalent that ordinary Germans could not have failed to notice it regardless of their attention to their own work and private lives. These slave labourers were mistreated, regarded as expendable and worked to death in many cases, to be replaced by more forced labour. Here too the inference is indifference and pursuit of personal interest on the part of ordinary Germans.

Some forced labourers were of course Jews, in the early concentration camps of the Third Reich in the 1930s and thereafter in the camps in Poland, where work was a means of avoiding extermination for a time. Even so, there is no evidence that the German electorate ever voted for antisemitic measures and certainly none indicating endorsement of the destruction of the Jews of the occupied territories. On the contrary, they voted for prosaic reasons associated with standard of living and identity, and then conformed to optimise their own personal outcomes, their attitude being one of indifference to what happened to the Jews.

Staub's reference to 'predisposing cultural characteristics' is then mistaken in its indication of some inclination towards radical mistreatment of the Jews, and seems to be reminiscent of Goldhagen's claim that ordinary Germans were culturally predisposed to eliminationist antisemitism. In fact, the evidence indicates that for ordinary Germans the Jews had a quality of 'otherness' that elicited indifference to what happened to them and a feeling that it was none of their concern, with primary and in fact exclusive attention to their own lives at work and home.

Staub also claims that a history of group conflict exacerbates the likelihood of perpetrator behaviour, but there was no record of conflict between ordinary

Germans and German or other European Jews, not least because of the Jews' ethos of assimilation and endurance of discrimination and even of pogroms without resorting to conflict. The inference is that Staub's reference to perpetrator behaviour here is meant to include the complicity of ordinary Germans in their passivity or opportunism in the context of the criminality of the Nazi regime, because his intention seems to be to identify the causes of the Holocaust, which was of course facilitated by ordinary Germans' inattention or indifference and their turning away to the depoliticised spheres of work and home. Staub claims that bystanders have the power to inhibit perpetrator behaviour but tend to remain passive and over time to become less concerned regarding the victims, even to the extent of becoming perpetrators themselves. The reference to the power to inhibit perpetrator behaviour is not realistic for totalitarian societies of atomised individuals under a repressive state apparatus, but bystanders do tend to remain passive. This is because they wish to avoid state sanctions themselves, but Staub does not refer to this motive. And bystanders who become perpetrators would tend to do so when their role requires it rather than through some process of moral corruption resulting from being a passive bystander. Their lack of concern for the victims reflects the salience of their own concerns and motive to optimise their personal outcomes and their relative indifference to what is happening to victims.

Staub's list of factors he claims predispose individuals and societies to perpetrator behaviour continues with reference to ideologies that exploit cultural 'devaluation of a group' and 'negative stereotypes', though he does acknowledge that such cultural devaluation may exist without genocide, as in imperial Russia with its pogroms. What may be said of such devaluation is that it could explain discrimination but not the extermination of a group, for 'cultural devaluation' of Jews was characteristic not just of interwar Germany but also of many other European nations, and did not result in popular approval of the extermination of the Jews in Germany.

Staub also cites German respect for authority and a culture in which there was no diversity but disregards the pluralistic nature of the Weimar Republic with its liberal democracy and democratic institutions and the alternative cultures of communism, socialism, conservatism and nationalism in interwar Germany. He conjectures that a cultural characteristic of assumed German superiority combined with recent experience of German exposed weakness and humiliation to elicit a need to enhance the conceptualisation of the race and culture on the part of Germans. There is no evidence that the majority of ordinary Germans had any such experience after German recovery from the Depression and disregard of the terms of the Treaty of Versailles and none that it had any causal connection to the Holocaust.

Staub's reference to the influence of past 'victimization' does not seem to have predicted intergroup conflict initiated by European Jews, for instance, despite their persecution throughout European history and not least in the pogroms in Tsarist Russia, and so does not seem to have had any autonomous influence on the incidence of perpetrator behaviour. In Germany by 1939 ordinary Germans had had years of enhanced prosperity under the Nazi regime, and no recent experience of 'victimization'.

Staub refers to a culture of aggressiveness and points to the violence of German veterans of the First World War in the interwar period, but these veterans did not represent the majority of Germans, who had after all voted for the social democrats rather than for nationalist militaristic groups. Staub's reference to scapegoating and ideology does not explain why the attitude of ordinary Germans to what happened to the Jews during the war was indifference rather than aggressiveness.

The case presented by Staub does seem to lack any appreciation of the nature of Nazi totalitarianism and the resulting nature of Nazi society, in which ordinary Germans were apprehensive of dissent or political involvement and felt powerless to protest even if they wanted to, and there is no evidence that they did for the sake of the Jews. Staub appears to believe that the German public could have stopped the escalation of mistreatment of Jews in the Third Reich by opposing it, but totalitarian governments deter dissent through their record of punitive violence against political opponents. Staub seems to lack any appreciation that human behaviour is dominated by pursuit of personal interest and the result is that Staub has expectations that are unrealistic for any population and for totalitarian societies in particular. He also refers to group conflict as a predictor of perpetrator behaviour, but there was no history of group conflict between ordinary Germans and German Jews, who were, even according to Staub's own admission, assimilated into German society. What Staub then resorts to is an argument similar to that of Goldhagen and referred to above, that there was a strain of eliminationist cultural antisemitism that was latent in ordinary Germans, though there is no evidence of it, presumably because it was latent. What there is evidence of is a German cultural antisemitism that was shared by many other Central European populations and governments in the interwar years, one that regarded the Jews as having a certain 'otherness' and so distinct from them. It was a form of antisemitism that countenanced a reduction in Jewish influence in German society but not one that advocated or supported their ghettoisation or extermination in the camps of the east or their shooting in numbers by the Einsatzgruppen.

The evidence of Christopher Browning's 'Ordinary Men' (referred to above) indicates that predisposing cultural characteristics are not a necessary condition to perpetrator behaviour of the most visceral and inhuman kind, murder by shooting of defenceless elderly Jews and of Jewish women and children. All that was required was the assignation of the murderous task even to a battalion of men with little Nazi indoctrination and mostly of an age that indicated socialisation before the Nazi period. For the majority conformed to meet the requirements of their roles to be approved of by the SS hierarchy, to be seen to be shouldering their part of a very unpleasant task assigned to the battalion, and to prove themselves to possess the necessary 'toughness' to commit such atrocities. For those who felt a more compelling abhorrence for the idea of shooting elderly Jews and Jewish women and children, desire for approbation and for avoidance of ostracism, ridicule, gossip and disapproval from the peer group resulted in their participation in the perpetrator behaviour of the battalion. These were different conformity responses. Those who participated in the shootings without apparent qualms were competitive and opportunistic, compliant with orders from the authority of the SS hierarchy above them for careerist reasons involving desire for enhanced status or to demonstrate ostensibly virtuous qualities (in the context of the SS) such as discipline and 'toughness'. Those who showed abhorrence and reluctance and initially at least chose not to participate in the shootings (their commanding officer had given the older men of the battalion the choice, indicating that any man could avoid involvement without sanction from the commanding officer) did in some cases eventually comply and participate in the shootings to avoid the social sanctions of the peer group, not least ridicule and ostracism. All the men in the battalion knew that refusal to shoot the elderly Jews and Jewish women and children would not have resulted in punitive official sanctions or in any threat to rank or to life, and the evidence of Browning's 'Ordinary Men' is indicative of the sufficient conditions for perpetrator behaviour, assignation of a task by some form of authority and individuals' desire to optimise their own outcomes as they perceived them to be.

The existence of a totalitarian social and political hierarchy one objective of which is perpetrator behaviour against a minority group and human optimisation of personal outcomes are then clearly when taken together a sufficient condition for perpetrator behaviour of the most immediate, visceral and inhuman kind. The issue of whether or not this combination is also a necessary condition may be answered by asking if anyone would defy authority and peer group where the task assigned was immoral as a consequence of any or all of the other predisposing factors Staub cites, for instance sociocultural predispositions, aggressiveness and experience of intergroup conflict. For there seems to be no indication that any or all of these other possible predisposing influences have ever been sufficient to cause perpetrator behaviour in defiance of authority and peer group, except in the isolated cases of psychopaths or genuine ideologues.

Staub's work may point to a number of antecedent factors that could predispose a population to intergroup conflict eventuating in perpetrator behaviour, but not all of these factors are functionally equivalent or necessary, and each particular case may have a different combination of the characteristics he mentions. The approach of attempting to find a general schema of antecedent factors that explains all instances of perpetrator behaviour seems to assume their presence and influence even where the evidence indicates otherwise.

Though Staub refers to bystanders and perpetrators as if they were groups with some uniformity of behaviour, experience and motive, they were not undifferentiated groups. For some bystanders were beneficiaries of Nazi repressive policies or perpetrator behaviour, for instance opportunists who appropriated Jews' homes and possessions or who systematically dispossessed them in the Jewish ghettoes, the careerists in the SS who achieved the status they aspired to by becoming functionaries in the extermination of the Jews, for instance Eichmann and the Einsatzgruppen, Einsatzkommando and Sonderkommando commanders, and the wives of SS perpetrators whose standard of living and social status depended upon their husbands' careers. Other bystanders by contrast did the bare minimum to meet the requirements of their roles to avoid Nazi state repression for themselves and their dependants, were not beneficiaries of Nazi perpetrator behaviour, became perpetrators only when changes in their roles required perpetrator behaviour of them, and if that happened conformed minimally to role requirements. Much of Staub's analysis employs concepts from social psychology that are abstractions for which there is no evidence in the record of the Nazi regime's bystanders and presumes a degree of reflection on the part of bystanders that ordinary Germans and ordinary people elsewhere in time and place seem unlikely to have engaged in, for normal life, not least given the habituation that Staub mentions, is a routinised experience, and, as has been indicated, one informed most decisively by attention to what is best for the individual concerned rather than by moral anguish and any need on the part of bystanders to rationalise and so justify their behaviour. Staub's argument could be that the individuals concerned would not have been aware of the processes to which he alludes, but that raises the issue of how conjectural such inferences are for human behaviour.

Staub's reference to Heider's consistency or balance theory, in the claim that ordinary Germans admired Hitler, attributed improved living standards and German racial status to him, and associated him with the extermination of the Jews, and that such association made the eradication of the Jews seem legitimate is an example of an attempt to impose an abstraction or concept on a reality in which there is no evidence to support it. Pragmatic optimisation of personal outcomes, not ideological commitment or personal commitment to Hitler, dictated the behaviour of bystanders, whom Staub characterises as 'semiactive participants'.

Staub claims that bystanders had and do have some power but has a very selective approach to the presentation of evidence on the issue. He cites social psychological research on bystander apathy to make the point that bystander intervention may alter the perception of the situation by other bystanders and induce them to intervene too, but the problem here is one of ecological validity, for what may be observed in experimental conditions may not be replicated in the real world, where the primary drive to optimise personal outcomes is the most compelling, for unlike experiential conditions there may in real life be genuine adverse consequences for bystander intervention to help another person. Staub does not refer to the social psychological research on altruism, which has found that even ordinary helping of others declines with rising cost to the helper, another indication of the primacy of optimisation of personal outcomes in human behaviour even when the cost involved is relatively trivial, unlike the situation facing ordinary Germans under Nazi rule.

Staub also cites the case of Denmark, where he claims that the resistance (which in fact never amounted to more than a minute percentage of the population of Denmark at the time) facilitated the escape of great numbers of Danish Jews, but the apprehension of Denmark's Jews appears not to have been a priority for the Nazi occupation relative to maintenance of a stable Denmark and of its valued exports, so the objective risk to the resistance may have been low and significantly the subjective risk as perceived by the resistance may also have been minimal. There is evidence that at least one member of the German authorities colluded in the escape of Jews from Denmark. The Danish case is then unique and one should not extrapolate from it to inferences regarding the possibilities of bystander inhibitory influence on perpetrator behaviour in general terms or in the case of Nazi German policies generally.

The other case Staub cites is that of Hitler, but the German public's view of antisemitic measures was only a concern to him early on in the Nazi period, before Nazi totalitarianism had become established. And there is no indication that Hitler was at any time considering the effect of German public opinion to the extent of halting discrimination against or persecution of the Jews or any other forms of perpetrator behaviour. Staub seems to have an interest in overestimating the possible influence of bystanders with liberal values, which may be part of a liberal humanitarian narrative of advocacy of protest against violations of civil and political rights that may be more applicable to liberal democratic societies than to totalitarian ones, but even he acknowledges that any possible effect of bystander opposition has to be early on and diminishes as totalitarian repression and rule become established. There does seem to be a general problem with extrapolation from limited evidence, social psychological or historical, to explain human bystander behaviour in great populations of people, and with Staub's not considering the effect of the motive to optimise personal outcomes that is to be found in all human behaviour.

Staub does then seem to identify the antecedents of a number of instances of perpetrator behaviour and to attribute causal influence to them, when some of the factors he mentions may be causally influential and some may be merely facilitative or may not have existed in the particular case, so there is a sense of a *post hoc ergo propter hoc* fallacy in his reasoning, some of which is contradicted by the historical record of what appears to be his primary case, the Holocaust. This search for common features and attribution of causal influence to them denies the particularistic nature of each instance of perpetrator behaviour and the reality of a different set of sufficient conditions in each case.

Staub does indicate a need to modify his conception for particular cases, but his references to the Nazi regime do not address the number of his factors that did not exert any decisive influence on German bystander behaviour, and he does not acknowledge the influence of pursuit of personal interest on bystander behaviour except to indicate that difficult life conditions may not be the only cause of or a necessary condition for intergroup violence in reference to violence perpetrated against primitive peoples to acquire their land, which he claims involves 'intense devaluation of the victim group'.

Staub goes on to identify 'ethnopolitical violence' associated with 'ideologies of antagonism' as another autonomous 'motivation for violence' by postulating an existential threat from another group in which anything gained by that adversarial group is seen as a loss, indicating a perception of advantage as constant sum and relative. Staub claims a group may be defined by its antipathetic relationship to another group, and cites the former Yugoslavia, Israel and Palestine, and Rwanda as examples. In these cases Staub claims that difficult life conditions are not necessary but would exacerbate the antagonism between groups. Yet in the Weimar Republic and the Third Reich the Jews represented no threat whatever to ordinary Germans or to any German government, and the lurid accounts of their deviousness and pervasive influence of Nazi propaganda were credible only to the antisemites of the Nazi movement.

Staub identifies possible predisposing influences on specific instances of perpetrator behaviour rather than necessary and sufficient conditions for all cases of perpetrator behaviour. Yet even here Staub claims that 'in generating group violence' the causal influences 'minimally include a history of devaluation of the other, the evolution of destructiveness (which has sometimes occurred over a long period preceding a flare-up of current antagonism), and the role of bystanders. Usually, some form of destructive ideology and the ideological justification for violence also exist'.

This account of minimal preconditions for extensive group violence is, as has been seen, challenged by the evidence of the Third Reich and the Holocaust. For in the interwar period Jews were assimilated into German society and the cultural antisemitism of the great majority of ordinary Germans was less intense than that found in other central and eastern European countries at the time, ordinary Germans were preoccupied with economic issues related to employment and standard of living rather than the Jews, and there was no history of destructive attitudes amongst ordinary Germans towards the Jews. There was Nazi ideological antisemitism, but even that was not eliminationist to begin with, not until the occupation of Poland and the western Soviet Union with their enormous concentrations of Jews, the failure of Jewish emigration schemes and the impossibility of exiling Jews to Siberia with the Red Army's defiance before Moscow in December 1941. And Nazi antisemitism was of an intensity that was not characteristic of the attitude towards the Jews of ordinary Germans, who were apathetic towards Jews, indifferent to their plight and attentive to their own concerns. The role of bystanders who attended to their own concerns and avoided involvement in political matters was a reaction to the advantages of Nazi rule in economic terms and to the Nazi state repression of the interwar years in Nazi Germany.

The evidence indicates that each instance of perpetrator behaviour had its own complex of causal influences. In the case of the Third Reich it was the sequence of events that brought Hitler to total power in Germany, including the Great Depression and German economic deprivation as a consequence, the arrogance and complacency of German conservatives in believing they could control Hitler, Hitler's own intransigence and opportunism, and the passive complicity of a German population that optimised its own outcomes by responding to Nazi totalitarianism by conformity in the form of avoidance of political dissent or involvement and attention to meeting role requirements and the private sphere.

Notes

[1] See Staub, Ervin, 'The Psychology of Bystanders, Perpetrators and Heroic Helpers', in *The Psychology of Good and Evil: why children, adults and groups help and harm others*, Cambridge, 2003.

[2] See Gordon, *Hitler, Germans, and the "Jewish Question"*, op. cit., pages 67–70.

Chapter Four

Other evidence of the decisive influence of pursuit of personal interest on human behaviour

The evidence of resistance movements in the Second World War

In France the numbers joining the Resistance increased sharply when in February 1943 the Germans introduced compulsory labour in Germany, for then the choice was between fleeing to the French countryside and joining the Maquis or being transported to Germany as labour at a time in the war when prospects of survival may have seemed greater in the French countryside than in German towns under aerial bombardment. The numbers in the French Resistance have been an issue of great controversy since the end of the war, and Wieviorka differentiates between the 'Resistance organisation, which obviously comprises only a very small minority, and a Resistance movement', which included all those who undertook individual actions to aid the 'organized Resistance'. How often and with what risk are not specified, but Wieviorka claims that the numbers in the Resistance movement were significant. The numbers who undertook regular genuine risk are of course those of whom it could be said there was some departure from optimisation of outcomes. The evidence of the rise in numbers in the Maquis when it became optimal to flee from the prospect of labour in Germany does appear to indicate the influence of pursuit of personal interest and so does the evidence of collaboration from the French population in the form of the minimal compliance inferred from the lack of an incidence of draconian reprisals from the Germans for resistance in France. The myth of the French Resistance has been propagated it seems to obscure the extent of French collaboration with the Germans and the collaborationist Vichy regime, 'a myth of people united in hostility to the Nazi occupiers, a nation of resistants'.[1]

In Poland the numbers in the various resistance groups have been estimated to be 410,000, with as many as 400,000 in the Home Army (the 'largest resistance organisation in Europe') in late 1943, which in a population of Poland in 1939 of 35.2 million gives a figure of 1.168 per cent of the population engaged in resistance rather than avoidance, minimal conformity or collaboration with the Nazis.[2]

The numbers in the Yugoslav resistance in late 1943 were 320,000, or about two per cent of the Yugoslav population (of 15,842,000 in 1948), a percentage not dissimilar to those of France and Poland and an indication of the small minorities of the populations of occupied Europe involved in resistance rather than minimal or more opportunistic collaboration with the Nazis (the figure for Yugoslav partisans rose to

650,000 in late 1944, it seems because of partisan control of the mountainous areas and the partisan victory over German forces in the summer of 1944).[3]

Though these percentages are of total populations that would have included children who could not have participated in the resistance to German occupation and so may understate the percentages of adults who could have joined resistance movements, the low percentages quoted are indicative of the minimal or opportunistic collaboration of the great majority in the occupied countries during the war. And of course it would have been advantageous to become a partisan in areas controlled by partisan groups, where membership would not have indicated attachment from principle but rather optimisation of outcomes. It is unfortunate that there is no figure for partisans as a percentage of the total population of the part of the Soviet Union occupied by the Nazis, it would seem because of difficulties in assessing the total population under German occupation from year to year.

The contrasting economic records of communism and capitalism

The failure of the communist societies of the eastern bloc in economic terms indicates that ideological exhortation to work for the collective good did not succeed in eliciting commitment and innovation from people, who engaged in minimal compliance with the dictates of totalitarian states to avoid punitive state sanctions and who were for instance far more productive on the small private plots permitted in Poland than on state-run enterprises there. By contrast the West with its free market economies and incentive societies of steep inequality has succeeded in optimising economic outcomes, predicated upon normative individual pursuit of personal interest in competition with others for wealth, status and power or influence that accords with the human attribute of individual optimisation of outcomes at the expense of others.

Obedience to the law

Though the question of why laws are obeyed seems to be controversial, with some sociologists claiming that legitimacy is a critical factor in popular compliance with laws and others arguing that laws are obeyed only to avoid sanctions imposed for their violation, the fact that all legal systems in all cultures and times have had both laws and sanctions does seem to indicate that the latter are regarded as a necessary condition to compliance with laws.

Tyler refers to the contrast between 'deterrence literature' that represents the 'instrumental perspective' and claims a deterrent effect on undesired behaviour from 'increasing the severity and certainty of punishment', and the 'normative perspective' that refers to the influence of 'distributive justice' and 'procedural justice'. Reporting on his 'Chicago Study', Tyler notes instrumental concern and some deterrent effect though also claims that personal morality exerts influence on the extent to which people obey the law through a belief in the moral legitimacy of the law and through a 'perceived obligation' to obey the law. Tyler claims that 'sanctions are of decidedly secondary importance in explaining compliance', indicating a role for sanctions but not their being 'the key defining feature'.[4]

The 'instrumental perspective' is that of my argument in this essay, and would expect human behaviour to reflect the perceived relative advantages to the self of compliance and non-compliance with laws and norms given what is known of the associated sanctions, so factors that could intervene would include the intensity of the drive to violate the law or norms, which may reflect the practices of peer groups in the case of compliance with the law, for the influence of drives and peer group norms on behaviour would of course represent optimisation of personal outcomes in material, social and psychological terms.

One criticism of Tyler's claims is that they are predicated upon self-report evidence (which he acknowledges), and many people may claim to obey the law for moral reasons when in fact if sanctions were removed they would not obey the law, for people may find it rewarding to believe themselves to be obeying the law for moral reasons when they are in fact observing it to avoid sanctions for violation of the law or may be engaging in presentation of self in the most favourable light to interviewers, a known tendency with such measures. For obeying the law is normative, not doing so may be seen to attract punishing informal sanctions from primary groups as well as from the legal system, and appearing to respect the law may be a form of positive presentation of self for those interviewed, in that it conforms to the norm of respecting the law. Tyler's reference to popular concern for fairness in the justice system may then be no more than a narrative seen to be normative and so conformed to in responses. Another criticism is that the average age in Tyler's interviewed populations was forty-two and forty-three, and Tyler himself acknowledges that 'older people regard the law as more legitimate', indicating that his findings should not be extrapolated to younger age groups.

There are other inconsistencies. Tyler finds mistrust of the performance of the police and the courts as fair but faith in their being so in the future, and though he points to 'several reasons why people obey the law', including 'instrumental concern with being caught and punished' or 'deterrence', 'personal morality' that sees 'law breaking is morally wrong' and a 'perceived obligation to obey the law', he notes that 'support for the police and courts was not particularly high, and neither were evaluations of their performance', which seems to indicate conformity in respondents to a protocol that dictates expression of acceptance of the law's legitimacy and of an obligation to obey the law to present a socially approved self. The fact that seems to be of some dissonance between expressions of generalised respect for the law and of lack of faith in its representatives and the workings of the legal system indicates that experience of the law was not the decisive causal influence on expressions of respect for the law, its legitimacy and the obligation to obey it. Tyler claims that there was no intense peer disapproval of law-breaking, possibly in an attempt to indicate that obeying the law could not be ascribed to peer-group influence and so to an 'instrumental' concern to avoid peer-group disapproval, ridicule, gossip or ostracism, though the evidence seems confined to 'more mundane cases' than drunk driving, for which he does find peer disapproval, indicating that his claim that moral dictates rather than avoidance of peer-group sanctions explain obedience to the law relates to mundane offences.[5]

The opposing view, that consonant with my own argument, is that of Schauer, who according to Kaufman claims that coercion is 'often necessary' to secure compliance with the law, that it is 'central to the very idea of law', that sanctions 'seem crucial' in securing compliance, and that coercion 'occupies center stage' in explaining obedience to the law. Kaufman goes on to criticise Schauer's exclusion of the law's moral legitimacy as a possible reason for obedience to the law, though for the Supreme Court case he mentions, Bush v. Gore, it seems that a perverse and unpopular decision did not elicit protest not out of respect for the moral legitimacy of the Supreme Court, as he claims, but because of the support for the Supreme Court from the coercive means of the legal system. Though that is an inference it is no less valid than Kaufman's inference, and more so when set in the context of the evidence presented here of the primacy of pursuit of personal interest in human behaviour.[6] Schauer does seem justified in claiming that 'sanction-independent genuine obedience to law is far less common than is often assumed'.[7]

To set the issue in context, if the perceived legitimacy of the law and an associated obligation to obey it were on their own sufficient to ensure that people obey the law, the sanctions of the legal system would not be necessary, and neither would the informal sanctions of gossip, ridicule, disapproval and ostracism to elicit conformity to the norms that govern social behaviour. The existence of such sanctions seems to indicate that self-interest is the primary influence on human behaviour, and that legal and normative systems elicit conformity because it avoids adverse consequences for the individual of not complying with laws or norms.

It cannot be argued that sanctions are needed to protect a majority who would obey norms of conduct or laws without the threat of sanctions for non-compliance from a very small asocial minority, for the incidence of tax avoidance indicates that those who are able to afford expensive tax accountants to find legal ways of evading tax do so. That indicates that norms that bear a cost such as paying taxes are obeyed only because of the sanctions imposed for violation and that where such sanctions may be avoided norms are disobeyed.

The end of communism in Europe

The demise of communism in the Soviet Union and eastern Europe is indicative of the relative influence of norms or ideology and sanctions or self-interest on human behaviour, for the communists of the eastern bloc seem to have transformed themselves into nationalists, democrats or populists to optimise their outcomes, and the peoples of those countries seem to have abandoned communism and its norms with ease to optimise their outcomes in the free democratic market societies that have replaced the communist regimes. Norms do then seem to exert influence on human behaviour only because of the sanctions associated with their violation rather than exerting any autonomous effect. For those socialised in the normative universe of the communist eastern bloc abandoned conformity to communist norms when it was optimal to do so.

The evidence of interaction and motivation in working and social life

Working and social life are governed by social protocols that require a camaraderie indicating togetherness and trust and preclude any reference to the reality of competitiveness in which status and well-being, both of which are zero-sum, are key influences on human behaviour. The imposition of informal social sanctions for violation of social protocols indicates a reality of competitive pursuit of personal interest at the expense of others, and observance of such protocols is optimal to avoid sanctions and to facilitate manipulation of other people.

Theories of motivation in human psychology

The theories that have been developed concerning human motivation all seem to involve implicit individual optimisation of outcomes. These include the drive theories of Hull and Freud, which postulate individual motivation to avoid adverse experience or to satisfy primitive desires. They also include, from humanistic psychology, Maslow's Need Hierarchy, in which, after meeting basic needs of hunger, thirst, shelter and security, love, belonging and self-esteem are claimed to be fundamental motivators. Love and belonging are of course a form of individual gratification and so a form of optimisation of personal outcomes, and their acquisition does necessitate a significant degree of compromise, with the other person, and conformity to the norms of social or peer groups for acceptance and belonging to occur. And self-esteem is related to enhanced social status, which is of course inherently relative and so competitive in nature, and may also require conformity in the form of presentation of self to manipulate social outcomes.

Arousal theory points to motivation as being derived from biological factors and related to the neurotransmitter dopamine, with individual differences in sensitivity to rewards resulting in differences in behaviour the objective of which is to assuage the desire concerned, with some people finding it impossible to delay gratification and others far more constrained by outcome and prudence. Most people do seem to be between these extremes, with a dominance of prudence and calculation of consequence, and delay of gratification, necessary to the cultivation of careers and relationships.

Developmental theories also appear to assume optimisation of individual outcomes as the primary influence on behaviour, as is the case with behaviourism, with its association of stimulus and response, and learning theories, which have postulated that children learn by emulating behaviour they see to be rewarded.

Incentive theory claims that primary motivation comes from extrinsic factors in the form of external rewards for behaviour, such as attention, social approbation, or enhanced career prospects, and the efficacy of incentive theory depends upon the self-esteem, locus of control motivation, the extent to which self-efficacy is a reward, and the neuroticism of the individual concerned. For the neurotic individual with low self-esteem and desire for self-efficacy and control, the external rewards mentioned may be very motivating, in that they would enhance self-esteem, assurance and a sense of being in control, and assuage a neurotic drive. Motivation may also come from intrinsic factors, that is, behaviours that are undertaken for their own sake, for the satisfaction that they proffer. These could include hobbies that give pleasure without external reward, but even behaviour initially undertaken for its own sake shall, if incentives to continue it are introduced, no longer be undertaken for its own sake and become dependent on external rewards, and most behaviour in ordinary life is extrinsically motivated, in working life with its inherent competitiveness in status hierarchies, where the motive is to maintain or enhance one's status, and in social life, where conformity to social or group norms reflects a desire for acceptance, approbation or admiration and for the avoidance of ostracism and ridicule. And even behaviour undertaken ostensibly for its own sake, for instance sport, may have a component of conformity to norms and competitiveness, both in team games, where there are group norms, and in more individualistic games, where rules must also be observed, and in most sport there is the desire to win or at least not to lose.

Cognitive and achievement approaches point to drives of need for achievement as motivating effort and achievement, which divides into an intrinsic motivation for mastery and comprehension, and performance objectives, which are extrinsic and involve instrumental commitment to tasks to obtain extrinsic rewards and to avoid punishing adverse outcomes. The difference is that the motive for mastery provides an enduring commitment, whereas the motive for achieve-performance objectives is contingent upon the achievement of external rewards and dissipates once rewards have been obtained unless needed for their maintenance. Of course human behaviour in most of working and social life reflects the primacy of extrinsic rewards.

Theories that trace human motivation from evolution also point to individualistic competitiveness within status hierarchies but with conformity as the optimal strategy to survive to reproduction age and pass genes on to the next generation for the great majority for whom dominance is not possible (the assumption in such theories is that all organisms are programmed to behave in ways that maximise their genes in the next generation and that genetic inheritance perpetuates that programming).

Theories of human motivation do then indicate the primacy of pursuit of personal interest in human behaviour and outcomes' being optimised by conformity to social or group norms in the majority of cases to avoid punishing formal and informal sanctions.

The self-serving bias

The self-serving bias is an indication of the primacy of self-interest in not just behaviour but also experience. Festinger's Theory of Cognitive Dissonance notes that it is not just the case that attitudes influence behaviour, the intuitive inference, but that attitudes reflect behaviour, which is counterintuitive. For Festinger found that when behaviour changed, for instance to conform to new role requirements (such behavioural change is of course a form of optimisation of outcomes), attitudes would change to reduce or eliminate the dissonance between the new behaviour and the pre-existing attitude, because dissonance between attitudes and behaviour causes discomfort, especially when the difference is between self-concept as a rational, moral person and behaviour that challenges such a concept of the self. An instance would be the commission of immoral acts with insufficient justification for them, which would be dissonant with a self-concept as moral and which has been seen to result in 'derogation of the victim' to eliminate dissonance. What Festinger seems to be indicating is that faced with a new situation the first human response is adaptation to optimise outcomes regardless of pre-existing attitudes and that the latter change to optimise psychological outcomes following optimising behavioural change. That seems to be another strand of evidence indicating the primacy of self-interest in human behaviour.[8]

Altruism

Another strand of evidence indicating the primacy of self-interest in explaining human behaviour is research on its opposite, altruism, for the evidence seems to be that much of what may seem altruistic is in fact a form of optimisation of personal outcomes by the individual concerned. Kin altruism in the form of care for children for instance would be predicted by the drive to maximise one's genes in the next generation claimed by evolutionary psychologists and so could be regarded as a form of self-interest. Here there is inadvertent optimisation of personal outcomes, for evolution seems to have programmed human beings to feel a drive to protect their children and possibly to feel acute discomfort if they feel they are not doing their best for their children. And of course it is normative to care for one's children and neglect is very much reproved societally, with punitive informal or even formal sanctions.

The difference between men and women in evolutionary terms is that for women maximising their genes in the next generation dictates care for their children and cultivating the protection of a socially dominant man (given that women can bear only a limited number of children), whereas for men the optimal stratagy to maximise the number of their children reproducing seems to be to impregnate as many women as possible. The explanation for paternal care and concern does then seem to be that referred to in the previous paragraph, that it is normative for parents to care for their children and that paternal care is indicative of fathers' conforming to a societal norm to avoid either the discomfort of not doing so, to the extent that the norm has been assimilated, or to avoid informal sanctions experienced as punitive. The same normative influence regarding parenting does of course also influence the behaviour of women who are like men socialised to obey norms and find sanctions punitive, and women may cultivate socially dominant men not just for the protection of children but also for the affluence and status such men provide.

Other forms of altruism have been identified as self-interested. Reputational altruism seems to have the objective of enhancing the self's reputation and so may be seen as a form of optimising social and psychological rewards. Reciprocal altruism is undertaken in the expectation of a return and so may be seen to be optimising personal outcomes by the individual concerned. And even the minor acts of helping behaviour that seem to be the cases cited as instances of altruism diminish when the cost to the individual helping is enhanced and so indicate the primacy of pursuit of personal interest in human behaviour.

Batson, an expert on altruism, addresses the evidence on helping behaviour and whether or not it indicates altruism. He concludes, 'proponents of altruism say not necessarily. Proponents of egoism say necessarily not' given their belief that all behaviour is for the 'ultimate goal of self-interest', for even where there is some 'material or physical cost' psychological egoists claim that 'there are social and self-rewards (praise, self-esteem) and avoiding social and self-punishment (censure, guilt). Proponents of altruism do not deny that motivation for helping is often egoistic.' Batson's very minimal claim is that 'psychological altruism does exist', though he does not claim any significant incidence of such altruism and his method of inferring 'psychological altruism' by ostensibly excluding all possible egoistic motives is open to challenge because excluding all possible motives of self-interest is not possible. Batson does not then dispute the primacy of self-interest in human behaviour, for his claim is no more than that it is possible for human beings to act in an altruistic manner when their empathy is engaged, with empathy being defined as concern for the experience of someone other than the self.[9] He does not challenge the argument that the great majority act to optimise their own outcomes.

Criticism of the concept of self-interest

The argument here has been that German popular complicity in the Holocaust reflected pursuit of personal interest and took various forms, avoidance of punitive Nazi state sanctions for dissent by turning away from anything political and attending to private life, preservation of one's position at work by compliance with role requirements, and for some opportunistic denunciations and taking advantage of the plight of Jews to misappropriate their possessions or perpetrator behaviour itself. The case is that German popular complicity in Nazi rule and the Holocaust reflected a universal human attribute of optimising personal outcomes rather than a German cultural attitude, and may be seen to be part of a wider controversy regarding the extent of influence from self-interest on human behaviour relative to other possible influences, such as claimed cooperativeness and altruism, and the claimed influence of morality, culture, creed, ideology and norms. Normative influence may though elicit cooperation or forms of apparent altruism because of the sanctions for violation of norms or because of the positive reinforcement of having observed in the socialisation process models who are rewarded for behaviour that is then emulated for similar motives. These cases would have to be considered as instances of pursuit of personal interest, and so would those members of ideological movements drawn to them for the psychological reward of belonging to such movements.

One enduring criticism of the concept of self-interest is that there is no evidence of it independent of the behaviour it seeks to explain, though support for its existence as a primary explanation for human behaviour comes from evolutionary psychology and the claim that evolution at the individual level results in hierarchical societies of competitive individuals who are programmed by natural selection to maximise their genes in the next generation and who optimise their chances of survival to reproduction age by dominance, possible only for the few, and compliance, the optimal stratagem for the many. The drive for status at the expense of others does then seem to be programmed in by evolution and selection of those best adapted to survive. Waller notes that there is a 'strain of selfish and aggressive traits that are part of our inherently self-centred human nature' and that 'sometimes altruism and cooperation turn out to be the most effective ways to compete'. The latter reference seems to be to conformity to group norms to enhance the survival of the group in competition with other groups for scarce resources. Waller relates ethnocentrism, xenophobia and desire for social dominance to evolutionary psychology and evolutionary selection of adaptive traits at the individual and the group level in what he refers to as the 'ancestral shadow'.[10]

Van Lange, De Cremer, Van Dijk and Van Vugt accept that self-interest is a 'powerful motivation' but argue that there is also evidence of 'cooperative choice' in prisoner dilemma situations, though they do not address the possibility that such evidence could indicate anticipated reciprocation or normative influence in circumstances with no real life consequences. They cite other prisoner dilemma evidence and a finding of empathy when participants are instructed to put themselves in the other's situation, though that seems to be empathy for the self in another situation with no real life consequences and with instruction that would never obtain in real life. Evidence is also presented of participants choosing fairness over 'self-enriching' outcomes, though there is no reference to 'reputational altruism' even though that seems an obvious possible explanation for such a finding and would constitute a form of optimisation of personal outcomes.

Reference to 'altruistic punishment' is to the tendency of people to punish violations of norms of cooperation in small groups even when there is a cost to the self, which is represented as evidence of a desire to '"do justice" to those who tend to exploit others'. That though is just one explanation, for another would be the psychological reward of punishment of those who violate norms and so threaten the psychological integrity and norm of compliance of the group. Another alternative explanation would be that all well-being is relative, so even an objective cost to the self of administering punishment to violators of group norms could, in the retributive nature of punishment, leave them worse off than they had been before their violation of the norms of the group, and so enhance the sense of well-being of those administering the punishment. Though the ensuing evidence of more intimate relationships presented by Van Lange, De Cremer, Van Dijk and Van Vugt does acknowledge selfish motivation as a possibility, there is an inference of altruism from the absence of 'recordkeeping' or reciprocity. That does of course not mean that reciprocity was not expected or influential on behaviour. A more compelling criticism is that the work does not address the effect of asymmetries of power in real life relationships on dominion and subjugation or on what is perceived to be optimal or normative by individuals who may seem to act without receiving reciprocation and so appear altruistic when in fact 'false consciousness', a belief in the legitimacy of the asymmetry concerned and its being optimal for that individual, is the explanation of the behaviour concerned.

In other words the possibilities of explaining the evidence presented by reference to self-interest are not explored. Van Lange, De Cremer, Van Dijk and Van Vugt refer to the 'myth of self-interest' (despite having acknowledged its influence on behaviour) and claim it is predicated upon the fact that 'people are more likely to reciprocate noncooperation than to reciprocate cooperation', though that could be seen to indicate a combination of vengeance and opportunism as motives in human behaviour.[11] For reciprocation of negative behaviours would require an incidence of such behaviour in the first place, that is, selfishness, and the contrast between selfishness and cooperativeness does not seem appropriate given that the latter could indicate pursuit of personal interest, for instance where the perception is that antagonism would result in adverse experience because of lack of power, or where cooperativeness is expected to elicit cooperativeness in return as others reciprocate in conformity to a norm of reciprocating overtures of cooperativeness to enhance the prospect of future exchanges.

Another criticism of self-interest as an explanation for human behaviour has been that the rational-choice theorists who advocate it do not ask the question, 'what explains this behaviour?', but rather 'can this behaviour be explained by reference to rational-choice theory?', which does not explore and so does not exclude alternative explanations for the behaviour concerned. That seems a reasoned criticism, but the approach of such critics is then to offer conjecture (not proof) regarding other possible explanations of the behaviour that are far less plausible than that of inadvertent or deliberate pursuit of personal interest, not least given that the latter has so much empirical support in the natural experiment of economic and social life outside of social psychology faculties. And of course if those challenging the explanation of self-interest for human behaviour are in fact attempting to find alternative explanations of human behaviour that is itself a form of bias.

For instance Millon et al find instances of 'trade offs' between 'justice concerns' and 'self-interest'. The first of these is the difficulty of victims for the idea of justice, which is resolved by the phenomenon of 'blaming the victim', though that seems to indicate the self-serving bias and the very 'self-interest' that is supposed to be traded in some way. In 'exchange fiction' people are more prepared to pay more than the worth of an object to help charities than they are to donate directly to charities, which is explained by reference to having to acknowledge with direct charity donations that the world is unjust and that injustice continues for those who are not helped by direct charity donations. Yet even with overpaying for products some charities may be helped and others not, and the more obvious explanation seems to be that the 'donation' in overpaying for goods is either less than would be required for a normative direct donation to charity or that such overpayment is less salient or seems less than direct donation to those donating. Another factor could be concern that direct donations to charities could elicit further requests for donations or result in some relationship that is not wanted. It is also possible that the 'justice concern' is in fact a concern to be seen to be concerned regarding justice, a form of presentation of self and a positive identity before audiences. The same could be said of 'derogation of the victim' to resolve the existence of victims without doing anything to help them. These explanations indicate primacy of concern for the self and are not it seems considered.

In 1990 two thirds of Europeans indicated preparedness to reduce their working hours and income (on average between ten per cent and twenty per cent) if it would create work for the unemployed, though in actuality they were not prepared to do so. The explanation offered is that there was no universality of preparedness to work less and take less income. That seems to be a rationalisation for not making the sacrifice in practice, and the more plausible explanation is that respondents sought to present a compassionate and selfless self when asked and that their apparent generosity was not authentic, both the presentation of self and declining to work less and have less income in practice being examples of self-interest, cultivating a positive impression and maintaining one's standard of living and socioeconomic status. The 'justice concern' that is decisive here seems to be justice for the self in relation to other prospective donors who decline to donate rather than for those who could have been helped, an indication of the influence of concern for the self over others, because if one were to work less and take less income and others did not one's socioeconomic status would be reduced in relative terms.[12] The evidence of this instance does then seem to indicate that when the cost of selflessness is anticipated to be significant self-interest is the primary influence on human behaviour. That is of course very similar to the finding in research on helping behaviour that is claimed to be evidence of altruistic motives, for when the cost to the self rises helping behaviour diminishes (see above). The controversy regarding the primacy of self-interest in human behaviour may in fact be to some extent semantic in nature, for there is no reference to self-interest in those who in conditions of starvation fight each other for food, and such behaviour is accepted as being entirely natural in such circumstances even though it is different only in context to other forms of pursuit of personal interest, not in process or motive. It is of course a minimal form of self-interest rather than one in which there was greater choice consistent with the survival of the individual, and as has been noted pursuit of personal interest forms a normal distribution in which the great majority conform to optimise personal outcomes either in a defensive way, to avoid risk of arrest or imprisonment or diminution in standard of living or status, or in a more opportunistic manner, taking advantage of their position in relation to those less fortunate. The relative numbers of those engaging in minimal and more active conformity, so relevant to any characterisation of the nature of human pursuit of personal interest as it manifests itself in human behaviour, are unknown. The inference is though that the very great majority engage in minimal conformity in the form of avoidance of risk and loss and that a percentage of that majority also engages in opportunism to enhance personal outcomes. The minimal case does though establish the existence of the motive to protect and enhance the interests of the self.

Discussion of the evidence presented in the context of Nazi Germany
The argument of the preceding chapter is that, given so much evidence from different and unconnected sources, some psychological and others from ordinary life in all societies, it is not plausible to claim that the German population was exempt from the primacy of personal optimisation of outcomes, that it was not the decisive influence on the behaviour of ordinary Germans. For that would be to claim some genetic abnormality inherited through evolution and natural selection that would have been maladaptive and have resulted in the perishing of Germans in the competitive process of natural selection because any lack of individual optimisation of personal outcomes would have resulted in poorer prospects of survival to reproduction age and the passing on of their genes to the next generation of Germans.

Some of the historical evidence presented here does not, it has to be admitted, isolate the influence on the behaviour of ordinary Germans of Nazi propaganda, a German cultural context of antisemitism and pursuit of personal interest at the expense of others from each other, for all these factors were of course present throughout the Nazi period. Goldhagen, Kershaw, Kulka, Bankier and Gellately indicate a prevalence of passive or more active complicity on the part of ordinary Germans under Nazi rule, though Goldhagen claims the cause was a German culture of eliminationist antisemitism, whereas Kershaw, Kulka and Bankier provide varying characterisations of ordinary Germans' indifference to the Jews, and Fitzpatrick and Fulbrook indicate a significant incidence of denunciation for reasons of pursuit of personal interest under communist totalitarianism.

Though these historians predicate their views on historical evidence, the inferences drawn by them do not isolate the effect of German cultural antisemitism or Nazi propaganda from that of pursuit of personal interest on complicity in the Holocaust on the part of ordinary Germans under Nazi rule. By contrast the evidence of Browning and Milgram does indicate the primacy of optimisation of outcomes for the self in human behaviour regardless of the cost to others and despite lack of ideological indoctrination that would legitimise the perpetrator behaviour observed. And so does the timing of perpetrators' endorsement of perpetrator behaviour, which seems to be part of their optimising careers in the elite SS, for before it became Nazi policy towards the Jews there is no evidence of eliminationist antisemitism in Nazi perpetrators. The same is true of ordinary Germans whose complicity was less direct, that there is no evidence of elimnationist antisemitism in them before it became Nazi policy towards the Jews, despite Goldhagen's claims. Taken with the evidence of all societies' depending upon legal systems that have formal sanctions for violation of norms and normative systems that punish breaches of norms (and the evidence of the extent of collaboration in occupied countries, where ideological indoctrination could not have been an influence), the indication is that the behaviour of ordinary Germans who became perpetrators and of those who had less direct complicity is explained by reference to human optimisation of outcomes. Ideological context seems to have been facilitative rather than decisive.

Notes

[1] See Wieviorka, Olivier, *The French Resistance*, Harvard University Press, 2016, p. 3, and Ousby, Ian, *Occupation: The Ordeal of France, 1940–1944*, Random House, 1999, p. xii.

[2] See Dallas, Gregor (1945), *The War That Never Ended*, Yale University Press, 2005, p. 79, and Chodakiewicz, Marek Jan, *Between Nazis and Soviets: Occupation Politics in Poland*, 1939–1947, Lexington Books, 2004, p. 347.

[3] See Cohen, Philip J., *Serbia's Secret War: Propaganda and the Deceit of History*, Texas A & M University Press, 1996, p. 96 for the numbers involved in the resistance in Yugoslavia in late 1943 and late 1944, and see *The Population of Yugoslavia*, Demographic Research Center, Institute of Social Sciences, Belgrade, 1974, p. 11, for the population of the country in 1948.

[4] See Tyler, Tom R., *Why People Obey the Law*, Princeton University Press, 2006, pp. 3 and 5, and Kaufman, Whitley, Review of Schauer, Frederick, 'The Force of Law', Harvard University Press, 2015, in *Law and Politics Book Vol. 26 No. 5* (September 2016).

[5] See Tyler, *Why People Obey the Law*, op. cit., pp. 40, 47, 50 and 56.

[6] See Kaufman, Whitley, Book Review of Schauer, Frederick, 'The Force of Law', Harvard University Press, 2015, in *Law and Politics Book Vol. 26 No. 5* (September 2016).

[7] See Schauer, Frederick, 'The Force of Law', Harvard University Press, 2015, p. 75.

[8] See Festinger, L., *A Theory of Cognitive Dissonance*, Row, Peterson, Evanston, Illinois, 1957, and Aronson, E., 'The Return of the Repressed: Dissonance Theory Makes a Comeback', *Psychological Enquiries 3*, 1992, cited in Metin, Irem, and Metin Camgöz, Selin, 'The Advances in the History of Cognitive Dissonance Theory', in the *International Journal of Humanities and Social Science Vol. 1 No. 6*, June 2011.

[9] See Sander, David, and Scherer, Klaus, *Oxford Companion to Emotion and the Affective Sciences*, Oxford University Press, 2014, pp. 26 and 27.

[10] See Waller, James, *Becoming Evil, How Ordinary People Commit Genocide and Mass Killing*, Oxford University Press, USA, 2007, pp. 158 and 200.

[11] See Van Lange, Paul, A. M., De Cremer, David, Van Dijk, Eric, and Van Vught, Mark, 'Self-interest and Beyond: Basic Principles of Social Interaction', in Kruglanski, Arie W., and Higgins, E, Tory (eds.), *Social Psychology: Handbook of Basic Principles*, Guilford Publications, 2013, pp. 544 and 545.

[12] See Millon, Theodore, Lerner, Melvin J., Weiner, Irving B., *Handbook of Psychology, Volume 5, Personality and Social Psychology*, John Wiley & Sons, 2003, pp. 541 and 542.

Chapter Five

A special case? The complicity of German women in the Third Reich

The view that women in Nazi Germany were victims of a patriarchal society that assigned women the role of rearing children and providing comfort for their men has been challenged to some extent by Koonz, Stephenson, Kompisch and Lower. It is true that the Nazi state regarded women as the bearers of the future of the German race merely in terms of reproduction and providing home comfort and support to Nazi men many of whom were perpetrators, a role German women were required to conform to in the same manner that German men were required to in their roles in the Nazi state apparatus, German businesses working for the Nazi state, the German army and the SS. Even so German women optimised their outcomes by conformity to the requirements of their roles to avoid informal sanctions and to obtain approbation and by various forms of voluntary collaboration and opportunism, for instance the inculcation of antisemitism in their children, unsolicited denunciations to the authorities, and benefitting materially from the dispossession of Jews.

Stephenson refers to Koonz's finding of the complicity of German women in providing a private sphere of normality for male perpetrators, conforming to the role of German women in Nazi Germany, and claims that such German women 'actively cultivated their own ignorance'. The inference is that women were not dissimilar to men in terms of conformity to role and complicity in the treatment of the Jews, and both German women's conformity to their assigned role and their avoidance of knowledge of the perpetrator behaviour of their men would have been optimal for such German women. For conforming behaviour would have ensured that German women benefitted from the status of Nazi or SS men and their avoidance of acknowledgement of their men's perpetrator behaviour would have precluded any discomfort regarding it or responsibility for it.

In addition to the women of SS and Nazi men in the Third Reich there is also now reference in the historiography to German women who boycotted Jewish shops and abandoned former Jewish friends, a form of minimal and defensive conformity that would have involved it seems the broad majority of German women and have reflected a concern to avoid informal sanctions of gossip, ridicule, disapproval, and ostracism and possible denunciation to the Gestapo. And there were German women involved in denunciations to the Gestapo and in the looting of the possessions of arrested Jews. These German women seem to have constituted at least a significant minority and their participation was more opportunistic. There was also a small minority of German women who became notorious as concentration camp guards.

Stephenson notes Gellately's finding of an extraordinary incidence of denunciations to the Gestapo, refers to women's use of entirely voluntary denunciations for personal reasons, and claims that lower-class women denounced middle and upper class women and that wives denounced husbands rather than the other way round. She quotes Wiggershaus's conclusion that the sadism displayed by German women perpetrators indicated 'no gender-specific difference in women's favour' and points to the latitude possible in the role of female warders indicated by what seem to be isolated instances of humane female warders who complied with the requirements of the role minimally. Her conclusion is that 'during the war, women were increasingly brought into traditional "male" environments, as professionals, as bureaucrats and clerical officers, and in prisons and concentration camps, and they often used their new opportunities for personal gain or to exert unaccustomed authority. In exercising agency, they, like men in Nazi Germany, often abused their power.'[1]

Despite producing evidence of German women's complicity and opportunism, with reference to Gestapo files from Dusseldorf that indicated that women would 'try to alter the power balance of the household by denouncing their husbands as spies', and to German women's brazen attempts to deny involvement in the Holocaust after the war, Kompisch makes the astonishing inference that women had suppressed their natural feminine attributes in such behaviour, though just what evidence there is for the existence for such natural moral attributes in women and not in men is unknown.[2] It is possible that the reference is to the supposed 'nurturing' qualities of women, though these are seen only in the context of rearing children, or the empathising expressive style of women that according to experimental evidence reflects women's conforming to the role requirements of female identity rather than greater kindness in women.[3] It is worth noting that Kompisch's work was published as late as 2008. In an indication of the idealisation of women's being a continuing theme, much earlier, in 1987, a *New York Times* article dated 2 March 1987, entitled 'Women in Nazi Germany: Paradoxes', discussing Koonz's work on German women in the Third Reich, had the following passage: 'Does Dr. Koonz believe that women are morally and emotionally superior to men? "No", she said, "I suppose that will make a lot of people angry."'

The article refers to another historian, Lerner, who is said to have commented, 'some women will find it very hard to take this bad news'.

Though Kompisch's and Koonz's work does not seem to have been affected by such apparent idealisation of women in academic life and in more general terms, in that both have identified the complicity of German women in Nazi society, Kompisch does refer to women's better nature, and Koonz indicates that German women were victims as well as collaborators in the Third Reich, though it would seem from the far greater numbers of German women who survived the war that German men suffered far more than German women under Nazi rule.

The recent literature does seem to indicate that there was no difference between

German men and women in terms of conformity or complicity in the treatment of the Jews and other work for the Nazi state or the SS. What was different was the role of women in Nazi Germany, which permitted them to benefit from the status of their men whilst requiring only that they support them and which made possible German women's deriving material or social advantage from the persecution of Jews. German men and women engaged in behaviour that reflected their respective role requirements to optimise personal outcomes or exceeded role requirements in opportunistic attempts to secure some advantage.

One difficulty seems to have been the idealisation of women in Nazi Germany as the bearers of a pure Aryan race. There seems no sense that women's motives would be similar to those of men. And even victims seem to have been appalled that women could have committed the heinous acts Nazi women perpetrated. After the war there was a continued idealisation of women's nature, one that was taken advantage of by German women perpetrators who presented themselves in as feminine a way as possible to post-war courts and so evaded justice. Lower, whose concentration is on a limited number of German women perpetrators in the east, notes that 'court officials noted when women cried during the questioning or proceedings. Such a display of emotion seemed to indicate humanity, sensitivity and presumably an empathy that was consistent with the nature or instinct of female innocence and caring.'[4]

The latter sentence is ambiguous. If it is intended to refer to some generalised female trait of kindness it seems to assume something for which there is no objective evidence, though it is possible that it is intended to refer to idealisation of the nature of women at the time. Elsewhere Lower refers to the dissonance between the perception of the nature of women at the time, as maternal, kind and caring, and the behaviour of 'nurses, mothers and wives who were accomplices and perpetrators', but also goes on to refer to women's role in social hierarchies in general, which she claims has been to enhance harmony and diminish aggression. She does not refer to the fact that the cultivation of harmony may be a form of complicity in immoral behaviour, as seems to have been so for German wives who provided comfort for perpetrator or complicit husbands selected for their status (the centrality of harmony was a factor in the perpetration of atrocities by Japanese troops in China in the late 1930s). And of course enhancing harmony optimised the outcomes of German women not just in terms of socioeconomic status but also of normative approbation for compliance with the requirements of their role in Nazi Germany. In these circumstances enhancing harmony is hardly a virtue.

Lower seems to explain women's perpetrator behaviour not in terms of natural pursuit of personal interest inherited from evolution but as a consequence of contextual influences that mitigated the influence of women's natural instincts, which she appears to claim without any justification were different to those of men. In its idealisation of German women, the lack of any reference to their motives or to the extent of their demonstrating agency in Germany during the war, Lower's work does not offer a plausible explanation for the behaviour of German women in the east during the war or for the behaviour of German women in general throughout the war.[5]

What is not known are the relative numbers of German women who conformed through providing the comfort of home life to German male perpetrators, through boycotting of Jewish shops or dissociating themselves from Jewish friends, and of German women who were involved through more direct agency by denouncing people to the Gestapo, obtaining the looted possessions of Jews, or by being doctors, nurses, secretaries, warders or camp guards in the east. That differentiation of the population of German women between those who minimally conformed and those who were more complicit or who engaged in perpetrator behaviour in compliance with or beyond the requirements of role seems decisive for any characterisation of German women's behaviour and complicity in Nazi Germany relative to German men. Much of the historiography relates instances of German women because there is no statistical evidence, and it is not legitimate to infer incidence from instance. That imposes a limitation on what may be concluded regarding the nature of the complicity of German women in quantitative terms, though the numbers in the east where so much actual perpetrator behaviour that took place are known.

Of the women in Nazi Germany those least interesting are the notorious female camp guards who exceeded the requirements of their role in their sadism, possibly enhanced by the dehumanised state of the Jews in the camps after the ghettos of Poland, by the receptiveness of such camp guards to crude Nazi propaganda vilifying Jews as enemies of the German race and state, and by their sense of impunity to adverse outcomes for perpetrator behaviour beyond the remit of the role. For such women were in statistical terms few and seem similar to psychopathic male guards. Of the 500,000 German women involved as nurses, secretaries and in other capacities in the German east according to Lower, there would have been few camp guards.[6] And of course Lower concentrates on a number of German women who chose to go or were sent to the east rather than addressing the totality of German women's complicity in the Third Reich. The numbers of German women complicit in the various ways referred to here would of course have been far greater. Lower claims that 'given the ideological indoctrination of the young cohort of men and women who came of age in the east in the Third Reich, their mass mobilisation in the eastern campaign, and the culture of genocidal violence embedded in Nazi conquest and colonisation, I deduced – as a historian, not as a prosecutor – that there were plenty of women who killed Jews and other "enemies" of the Reich, more than had been documented during the war or prosecuted afterwards.' And, acknowledging the numbers of killings by German women that were documented were 'not numerous', Lower continues, 'they believed that their violent deeds were justified acts of revenge meted out to enemies of the Reich' as 'expressions of loyalty'.[7]

Though the statement seems to be limited to German women's actual participation in murder of Jews rather than indicating the extent of more general complicity of German women in the Third Reich, it seems to assume an effect from Nazi ideological indoctrination and culture rather than producing evidence that might establish that German women's complicity was caused by ideological indoctrination, which seems to be a form of *post hoc ergo propter hoc* reasoning.

Lower notes that a woman named Petri explained her involvement in perpetrator behaviour by reference to 'the anti-Semitism of the regime and her own desire to prove herself to the men', an indication of both ideological indoctrination and of her desire to conform for reasons of personal interest in the form of enhanced status, though, in what seems to be a specific attempt at self-exculpation, Petri also claimed, 'I had been so conditioned to fascism and the racial laws, which established a view toward the Jewish people. As was told to me, I had to destroy the Jews.'[8] Though Lower does expatiate upon the indoctrination of young women in Nazi Germany as part of their socialisation and role, she also notes the aspirational character and purposes of the young German women who went east upon whom she concentrates, so it is difficult to see how she infers that ideological indoctrination was the decisive influence on their behaviour. In fact conditioning is effective only because of the human drive to optimise outcomes by avoiding sanctions imposed for violations of norms and even normative influence on behaviour occurs as a result of human optimisation of outcomes. For in socialization, behaviour that is seen to be rewarded is that learned and emulated.

Though Nazi socialisation and indoctrination may have been part of the prelude to perpetrator behaviour in the east for many German women, that does not mean that eliminationist antisemitism was the cause of such perpetrator behaviour by German women, and in fact Lower notes that 'most women who went east were not rabid anti-Semites'. Lower's intention seems to be to indicate the effect of conditions in the east on young German women, though part of that experience would have been a desire to conform to norms there.[9]

There seems to be no convincing evidence that women are more moral than men or explanation of why evolution would have selected greater morality in women than in men. What evidence there is seems of dubious value, in that it appears to be either in the form of responses to self-report measures that permit the individual to misrepresent actual motives to accord with normatively approved stereotypes, in the case of women a caring and empathising identity concerned with the welfare of other people, or responses to propositions that indicate little if anything as to women's behaviour in real life, where choices have consequences, and the findings have been contradicted by the evidence of neuropsychological measures that do not reflect presentation of self to conform to gender stereotypes. Research also indicates that women above a certain age tend to be more conforming to norms than men and that women are biologically as well as sociologically motivated to conform or engage in prosocial behaviour.[10]

Notes

[1] See Stephenson, Jill, *Women in Nazi Germany*, Pearson Education, 2011, pp. 113–15.

[2] See Kompisch, Kathrin, *Perpetrators: Women under National Socialism*, Bohlau Verlag Cologne Weimar, 2008.

[3] See Baez, S., Flichtentre, D., Prats, M. et al, *Men, Women ... who cares? A population-based study on sex differences and gender roles in empathy and moral cognition*, PLoS One. 2017: 12/61: e0179336 for reference to the fact that though 'experimental and neuropsychological measures show no consistent sex effect, self-report data consistently indicates greater empathy in women' and for the claim that

'self-reports may induce biases leading individuals to assume gender-role stereotypes'.

[4] Lower, Wendy, *Hitler's Furies, German Women in the Nazi Killing Fields*, Vintage, 2014, p. 168.

[5] See ibid, pp. 158–60.

[6] Ibid, p. 6.

[7] Ibid, p. 4.

[8] Ibid, pp. 4 and 156.

[9] Ibid, p. 163.

[10] See Baez, S., Flichtentrei, D., Prats, M. et al, *Men, Women … who cares? A population-based study on sex differences and gender roles in empathy and moral cognition*, op. cit., for reference to misrepresentation to accord with gender stereotypes and especially that of women in self-report measures. See also Eisenberg, Nancy, and Strayer, Janet (eds.), *Empathy and Its Development*, CUP Archive, 1990, pp. 197 and 203, for reference to large gender differences in self-reports regarding empathy and no gender differences in physiological measures and to their finding that though 'prevailing stereotypes lead one to expect females to exhibit greater physiological responsiveness' there is 'little empirical support for this expectation'. See Eagly, Alice H., and Chrvala, Carole, 'Sex Differences in Conformity: Status and Gender Role Interpretations', in *Psychology of Women Quarterly*, September 1, 1986 for the finding that 'females conformed more with surveillance than without it' and that 'older females (it seems older than 19 years old) were significantly more conforming than older males under surveillance'. That seems to be a reference to the greater social awareness of women and their greater tendency to conform to social norms in their behaviour because of an enhanced susceptibility to informal sanctions such as gossip, ridicule, disapproval and ostracism. And see Soutschek, A., Burke, C. J., Raja Beharelle, A. et al, 'The dopaminergic reward system underpins gender differences in social preferences', in *Nature Human Behaviour, Vol 1*, November 2017 for the finding that 'the neural reward system appears to be more sensitive to prosocial rewards in women than in men', though there is acknowledgement that the difference between men and women in prosocial behaviour could be the consequence of 'cultural expectations and gender stereotypes'. The indication is that women conform to optimise their material, social and psychological outcomes just as men do.

Chapter Six
Conclusion

The evidence presented here, especially the historical evidence of Browning and the experimental evidence of Milgram (and the need for sanctions to enforce norms and laws in all societies in all historical periods), indicates that individual optimisation of outcomes in the form of avoidance of consequences perceived to be punitive or in the form of taking advantage of opportunities is sufficient to explain both the passive, minimal conformity and the opportunism of ordinary Germans under Nazi totalitarianism. Such pursuit of personal interest at the expense of others seems to be the decisive influence on normal human behaviour in all societies, as is indicated by the fact that Milgram's experimental findings have been replicated so many times in different time periods and cultures, by the evidence of ordinary human behaviour under totalitarian regimes, and by the success of market societies with individual incentives contrasted with the failure of the ideological incentives of communism. Attitudinal disposition derived from culture or from ideological indoctrination seems to be a facilitative rather than a decisive influence on human behaviour and does not seem to be a necessary condition to minimal or active conformity. The indication is that ordinary Germans reacted to the Nazi regime and the Final Solution in much the same way that people in general do, optimising personal outcomes by a combination of conformity, adaptation and opportunism, characteristics inherited through the evolutionary process as optimally adaptive. What was different was context and consequence.

The behaviour of German women in the Third Reich is explained by a combination of assigned role, as supportive wives and mothers, which distanced most German women from perpetrator roles, and exactly the same self-interested motive that explains male adaptive minimal conformity and opportunism, for the evidence indicates that the behaviour of German women reflected the same motive of optimisation of personal outcomes as the behaviour of German men.

For ordinary German men the manifest universality of compliance in society and in the Nazi bureaucracy, the German Army and the SS must have made it difficult even to conceive of resistance to compliance with role requirements given the known difficulty of being the first or only one not to conform found by Asch and Milgram even in experimental settings. For ordinary German men there was also the reality of the Führerprinzip that legitimised every order from above by conferring on it the force of law from an inference of its being Hitler's wish. Such circumstances set in a context of the often unreflective, inadvertent conformity that is the means by which individual outcomes are optimised for the great majority of people may explain the perpetrator behaviour and less direct complicity of ordinary German men. There was also of course the threat of demotion and loss of socioeconomic status for the individual and his family with any defiance of role requirements under the Nazi state. For German women there seems to have been greater latitude, for there was no organisation in which conformity was expected and universal, and there seems to have been a greater voluntarism in German women's unsolicited denunciations to the Gestapo and obtaining of the looted possessions of Jews, for neither was a requirement of their role.

Perspectives on Eichmann
Explaining Perpetrator Behaviour

The purpose of this book is to assess the existing explanations of Adolf Eichmann's perpetrator behaviour. These include Eichmann as a monster of abnormal personality, Arendt's influential and controversial claim that Eichmann was entirely normal but devoid of capacity for moral reasoning, and Stangneth's and Cesarani's characterisation of Eichmann as an eliminationist antisemite. Arguments against these explanations are presented and the book argues that Eichmann was entirely normal not in the cognitive sense of limited moral awareness and poor appreciation of the consequences of his actions but in the sense of optimisation of his own outcomes in material, social and psychological terms regardless of the cost to others. This new argument is supported by reference to the social psychological experiments of Milgram on obedience to immoral authority and Zimbardo on the influence of role on behaviour, by reference to Browning's research on the perpetrator behaviour of a German police reserve battalion in Poland, and by reference to research on Einsatzgruppen commanders.

Chapter One
Introduction

Eichmann has been the subject of considerable controversy within academia and in the media since his apprehension by Mossad in Argentina and his abduction to Israel in 1960, a public trial that attracted worldwide attention in 1961 and his execution in Jerusalem in 1962. The opposing views on Eichmann seem to be well-represented by Hannah Arendt, a German American social philosopher and political theorist, who has claimed that Eichmann was entirely normal, and David Cesarani, a historian of the Holocaust, who claims that Eichmann's involvement in the destruction of Europe's Jews is explained by Eichmann's eliminationist antisemitism. Cesarani neatly sums up the sequence of historiographical perspectives on Eichmann over time, identifying an immediate post-war period in which Eichmann was perceived as an 'aberration – a pathological type', an ensuing perception, influenced by Eichmann's trial in Jerusalem in 1961, of Eichmann as an unreflective, compliant 'totalitarian man', a view of him as representing the tendency of bureaucracies to isolate individuals from the consequences of their actions and to facilitate immoral activity, an ensuing correction in the Eichmann case indicating the immediacy of the destruction of Europe's Jews for him, and Cesarani's own view, in 2005, that Eichmann 'appears more and more like a man of our time. Everyman as genocidaire', referring to the recent prevalence of brutal ethnic cleansing.[1] The inference is that Cesarani is referring to the influence of racial hatred on perpetrator behaviour, in the form of Nazi eliminationist antisemitism in Eichmann.

There have been various views on Eichmann from within the discipline of psychology. These moved from an initial view of him as a Nazi monster to a perception of Eichmann that has been very much influenced by the pioneering experiments on compliance with immoral commands of Stanley Milgram, an American social psychologist. Milgram's experiments, devised with variations to isolate the influences on obedience to immoral authority and conducted in the early 1960s, were intended to investigate the obedience to immoral authority of Eichmann and other Nazi perpetrators, and the astonishing levels of compliance with immoral authority Milgram found exerted enormous influence on the general understanding of Eichmann and of perpetrator behaviour for decades. More recently though Lang has claimed that Milgram's referring to the Holocaust as a historical example of such compliance has 'inadvertently deprived the Nazi genocide of its historical meaning and relegated perpetrator behaviour to a function of hierarchical social structures' and has diminished any sense of human agency or personal responsibility because causation is attributed to organisational factors. I shall return to Milgram below, though it should be noted here that Lang seems to be rejecting the link between Milgram's findings and Nazi perpetrator behaviour because the latter was located in a historical setting that exerted influence on perpetrators and because Milgram's findings seem to deny any individual responsibility. Rejection of a theory because it denies individual responsibility is not of course a coherent argument against its causal validity. The reference to a specific historical setting is more germane, not least in the context of the Führerprinzip and the SS code of obedience and discipline. Such views challenge the earlier consensus so influenced by Arendt and Milgram and the view that Eichmann was normal rather than a historical construction of the Nazi state.[2]

In what follows I shall discuss the evidence for the two main views of Eichmann that have endured, with a detailed assessment of Arendt's attribution of a banality of absence of moral reasoning to Eichmann and an assessment of Cesarani's and Stangneth's attribution of ideological antisemitism to Eichmann (derived from a specifically Nazi ideological context) as the decisive influence on his behaviour.[3] In contradistinction to both these views I shall argue that Eichmann's behaviour is explained by a combination of a trait dominant in almost all human behaviour in all cultures, inadvertent or calculated optimisation of outcomes for the individual concerned, and societal context that dictates what is rewarded and what is punished in material, social and psychological terms. My argument does then take account of ordinary human characteristics and of the context of Nazi Germany, and to support it I shall present contextual evidence from Nazi Germany and from Milgram's social psychological experiments on immoral behaviour.

For the purposes of this essay the term 'eliminationist antisemitism', originally used by Goldhagen in 'Hitler's Willing Executioners', shall be understood as differentiating an antisemitism that dictated the extermination of the Jews of Europe from a cultural antisemitism of Jewish 'otherness' of the sort found in many European countries in the interwar period.[4]

Before considering the different explanations of Eichmann's perpetrator behaviour, reference to Eichmann's background and upbringing would seem to set the context for his trajectory to SS officer and Jewish expert and thence to arranging transportation of Jews to extermination camps. Eichmann was born into a middle-class Protestant family in Solingen, Germany, in 1906. His father was a bookkeeper who exerted strict patriarchal control over the family and there were four more children after Eichmann himself. In 1913 the family moved to Linz in Austria as Eichmann's father had obtained a better job, as a manager, and in 1916 Eichmann's mother died. His father remarried into an affluent family, and Eichmann's stepmother was a strict Protestant. At school Eichmann had a Jewish friend but also other friends in a childhood that seems to have been entirely normal for the time. Eichmann did poorly at school and was removed by his father in 1921. At vocational college he did no better, left without qualifications and worked for his father in his various enterprises, many of which failed, though the family was never poor. In all these endeavours Eichmann seems to have done just what his father told him to do, which may also have been normal for the time. Eichmann was then found a job at an oil company by relatives of his stepmother, who had wealthy Jewish friends in Austria. There, between 1927 and 1933, Eichmann worked as a sales representative and in scheduled deliveries. There was then nothing in Eichmann's childhood to indicate any abnormality of personality or upbringing that could explain his ensuing perpetrator behaviour. Cesarani concludes that Eichmann had a 'normal upbringing and education' and 'an active social life, girlfriends, and, later, a wife and family', that he was 'conventionally bourgeois', and that his 'politicization' was 'normal' in its right-wing nationalism and cultural antisemitism,[5] though the latter seems to have had no effect on his friendships or on his using Jewish family connections to obtain work. Eichmann's joining the Nazi Party and SS in 1932 seems to have reflected the influence of friends of his father, for it was Ernst Kaltenbrunner, the son of a friend of Eichmann's father and at the time a leader in the SS, and a long-time national socialist named Andreas Bolek, another of his father's friends, who introduced Eichmann to the Nazi Party and the SS.[6]

Notes

[1] See Cesarani, David, *Eichmann: His Life and Crimes*, Vintage Books, 2005, p. 368.

[2] See Miller, Arthur G. (ed.), *The Social Psychology of Good and Evil*, Second Edition, Guilford Publications, 2016, pp. 189 and 190.

[3] See Deutschlandfunk.de, for Rolf Pohl's review of Irmtrud Wojak's 'Eichmann's Memoirs – A Critical Essay', for reference to Wojak's claim that Eichmann was a 'fanatical National Socialist' and that ideology was a decisive influence on Eichmann. For Wojak mere bureaucratic imperatives were not the decisive influence on Eichmann's sending Jews to extermination centres. Though Wojak predicates her work on primary sources from Eichmann in the form of his memoir from Jerusalem and the Sassen interviews in Argentina and counsels against trusting anything Eichmann claims given his motives, the evidence of the Sassen interviews seems to be accepted as evidence of Eichmann's antisemitism without interrogation as to context, an indication of biased treatment of evidence and selection of evidence that supports the case being made.

[4] See Goldhagen, Daniel Jonah, *Hitler's Willing Executioners: Ordinary Germans and the Holocaust*, Little, Brown, New York, 1996. See also Eley, Geoff (ed.), *The 'Goldhagen Effect': History, Memory, Nazism – facing the German Past*, University of Michigan Press, 2000, p. 5.

[5] See Cesarani, *Eichmann*, op. cit., pp. 16 and 19–23.

[6] Ibid, p. 26.

Chapter Two

The initial impression. Arendt: Eichmann's lack of moral reasoning

A rendt was the author of the phrase 'the banality of evil' to describe her impression of Eichmann at his trial in Jerusalem. The phrase was enormously influential in arguing against the idea that the Nazi hierarchy was composed exclusively of people of monstrous evil rather than mostly of ordinary human beings who would in other circumstances have lived entirely ordinary lives. The consensus in the psychological literature now is that the great majority of the major Nazis were entirely sane and rational, with just isolated instances of psychological abnormality, such as Hess, and one of the legitimate if hardly novel points in Goldhagen's controversial 'Hitler's Willing Executioners' was his noting that the extermination of the Jews involved great numbers of ordinary Germans in both passive and active complicity, the latter as lawyers, doctors, nurses, bureaucrats, camp guards, workers and in other professions. Goldhagen goes on to attribute the involvement of ordinary Germans in the destruction of the Jews of Europe to a German 'cultural norm' of 'eliminationist antisemitism' that preceded the Nazis' obtaining power in Germany, though nothing more than conformity to societal norms to avoid sanctions or meeting of role requirements to optimise personal outcomes was required for the passive or active complicity in the Holocaust of great numbers of ordinary Germans. The claims made by Goldhagen as to the motivation of German perpetrators shall be discussed in Chapter Eight below in connection with Browning's work, which was the stimulus for Goldhagen's 'Hitler's Willing Executioners'.[1]

Arendt's assessment of Eichmann reflects her disciplinary background in social philosophy, from which Arendt attributed Eichmann's perpetrator behaviour to a failure to reflect on what he was doing and its consequences, to 'Eichmann's moral and intellectual shallowness, his inner void'.[2] Arendt claims that Eichmann 'was obviously also no case of insane hatred of Jews, of fanatical anti-Semitism or indoctrination of any kind. He "personally" never had anything whatever against Jews', and that he was 'normal insofar as he was "no exception within the Nazi regime"'.[3]

Arendt claims that the effect of moral reasoning on behaviour regarding the Jews is established by the Danish resistance to the surrender of Jews for deportation to the camps. In Denmark ninety-nine per cent of the country's Jews survived the war, many having been helped to escape to neutral Sweden by the Danish resistance in 1943, and Danish Jews were received back into their pre-war positions in Danish society after the war.

The context is though indicative, for in the war Nazi control in Denmark was liberal by comparison with other countries in German-dominated Europe, in part it seems aimed at minimising the numbers of German troops needed to keep order there. The Danish government realised the hopelessness of resistance and surrendered to German occupation forces in hours, and the relationship between the local Nazi authorities and the Danish government was good. The result was that the Danish government remained in control of the country. There was also the value of Danish exports of agricultural products to Germany.

That relationship continued, despite the Wannsee Conference decision to eradicate the Jews of Europe and put pressure on the German authorities in Denmark to act against its Jewish population, to which they responded with 'delaying tactics', until August 1943.[4] Thereafter, following the major German defeat at Stalingrad and other reverses in the east and in North Africa, the Danish resistance began to be more active, and the result was the imposition of German rule and an order to round up Jews for deportation. Arendt notes that the Danish government gave the Danish Jews notice of their imminent arrest and deportation following a warning to that effect from a German shipping agent who could have been notified by Best, the Nazi Plenipotentiary in Denmark, who according to Arendt also went to Berlin to plead for Denmark as a special case (the Danish government would have been undertaking no risk as the source of the information on the imminent arrest and deportation of the Jews would have been very difficult to ascertain). Arendt notes too that von Hannecken, the German military commander in Denmark, refused to provide troops to Best.[5] Powers and Vogele claim that Best was 'interested in maintaining the relative political peace of the country' 'to his own benefit', which is consistent with Arendt's reference to Best's having claimed that the German objective had not been to 'seize a great number of Jews but to clean Denmark of Jews' and that the objective had been 'achieved' following the Jews' escape to Sweden.

Powers and Vogele also claim that Best made it 'known clandestinely that the seizure of Jews was about to begin', which confirms Arendt's reference to Best's possible warning through a German intermediary of the imminent deportation of Denmark's Jews.[6] From her own evidence Arendt concludes that it was the Danish resistance that was the cause of Nazi leniency, and even seems to indicate some moral influence from the Danes on the Germans in Denmark, rather than the more obvious inference that Nazi leniency predicated upon local Nazi interest in maintaining peace in Denmark resulted in a sense of no risk for aiding the Jews to escape amongst Danes, for instance because there would be no Nazi desire to apprehend those involved or to punish them. Arendt's conclusion seems to be an indication of her treatment of evidence and tendency towards assertion without consideration of alternative explanations.[7]

The wartime context explains the relationship between the Danish government and the Nazi authorities in Denmark. The political context of Denmark was one of a tradition of liberal democracy, of individual rights and respect for minorities, and the cultural and social context was one of thorough integration into Danish society of the relatively small Jewish population of Denmark. There was then no history of 'otherness', separatism or pariah status for Danish Jews. Though the Danish case seems to indicate that there may have been some influence on the treatment of Jews from their low numbers, from the status of the Jewish population in terms of their integration rather than 'otherness', and from liberal cultural and political traditions, the most decisive factor would seem to be the extent of perceived risk of adverse consequences for assisting Jews to escape. For it seems plausible that the extent of Danish assistance to Jews was decisively influenced by there being no apprehension of adverse consequences for providing help to Jews to flee to Sweden, an inference drawn from the relative leniency of the Nazi occupation of Denmark and from the Danish government's having been left to run the country.

The permissiveness of the German occupation may have reflected the German sense of the Danes as fellow Aryans and the lack of any racial or ideological objective in the German occupation of Denmark. There was in fact an extraordinary extent of collaboration between the German presence in Denmark and a Danish government that compromised over censorship, arrests of communists and orientation of trade to Germany, that governed a country characterised by a general lack of resistance and that remained in power with popular support until 29 August 1943. Though the Danish government was in the end dissolved by the Germans because of its declining to introduce repressive civil and legal constraints following an enhanced incidence of strikes and civil disturbances after Stalingrad, earlier that year 'a majority of the Danish people continued to support collaboration, voting overwhelmingly in March 1943 to support Denmark's collaborationist foreign minister'.[8]

Lidegaard refers to 'record numbers of voters massively supporting the parties behind the policy of cooperation' and claims that growing resistance in 1943 'did not put an end to cooperation, which actually expanded over the last years of the occupation', an indication that the assistance rendered the Jews to evade deportation by a certain percentage of the Danish population did not affect the general policy of cooperation between Danes and the Nazi presence in Denmark. Lidegaard also notes that 'after the action against the Jews in October 1943', though sympathy for the resistance was enhanced, 'probably most people at the same time maintained their support for cooperation, wanting both to uphold normality as much as possible and yet also to get rid of the occupants as soon as possible', though apparently without undertaking any personal risk. It is then incongruous that he quotes without adverse comment a Swedish view that the Danish assistance to the Jews to evade deportation represented 'the first time you saw a whole people rise up as one against the disgrace of racial persecution'.[9] For it cannot be that the majority of the Danish population endorsed continued collaboration and yet also participated in resistance in the form of helping Jews. In fact Jespersen claims that the numbers in the Danish resistance were 'only a few hundred in 1943', rising to well over 10,000 in late 1944 and reaching 'nearly 50,000 or around one per cent of the Danish population only by the end of the war'.[10] So low a percentage of the Danish population involved in the resistance is what would be expected in a normal distribution of preparedness to entertain some measure of risk and does not support Arendt's reference to the Danes' representing the possibility of popular defiance of oppression by greater force because of moral reasoning. Though the figure for the Danish population would be expected to include children, so the Danes who did join the resistance could well have been a higher percentage of those who could have joined, the low percentage of Danes in the resistance even at the end of the war is indicative of generally limited resistance and collaboration by the great majority in Denmark throughout the war. And of course the number of Danes in the resistance at the time of the deportation of Jews, in 1943, the period to which Arendt refers, was no more than 'a few hundred', a minute minority of Danes.

It is also possible that even the small numbers of Danes who did assist Jews to escape to Sweden would have been reduced had the German occupation of the country been more repressive, for there was in Denmark a context of Nazi leniency (epitomised by Best's own warning of the impending deportations of Jews). Even after the Jews' escape to Sweden there was an absence of reprisals from the Nazis and Best's own claim that the Jews' flight to Sweden achieved the Nazi objective of clearing Denmark of Jews, though that is to infer Danish perceptions of possible adverse consequences at the time of helping Jews from ensuing outcomes. What does seem obvious is that Arendt's inference of Danish influence on German leniency is one that has no evidence to support it (and she provides none).

The evidence indicates that the great majority of the Danish population collaborated with the Nazi occupation, responding to the ordinary levers of human motivation, material affluence or security, enhanced or protected status, influence or power. That indicates at least a pragmatic passive complicity in the majority of the Danish population and is of course consistent with the speed of the Danish surrender to the Nazis and their political and economic collaboration with the Nazi occupation of Denmark.

Arendt's claim that moral reasoning was the cause of the Danish resistance to the surrender of Jews, confined to a small number of Danes though it seems to have been, is in fact no more than an inference, for there is no proof of the process involved, which is in any event more likely to have been normative or associated with personality factors rather than one of explicit moral reasoning. And she does not establish that moral reasoning would have been influential on behaviour if the anticipated consequences of resistance had been far more adverse. Her claim that it was the lack of such moral reasoning that made Eichmann banal, complicit and normal is also conjecture.

Arendt does not seem to refer to the assistance to Danish Jews from the Danish resistance merely to indicate the possible existence of moral choice in behaviour, nor to establish its possibility in a small percentage of a population, but rather to demonstrate its possibility as a general characteristic, for she claims that 'the behavior of the Danish people and their government was unique among all the countries of Europe' and indicated the 'enormous power potential inherent in non-violent action and in resistance to an opponent possessing vastly superior means of violence',[11] for it indicates that a small minority of the Danish population helped the Jews in a possible context of low salience of risk of adverse personal outcomes because of experience of the generally indulgent nature of the Nazi occupation of Denmark and the lack of enthusiasm for deporting the Jews of Denmark on the part of the Nazi presence there.

Arendt does seem to contradict herself, in that she seems to be both claiming that

Eichmann was normal in not understanding the nature of the moral choice facing him or its consequences and asserting that the Danish population in general resisted German deportation of Jews, indicating that such resistance was normal in the Danish population so far as the Jews of the country were concerned. Eichmann would not then have been normal in Danish society at the time, which suggests a cultural or unusual personality influence on Eichmann's behaviour and complicity, something in German culture or in Eichmann's character, though that does not seem to be Arendt's intention. Rather, she seems to claim that Eichmann was normal in psychological terms and would be considered so in any society.

In such a context of claimed capacity for moral understanding and reasoning amongst the Danish population during the war and its reflection in Danish behaviour, Arendt claimed that Eichmann failed to reflect upon his situation and to understand the nature of the moral choices facing him. Though a self-professed political theorist rather than a moral philosopher, and claiming to be concerned with aggregates of individuals rather than individuals on their own, Arendt's academic career seems to have been in philosophy and her 'primary concern' seems to have been 'moral reasoning'. The consequence seems to be that Arendt attributed Eichmann's role in the destruction of Europe's Jews to what she saw as his failure of moral reasoning and lack of understanding of the consequences of his actions for the Jews.[12]

Arendt seems to have been a victim of her own intellectual and moral disdain for Eichmann in ascribing Eichmann's behaviour to what she sees as his limited capacity for moral reasoning and for understanding the consequences of his actions. Elon, who wrote the introduction to the 2006 edition of 'Eichmann in Jerusalem', notes Arendt's being 'brash', 'insolent', 'professorial' and 'imperious', and having an expressive style characterised by 'sarcasm'. These characteristics are in fact apparent in her view of Eichmann, in her scathing criticism of the Jewish leadership in Europe in the war and in her contempt for the prosecution in the Jerusalem trial. Though Elon notes that Arendt had a 'tendency to draw absolute conclusions on the basis of casual evidence', to which he could well have added avoidance of consideration of alternative explanations to her own, he does not note that these very characteristics in Arendt resulted in her misjudging Eichmann in believing that failure of moral reasoning explained Eichmann's perpetrator behaviour.[13]

Arendt does note that Eichmann had 'an extraordinary diligence in looking out for his own personal advancement', though that does not indicate that Arendt understood pursuit of personal interest to be the decisive influence on Eichmann's behaviour, for she says that other than self-interest Eichmann 'had no motives at all', an indication of her lack of understanding of the influence of inadvertent or deliberate pursuit of personal interest on human behaviour. Instead, seemingly influenced by her disciplinary background, she seems to concentrate on 'conscience' as something innate in human beings and a decisive influence on human behaviour, when that is a supposition that seems to be predicated upon her view of herself as part of a moral and intellectual elite, and she proffers no evidence for its being a decisive influence on the behaviour of ordinary human beings at all.[14]

Arendt does acknowledge that between the Wannsee Conference in January 1942 and Himmler's order in the summer and fall of 1944 to cease deportations of Jews to extermination centres 'Eichmann was troubled by no questions of conscience', though she seems to argue that in Hungary in 1944, when Eichmann 'sabotaged' Himmler's new, 'moderate' policy towards the Jews 'as much as he dared', Eichmann was displaying a form of conscience in following what he perceived to be the law and legitimate authority in Nazi Germany under the Führerprinzip. Arendt makes no reference to the psychological rewards to Eichmann of the Führerprinzip in terms of attribution of responsibility for decisions, nor to those of the SS code and SS identity that obligated Eichmann to follow the Führerprinzip but left him with no responsibility for his behaviour in his role. Nor does Arendt allude to the effect of universality of acceptance of the Führerprinzip in Nazi Germany and especially within the Nazi state apparatus and the SS, or to the perceived sanctions for not accepting the Führerprinzip, on Eichmann's conformity to what he perceived to be the requirements of his role in the SS.

In other words Arendt makes no attempt to understand Eichmann's experience of the Third Reich, the SS and his role in the SS in the context of his personality, attitudes, objectives and background, and does not address the possibility that Eichmann's perpetrator behaviour is explained by unreflective conformity to the norms and requirements of the Nazi state apparatus and the SS hierarchy to optimise his material, social and psychological outcomes. Though she derogates Eichmann as ordinary, unexceptional, banal, careerist and self-interested, she does not consider that these very attributes would result in unreflective conformity to maximise advantage to himself. Arendt does though note Wisliceny's conviction that Eichmann must have had some written authorisation from Müller and Kaltenbrunner to continue with a policy that defied Himmler (see below).[15] That of course indicates that Eichmann may have been responding to the most proximate SS authority in Hungary in 1944.

Arendt claims that, in relation to the annihilation of the Jews, 'he merely, to put the matter colloquially, never realized what he was doing'.[16] That was even at the time of Arendt's writing 'Eichmann in Jerusalem' known to be untrue, because Hoess, the commandant at Auschwitz, had told the Nuremberg court in 1946 that 'Eichmann came repeatedly to Auschwitz and was intimately acquainted with the proceedings'.[17] Though Hoess's testimony has, as Cesarani points out, proved to be inaccurate in several respects in relation to Eichmann's involvement in the Holocaust, more it would seem from misremembering than intent, even Eichmann admitted that he had visited, on Heydrich's instruction, the SS Police Chief in the Lublin area, Globocnik, who passed him on to an Einsatzkommando commander in the Lublin area, and that he had been sent by Müller, his immediate boss in the SS, to Chelmno near Lodz, to an Einsatzkommando in Minsk and to Auschwitz. Though Cesarani notes that the dates Eichmann ascribes to these visits are contradicted by other, objective evidence, he does not seem to be challenging their having taken place, for he refers to Eichmann's having 'admitted that Müller sent him to Auschwitz' and to Eichmann's having 'admitted that he knew what happened in "the east" and in Auschwitz'.[18] Arendt is then incorrect in claiming that Eichmann did not understand the consequences of his transporting Jews to Poland's extermination centres, and in fact she recites the evidence Eichmann gave in what she refers to as the 'police tapes' played at his trial in Jerusalem, which seem to be the record of his interrogation prior to trial by the Israeli police officer Less, in which Eichmann recounts his having visited Globocnik in Lublin, where he was shown the mass murder of Jews, Chelmno, Minsk and Treblinka, and his horror and revulsion at what he witnessed there.[19]

It could be that Eichmann's reference to such visits was intended to establish that the decision to murder the Jews of Europe had been taken by Hitler, Goering, Heydrich and Himmler and that Eichmann was under instruction to report on such places, not least as according to Cesarani reference to the visits was in a context of Eichmann's testimony to the effect that he had been told what was intended by Heydrich. It was in a context too of Eichmann's recalling his being appalled by what he saw and saying so to Müller on his return, indicating aversion for the process of murdering Jews.[20] Such experience did not though prevent Eichmann from transporting Jews to extermination centres, indicating either indifference to what he knew would happen to the Jews or the dominant influence on his behaviour of considerations of his SS career and the approbation of his peers and bosses in the SS despite reservations over the task.

Arendt does seem to have misjudged Eichmann in claiming that his banality was composed of a failure to understand the moral implications of what he was doing, for Eichmann's banality and normality seem to be in his pursuit of personal interest at the expense of others to whose plight Eichmann was indifferent.

Notes

[1] See Dimsdale, Joel, E., *Anatomy of Malice: The Enigma of Nazi War Criminals*, Yale University Press, 2016 for reference to the view of Gustave Gilbert, the US psychologist at Nuremberg, that the Nuremberg defendants were 'depraved psychopaths', though see Searls, Damion, *The Inkblots*, Simon and Schuster, 2017 for the contrasting view of Douglas Kelley, the US psychiatrist at Nuremberg, that 'insanity is no explanation for the Nazis', who were 'simply creatures of their environment', concluding 'not only that such personalities are not unique or insane, but also that they could be duplicated in any country of the world today', though he acknowledged that the senior Nazis were 'dominant, aggressive, egocentric personalities'. And see Zillmer, Eric A., Harrower, Molly, Ritzler, Barry A., and Archer, Robert P., *The Quest for the Nazi Personality: A Psychological Investigation of Nazi War Criminals*, Routledge, 2013, pp. 90, 91 and 93 for the view that there was 'no common denominator reflecting some type of psychopathic personality', that the Nazis arraigned at Nuremberg were 'as diverse a group as we might find in our government today', that 'the Nazis were quite similar to an average group of U.S. citizens' and that 'productive and well-integrated personalities may become involved in large-scale "horrors"'. See also Goldhagen, *Hitler's Willing Executioners*, op. cit.
[2] Arendt, Hannah, *Eichmann in Jerusalem, A Report on the Banality of Evil*, Penguin, 2006, pp. xiii and xiv.
[3] Ibid, p. 26.
[4] See Powers, Roger S., and Vogele, William B., *Protest, Power and Change: An Encyclopedia of Nonviolent Action from ACT-UP to Women's Suffrage*, Routledge, 2012, pp. 145 and 146.

[5] See Arendt, *Eichmann in Jerusalem*, op. cit., pp. 171–75.

[6] See Powers and Vogele, *Protest, Power and Change*, op. cit., pp. 145 and 146, and Arendt, *Eichmann in Jerusalem*, op. cit., pp. 174–75. One minor point of difference is that Powers and Vogele claim that the German intermediary informed Danish Social Democrats rather than the Danish government directly.

[7] See Arendt, *Eichmann in Jerusalem*, op. cit., pp. 171–75.

[8] See Axelrod, Alan, and Kingston, Jack A., *Encyclopedia of World War Two, Volume I*, H. W. Fowler, 2007, p. 271.

[9] See Lidegaard, Bo, *Countrymen: The Untold Story of How Denmark's Jews Escaped the Nazis*, Atlantic Books, 2014.

[10] See Jespersen, Knud J. V., *From Arsonist to Fire Brigade: Special Operations Executive and Danish Resistance, 1940-1945*, in Sevaldsen, Jørgen, Bjorke, Bo, and Bjorn, Claus (eds.), *Britain and Denmark: Political, Economic and Cultural Relations in the 19th and 20th Centuries*, Museum Tusculanum Press, 2003, p. 284.

[11] Arendt, *Eichmann in Jerusalem*, op. cit., p. 171.

[12] See Aschheim, Steven E. (ed.), *Hannah Arendt in Jerusalem*, University of California Press, 2001, p. 88.

[13] See Arendt, *Eichmann in Jerusalem*, op. cit., p. xvii.

[14] Ibid, pp. 287, and 93 to 97. Festinger's Theory of Cognitive Dissonance, that predicts that attitude follows behaviour undertaken to optimise outcomes through conformity to role requirements, would indicate rather less influence from 'conscience' on behaviour.

[15] Ibid, pp. 145 and 151.

[16] Ibid, p. 287.

[17] http://law2.umkc.edu/faculty/projects/ftrials/nuremberg/hoesstest.html, Testimony of Rudolf Hoess, Commandant of Auschwitz, to the Trial at Nuremberg, 15 April 1946.

[18] See Cesarani, *Eichmann*, op. cit., pp. 98–102 and 366, for reference to the authority to exterminate the Jews of Europe from Goering to Heydrich, for Eichmann's account of his visits to the east under orders and his reaction to them, and for the errors in Hoess's claims regarding Eichmann. For the American psychologist at Nuremberg Gustave Gilbert's claim that Hoess's testimony was what Hoess believed to be the truth given Hoess's apathetic character, see the transcript of the Eichmann trial in Jerusalem on NIzkor.org., though it is worth noting that testimony as to Hoess's honesty seems to have been presented as evidence of the veracity of his testimony, when as Cesarani points out Hoess's account was often inaccurate.

[19] See Arendt, *Eichmann in Jerusalem*, op. cit., pp. 86–89.

[20] See Cesarani, *Eichmann*, op. cit., pp. 99–102 for an account of Eichmann's visits to the east and his reporting back to Müller.

Chapter Three

Stangneth. The Eichmann of the war years, the Eichmann of the Sassen interviews in Argentina in 1957, and the Eichmann of the Jerusalem trial in 1961

Stangneth, a German philosopher, in a recent account of Eichmann's life that concentrates on the period between the end of the war and his abduction by the Israelis and trial in Jerusalem, claims that Arendt was the victim of her own expectations of Eichmann. Stangneth claims that there is a radical difference between the confident Eichmann, whom she portrays as having presented himself as a Jewish expert and as having attended to his 'public image' and 'growing reputation', noticed by Heydrich for his aptitude for organisation and possibly his expertise on the Jews, and the impression she claims Eichmann deliberately cultivated in Jerusalem, as a colourless bureaucrat compliant with the requirements of the role he had been assigned and with orders received in a military hierarchy in time of war, that is, as no more than a functionary in the resolution of the Jewish problem, initially in planning their emigration and then in their transportation from ghettoes to extermination camps.

Though Eichmann attempted after his abduction by the Israelis to portray himself as a 'small cog in the machine',[1] Stangneth claims other evidence of his dealings with Jews before and during the war, and his interviews with Sassen in Argentina after the war, in which he boasted of his role in the genocide of the Jews and in which his desire for the admiration of the audience was apparent, indicates a very different personality of great confidence and arrogance.[2] Some of Stangneth's references to evidence of antisemitism in Eichmann, for instance in the Sassen interviews, are accompanied by commentary regarding Eichmann's absurd claims of responsibility and influence in Nazi Germany and the SS and his tendency to brag and to present himself as the archetypal senior SS officer to an audience of Nazi sympathisers, though she does also indicate a 'radical anti-Semitism' in Eichmann without such commentary on Eichmann's presentation of self.[3]

On the face of it Stangneth seems to be justified in her attribution of great confidence and arrogance to Eichmann, for there is extensive wartime evidence of Eichmann's taking pleasure in his power over the Jews and in his reputation with them, and evidence of his arrogance as an SS officer of some rank and authority over the Jews. That does not though establish that Eichmann behaved as he did towards the Jews because he was an eliminationist antisemite, because an alternative explanation is that he took pleasure in the power over the Jews of his role in the SS and the fear he elicited in the Jews because of the seductive nature of power in general and especially because of his previous anonymous background with its lack of influence, power, belonging, identity and status.

As to the evidence of the Sassen interviews, which took place over several months in Argentina in 1957, Eichmann has been quoted as having said, 'if we would have killed 10.3 million Jews, then I would have been satisfied and would say, good, we have annihilated any enemy', and 'I wasn't only issued orders', 'I rather anticipated, I was an idealist'.[4] In other evidence of Eichmann's enthusiasm for his role, in the record of the interviews Sassen sold to *Life Magazine* Eichmann recalls having said to his men on departure from Berlin in 1945, 'I will gladly jump into my grave in the knowledge that five million enemies of the Reich have already died like animals ('Enemies of the Reich', I said, 'not Jews') and remembers the 'extraordinary sense of elation' it gave him. Cesarani refers to the quotation, though he does not interrogate it for meaning in the context of Eichmann's personality and does not consider the possibility of its being no more than bravado. On the contrary, he seems to treat it as evidence of Eichmann's eliminationist antisemitism.[5] Yet there is extensive evidence of Eichmann's tendency to brag, and Arendt refers to Eichmann's absurd grandiosity and claims of voluntary and enthusiastic responsibility for the Holocaust repeated in Argentina. According to Arendt Eichmann also claimed to have 'invented' the ghetto system and to have 'given birth to the idea' of shipping all European Jews to Madagascar.[6]

Evidence of apparent agency and eliminationist antisemitism in Eichmann is not convincing both because Eichmann's claims to have been the originator of certain policies regarding the Jews and of decisive influence on the extermination of the Jews of Europe have been discredited by evidence (see below) and because Eichmann was, before he joined the SS, an anonymous personality whose antisemitism was no more than the ordinary cultural antisemitism of many Germans of the time and for whom a career in the SS conferred an elite identity, a code of conduct that included expressed attitudes, a sense of order, involvement, freedom from responsibility and a sense of belonging.

Lang notes the attractions of SS membership for recruits, which included 'power and recognition to the disappointed who felt powerless', an SS 'aristocratic status', and 'great prestige, honor, and power within German society', for 'it was precisely a desire for status, recognition, dignity, and power' 'that drove many to volunteer in the first place'.[7]

An explanation more consonant with evidence of Eichmann's indifference to the Jews, record of vigour and enthusiasm in arranging their emigration from Germany earlier in the Third Reich, and arranging the deportation and transportation of Jews to extermination centres only when that was the direction he received in his role in the SS, is that Eichmann embraced the historic mission of the SS to eliminate the Jews of Europe when that was necessary to preserve his elite SS status, identity, privilege, sense of belonging and purpose, and the approbation of bosses and peers.

In the Sassen interviews Eichmann also claims that 'Müller said to me once, if we'd had fifty Eichmanns, we'd have won the war for sure', and goes on 'and I was proud.

That shall have given you an insight into my interior – since you don't know me from within, and that is important'. Another claim was that he had indicated at the end of the war that he did not need forged identity papers as he intended to commit suicide with his revolver, apparently disregarding the fact that he was in Argentina as a consequence of having fled from Germany. The exclusive regard for himself and his own experience and tendency to boast is typical of Eichmann in the Sassen interviews. Eichmann also claims, 'they knew me wherever I went. Through the press, the name Eichmann had emerged as a symbol', and, commenting on his role in Hungary, 'as my chief, Gruppenführer Müller expressed it, they were sending in the master himself, so I wanted to become like a master', so 'an SS (Obersturmbannführer) Eichmann came to Hungary'.

Regarding the foot marches of Jews from Budapest when the rail line was broken, Eichmann said it was 'to show my iron fist to the Allies and also to tell them at the same time it is not going to change anything even if you destroy the lines of communication to the Reich and bomb them to pieces, we will still march'. Despite this apparent evidence of Eichmann's grandiosity and autonomy in Budapest in 1944, Eichmann does refer in the Sassen transcript concerned to his involvement in the foot marches as having been under an 'order from the Chief of the Security Police and the Security Service to this effect'.[8] Even when trying to impress a receptive Nazi sympathising audience with his SS identity Eichmann does then indicate that he was under orders rather than acting with any genuine autonomy. The Chief of the Security Police and the Security Service at the time was Kaltenbrunner.

Another statement by Eichmann in the Sassen interviews was that 'the men in my command had the sort of respect for me that prompted the Jews to effectively set me on a throne'. Commenting on these quotations Stangneth notes that 'Eichmann boasted about anything that seemed at all plausible to him'.[9] The evidence of the Sassen interviews does then seem to be more indicative of Eichmann's tendency to brag and desire to impress audiences than of his having been an eliminationist antisemite. Had Eichmann's SS role required him to continue to arrange Jewish emigration he would it seems have done so with undiminished zealotry.

In fact the evidence of the Sassen interviews is quite mixed, for Eichmann also refers to his shock at being witness to Einsatzgruppen murders of Jews in Minsk and to his having protested over them to Müller, though Eichmann acknowledged that 'the Führer' had decreed that the previous policy of a political solution to the Jewish problem, which seems to be a reference to emigration, was to be replaced by a 'physical solution', and accepted that an order from the Führer had to be carried out.[10] Cesarani notes Eichmann's shock and 'qualms' regarding the 'physical annihilation' of the Jews, though he claims that he dismissed them.[11] Such recollections challenged Sassen's agenda of Holocaust denial and minimisation of Hitler's responsibility for the destruction of the Jews, but though they could not be said to reflect Eichmann's attempting to please his audience they could be seen to represent Eichmann's understanding of his own status within the group in the Sassen meetings as the major SS presence there.[12] They are indicative of Eichmann's having assimilated the SS code of obedience to Führer orders and of the centrality to

Eichmann in his Argentinian obscurity of his SS identity and the SS code. And they could be seen to indicate Eichmann's self-aggrandisement over his wartime role in emphasising his credentials as the ideal SS officer following the SS code and the Führerprinzip no matter how difficult the task assigned him.

Even Cesarani, whose view is that Eichmann was an eliminationist antisemite, acknowledges both that Eichmann was 'moderately inebriate' at the time of the Sassen interviews and Eichmann's desire to aggrandise himself and his role in the SS before what he conceived of as a receptive audience, the implication of which is that Eichmann's eliminationist antisemitic rhetoric in the Sassen interviews should not be taken as evidence of his being an eliminationist antisemite.[13] As has been indicated, the more plausible inference seems to be that the Sassen interviews represent evidence of Eichmann's continuing attachment to his SS identity and career and the sense of elite purpose and belonging it gave him, which he seems to have missed in his post-war obscurity and poverty in Argentina when he was interviewed by Sassen, rather than evidence of eliminationist antisemitism in Eichmann.

Stangneth denies the claim that Eichmann was drunk for much of the Sassen interviews, insisting that 'alcohol didn't play an important part at these meetings', though she goes on to acknowledge that 'in the 1950s, almost all social gatherings involved alcohol, and these were no exception', before claiming that there were 'no slurred words', apparently disregarding the disinhibiting effect of drink long before words become slurred, especially for Eichmann in company sympathetic to Nazism, and disregarding too the evidence of bravado before peers. And even if Eichmann had been sober, Stangneth herself acknowledges that the Sassen interviews provide evidence of Eichmann's insistence, despite Sassen's agenda of denial of the Holocaust and Hitler's responsibility for it, that in his role in the extermination of the Jews 'he had been acting on Hitler's orders' and that he 'had implemented exactly what Hitler wanted', a clear indication of Eichmann's sense of the ultimate authority of Hitler in the extermination of the Jews and of Eichmann's attachment to the SS code of giving effect to Hitler's decisions. It seems also to be an indication of Eichmann's continuing attachment to his SS identity and code, and to the sense of belonging to an elite that his identity as an SS officer conferred upon him.

It follows that Eichmann's doing what Hitler had decreed is not evidence that Eichmann was an eliminationist antisemite, and though the Sassen evidence does not on its own establish that Eichmann was not an eliminationist antisemite before his understanding that Hitler had authorised the extermination of the Jews, it does indicate Eichmann's having been unprepared to act without legitimate authority in the form of Hitler as Führer and of his bosses in the SS. It is then not inconsistent with the thesis that Eichmann performed his role in the Holocaust to preserve the psychological rewards of his career in the SS, its privilege, status, power, aggrandisement, involvement, belonging to an elite, and identity.

Stangneth does not seem to acknowledge that if, as she claims, Eichmann was adept at presenting himself as a compliant and anonymous bureaucrat and functionary in the Nazi hierarchy to optimise his chances of survival when on trial in Jerusalem, it is altogether probable that he was just as adept at presenting himself as a senior SS officer committed to the eliminationist antisemitic task of the SS (even to the point of making ludicrous claims of influence on Nazi policy towards the Jews) when in the company of Nazi sympathisers, fellow Nazis and SS men in Argentina. Stangneth contrasts the bragging and very confident behaviour of Eichmann with Jews and peers during the war and in Argentina and his presentation of self as minor functionary complying with orders in time of war in Jerusalem, and claims that the wartime Eichmann and the Eichmann of the Sassen interviews represent the real Eichmann and that the man he represented himself as being in Jerusalem was a fraud. She claims that 'the writings and discussions from Argentina are conclusive proof' of Eichmann's distorted presentation of self as 'Cautious Bureaucrat' in Jerusalem, for 'the Argentina Papers allow us to see behind the mirror. They reveal a man who was practised in the art of manufacturing and conveying stories with an inner coherence' 'though they had little to do with reality'. And though she acknowledges that in Argentina, 'to gain the respect and assistance of his old comrades, he confirmed their expectations that National Socialism could be separated from the imperative to exterminate', and that Eichmann boasted over his role as an SS officer, Stangneth does not refer to the obvious corollary that Eichmann's entire presentation of self in Argentina was designed to cultivate the desired impression of the ideal committed SS officer.[14]

What Stangneth does not seem to address is the possibility that Eichmann presented different selves to different audiences to optimise social and psychological outcomes for himself, which would be consistent with his taking pleasure in his power in relation to the Jews in the war, when he seems to have found his reputation with them and the terror he inspired in them rewarding, his ridiculous bravado in the Sassen evidence, and his abject persona in the Jerusalem trial. Establishing that Eichmann's demeanour and presentation of self and his role in the war with the Jews when on trial in Jerusalem were fraudulent does not prove that he was an eliminationist antisemite. Nor does the Sassen evidence even if Eichmann is assumed to have been sober.

Though Stangneth herself refers to Eichmann's claim in prison in Jerusalem in 1961 that 'the mental burden resulting from the anonymity of my person' was the most difficult aspect of his post-war existence,[15] she does not seem to make the natural inference that the psychological reward of the admiration and respect shown to him by Sassen and the other Nazi sympathisers present may explain Eichmann's grandiose eliminationist antisemitic statements in the Sassen evidence, for they indicated his seniority and influence in the major task assigned to the elite SS at a time at which his status was in dramatic contrast to his anonymous existence in Argentina. They also indicate Eichmann's continuing attachment to the SS code and to his SS identity, again from a time when his life was far more rewarding in terms of belonging, hierarchy, status, approbation, identity, power and influence. There are in fact some contradictions even in the evidence Stangneth produces of the Sassen interviews, for amongst the evidence of Eichmann's eliminationist antisemitic bravado there is other evidence that is dissonant with the inference of eliminationist antisemitism in Eichmann, for instance his indicating indifference as to what happened to the Jews, whether they went to Madagascar, Riga or Auschwitz, his shocked reaction to the extermination process, his sense of 'comradeship' and having 'supported his fellow officers' in enduring the visits to extermination centres such as Auschwitz, and his reference to the obligation to carry out orders and tasks in the SS regardless of personal reservations, a reference indicative of Eichmann's attachment to the SS code even in Argentina in 1957 because of the status and identity it conferred on him.

Eichmann's extensive writings corroborate the Sassen evidence in their absurd grandiosity and self-regard, their claims of having done his duty according to Nazi legality, their reference to war morality that made everything permissible, and their reference to the 'oath of allegiance' that dictated compliance with Nazi-defined laws and orders. Here too Eichmann attempts to aggrandise himself to obtain the psychological rewards of justification and approbation he found in the SS, in the cultivation of a ridiculous narrative of himself, composed in a posturing style and with a moralising sanctimonious content.[16] Eichmann's pseudo-philosophical jottings and notes do seem to have been characteristic of him before his apprehension in Argentina and in captivity in Jerusalem to expound on the philosophical morality of what he had done and refer to philosophers not out of any post-transgressional response indicating anguish of conscience but rather to justify himself in a manner indicative of endless fascination with his own personality and no consideration for the Jews.

The question of Eichmann's inebriation during the Sassen interviews does not then seem to be relevant to the extent to which the views, attitudes, perceptions and motivations apparent in Eichmann in them are representative of Eichmann's real attributes. For Eichmann would not have had to have been drunk during the Sassen interviews for his behaviour and expressed views to be affected by desire to impress a Nazi audience for someone whose retreat into obscurity could have made his SS identity and the prestige it once accorded him that much more valuable. What reference to such motives in Eichmann does mean is that the Sassen evidence has to be discounted, including that which lends itself to the argument being presented here, that Eichmann did what he did in transporting Jews to extermination centres because he perceived the policy to be what Hitler had decreed and had made mandatory for Eichmann in his role in the SS, and that was as a consequence imperative to Eichmann's SS identity and career.

Stangneth does not seem to locate Eichmann in the context of the Nazi and SS hierarchy before and during the war, when he was regarded as of use to senior SS officers such as Heydrich and Himmler, who formulated policy towards the Jews, and to Kaltenbrunner, Heydrich's successor, and Müller, Eichmann's immediate boss in the SS, or to identify Eichmann's role as a transport expert whose job was to implement policy decided upon above him in the Nazi and SS hierarchy. To such senior SS officers Eichmann would have seemed the perfect subordinate, willing, orthodox, careerist, aspiring, wanting the good regard of his bosses and efficient at administration and especially at management of transports. The evidence that Stangneth produces of the good impression Eichmann produced on his SS peers and bosses is not evidence of Eichmann's being influential in the formulation of the Final Solution, which had been decided above his level before and communicated by

Heydrich at the Wannsee Conference, where Eichmann was present to take the minutes rather than to contribute.

Eichmann's persona at his trial in Jerusalem does seem radically different from the evidence of Eichmann as a confident careerist wartime SS officer diligent in his meeting of role requirements defined by the SS hierarchy and of Eichmann's apparent pleasure in recollection of his 'success' as an SS officer in transporting Jews to their annihilation in conversation with Sassen in Argentina, though all that does is to establish that Eichmann enjoyed the power of his role as an SS officer specialising in transports of Jews and that he was sensitive to audience, as would be expected of an individual with a need to belong and to be approved of by peers and bosses, for when Nazi policy had been Jewish emigration Eichmann had implemented that with similar vigour. Stangneth's evidence does not establish that Eichmann was an eliminationist antisemite or that he exerted any autonomous influence on the destruction of Europe's Jews, and establishing that he manipulated his presentation of self to accord with his purposes before different audiences is to indicate how normal Eichmann was, as such presentation of self to obtain desired outcomes is ordinary.

Though in Jerusalem Eichmann had an interest in portraying himself as a mere bureaucrat following orders in an SS hierarchy in time of war that does not mean that he was not just that. None of what Stangneth seems to be presenting as new is in fact inconsistent with the view that Eichmann behaved as he did to optimise his material, social and psychological outcomes, in terms of the good regard of his SS peers and bosses, in terms of the maintenance of his SS elite status, identity, privileges and prerogatives, and in terms of the enjoyment Eichmann seem to have taken in his power over Jews.

Lang claims that for Himmler 'the SS community was to be united by an intense feeling of comradeship, and their feeling of belonging should inspire unconditional loyalty and obedience', the latter being not passive compliance but a desire to do their duty. This appears to be a reference to the motive in SS officers to conform to the requirements of the roles assigned them in the SS to maintain the approbation of peers and bosses in the SS. The importance of this elite SS officer identity to Eichmann is indicated by his pride in his perpetrator behaviour before an audience of SS sympathisers in Argentina as recorded on the Sassen tapes, and in fact pride is the attribute Lang claims has been underestimated in Nazi perpetrators.[17]

Notes
[1] See Stangneth, Bettina, *Eichmann Before Jerusalem: The Unexamined Life of a Mass Murderer*, The Bodley Head, 2014, pp. 25 and 26, for Eichmann's wartime attention to his image (and doing his 'best to influence it') and interest in his reputation, and p. 3 for his attempt to portray himself as a mere functionary carrying out orders after his capture by the Israelis.
[2] See ibid, p. 28, for reference to Eichmann's confidence in himself in January 1941, and pp. 38 and 441 for reference to Eichmann's claiming, during the Sassen interviews, that 'I was here, there and everywhere. You never knew when I was going to show up', a typically aggrandising statement regarding his role in the war.

[3] See ibid, p. 25 for reference to Eichmann's 'anti-Semitic paranoia' in 1961, p. 49 for reference to Eichmann's eliminationist antisemitic discourse in the company of Sassen, though in the context of Stangneth's appreciation of Eichmann's bravado before a Nazi sympathising audience, p. 96 for reference to Eichmann's 'fanatical hatred of Jews' though only in a context of Eichmann's reputation, p. 211 for reference to Eichmann's 'radical anti-Semitism' without such commentary, and p. 226 for reference to 'the dedicated anti-Semite Adolf Eichmann'.

[4] Wojak, Irmtrud, *Eichmanns Memoiren: Ein Kritischer Essay*, Zuerst, 2001, Frankfurt: Fischer TB, 2004. See also Stangneth, *Eichmann before Jerusalem*, op. cit., p. 304.

[5] See *Life Magazine*, Vol. 49, No. 23, 5 December 1960, pp. 150–52. For Cesarani's use of the quotation concerning Berlin see Cesarani, *Eichmann*, op. cit., p. 367. And see Nazi Conspiracy and Aggression, Volume VIII, Office of United States Chief of Counsel for Prosecution of Axis Criminality, United States Government Printing Office, Washington, 1946, Affidavit of Dieter Wisliceny, p. 610 for Wisliceny's claim that Eichmann had said, at their last meeting in February 1945, 'I laugh when I jump into the grave because of the feeling that I have killed 5,000,000 Jews. That gives me great satisfaction and gratification.' The account in 'Affidavit C', dated 29 November 1945, is claimed to be 'substantially the same as his testimony on direct examination before the International Military Tribunal at Nurnberg, 3 January 1946'.

[6] Arendt, Hannah, *Eichmann in Jerusalem*, op. cit., pp. 46 and 47.

[7] See Lang, Johannes, 'The Proud Executioner: Pride and the Psychology of Genocide', in Brudholm, Thomas, and Lang, Johannes (eds.), *Emotions and Mass Atrocity: Philosophical and Theoretical Explorations*, Cambridge University Press, 2018, p. 72.

[8] See The Nizkor Project – The Trial of Adolf Eichmann – Session 104.

[9] See Stangneth, *Eichmann Before Jerusalem*, op. cit., pp. 14, 25, 49, 255 and 256. See also Westermann, Edward B., 'Ordinary Drinkers' and 'Ordinary "Males"? Alcohol, Masculinity, and Atrocity in the Holocaust', in Kaplan, Thomas Pegelow, Matthäus, Jürgen, and Homburg, Mark W. (eds.), *Beyond Ordinary Men: Christopher R. Browning and Holocaust Historiography*, Ferdinand Schöningh, 2019, pp. 30 to 38 for reference to the prevalence of alcohol use in Nazi Germany in general and amongst perpetrators in particular and its association with male drinking sessions and a Nazi ideal of 'hypermasculinity' that dictated violence. This raises the possibility that in the Sassen evidence Eichmann was behaving in ways consonant with his aspirational SS officer identity before an audience sympathetic to Nazi attitudes rather than indicating his own attitudes towards the elimination of Jews. For Eichmann the violence was of course attitudinal and verbal rather than the sort of physical violence of those who actually murdered Jews.

[10] See Cesarani, *Eichmann*, op. cit., p. 106.

[11] See ibid, p. 367.

[12] This alludes to a possible argument in support of Stangneth's claim that the Sassen transcripts are evidence of Eichmann's real attitudes rather than his attempting to please an audience of Nazi sympathisers, that is that Eichmann did refuse to support Sassen's agenda of Holocaust denial, which could be regarded as an indication that

Eichmann was not motivated to please his audience. This argument is not tenable because it disregards Eichmann's sense of his own status as a relatively senior SS officer with special responsibility for the Jews, and does not take account of Eichmann's desire, apparent also in his behaviour in Hungary in 1944, to impose himself upon audiences and to impress them with his SS rank and identity from the only time in his life in which he had an elite status, rank and identity. What the Sassen transcripts do indicate is that Eichmann did in fact present different selves to different audiences before, during and after the war, in the SS in Germany and the occupied territories, in Argentina and in Jerusalem.

[13] See ibid, p. 219. See also The Nizkor Project – The Trial of Adolf Eichmann – Session 104 for Eichmann's response to the Sassen transcripts in court in Jerusalem, that they reflected his 'expansive mood inspired by wine and an alcoholic atmosphere, and it is truth and mixed up with fiction'. This explanation was of course expedient to Eichmann's defence because it invalidated the Sassen transcripts as evidence of Eichmann's true attitudes towards the Jews and the reasons for his complicity in the Holocaust, but that does not of itself mean that it is untrue.

[14] Ibid, pp. 366 and 367.

[15] Ibid, p. 101. On the same p. Stangneth refers to 'Eichmann's need for action and admiration'. See p. 365 for Stangneth's reference to Eichmann's 'ability to inhabit and perfect a role', and for extraordinary reference to Eichmann's capacity for attachment to people even when in Jerusalem and Eichmann's 'winning ways'.

[16] See ibid, pp. 200, 203, 215, 216, 217, 263, 264, 266, 267 and 278.

[17] See Lang, *The Proud Executioner*, op. cit., p. 70. Lang's reference to 'pride' is in fact consonant with the prestige and value placed on an SS officer identity found in Eichmann. Lang claims a role for 'pride' in SS perpetrator behaviour that has not been appreciated because of a portrayal of Nazi perpetrators as emotionless, which Lang sees as derived from the SS code and identity advocated by Himmler of toughness and hardness in avoidance of sympathy for the victims of the SS. There does in fact seem to have been some diversity of experience in SS perpetrators, including genuine distress and psychological disturbance in some cases (which does seem incompatible with a decisive influence from 'pride'). What unites SS perpetrators in terms of influence on their actual behaviour is conformity to the requirements of the role SS perpetrators were assigned, to maintain the approval of their SS peers and bosses.

Chapter Four

Cesarani: Eichmann's journey to eliminationist antisemitism

Cesarani notes that Arendt, in a letter to the German philosopher Karl Jaspers, described the Israeli prosecutor Gideon Hausner, who was Jewish and from Galicia, as a 'typical Galician Jew' 'constantly making mistakes', an attitude he claims was typical of bourgeois German Jews in relation to Ostjuden. Challenging Arendt's view of Eichmann as ordinary and banal, a passive recipient of orders from above him in a military hierarchy in time of war, Cesarani points out that Arendt was in fact present at Eichmann's trial for no more than four days and so was dependent upon court transcripts, and that as a consequence she missed evidence of Eichmann's sharpness with Hausner at certain moments in the trial that were indicative, Cesarani claims, of Eichmann's real attitude and of his attempt to deceive the court as to his own personality, which he presented as passive and compliant with orders received in a military hierarchy in time of war and attitudinally not antisemitic in the eliminationist sense. Cesarani even goes so far as to claim of Eichmann and Arendt that 'because his disdain for Jews found more than an echo in her attitudes towards them, she was pre-programmed not to register his anti-semitism or not to take it seriously'.[1]

Though Cesarani does produce evidence of Eichmann's obdurate resistance and flashes of irritation during Hausner's cross-examination of him, his inference that such evidence indicates Eichmann's having attempted to deceive the court as to his own personality is not justified, for the evidence Cesarani produces is of Hausner's having on occasion accused Eichmann of responsibility quite unfairly and of Eichmann's having responded in ways that do not indicate antisemitism of any kind or anything other than a perfectly normal reaction to Hausner's general accusatory demeanour throughout the trial and extensive use of testimony regarding the suffering of the Jews under the Nazis that was extraneous to the issue of Eichmann's guilt or innocence, so much so that he was rebuked by Judge Landau, who noted that he had been indirectly reproached before regarding such tactics. In any case it is accepted here that Eichmann did assume a different demeanour, when on trial in Jerusalem, to that he had exhibited in the Sassen interviews and in his role as Jewish emigration and then transportation expert, and it is in fact the argument here that Eichmann optimised his outcomes in material, social and psychological terms by adapting to different audiences, a form of conformity. In that context his being driven to acrimonious exchanges with the flamboyant Hausner when on trial for his life is not evidence of Eichmann's having been anything other than a careerist who optimised his outcomes through conformity in the SS. Nor is it evidence of Eichmann's having had any sense of agency during the war.[2]

Cesarani claims that Eichmann did had have some agency and choice and that he was a willing participant in the annihilation of Europe's Jews because he became a 'radical' antisemite, though Eichmann had not acted as an eliminationist antisemite before such a policy had been decided upon above him in the Nazi hierarchy, in fact having been an agent in the emigration of Jews from Germany, and only endorsed eliminationist antisemitism when it became part of SS ideology and the historic mission of the SS. Cesarani notes, 'it was in the nature of radical Nazi antisemitism that on the surface its adherents appeared to be coldly performing a job and obeying orders', though that means that 'radical' or 'eliminationist' antisemitism may be attributed to individuals in the Nazi and SS hierarchy without any objective evidence in behaviour or attitude of such antisemitism. That is an extraordinary inference from no evidence, and in fact from evidence of careerism in the SS. The alternative interpretation, more consistent with the timing of Eichmann's seeming to embrace eliminationist antisemitism, is that Eichmann assimilated the eliminationist ideological agenda of the SS to avoid the possibility of loss of the good regard of his peers and bosses in the SS and to preserve his elite SS status with its power, influence, involvement, identity and prerogatives.[3]

Lang notes that in the SS 'social recognition and the feeling of superiority that came with the status and power of the SS made its members want to live up to its ideals, just as it made them dread the prospect of being excluded from this exclusive community.'[4]

Even Cesarani, whose claim is that Eichmann was after a certain time motivated by eliminationist antisemitism, notes of Eichmann that 'there is reason to believe his statements in captivity that he was uncomfortable with the policy of "physical annihilation"' and that 'it was neither mendacity nor self-deception for Eichmann to proclaim that he clung to a "territorial solution" for European Jewry until late autumn 1941. Such a policy, after all, offered him more chance of prestige and promotion than mass murder,' for 'the decision to embark on the "physical annihilation" of Jewish populations was potentially a disaster for him and his office', in that it meant that the policies with which Eichmann had been intimately involved, 'emigration, forced migration and territorial solutions were no longer on the agenda'. Cesarani then acknowledges that Eichmann was disappointed when his 'territorial solution' to the 'Jewish problem' was replaced by a policy of 'physical annihilation', which threatened his position and reputation as an expert on the Jews, for careerist reasons.

Cesarani goes on to claim that Eichmann was 'relieved' to find that he had a role in the 'new phase of "Jewish policy"' after his job as an "emigration expert" disappeared, that he was "still in business"', which does of course attribute decisive influence on Eichmann's ensuing perpetrator behaviour and in fact on his ensuing apparent assimilation of eliminationist antisemitism to his pursuit of his own interests in the form of his SS career.[5] Cesarani's argument that Eichmann became an eliminationist antisemite once the physical annihilation of the Jews had been decided upon above him in the Nazi hierarchy as Nazi racial policy and an SS objective does then indicate Eichmann's assimilating eliminationist antisemitism to optimise his career prospects and the regard of his peers and bosses in the SS. That ascribes decisive causal influence to Eichmann's pursuit of his own interests rather than to eliminationist antisemitism derived from an autonomous ideological conviction and tends to indicate that Eichmann's ensuing commitment in the transporting of Jews to extermination centres and antisemitic utterances reflected Eichmann's desire to maintain or enhance his reputation in the SS and to secure the approbation of peers and bosses in the SS, and that after the war his statements in the Sassen interviews were designed to impress an audience sympathetic to Nazism with his SS officer identity.

Cesarani does in fact acknowledge that Eichmann was 'a normal person' whose form of antisemitism was not uncommon in Austria in the 1920s, void as it was of any eliminationist or violent intent, that his 'move to the right' was 'gradual', beginning with joining a right-wing organisation and reading Nazi newspapers, that 'Eichmann was probably being quite honest when he said at the moment he joined the Nazi Party, he didn't hate Jews', and that as an SS officer early in his career dealing with German Jews Eichmann had 'cordial' relations with Zionists in promoting Jewish emigration from the Reich.[6] Eichmann's father mixed in right-wing nationalist circles, and as has been seen when Eichmann joined the Nazi Party in 1932 it was due in part to the recommendation of Kaltenbrunner, at the time an SS leader and the son of one of his father's friends, and to the influence of Andreas Bolek, another national socialist and friend of Eichmann's father, indicating that the continuing influence of Eichmann's father on Eichmann.[7] Eichmann became a member of the SS later the same year.

Though in the election of July 1932 the Nazi Party won more seats in the German Parliament than any other party, in Austria the Nazi Party had not achieved anything like such popularity, so Eichmann's motive for joining does not seem to have been instrumental in the sense of optimising economic or social advantage. One factor does seem to have been the combination, referred to above, of right-wing nationalist sentiment not uncommon in the German and Austrian middle-classes of the time in his family background and the personal influence of Eichmann's father's friends. Another could be Eichmann's tendency to want to join organisations in what seems indicative of a desire to belong and to be part of something, for an identity and role, a trait that was to reappear in his SS career, as was cultivation of the approval of father figures, that is, to optimise psychological outcomes for himself.

Eichmann then lost his job with the oil company not long after the Nazis assumed power in Germany, in June 1933, whereupon he returned to Germany, possibly because as a Nazi Party member his prospects seemed better there. In Germany he joined an Austrian exile SS unit, before joining the SD in Berlin in 1934, it seems to escape the tedium of military life. Cesarani notes that at the time of Eichmann's joining the SD it was 'an agency that came later to specialise in Jewish affairs' and 'bore no resemblance to the sinister machine it became', with 'little influence on anything, let alone the formation of policy towards the Jews'. Though a few years later the SD became 'the driving force of "Jewish policy"', 'this was not obvious to Eichmann at the time', and though the prosecution at Eichmann's trial alleged that Eichmann was 'honing his Jew hatred', 'nothing could have been further from the truth'. For in 1934 Eichmann was employed in the SD compiling a 'register of

Freemasons', from which he joined a unit specialising in Jewish affairs under Mildenstein, possibly because of the nature of the work on Masons, though Cesarani notes that Eichmann 'was not deterred by the prospect of working in a secret service department devoted to combating the Jewish enemy'. Cesarani claims that Mildenstein was another case of Eichmann's having found a 'mentor in an older man'.[8] Eichmann's work under Mildenstein was to study Zionist movements, and though when Mildenstein left Eichmann was not immediately promoted, he was assigned to an office that became Reich Main Security Office Section IV B4 on 1 March 1941, with a task of dealing with 'Jewish matters, evacuation matters', and reporting to Heinrich 'Gestapo' Müller of Amt IV, who reported to Heydrich and above him to Himmler.

Nazi policy at that time, decided upon in the upper echelons of the Ministry of the Interior and the Ministry of Finance together with the Führer's Deputy, was to encourage Jewish emigration by systematic exclusion of Jews from German economic and social life through a series of discriminatory measures. Longerich notes the 'intensifying of the persecution of the Jews', an objective of 'emigration of Jews under all circumstances', and punitive taxation against Jews, the result of which was that 'the assets of Jewish businessmen were systematically appropriated by the state'.[9] Eichmann was then in his role in the SD of arranging Jewish emigration doing no more than implementing a policy decided upon above him in the Nazi state hierarchy, meeting the role requirements of a middle ranking functionary and having no influence on policy whatever.

Even if it is assumed that Eichmann joined the Austrian SS unit in Germany because he perceived that to be his best opportunity for work at the time rather than for an elite identity, it does not follow that Eichmann would not have been attracted to the privilege and status of being part of the SS as it became an elite identity in Germany under Nazi rule. And it seems that Eichmann's expressed antisemitism developed from the period before he joined the SS, when he does not seem to have been especially antisemitic, through the period of arranging Jewish emigration, to use of a more eliminationist antisemitic vocabulary appropriate to the altered Nazi enterprise of annihilating the Jews, indicating that the motive was to enhance his career and to be approved of by his peers and bosses in the SS. Cesarani claims that Eichmann assimilated the SS conviction that Jews represented a threat to the German race and state and that by 1938 Eichmann was using 'terror' to encourage Jews to emigrate, though he admits that in Poland in 1939 Eichmann's target was not just Jews.[10]

Though Eichmann had been involved in 1938 in plans for the voluntary emigration of Jews from Austria to Palestine, Arendt claims that policy changed to forced emigration in February 1939. During September 1939, following the Nazi invasion and division of Poland under the Ribbentrop-Molotov pact, the western part of Nazi-occupied Poland became part of the German Reich, and the Nazi intention was to resettle ethnic Germans there and to deport Poles and Jews to the east, to the General Government under Hans Frank. To begin with there was to be an intermediate step of ghettoisation of Jews in the east to enhance control over them and to facilitate ensuing deportations. To give effect to this decision, on 6

October 1939 Müller instructed Eichmann to deport Jews from East Upper Silesia. In his implementation of Müller's order Eichmann chose Nisko, a swampy area in the Lublin district near to the German-Soviet demarcation line, as the destination for deported Jews, and extended the transports to include Jews from the Protectorate and Vienna.

On 19 October Müller indicated that central coordination of the deportations was needed and then directed that they should be halted. Browning's view is that the main reason for the halting of the deportations under the Nisko Plan was Himmler's prioritisation of the resettlement of ethnic Germans in the east, though deportations of Jews to the Lublin reservation continued under Hitler's directive of 18 October 1939 to expel 'Jews, Polacks and riff-raff' to what remained of Poland. The plan was for a more gradual deportation of Jews to the east, with an anticipated 550,000 Jews to be deported to the Lublin reservation and accompanied by Poles to make a total of 1,000,000 deportees over the next four months.[11]

The evidence indicates that Eichmann was not involved in the decision to deport Jews to eastern Poland in 1939, that the decision was made above him in the Nazi state and SS hierarchy, and that Eichmann was instructed by his immediate boss, Müller, to implement the decision and arrange the deportations of Jews to the east. Though it seems to have been Eichmann who decided upon Nisko, that was no more than a decision as to the precise location for the deportations, and though there is evidence of a possible excess of zeal on Eichmann's part in adding Jews from the Protectorate and Vienna to the instruction from Müller to deport Jews from East Upper Silesia the likelihood is that Eichmann's initiative was intended to impress his bosses in the SS by giving effect to Hitler's intention of deporting Jews from the Reich to the east of the part of Poland occupied by the Nazis. And Eichmann obeyed the ensuing order from Müller to halt the deportations of Jews to the east.

According to Cesarani, 'Nazi population policy in Poland' attempted to populate western Poland with ethnic Germans and to deport Poles and Jews from western Poland to the east to make room for them, and Eichmann was involved in the deportations between December 1939 and March 1941 and so moved from being an emigration expert to an expert in mass deportations.[12] Here too Eichmann may be seen to be a middle-ranking functionary responding to decisions made, and acting in compliance with orders from, above him in the Nazi state and SS hierarchy.

In 1940 another plan for Jewish emigration emerged, which was to transport western European Jews to Madagascar. This was not new, for the French had planned to deport Jews to Madagascar in December 1938, and the proposal to compel France to make Madagascar a destination 'for the solution of the Jewish question' came from Rademacher, the German Foreign Office's 'expert' on Jewish issues, on 3 July 1940, following the surrender of France on 22 June 1940. The plan was endorsed by Hitler and by the SS, and Heydrich regarded it as a 'territorial Final Solution', but by September 1940 it was obvious that the plan would be impossible to implement because of the control of the seas by the British Navy. The result was that 'forced emigration' ceased to be a possible means of getting rid of European Jews.[13] The Madagascar Plan had prompted a halt on ghetto construction in the east, with Frank expressing 'colossal relief' that the plan would end the deportations into the

General Government in Poland, but its abandonment left European Jews in Germany and the occupied territories to be dealt with by the Nazi authorities in Europe.[14]

Thereafter the German attack on the Soviet Union on 22 June 1941 (Operation Barbarossa) involved the 'inheritance' of immense numbers of Jews in eastern Poland and the western part of the Soviet Union and Goering's authorisation to Heydrich, on 31 July 1941, to produce a plan for the 'total solution of the Jewish question in the German sphere of influence in Europe'. In the meantime Heydrich had authorised the elimination of Bolsheviks, partisans and Jews behind the German lines, the result of which was the mass murder of Bolsheviks and Jews by Einsatzgruppen (this is discussed in some detail in Chapter Seven below). In October 1941 Jewish emigration from the Reich was forbidden, ending Eichmann's policy of emigration for Jews.[15]

The Soviet counteroffensive of 5 December 1941 was followed by the Japanese attack on Pearl Harbour on 7 December and a German declaration of war on the US on 11 December. On 12 December a meeting took place at the Reich Chancellery between Hitler, Himmler, Goebbels, Bormann, Frank, and other 'Reich leaders and Gauleiters'. Though there is no official record of the meeting Goebbels' lengthy reference to it in his diary notes Hitler's having 'prophesied to the Jews that if they brought about another war they would experience annihilation. That was not empty talk. The world war has happened. The annihilation of Jewry must be the inevitable consequence.' Goebbels goes on to refer to Hitler's having advocated avoidance of sentimentality and for the 'originators' of the war 'to pay for it with their own lives'. The fact that Goebbels' diary entry would have been contemporaneous with the meeting being recalled enhances its credibility as evidence of Hitler's having indicated his decision in December 1941 that the Jews should be exterminated, though Longerich notes that Hitler had given several earlier indications that he wanted the Jews of Europe to be eliminated. The Wannsee Conference followed on 20 January 1942, at which Heydrich referred to Goering's authorisation letter of 31 July 1941 to develop a plan for the final solution to the Jewish question in Europe and to the development of such a plan being within the domain of the Reichsführer-SS, Himmler. Given that Eichmann reported to Müller, who in turn reported to Heydrich and then to his successor, Kaltenbrunner, who reported to Himmler, Eichmann was a long way away from the locus of decision-making regarding the Jews of Europe.[16]

Cesarani notes that Eichmann never made policy and was limited to implementing it in arranging deportations of Jews between 1942 and 1944, though he claims that Eichmann became an eliminationist antisemite through a combination of 'ideas' reflective of 'society' and supported by the 'political system', the 'dehumanization of the Jews' and their being considered a threat to the German race and state, and a 'disabling of inhibitions' regarding murder. Cesarani claims that 'anyone subject to these processes might have behaved in the same way, be it in a totalitarian state or a democracy', which indicates Cesarani's belief in Eichmann's being 'normal'.

Cesarani does not though address why Eichmann and people in general are so susceptible to societal influence, that is, he does not consider the possibility that the explanation is that Eichmann optimised his material, social and psychological outcomes in the form of careerism and securing the approbation of bosses and peers in the SS by conformity, just as people in general do in all societies.

In an indication that Eichmann was not an eliminationist antisemite in the ordinary understanding of Nazi perpetrator behaviour, Cesarani claims that Eichmann either wanted to murder the Jews or did not care if they 'perished'.[17] Though Cesarani's claim is then that ideological and circumstantial considerations are key to explaining why Eichmann did what he did, he seems to claim for Eichmann either an ideological desire to exterminate the Jews or indifference to their annihilation. This lack of differentiation between indifference to what happened to the Jews, which Kershaw has found to have been the common attitude amongst ordinary Germans in Nazi Germany and which Kershaw has associated with ordinary Germans' having more compelling interests than the Jews (and one which seems to indicate, or at least is entirely consistent with, pursuit of personal interest as the decisive influence on Germans' behaviour), and eliminationist antisemitism in the form of desire to exterminate Jews, seems to be a key difficulty in Cesarani's case. For an attribution of indifference to what happened to the Jews would indicate that Eichmann optimised his own outcomes in his perpetrator behaviour by meeting the requirements of his role, whereas the claim that Eichmann wanted to murder Jews would indicate a primary ideological influence of eliminationist antisemitism on Eichmann's perpetrator behaviour.[18]

Cesarani is meticulous in his consideration of all the evidence on Eichmann's SS career and on his attitudes and behaviour. He points to the very different assessments of Eichmann's psychological state, which have varied between characterisation of Eichmann as murderous and lusting after power and as being altogether normal, and notes what he refers to as Brunner's psychoanalytic interpretation that Eichmann sought to annihilate himself and so achieve a form of 'narcissistic self-mastery' over himself. Cesarani claims that 'Manvell and Fraenkel were closer to the mark (than claims that Eichmann was abnormal in upbringing) when they argued, contrary to many other writers in the 1960s, that "Eichmann adopted anti-semitism as a career; he was not personally anti-semitic", and notes Eichmann's 'aptitude for power games within the Third Reich and his willingness in 1944, at least, to play one power centre against another'. Here Cesarani seems to indicate that Eichmann was motivated by careerism rather than ideological motives.[19]

Turning to the sequence of events in Eichmann's career, Cesarani then refers to evidence from a lecture in 1937 that Eichmann conceived of the Jews as enemies of the German race, though by that time antisemitism of that sort would have been prevalent within the Nazi Party and the SS and so could have been no more than conformist. Cesarani notes Eichmann's taking pleasure in his power over Jews when arranging their emigration from the Reich, which is evidence of the psychological rewards for Eichmann of SS rank and his role in relation to the Jews, and Eichmann's ensuing role in the removal of Jews from Europe in the form of the Madagascar Plan and after its failure and the invasion of the Soviet Union in 1941 the evacuation of Jews to the east. Cesarani believes in the genuineness of Eichmann's shock at the change in Nazi policy to annihilation of the Jews, and as has been seen regards Eichmann as having been relieved to remain 'in business' in his new role of transporting Jews to extermination centres, which is of course an indication of careerism and optimisation of outcomes as the explanation for Eichmann's perpetrator behaviour. Cesarani infers that Eichmann did not object to being part of the extermination process, concluding, as has been indicated above, that Eichmann either wanted to murder Jews or did not care if they 'perished'. He then claims that Eichmann's 'genocidal intentions are implied by Eichmann's last speech in Berlin', when Eichmann is claimed to have said he would gladly go to his grave knowing that millions of enemies of the Reich had preceded him (see above), and by Eichmann's statement in the Sassen interviews that he regretted not having murdered all 13.5 million Jews in the world, ignoring his own reservations regarding the credibility of the Sassen records and the possibility of their representing nothing more than bravado. Cesarani then refers to a completely 'indoctrinated Eichmann', though that does not seem to follow from Cesarani's own evidence, which indicates that Eichmann transported Jews to extermination centres for careerist reasons. For Cesarani then ideological indoctrination and eliminationist antisemitism explain the role of Eichmann, despite producing evidence and drawing inferences indicating careerism.[20]

Despite Cesarani's claim that Eichmann was antisemitic in the eliminationist sense, it seems that his expressions of eliminationist antisemitism represented nothing more than conformity to Nazi and SS ideological identification of Jews as enemies of the German race and state in time of war, an ideological conformity to maintain his identity as a senior SS officer and an integral part of one of the major enterprises of the Nazi state and to enhance his career and the regard of his peers and bosses in the SS hierarchy. For the evidence is that Eichmann was indifferent to the fate of the Jews, facilitating their emigration when that was considered the desired means of ridding Germany of its Jews, and arranging their transportation to extermination centres when Nazi policy and the role of the SS changed. In other words evidence of Eichmann's apparent eliminationist antisemitism once the extermination of the Jews had been decided upon reflected his desire to maintain his position in the middle to upper echelons of the SS and to be involved in what became one of the major enterprises of the Nazi state, rather than ideological eliminationist antisemitism's being the cause of Eichmann's perpetrator behaviour. Eichmann's expressed attitudes and behaviour seem to have reflected his desire to belong, for order, hierarchy, and the good regard of his peers and bosses in the SS.

Ian Kershaw, in a review of Cesarani's *Eichmann: His Life and Crimes*, supports Cesarani's rejection of Arendt's characterisation of Eichmann as an 'archetypal middle-manager on the lookout for career advancement, but otherwise without motive', or, in Cesarani's phrase, 'the classic desk-killer who mechanically and thoughtlessly arranged for millions to die as the culmination of a routinized and sanitized process of destruction'. On the contrary, Kershaw claims that 'far from being merely an industrious underling dispassionately implementing orders, Eichmann was a convinced anti-Semitic ideologue' 'who could "initiate action"', and though Kershaw acknowledges that Eichmann had not joined the Nazi Party 'specifically because of its anti-Semitic message', he claims that once Eichmann was in the Security Service and was 'exposed to Nazi anti-Jewish ideology' he 'swiftly became a fervent believer' that the Jews 'had to be removed one way or another'. Kershaw claims that 'the ideological context, organisational structure of the Nazi security apparatus, and the opportunity of a "war of annihilation" made Eichmann what he was', an indication of Kershaw's belief that circumstantial factors associated with Nazi ideology and its implications in time of war were the decisive causal influence on Eichmann's perpetrator behaviour.[21]

In his support for Cesarani and criticism of Arendt, Kershaw does then seem to concentrate on the influence of the ideological context and to disregard the influence of Eichmann's personality, background, and motives, not least Eichmann's desire to belong, for an elite identity, for hierarchy, order, and for the sense of involvement and the privileges of SS membership and rank. Yet just four years later, in 2008, Kershaw claimed that 'within the SS-SD-Gestapo organisational complex, it was less the outright racial fanatics so much as the ambitious organizers and competent administrators like Eichmann and ice-cold executioners like Höss who turned the hellish vision into hell on earth', adding that 'Arendt's controversial report of the Eichmann trial ended: "The trouble with Eichmann was that so many were like him, and that the many were neither perverted nor sadistic, that they were, and still are, terrifyingly normal"', and, noting that Höss too had been found to be a 'petty bourgeois, normal person', Kershaw concludes, 'ideological anti-semitism seems at best to have provided a secondary motive in these cases, as it does in the career of Franz Stangl, Commandant at Treblinka death-camp'. And though Kershaw adds, 'there is no intrinsic contradiction between ideological conviction and managerial talent', he ignores part of his own attribution, that is to individual aspiration and careerism rather than ideological motives.[22]

In another review of Cesarani, Walter Laqueur notes that 'Eichmann only gradually became an instrument of mass murder' and had been no more antisemitic than many others on the far right in Germany at the time. He notes that Eichmann had been content to arrange Jewish emigration from Germany and had been surprised by the decision to exterminate the Jews of Europe, and that 'Eichmann slouched slowly towards genocide', a view with which he claims Cesarani agrees. Such evidence is an indication of the timing of and reason for Eichmann's becoming an apparent eliminationist antisemite. He notes too that in his involvement in transporting Jews to extermination centres Eichmann used, to refer to Cesarani's own phrase, 'the same problem-solving, can-do, corporate mentality' he had shown before becoming an SS officer, an indication of Eichmann's concentration on efficient task completion and indifference to rather than hatred of Jews.[23]

Notes

[1] See Cesarani, *Eichmann* op. cit., pp. 345 and 346. Despite these claims of anti-Ostjuden prejudice towards Hausner in Arendt, on p. 282 Cesarani describes Hausner's cross-examination of Eichmann as a 'shambles', which seems to corroborate Arendt's criticism of Hausner. See also Mulisch, Harry, *Criminal Case 40/61, The Trial of Adolf Eichmann: An Eyewitness Account*, University of

Pennsylvania Press, 2009, p. 141 for reference to Hausner's incompetence as Prosecutor and Eichmann's adeptness as defendant.

[2] See ibid, pp. 281–98, and Shaked, Michal, *The Unknown Eichmann Trial: The Story of the Judge, Holocaust and Genocide Studies*, Volume 29, Issue 1, Spring 2015, pp. 1–38.

[3] See ibid, p. 157. Cesarani seems to use the word 'radical' to indicate an antisemitism extreme enough to explain systematic extermination of the Jews of Europe, in place of the term 'eliminationist' and with the same meaning in regard to antisemitism. Cesarani claims that Eichmann was not 'sentimental' regarding the Jews and that he saw them as a 'germ', a 'disease' to be destroyed, though the evidence he presents in support of that contention is Eichmann's admission that the Jews were regarded in that way by Nazi ideology and policy, which is not evidence of its being the view of Eichmann personally or of its being the decisive causal influence on his perpetrator behaviour.

[4] See Lang, *The Proud Executioner*, op. cit., pp. 72 and 73.

[5] See ibid, pp. 115 and 116. See p. 281 for reference to Eichmann's claims in court in Jerusalem that, having been sent with *ex post facto* authorisation of the extermination of Jews to Globocnik in mid-1942, he asked 'to be relieved of his new duties' and that he would have been executed if, having exhausted the possibilities of transfer, he had 'stayed in post and disobeyed orders'. Such claims were part of Eichmann's defence that he could not have done other than he did and are dissonant with the attribution of careerism to Eichmann by Cesarani, who notes on p. 293 that Eichmann could provide no 'direct evidence' of having requested a transfer.

[6] Ibid, pp. 16, 30 and 34.

[7] Ibid, p. 26.

[8] See ibid, pp. 39, 45 and 47.

[9] See Longerich, *Holocaust: The Nazi Persecution and Murder of the Jews*, Oxford University Press, 2010, pp. 62 to 65. See also p. 67 for reference to the numbers of Jews who emigrated from the Reich between 1933 and 1937 in accordance with the Nazi objective of expelling the Jews, and pp. 68 and 69 for reference to the SD section dealing with the Jews coming under Wisliceny in April 1937 and attempting to take control of Jewish policy though having to abandon emigration to Palestine because of opposition to the creation of a Jewish state from the Nazi hierarchy.

[10] See Cesarani, *Eichmann*, op.cit., p. 16.

[11] See Browning, Christopher R., *Nazi Policy, Jewish Workers, German Killers*, CUP, 2000, pp. 5 to 9. See also Rubenstein, Richard L. and Roth, John K., *Approaches to Auschwitz: The Holocaust and Its Legacy*, Westminster Knox Press, 2003, pp. 150 and 151 for reference to Hitler's speech to the Reichstag on 6 October 1939 regarding the obtaining of *Lebensraum* for Germans and ethnic Germans by expulsions of Poles and Jews to the east, to Heydrich's having informed RSHA leaders on 29 September 1939 of a plan to expel Poles and Jews to a 'Reich ghetto' between Warsaw and Lublin, to the postponement of the plan due to Wehrmacht opposition and to Himmler's prioritisation of the assimilation of ethnic Germans into the Reich over the expulsion of Poles and Jews and halting the deportations on 26 October 1939.

[12] See Cesarani, *Eichmann*, op. cit., p. 8.

[13] See Browning, Christopher R., *The Origins of the Final Solution: The Evolution of Nazi Jewish Policy, September 1939–March 1942*, University of Nebraska Press, 2007, p. 88, and Rubenstein and Roth, *Approaches to Auschwitz*, op. cit., p. 163 for the source of the Madagascar Plan.

[14] See Browning, Nazi Policy, *Jewish Workers, German Killers*, op. cit., p. 16.

[15] See Stackelberg, Roderick, and Winkle, Sally A., *The Nazi Germany Sourcebook: An Anthology of Texts*, Routledge, 2013, p. 340, for Goering's instruction to Heydrich dated 31 July 1941. And see Browning, *Nazi Policy, Jewish Workers, German Killers*, op. cit., p. 40 for reference to the date of the end of emigration for Jews from the Reich. Emigration for Jews in the occupied territories had, Browning notes, been forbidden 'after the outbreak of war'. See also Fischel, Jack R., *Historical Dictionary of the Holocaust*, Rowman and Littlefield, 2020, p. 262 for a more precise date for the ban on Jewish emigration from the occupied territories. Fischel notes, 'the ban on Jewish emigration from Poland was issued by the Reich Security Main Office (RSHA) on 23 November 1940, shortly after the creation of the Warsaw Ghetto. The ban heralded a change in Nazi policy toward the Jews, from officially encouraging their emigration to forbidding it.'

[16] See Longerich, Peter, *Goebbels*, Random House, 2015, pp. 506 and 507 for reference to Goebbels' diary entry concerning the meeting at the Reich Chancellery on 12 December 1941. And see Lehrer, Stephan, *Wannsee House and the Holocaust*, McFarland, 2015, pp. 70 and 71 for reference to Heydrich's referring to the authority of Goering and to the treatment of the Jews as being Himmler's domain. Lehrer notes the sanitised language of the Wannsee Protocol in the reference to 'emigration' being replaced by the 'forced evacuation' of Jews, though there is reference to Jews' being lost through being used as labour in the east.

[17] See Cesarani, *Eichmann*, op. cit., pp. 367 and 368.

[18] See Kershaw, Ian, *Hitler, the Germans and the Final Solution*, Yale University Press, 2008, p. 148 for Kershaw's claim that the instinct for 'self-preservation' is enhanced by a 'climate of repression and terror' and in such circumstances is more influential on human behaviour than 'the instinct to preserve others', and is related to 'moral indifference and apathetic compliance'. See also p. 7 for Kershaw's addressing the semantic issues regarding terms used to describe the reactions to the treatment of the Jews in Nazi Germany and the nature of popular German complicity. And see p. 147 for Kershaw's view that Germans attended to other matters that seemed more compelling to them than the treatment of the Jews.

[19] See Cesarani, *Eichmann*, op. cit., pp. 360 and 361.

[20] See ibid, pp. 357–68.

[21] See 'Nothing banal about his evil', Ian Kershaw, Review of 'Eichmann: His Life and Crimes', in *The Telegraph*, 25 July 2004. And see Cesarani, *Eichmann*, op. cit., pp. 343 and 344 for the quoted passage.

[22] See Kershaw, *Hitler, the Germans and the Final Solution*, op. cit., p. 270 and p. 281*n*, *Arendt, Eichmann in Jerusalem*, op. cit., p. 276 for the quotation from Arendt, and Kershaw, Ian, *The Nazi Dictatorship: Problems and Perspectives of Interpretation*, Bloomsbury Publishing, 2015, p. 154 for a verbatim reiteration of Kershaw's view in 2008. See also Cesarani, *Eichmann*, op. cit., p. 46 for reference to the young,

educated, rational, objective and aspiring middle-class men selected by Heydrich and Himmler into the SD and SS who valued hardness and objectivity and who according to Cesarani were influenced by ideological 'völkisch nationalism'. That is though very different from eliminationist antisemitism.

[23] See 'Four pfennige per track km', Walter Laqueur, *London Review of Books, Vol. 26, No. 21*, 4 November 2004. See also Cesarani, *Eichmann*, op. cit., p. 16.

Chapter Five

Eichmann in Hungary in 1944. Evidence of eliminationist antisemitism?

The behaviour of Eichmann in Hungary is worth addressing separately because it has been interpreted as a compelling instance of Eichmann's displaying autonomy in defiance of Himmler's orders. It is then germane to the argument here that Eichmann engaged in eliminationist antisemitic behaviour only to enhance or protect his SS career with all the material, social and psychological rewards it afforded him, the latter including approbation from those above him in the SS hierarchy, rather than because he was or had become an eliminationist antisemite.

Arendt's claim that Eichmann 'sabotaged' Himmler's order to cease transportations of Jews from Hungary in the summer and fall of 1944 has been referred to above. Referring to the unprecedented speed and intensity of the deportations of Jews from Hungary and to the multiplicity of German agencies associated with the Jews in Hungary in 1944, Arendt claims that Eichmann came into 'open conflict with orders from his superiors' in his organising the notorious 'foot marches' of Jews from Budapest even in the knowledge that Himmler had ordered the 'dismantling' of the 'extermination facilities' at Auschwitz.[1] Though such evidence could be taken to indicate that Eichmann was driven more by eliminationist antisemitism than by concern to maintain the regard of his bosses in the SS and the elite identity and status his SS career afforded him, Eichmann did have support for continuing to transport Jews from his immediate boss, Müller, who was known to exert close control over his subordinates, and from Müller's boss, Kaltenbrunner, who had long standing personal ties to Hitler and often bypassed Himmler and reported directly to Hitler (not least it seems towards the end of the Third Reich) and whom Himmler feared would denounce him to Hitler over his planned arrangements to exchange Jews for war materiel. And it seems that Kaltenbrunner was the most proximate SS authority in Hungary in 1944, arriving in Budapest three days after the German occupation, insisting upon the installation of two 'notorious anti-Semites' to control 'Jewish affairs' and arranging for them to deport as many as 381,600 Jews from Hungary between mid-May and 30 June 1944, indicating that 'even as the Third Reich began to collapse around him, Kaltenbrunner did not slacken his attempt to annihilate the Hungarian Jews'.[2]

Cesarani concurs over the extent of Kaltenbrunner's influence on Nazi policy towards the Jews of Hungary, noting that 'Eichmann was telling the truth when he swore that policy was laid down before he even arrived' in Hungary, that Kaltenbrunner 'was in Budapest well before Eichmann' and settled policy towards the Jews with the new Hungarian government, and that 'Kaltenbrunner consistently applied pressure to accelerate the deportations once they were under way, and Eichmann did his bidding'. And in another indication of the proximate influence of Kaltenbrunner on Eichmann in Hungary in 1944, it was Kaltenbrunner who ordered Eichmann to leave Budapest just before the Red Army arrived.[3]

Arendt's explanation for Eichmann's behaviour in Hungary in defiance of Himmler's orders is that he did display genuine autonomy from Himmler in following what he perceived to be Hitler's intentions as Führer and what he conceived to be the law in Nazi Germany. As has been seen Arendt refers to Wisliceny's inference that 'Müller and Kaltenbrunner must have covered him', which seems to indicate Eichmann's having displayed some autonomy from Himmler in compliance with what he understood to be Hitler's wishes (and by implication the Führerprinzip and the SS code, which seems to have been part of an SS identity Eichmann found psychologically rewarding). There are though two reservations here. One is that Arendt does acknowledge in a different context that Wisliceny was a 'dubious' source. The other is that Eichmann was even in Arendt's account supported by the most proximate SS authorities in Hungary in the form of Müller and Kaltenbrunner.[4]

The documentary evidence of Wisliceny's testimony at the International Military Tribunal at Nuremberg is more specific, indicating Wisliceny's view that Eichmann was 'cowardly' and 'went to great lengths to protect himself from responsibility. He never made a move without approval from higher authority and was extremely careful to keep files and records establishing the responsibility of Himmler, Heydrich and later Kaltenbrunner.' Wisliceny continued, 'every move taken by Eichmann in executing measures against the Jews was submitted to Heydrich and later to Kaltenbrunner for approval.' Though it may be the case that Wisliceny was an unreliable witness when it came to obtaining some advantage for himself, it is difficult to see how his testimony regarding Eichmann's avoidance of responsibility for policy towards the Jews would have assisted him. It does then seem credible evidence of Eichmann's personality and of his sense of his role in the SS. In a specific indication of Eichmann's appreciation of the ultimate authority in the Third Reich and so of the locus of responsibility for the extermination of the Jews, Wisliceny refers to Eichmann's having told him, at a meeting in Berlin in July or August 1942, that 'on written order from Himmler all Jews were to be exterminated', and to Eichmann's having shown him a Himmler order stating that 'the Führer has decided that the final solution of the Jewish question is to start immediately'. Wisliceny's testimony provides some context to Eichmann's behaviour in Hungary, for it is indicative of Eichmann's understanding that his role there in deporting Jews to their extermination was giving effect to an order from the Führer and of Eichmann's responsiveness to the immediate chain of command above him in the SS. Despite its being critical of Eichmann, claiming that Eichmann 'gave no indication of any human feeling' towards the Jews (which itself could be interpreted as indicating indifference in Eichmann to the fate of the Jews rather than ideological eliminationist antisemitism), Wisliceny's testimony is in fact consistent with Eichmann's defence of obedience to orders under the Führerprinzip and with the argument presented here that Eichmann was not an eliminationist antisemite but rather someone with little desire for, or actual, personal agency, with an aversion to responsibility, with a careerist orientation and an attachment to his SS rank and identity that made him the ideal, zealous and obliging subordinate. Wisliceny's evidence on Eichmann in Hungary in 1944 is that 'late in 1944, Himmler directed that all executions of Jews were to cease, but Eichmann did not carry out this order until he received a written directive signed by Himmler'.[5]

McKale claims that Kaltenbrunner arrived in Budapest on 22 March 1944, following the German occupation on 19 March, arranged collaboration from the new Hungarian regime over sending Jews as labour to Auschwitz, and left 'the details of the deportations to Eichmann'. He also claims that 'Kaltenbrunner had opposed even Himmler when, in the fall of 1944, the Reichsführer ordered that the deportations of Hungary's remaining Jews be suspended', and that 'even as Soviet troops approached Budapest to liberate it from Nazi rule, Kaltenbrunner demanded further deportations of Jews', clear indications that Kaltenbrunner was the decisive influence on Eichmann both in the initial and in the continued transportation of Jews from Hungary to Auschwitz in 1944.[6]

The influence of Kaltenbrunner could have been enhanced by the fact that he was an Eichmann family friend and had introduced Eichmann to the SS, and because both men were from Linz in Austria. Eichmann could then be seen to have continued with the transports of Jews because of the insistence of Müller and Kaltenbrunner as the most proximate form of authority in the SS, and with the implicit authority of Hitler, rather than because of eliminationist antisemitism.

Even Cesarani, whose view is that Eichmann's behaviour reflected eliminationist antisemitism rather than banality or compliance with military orders and who claims that in his trial in Jerusalem Eichmann admitted, 'I proposed the foot marches', notes Müller's support for Eichmann's defiance of attempts to halt the foot marches of November 1944. Cesarani refers to the testimony of SS Standartenführer Kurt Becher, whom Himmler had sent to 'look after the economic interests of the SS' in Hungary and who reported direct to Himmler, that Himmler told Eichmann in early December 1944 that he (Himmler) was in command, not Müller or Eichmann, indicating 'that Eichmann was not acting alone when he persisted with the harshest treatment of the Jews'. Cesarani claims that 'Müller and Kaltenbrunner were at odds with Himmler on the Jewish issue and had no truck with the Reichsführer's efforts to use Jews as conduits to the Allies'.[7] Such evidence would seem to support the view that Eichmann was responding to the most proximate and what he may have seen as the most legitimate authority in Hungary in 1944, given Kaltenbrunner's relationship with and apparent access to Hitler, whose insistence upon no negotiations with wartime adversaries was known, and would seem to support Eichmann's defence of compliance with Hitler's wishes under the Führerprinzip and to indicate that Eichmann did what he did in Hungary to maintain his SS identity and the approbation of Müller and Kaltenbrunner, not because he was an eliminationist antisemite. Even if Eichmann did propose the foot marches it would have been in a context of knowing of Müller's and Kaltenbrunner's general orientation to continue with deportations of Jews from Hungary, so Eichmann's motive may have been to secure the approbation of his bosses in the SS for an initiative that was consonant with their wishes.

Cesarani does in fact note Eichmann's 'susceptibility to father figures' in his relationship with Heydrich and Müller, and Eichmann's relationship with Kaltenbrunner could be seen in a similar light. Such susceptibility to 'father figures' combined with a desire to be approved of by his immediate bosses in the SS could then explain Eichmann's behaviour in the SS in general and his defiance of Himmler over the deportation of Hungarian Jews in particular, and explain too Eichmann's mastering the rhetoric of eliminationist antisemitism whilst really being indifferent to what happened to the Jews.[8]

There is a distinction to be drawn between the policy of deportations of Jews from Hungary, which seems to have been dictated by Eichmann's immediate bosses in the SS, Müller and Kaltenbrunner, not least given the latter's relationship with Hitler, and which Eichmann carried out to ensure the approbation of his immediate bosses in the SS, and Eichmann's interpersonal behaviour with Hungarian Jews. For the evidence is that Eichmann's behaviour in his dealings with Jewish representatives in Hungary was imperious, dictatorial, threatening and grandiose, and indicative of Eichmann's taking some pleasure in his position of power in relation to them. That does not though indicate eliminationist antisemitism autonomous of Nazi and SS policy in Hungary, or that Eichmann was abnormal, for such arrogance and bravado are just what would be expected of an individual incentivised by status, involvement and power over other people, and the evidence on Eichmann's personality indicates that he would have been very similar in behaviour with Poles or other Slavs who found themselves in similar circumstances to Hungary's Jews, indicating that eliminationist antisemitism was not the decisive causal influence on Eichmann's behaviour towards Jews in Hungary. For a man of Eichmann's ordinary background of relatively unpromising beginnings the power and status of SS identity, rank and role in relation to helpless Jews would have been seductive. In very different circumstances Eichmann would be expected to have found pleasure in some form of corporate behaviour that involved cultivating the good regard of his bosses and peers and imperious domination of and indifference to the welfare of subordinates or those over whom he believed he had some form of control.[9] It is worth noting that after the war Eichmann never engaged in any behaviour against Jews which could have been criminal under legal codes outside that of the Third Reich, indicating that under different circumstances he would have sought rank, status, approbation and a sense of belonging in work that would have been normative in the society in question, so in a liberal democratic capitalist society he might have aspired to the middle echelons of the bureaucracy or corporate business. In other words Eichmann's desire for status, rank, approval and belonging and avoidance of low status and obscurity would have been met by very different behaviour reflective of what was optimal for him in the circumstances.[10]

During his stay in Hungary Eichmann did have dealings with Jewish representatives Brand and Kasztner, ostensibly to arrange for the exchange of Jews for money or war materiel, though Cesarani claims that Eichmann 'never relented one iota from the extermination schedule', that, other than the Kasztner train, 'Eichmann merely toyed with his Jewish interlocutors', and that Eichmann's motivation in appearing to endorse the negotiations with Brand and Kasztner and offering to save 1,000,000 Jews in return for war materiel was 'rivalry with Becher'. Cesarani claims that even the transport of Jews to Vienna was the consequence of an arrangement with the mayor, who was a friend of Kaltenbrunner, to provide Jewish slave labour, which makes it another indication of Kaltenbrunner's influence on Eichmann. The interlude of negotiations to save Jews does seem to indicate Eichmann's intense competitiveness and sense of entitlement, which is supported by Cesarani's observation that Eichmann's behaviour in Hungary reflected 'his vanity as much as his fanaticism'. That was of course in a context of competing influences from various parts of the Nazi hierarchy in Hungary at the time. And there was Eichmann's responsiveness to Kaltenbrunner. Cesarani even wonders if Eichmann was opposed to Jewish emigration, not least to Palestine, because of 'hatred of Jews and a desire to see them annihilated' or because their emigration had been organised by a 'rival'.[11] That is despite Cesarani's claim that Eichmann became an eliminationist antisemite over time in the SS, for the period in Hungary was towards the end of the war.

There was an interval of idleness for Eichmann in Hungary following Horthy's suspension of deportations of Jews and Himmler's confirmation of the suspension of deportations on 25 August 1944, a period during which Eichmann seems to have enjoyed a sybaritic lifestyle of great privilege, and there was also Eichmann's brief mission to evacuate Volksdeutsche from the path of the advancing Red Army, prior to a 'delighted' Eichmann's return to work on 18 October following the change of Hungarian government imposed by the Nazis, announcing to Kasztner, 'well, as you can see, I'm back again'. Cesarani claims that 'Eichmann revelled in the cruel disappointment of the stricken Jews, who had hoped Hungary would be able to wriggle out of the war' without the loss of its Jews. What followed was Eichmann's 'fanatical insistence on the foot marches' from Budapest to Vienna that have been referred to above. Cesarani notes Kasztner's comment that 'in that moment he seemed to be the happiest man on earth', and that 'besides, as usual in that period, he was drunk'. The chaotic context is worth noting, with the Red Army approaching Budapest.[12]

The evidence of Hungary in 1944 seems to indicate that Eichmann's behaviour there was influenced by a combination of factors. There was the influence of the inferred or expressed wishes of his immediate bosses in the SS, Müller and Kaltenbrunner, indicating Eichmann's careerism and desire for the approbation of his immediate bosses in the SS and the ultimate authority of Hitler. There was Eichmann's sense of entitlement over what should happen to the Jews of Budapest, his intense competitiveness with other Nazi agencies and resentment at what he regarded as their interference in his domain. And there was Eichmann's taking pleasure in his status relative to the helpless Jews, evidence of an enjoyment of power that had been apparent when he had been arranging Jewish emigration from the Reich and that reflected the lack of status and power in his background. Though some of the Hungarian evidence could on its own be taken to be indicating eliminationist antisemitism in Eichmann, the evidence of Eichmann's previous record of cultivating the regard of Müller and Kaltenbrunner as his immediate bosses in the SS, of Eichmann's competitiveness with other Nazi agencies in Hungary, and of the pleasure he derived from his status and power over the Jews in the period of Jewish emigration provide a context that indicates optimisation of social and psychological outcomes for Eichmann being the cause of his behaviour in Hungary in 1944.

Notes

[1] See Arendt, *Eichmann in Jerusalem*, op. cit., pp. 137, 138, 139, 140 and 145. And see p. 202 for reference to the 'foot marches' of November 1944 having been stopped by Himmler rather than Eichmann, an indication for Arendt of Eichmann's defiance of orders.

[2] See Black, Peter R., 'Ernst Kaltenbrunner and the Final Solution', in R. L. Braham (ed.), *Contemporary Views on the Holocaust*, Springer Science and Business Media, 2012, p. 192.

[3] See Cesarani, *Eichmann*, op. cit., pp. 164, 170 and 195.

[4] See Arendt, *Eichmann in Jerusalem*, op. cit., pp. 145 and 146. And see pp. 148 and 149 for reference to the nature of law in Nazi Germany.

[5] See *Nazi Conspiracy and Aggression*, Volume VIII, Office of United States Chief of Counsel for Prosecution of Axis Criminality, United States Government Printing Office, Washington, 1946, 'Affidavit of Dieter Wisliceny', op.cit., pp. 606, 607, 608, 609 and 610.

[6] See McKale, Donald M., *Nazis After Hitler: How Perpetrators of the Holocaust Cheated Justice and Truth*, Rowman & Littlefield, 2012, p. 142.

[7] Cesarani, *Eichmann*, op. cit., pp. 163, 192 and 193, though see p. 13 for reference to Eichmann's deportations of Jews in the autumn of 1944 being 'unmistakable signs of fanaticism'. See p. 184 for Cesarani's reference to Eichmann's behaviour in Hungary as indicating 'signs of fanaticism', though he notes that though Eichmann was 'consumed with a desire to finish what he had begun' 'he could follow his impulses in the knowledge that Kaltenbrunner and Müller were right behind him'. And see p. 297 for reference to Eichmann's admission of having proposed the foot marches in court in Jerusalem in 1961.

[8] See ibid, p. 16.

[9] See ibid, pp. 159, 167, 175, 176, 179 and 180, and Stangneth, *Eichmann Before Jerusalem*, op. cit., pp. 49 and 50 for evidence of Eichmann's general bravado and arrogant behaviour with Jews in Hungary. See also Westermann, '"Ordinary Drinkers" and Ordinary "Males"? Alcohol, Masculinity, and Atrocity in the Holocaust', in Kaplan, Matthäus and Homburg (eds.), *Beyond Ordinary Men*, op. cit., pp. 30 to 38 for reference to a norm of alcohol use, which was true of Eichmann in Budapest in 1944, and to a Nazi ideal of 'hypermasculinity' that was associated with violence. These factors could explain the behaviour of Eichmann with Jewish representatives in Hungary in 1944 and would indicate Eichmann's susceptibility to the attractions of an SS officer identity.

[10] See Lang, 'The Proud Executioner: Pride and the Psychology of Genocide', in Brudholm and Lang (eds.), *Emotions and Mass Atrocity*, op. cit., pp. 64–80 for Lang's

argument that 'pride' and 'arrogance' explain Nazi perpetrator behaviour because they were accompanied by a sense of German racial entitlement and indifference to Jews who were seen as not being entitled to treatment as human beings. Lang's claim disregards the evidence of Browning's 'Ordinary Men', who were not motivated by racial 'pride' or 'arrogance', as is indicated by their reservations and distress over the task of murdering Jewish old people, women and children, by the fact that the battalion was more used for deportation duties after the initial massacre of Jews Browning describes, and by the ensuing use of Hiwis, eastern European 'volunteers', for the most visceral work of actual shooting of Jews.

Lang also disregards evidence of heterogeneity of experience amongst Browning's 'Ordinary Men', which would also be inconsistent with the role of 'pride' and 'arrogance' Lang claims existed. And other evidence, of the Order Police and the Einsatzgruppen, is indicative of no decisive role for 'pride' and 'arrogance' in explaining Nazi perpetrator behaviour, for there was general use of alcohol (as described above) in the east and of Hiwis for the shooting of Jews. There is no doubt that some SS personnel took pleasure in their power over local populations in the east, not least but not only the Jews, or that they misused that power to their own ends, but that was in the form of monstrous social behaviour and general brutishness of the sort found in Eichmann in Budapest in 1944, and the policy followed by Eichmann was one that reflected the wishes of his immediate bosses in the SS, Müller and Kaltenbrunner, not SS 'pride' and 'arrogance'. Eichmann acted in Budapest in 1944 for the same motives apparent elsewhere for him and other Nazi perpetrators, optimisation of personal outcomes in the form of career, approbation of bosses and peers and avoidance of any sanctions for failure to meet the requirements of his role.

There are other difficulties with Lang's argument. He argues that the SS conferred on its members an elite status and social recognition (both of which are true) that was dependent upon the SS's being efficient and disciplined in the implementation of the policies of the Nazi state. But that argument would indicate conformity to the requirements of role within the SS to retain rank and status in the SS, not the 'pride' and 'arrogance' to which Lang refers. Lang also argues that the 'pride of belonging to the SS' inspired a 'passionate willingness' to meet the obligations of 'duty' and the requirements of the role of the SS, but the evidence indicates that desire for approbation from bosses and peers and fear of informal sanctions were the causes of conformity to role requirements in the SS. Lang also argues that the same SS 'pride' and 'arrogance' were the cause of indifference to the Jews, but that indifference was pervasive amongst ordinary Germans outside the SS and was autonomous of 'pride' and 'arrogance'.

[11] See Cesarani, *Eichmann*, op. cit., p. 186.

[12] See ibid, pp. 174–93.

Chapter Six

Psychiatric and psychological assessments of Eichmann and their relationship to the evidence of Eichmann's personality in his career in the SS

Eichmann was assessed in Israel by a psychiatrist, Kulcsar, and his psychologist wife, who were appointed by the court. Though certified fit to stand trial, according to Brunner Eichmann was found by the Kulcsars to be to be 'weak' and 'docile' and to compensate by developing an appearance of toughness to conform to the Nazi ideal. The implication seems to be that he presented himself as confident and dynamic during the war rather than passive to secure the approbation of his peers and bosses in the SS. Eichmann's 'role-playing' was found to be so natural to him that it was seen as a fundamental personality trait, which is of course consistent with the argument that Eichmann was adept at presenting himself before different audiences to secure the admiration and regard he seems to have needed. The Kulcsars also found that Eichmann's 'enacting' and 'identifying' with 'a certain role' 'for months or years' 'to such a degree' meant that 'it is doubtful if he could still be frank, even if he wanted to', which seems to be a reference to his roles in the SS and the intensity of his identification with the role of SS officer, and which seems also to call into question any account Eichmann would give of himself and his own motives.

Eichmann was also seen by the Kulcsars as having been disconcerted by his own aggressive tendencies and afraid of retaliation by others, and as having resolved such conflict by assimilating the role of a 'totally devoted, completely rational, and idealist bureaucrat' involved in genocide. Brunner quotes the Kulcsars' conclusion that by 'choosing his role of punctuality, lifeless chilliness, cynicism and superficial adaptivity, he (Eichmann) could gratify his own destructive instincts while executing the destructive tasks bestowed on him'. That does not though explain why Eichmann was so content to carry on with his plans for Jewish emigration, which did not involve violence, or why he was unpleasantly surprised by the decision to exterminate the Jews given its possible effect on his career, which seems to have been more compelling than any possible desire for violence against the Jews. The inferences of psychiatric and psychological evaluations from a series of personality tests do then have to be interrogated, not least by use of the context of Eichmann's actual behaviour.

Kulcsar and his psychologist wife seem to have had some doubt as to whether or not Eichmann's aversive reaction to aggressive images was part of an attempt to present a personality who abhorred violence to manipulate the court, but though that remains a distinct possibility it is also possible that the inference that Eichmann was aggressive was reflective of Freudian influence on the practice of psychology and psychiatry at the time. The more convincing part of the Kulcsar evidence is that relating to Eichmann's capacity for embracing and identifying with a role, in his case in the SS as a Jewish and then a transportation expert.

There was some dissonance between Kulcsars' finding that Eichmann's 'inner world was inhuman, biological at best, and fundamentally mechanical' and his wife's inference, though she agreed with her husband that Eichmann could not form 'direct human relationships', that Eichmann possessed 'sensitivity, talent, and spontaneous empathy', which he rationalised by claiming that Eichmann's empathy came over time to be used in an exploitative manner against other people, for whom Eichmann had no concern because of his egocentric preoccupation with his own experience and agenda. The conclusion was that Eichmann's 'conformism' was 'learned' and permitted 'personal volition'. Brunner's conclusion is that the psychiatric and psychological evaluations of Eichmann left a great deal to be desired, even when account is taken of the state of psychiatric and psychological evaluation at the time (for some of the inferences do seem to have been very conjectural and to be supported by evidence that today would not even be considered to be indicative), though he does attribute some of the blame to Eichmann's deviousness.[1]

In other appreciations of Eichmann's psychological state, Cesarani notes that Arendt claims that 'half a dozen psychiatrists had certified him as "normal"' and that Bruno Bettelheim, the renowned child psychologist, agreed with Arendt that Eichmann and most other Nazi perpetrators 'were people who, under other circumstances, would be considered normal, ordinary persons'. Cesarani notes other assessments of Eichmann, including that of one-time Israeli military spokesman and thereafter writer Moshe Pearlman that Eichmann was 'servile to his superiors, bullying to his subordinates and victims' and 'an opportunist with an eye on the main chance'. Though just what credibility Pearlman might have is not elucidated, such an assessment seems consistent with the portrayal here of Eichmann as careerist, opportunist, and exclusively concerned with his own psychological and social welfare.[2]

By contrast Szondi, a practising psychoanalyst to whom Kulcsar sent the Eichmann file without identifying him, found Eichmann to be obsessed with desire to murder, though Brunner notes that Szondi's background and training were not in psychiatry or psychology and that his test is no longer regarded as of clinical or diagnostic value. Brunner's article indicates that the Kulcsars' attribution of homicidal aggression to Eichmann was derived from Szondi's interpretation of the Szondi test, so the attribution of such a drive to Eichmann is less credible than the rest of the Kulcsar evidence.[3]

Gustave Gilbert, the American psychologist at Nuremberg, claimed that Eichmann's answers to the Rorschach test indicated that he was 'a fairly well discernible personality type – the murderous robot of the SS', though that is challenged by Zillmer, Harrower, Ritzler and Archer, who claim that the Rorschach test for Eichmann indicated an ordinary, banal, socially distant, inflexible person who could have been an organization man.[4]

Minerbi claims that Kulcsar regarded Eichmann as 'obsessed with killing', an 'ambitious sadomasochist with average-to-good intellect, devoid of any moral values, who acts under the influence of his egocentric and impulsive motives and attempts to find a real and rational justification for his actions instead of seeking moral approval' and who had derived from his relationship with his father the idea that 'to be weak and passive is dangerous' and who tried to 'prove his virility by forceful positions and actions'. The consequence for Eichmann was 'formal adaptation to doing what was asked of him while he actually rebels and follows his own will'. Minerbi also quotes Szondi as having found Eichmann's 'defense mechanisms so weak that they left him completely at the mercy of his instincts'.[5]

There do seem to have been inadequacies in the psychiatric and psychological evaluations of Eichmann, not least Kulcsar's failure to interpret a Rorschach test, very different inferences regarding Eichmann between Kulcsar and his wife that seem to have been rationalised to achieve consistency, very contrasting inferences regarding Eichmann's personality from the Rorschach test, and serious doubts as to the validity of the Szondi test and Szondi's credentials. The evidence of Eichmann's having had aggressive and murderous tendencies seems very much at variance with his anonymous record prior to joining the SS and whilst in it before the annihilation of the Jews became Nazi racial policy and the major task of the SS. It is worth adding that even if it were true that Eichmann had aggressive or murderous drives that would not attribute his participation in the Holocaust to eliminationist antisemitism, that is, ideological genocide of the Jews of Europe. On the contrary, it would tend to indicate that Eichmann's transporting Jews to extermination camps represented a form of pursuit of personal interest for Eichmann. For the Kulcsars' reasoning above would postulate that Eichmann's aggressive and murderous drives could have been satisfied by violence against any group sanctioned by the Nazi state and endorsed by the SS as consistent with or dictated by SS identity and role. There is evidence of Eichmann's use of, and taking pleasure in, his power over the Jews, but that seems to be explained not by aggression but by reference to a drive for power and status and attachment to his SS role and identity reflective of his previous anonymous identity that afforded him no positive social status or power. And there is the evidence of his less aggressive relationships with Jews when emigration was the Nazi plan for the Jews and Eichmann's responsibility in the SS.

The psychiatric and psychological evaluations do not challenge the explanation that Eichmann was careerist, that he optimised his personal outcomes in material, social and psychological terms, which included maintenance of the approbation of his peers and bosses in the SS and of his rank and identity as an SS officer, and that he was behaviourally and attitudinally responsive to the reinforcement contingencies of his immediate circumstances, both in an arrogance towards Jews consonant with his SS role and identity, and in the weakness and docility observed in him on assessment in Israeli custody. Eichmann's 'conformism' is then seen as an adaptive stratagem that optimises outcomes for him. Such self-serving behaviour extends even to his memoir, where Brunner notes that 'Eichmann used mechanistic hyperbole, metaphors and analogies in describing his psychic processes and his conflict with the Nazi hierarchy', and the passages he quotes from Eichmann's memoir do seem a ludicrous, self-absorbed and self-exculpating account of his relationship with the Third Reich, with absurd pseudo-philosophical overtones.

Brunner notes for instance that Eichmann claims in his memoir to have found himself at a desk job by some quite implausible mistake, though he then did his 'duty' despite the fact that the work 'suited me neither physically nor psychically; that it was a pain for me: from which I had to struggle and overcome myself every day anew, before I began the task that I was ordered to do'. Brunner comments that 'in his words, he was willing to sacrifice himself unconditionally for the Fatherland and its liberty', though he notes that Eichmann expatiates that 'I shielded my soul', for though he conformed externally he never let the 'False Gods' into his 'soul', because he was 'stubborn like the new heavy tanks'. Eichmann goes on—

'One's own attitude, one's own reaction to the events of the day, is subject to spiritual self-observation, in which the external "I" carries on a kind of dialogue with my inner "I" – which could also be called conscience. Then, on the basis of this "conversation", my inner "I" takes up its position, a position that I register as "calming" or "upsetting". Depending on my psychic condition, I then sense a resonance in my psychical condition. If one treasures inner calm and a certain pulsating harmony, as I do, to use a familiar saying of my pre-war years, if one cherishes "inner quiet serenity" more than anything else, then one will do everything to restore order in the inner disarray, or at least try to do so.'

Brunner notes that Eichmann claims to have the moral sense that Arendt claims he lacked and that he claims that powerlessness rather than a lack of moral reasoning or appreciation of the nature and consequences of his actions explains his perpetrator behaviour. Though Brunner seems to regard some of Eichmann's memoir as being other than self-serving or self-indulgence in its references to a supposed inner life, and as being consonant with the Kulcsar's finding of Eichmann's unresolved conflicts with aggressive drives, the latter do in fact derive, as has been seen, from Szondi's interpretation of his own tests, which have been discredited since, and Brunner does acknowledge the difficulty of drawing accurate inferences given Eichmann's deviousness. My own view is that Eichmann's memoir is a self-indulgent and self-parading document intended either to assist a plea for clemency or for posterity and a testament to his psychological egoism. It is of course possible that Eichmann had by the time of Jerusalem convinced himself of the veracity and authenticity of the account he was writing in his memoir, though that would only be more evidence of psychological egoism in adapting to new circumstances. As may have been the case with Eichmann in the SS, Eichmann in Jerusalem may have believed what was expedient for him at the time. What is apparent is Eichmann's preoccupation with himself and his lack of any reference or attention to the victims.[6] The memoir is dissonant with the evidence of Eichmann's behaviour and attitudes before the war, during it and after it in the Sassen interviews, in which there is no evidence of Eichmann's having experienced the sort of moral anguish he refers to in his memoir.

There is though a major difficulty with most of the evidence on Eichmann. For the Sassen interviews, the notes of Eichmann's interrogation by Less in Israel, and Eichmann's memoir composed in Israel reflect Eichmann's sensitivity to very different audiences and motivation and capacity to optimise his material, social and psychological outcomes. In the Sassen interviews Eichmann seems to have attempted to impress a circle of Nazis and Nazi sympathisers by acting the unrepentant senior SS officer, enjoying being the centre of attention and the object of respect, whereas in the Avner Less Israeli police interrogation and his memoir composed in prison in Israel Eichmann seems to have attempted to present himself as having done no more than arrange transportation of Jews to extermination camps following orders from above him in the SS and the Nazi hierarchy, that is, as having been no more than a functionary in the Holocaust. Though Less's technique seems to have been to obtain Eichmann's self-exculpating account and then present him with documentary evidence that invalidated it on specific points, for instance knowledge or responsibility, Eichmann's narrative in his interrogation by Less does in fact seem to be close to the truth, for he was, as he presented himself to Less, no more than a functionary receiving and carrying out orders given him by his bosses in the SS to give effect to decisions made far above him in the Nazi and SS hierarchy,[7] though he neglected to mention that his careerism and desire for the approbation of his bosses and peers in the SS, and his attachment to the SS code as part of his affiliation for his SS identity, made him a willing accomplice, though not dissimilar in that regard to the majority of careerist SS officers or others in the Nazi hierarchy in Nazi Germany.

One aspect of Eichmann's behaviour that does seem odd in the context of his propensity for adaptation to different audiences is Eichmann's demeanour when on trial in Jerusalem. For though Eichmann's calm and detached equanimity when faced in court with extensive evidence of the Holocaust could be explained by reference to Eichmann's being an eliminationist antisemite or being indifferent to what happened to the Jews, or by the fact that Eichmann was a 'desk murderer' and so could have conceived of himself as just a link in a long chain of command between those who decided upon the extermination of the Jews and those who carried out the murders, Eichmann's calm demeanour in a courtroom in which he was the object of intense and hostile scrutiny, obloquy and interrogation for monstrous crimes hour after hour in his glass box cannot be explained by reference to adverse attitudes towards Jews or some limited sense of his own involvement, for such attitudes would affect his reaction to evidence of what happened to the Jews, not to what was happening to him in the courtroom or to what Eichmann seems to have known of the most plausible outcome of the court, for Brunner notes from Eichmann's self-serving memoir, written in prison in Israel, 'in the shadow of the gallows', that 'Eichmann was aware of the fact that his execution was a possible, or even probable, outcome of the trial.'[8]

Even Arendt, who claims Eichmann was normal, notes that 'Eichmann went to the gallows with great dignity' and was 'in complete command of himself', whereas a normal person would be expected to react with involuntary, intense distress. Cesarani agrees that Eichmann 'died with courage and as much dignity as a hanging allows'. And Gellhorn, who was present at the trial, notes of Eichmann that 'day after day he leans back in his chair, impassive, and listens to the testimony of the men and women he tormented. Usually their words seem to weary him; sometimes there is a flicker of irritation, a frown.' She notes that Eichmann paid real attention only when documentary evidence was presented, when he would 'make notes'. Adams and Balfour note of Eichmann at the trial an 'almost eerie calmness to his voice',[9] and 'there is in fact considerable evidence of Eichmann's calm demeanour at his trial in Jerusalem on film'.

One explanation is that Eichmann had remarkable self-control even over such long periods of time in the courtroom. Another could be that Eichmann's personality was such that he experienced no anxiety despite the hostility of the courtroom and the certainty of its outcome, though the Israeli interrogator Avner Less describes Eichmann as a 'bundle of nerves' at their first meeting, claiming that 'the left half of his face twitched' and that 'he held his trembling hands under the table', evidence that seems to indicate that Eichmann must have developed good control over his emotions by the time of the ensuing trial in court or must have habituated to the obloquy in Jerusalem during the long period of his interrogation by Less, which according to Less amounted to 275 hours.[10] Though Less's observation of Eichmann was at close quarters and over an extended period, and so would seem to have greater credibility than other impressions of Eichmann, Less was clearly antipathetic towards Eichmann and motivated to disparage him, and his impression of Eichmann's anxiety could be interpreted as indicating Less's expectation of a more impressive man as a senior SS officer than he found Eichmann to be in person, and the experience of an asymmetry of a Jew over a Nazi perpetrator.

Aharoni and Deitl claim that Eichmann expected execution at the time of his arrest in Argentina and had even expected eventual capture,[11] evidence that would tend to support the view that by the time of his trial in Jerusalem Eichmann, having been in Israeli custody for several months and interrogated over that period, with his account being challenged by contradicting evidence, may have become habituated to hostile Israeli treatment and interrogation and have become reconciled to the loathing of the courtroom and certainty of execution. Eichmann's situation on his own in Jerusalem was of course more isolated than that of the defendants at Nuremberg, who were tried together and sat together in the courtroom, and the Nuremberg defendants were in defeated western Germany, whereas Eichmann was the sole object of loathing in Israel, a state the very purpose of which was to provide a safe haven from persecution for Jews, so it would not be legitimate to claim that as many of the Nuremberg defendants were calm Eichmann's calmness in Jerusalem was not unlike that of many defendants at trials for war crimes.

Eichmann's demeanour in the courtroom does seem at variance with the Israeli psychiatric and psychological assessment of Eichmann as 'anxious', which challenges the general validity of their other inferences regarding Eichmann. Eichmann's attachment to the dictates of the SS code and SS identity would have required dignity and courage in the face of adversity, though that would be more plausible if there were evidence of Eichmann's struggling to control his anxiety in the hostile courtroom, and there seems to be none. It cannot be attributed to a lack of empathy in Eichmann, regardless of whether or not that was one of his attributes, because even those who lack empathy retain concern for personal outcomes.

The only part of Eichmann's record that seems other than entirely 'normal', that is, other than aspiring, careerist, reflective of a desire for the approbation of his bosses and peers in the SS, for the maintenance or enhancement of an elite SS identity, and for involvement with senior figures in the SS in a major task of the Nazi state, is his demeanour in court in Jerusalem, and that has been explained by reference to his lengthy period of incarceration and interrogation in Israel and his habituation to hostile accusations and challenges and obloquy in that time. The other possible explanation is just weariness at hours of listening to the accounts of Jewish suffering in the Holocaust regardless of their relevance to his guilt or innocence. The conclusion is that entirely normal people may seem calmer than would be expected in court after long periods of hostile detention and interrogation because habituation diminishes the response to repeated exposure.

Regardless of its derivation, Eichmann's apparent calmness in the courtroom in Jerusalem does not bear upon the discussion above concerning the explanation of his perpetrator behaviour, for even if Eichmann really was very calm in the courtroom despite the adverse circumstances that does not mean that he was not motivated by the privileges, status and elite identity of SS membership, and by desire for approbation from peers and bosses in the SS. Calmness does not in other words indicate autonomy from and indifference to the social universe of bosses and peers, and is not inconsistent with conformity to role requirements and ideological conformity to optimise personal outcomes in the form of obtaining rewards and avoidance of sanctions. In fact Eichmann's composed demeanour in the courtroom could be seen as another instance of his presenting a certain self, one in this case consistent with the one identity in his life that conferred on him any status, that is, the identity of an SS officer, before an audience, in this case posterity. That inference is consistent with Less's finding of Eichmann's military bearing and demeanour in the interrogation period. It is also consistent with Eichmann's defiance of Hausner.

Notes

[1] See Brunner, José, 'Eichmann's Mind: Psychological, Philosophical and Legal Perspectives', in *Theoretical Inquiries in Law 1.2* (2000), pp. 434–37. In an indication of how much credence may be placed on the results of the tests Brunner notes that Kulcsar omitted the crucial inquiry stage of the Rorschach test, which seems to indicate that there was no interpretation of the responses given by Eichmann.

[2] See Cesarani, *Eichmann*, op. cit., pp. 357 and 358.

[3] See Brunner, 'Eichmann's Mind', op.cit., p. 440 for reference to the influence of Szondi on the Kulcsar's attribution of homicidal tendencies to Eichmann, for Szondi's disciplinary background, and for the more recent adverse view of the Szondi test.

[4] See Cesarani, *Eichmann*, op. cit., p. 358, Zillmer, Harrower, Ritzler, and Archer, *The Quest for the Nazi Personality*, op. cit., p. 9, and Szasz, Thomas Stephen, *Ideology and Insanity: Essays on the Psychiatric Dehumanization of Man*, Syracuse University Press, 1991, pp. 120 and 121 for Szasz's case that psychiatric diagnosis may reflect 'psychiatric propaganda and rhetoric' and that 'Eichmann was examined by several psychiatrists, all of whom declared him be normal', though Hausner, the Israeli prosecutor, claimed that psychiatrists had diagnosed Eichmann as 'a man obsessed

with a dangerous and insatiable desire to kill', 'a perverted, sadistic personality', an indication of psychiatry being misrepresented for propagandistic purposes.

[5] See Minerbi, Sergio, *The Eichmann Trial Diary: A Chronicle of the Holocaust*, Enigma Books, 2011, pp. xiii and xiv.

[6] See Brunner, 'Eichmann's Mind', op. cit., pp. 458–63.

[7] See von Lang, Jochen (ed.), *Eichmann Interrogated: Transcripts from the Archives of the Israeli Police*, The Bodley Head, 1983, pp. 96 to 102 for Eichmann's insistence that he was involved only in 'evacuation' of Jews and that he never ordered or had any involvement in killing of Jews, and see p. 157 for reference to Eichmann's claim that 'I just did as I was told' and that if he had been told that his own father was a traitor he would have murdered him, an indication that he obeyed orders and was motivated to do so regardless of whether or not the 'victim' was Jewish. The evidence seems to indicate that Eichmann's position was that had he been ordered to murder Jews he would have done so but that he was not ordered to do so because his role was to arrange the transportation of Jews to the east.

[8] See Brunner, 'Eichmann's Mind', op. cit., p. 456. And see von Lang, *Eichmann Interrogated*, op. cit., p. 291 for Eichmann's rather dramatic and self-regarding concluding statement in his interrogation by Less, in which he said, 'I know the death penalty awaits me', and offered to hang himself in public as an 'example and deterrent to all the anti-Semites of the earth', though that did not prevent him from trying to escape the gallows thereafter in court, in an appeal against the death sentence of the court, and in an ensuing appeal to the Israeli President for a pardon, so the quotations have to be taken as no more than evidence of Eichmann's understanding that execution was a distinct possibility rather than a certainty. They represent Eichmann's proclivity for grandiose rhetoric and presentation of self.

[9] See Arendt, *Eichmann in Jerusalem*, op. cit., p. 252, Cesarani, *Eichmann*, op. cit., p. 322, Gellhorn, Martha, 'Eichmann and the Private Conscience', *The Atlantic Online*, February 1962, whose lack of impartiality is indicated by her choice of the inappropriate word 'tormented', though that does not mean her impression is inaccurate, and Adams, Guy, and Balfour, Danny, *Unmasking Administrative Evil*, M. E. Sharpe, 2015, p. xxiii.

[10] See von Lang, *Eichmann Interrogated*, op. cit., pp. (vi) and (vii). See also p. (ix) for Less's experience of Eichmann's egregious insensitivity, in his attempting to find common ground with Less in his background as a policeman and in his apparent shock at Less's father's having been sent east on one of the last transports out of Berlin. Less infers that Eichmann 'had no feeling for the monstrousness of his crimes'.

[11] Aharoni, Zvi, and Dietl, Wilhelm, *Operation Eichmann: The Truth about the Pursuit, Capture and Trial*, Wiley, 1997, p. 174.

Chapter Seven

Social psychological experimental evidence on human behaviour. The Milgram experiments and Zimbardo's Stanford Prison Experiment

Milgram's Experiments on Obedience to Authority

The relevance of Milgram's experiments on obedience to immoral authority to explaining Eichmann's perpetrator behaviour is to be found both in the astonishing levels of obedience to immoral authority Milgram found, which seem to indicate that Eichmann's compliance with orders from above him in the SS was entirely normal, and in what does seem to be indicated regarding the causes of perpetrator behaviour on the part of normal people. The following discussion of Milgram's results and their interpretation is lengthy and reflects the centrality of his findings and the possible explanations of them for any explanation of perpetrator behaviour in normal people.

The inference from what Arendt claims is that had Eichmann been more morally aware, and had he had more understanding of the consequences of his actions, he would have acted differently. That does not seem plausible, for Milgram's experiments on compliance with immoral authority found that ordinary people drawn at random from a liberal democratic society with respect for individual rights were prepared to inflict severe pain on, and to risk serious harm to, an individual of whom nothing negative was known, just to avoid the embarrassment of having to decline to continue to an authority figure and of being seen to have failed at a task voluntarily undertaken by that authority figure, even though there were no consequences for declining to comply outside the experiment.[1] The participants in the Milgram experiments did exhibit significant levels of distress in continuing to administer what they believed were electric shocks to 'victims' but even so most continued to comply with the immoral command. Their capacity for 'moral reasoning', implicit in their distress, did not preclude their inflicting electric shocks on 'victims', which seems to be a form of perpetrator behaviour, even though there were no real-life consequences for them for declining to do so. The fact that Milgram's experiments have been replicated in many different cultures and time periods with identical results indicates that the experiments revealed something that is a fundamental influence on human behaviour.

Milgram's findings regarding behavioural compliance with immoral authority are then established, and though there have been criticisms of his experiments the findings do seem conclusive. The more controversial area is that of the explanation for such findings, that is, inferences regarding the causes of the behaviour of Milgram's participants in the original experiment and in variations undertaken to identify the causes of the behaviour witnessed. Though Milgram himself postulated the influence on participants of an 'agentic state' that precluded any sense of responsibility for the administration of the electric shocks or their consequences, the nature of participants' distress when continuing to administer shocks or when refusing to do so seems to indicate that participants did feel responsible, that they did have a capacity for 'moral reasoning', and that their behaviour reflected their putting their own avoidance of embarrassment at having to decline to continue to an authority figure and of being seen to have failed by that authority figure before the pain, suffering and risk to health of a person against whom nothing adverse was known. For the evidence is that of the forty participants all were prepared to shock to 300 volts despite evidence of severe distress and of risk to health from 'victims' long before 300 volts was reached, that five refused to go on beyond 300 volts, that four refused to go beyond 315 volts, that two refused at 330 volts, one at 345 volts, one at 360 volts and one at 375 volts, with Milgram noting that one participant who refused to go on referred to the 'learner's' 'knocking', said it was 'not fair to shock the guy', and criticised the experiment for not being 'very humane', and that another who refused to continue said, 'he's banging in there', 'I'm gonna chicken out', and 'I can't do that to a man'.[2] The reference to 'chickening out' seems indicative of the sense of failure and embarrassment experienced by a participant who then declined to continue to administer shocks and of the primary causal influence on those who continued to obey and shock to the maximum indicated by the experimenter. Though in the instance referred to there was extreme concern for the welfare of the 'victim' there was also concern as to how refusal to continue would seem to the experimenter and in fact how it seemed to the participant himself, and though pursuit of personal interest in the form of avoidance of a sense of failure and embarrassment before the authority figure was not the dominant influence on behaviour for that participant at the voltage concerned (though not before) it is indicative of the influence of personal social and psychological outcomes on participants' behaviour in general terms.

Criticism of the Milgram experiments as unrealistic is challenged by the detail of the Milgram experiments, for with a volunteer population of participants drawn from the normal population and divided on what seemed to be a random basis into 'teachers' (referred to here also as 'participants') and 'learners' (referred to here also as 'victims') in what was described as an experiment on the effect of punishment on learning, 'teachers' or 'participants' were instructed to administer electric shocks of increasing magnitude for each incorrect response from 'learners' or 'victims', who were in fact confederates of the experimenter (referred to here as the 'authority figure' because of his status relative to participants) and who would deliberately give incorrect responses. The experimenter would then observe the 'teacher' administering shocks to the 'learner' for incorrect responses and instruct the 'teacher' to continue when the 'teacher' showed hesitancy, uncertainty, reluctance, distress or extreme distress. Referring to shocks especially at the higher levels Milgram notes that participants 'were observed to sweat, tremble, stutter, bite their lips, groan and dig their fingernails into their flesh. These were characteristic rather than exceptional responses to the experiment.' Milgram also observed inappropriate laughter, and even seizures in three participants. The reactions from the 'learner' to the gradual escalation of 'shocks' included involuntary exclamations of pain ('ugh') between 75 volts and 135 volts ('teachers' had been given sample shocks prior to administering them, so they knew experientially what the pain was like), followed by refusal to go on, pleas to be let out and reference to having heart trouble and symptoms at 150 volts and 195 volts, screaming to be let out at 270 volts and 300 volts, more intense, prolonged screaming to be let out at 330 volts, then, between 345 volts and 450 volts (the latter of which was designated 'XXX', and was two steps beyond the designation 'Danger: Severe Shock'), silence. The experimenter's exhortation to the 'teacher' would escalate from 'please continue' through 'the experiment requires you to continue', to its being vital that the participant continue and finally to there being no choice except to continue for the participant. Though the existence of choice is evidenced by the fact that thirty-five per cent did resist shocking 'victims' to the maximum voltage, all participants were, as has been seen, willing to shock to 300 volts, a very high level of shock and one known to inflict great pain and even to be dangerous, and sixty-five per cent continued to shock to the maximum and administer that level of shock three times, at which point the experiment was halted. It is worth noting that those who did resist, the thirty-five per cent, did not insist the experiment should be halted or check on the welfare of the 'learner' before leaving, indicating that they were exclusively concerned regarding their own responsibility for involvement rather than for the welfare of the victim, in other words, concerned for their own welfare.[3] Waller claims that participants in replications of the Milgram experiments have included individuals of different classes, gender and educational backgrounds and that such differences have had no effect on levels of compliance found.[4]

The evidence of 'victims'' pain, distress and pleas would have challenged any reassurance from the experimenter as to the long-term welfare of the 'victim', especially in the variation on the experiment in which the 'teacher' believed from the 'learner's' shouts that he had a heart problem, though even that variation seems not to have changed the percentage administering electric shocks to the maximum.[5] Though Milgram notes that participants were told that the shocks were 'painful but not dangerous', Blass observes that experimenter assurance of there being no danger to the 'learner' would have been challenged by 'contradictory and sinister messages' from 'learners'' reactions that indicated extreme pain and risk of severe harm.[6]

What the detail of the Milgram experiments' procedures establishes is that sixty-five per cent of participants were prepared to inflict severe pain to the maximum possible and to entertain the risk of causing serious harm to or being responsible for the death of 'learners' just to avoid the embarrassment of having to decline to comply with instructions from an authority figure and to avoid being seen to have failed to complete a task voluntarily undertaken by that authority figure, even though there were no real-life consequences for participants (Milgram notes that there was 'no material loss' for participants who refused to comply and that 'no punishment would ensue').[7]

Milgram found that when the experimenter was replaced by an ordinary member of the public without a lab coat, compliance from participants diminished from 65 per cent to a mere 20 per cent, and when the location was changed from the prestigious Yale University campus to a rundown downtown location compliance fell to 47.5 per cent prepared to administer shocks to the maximum, indicating that the experience of having to defy the experimenter and of being seen to have failed at the task was far more adverse with authority figures of greater prestige, and to a lesser extent in more prestigious locations, as would be expected.[8] The Milgram evidence is then indicative of the primacy of pursuit of personal interest even when the advantage is objectively minimal, exclusively social or psychological and confined to the experimental setting, and even when the perceived harm and risk to someone of whom nothing adverse is known is very great, and is very relevant to an explanation of Eichmann's perpetrator behaviour in indicating that compliance with immoral authority is normal for human beings regardless of culture (for the population of New Haven, Connecticut in the early 1960s would not have been one in which conformity was valued more than in other cultures),[9] and for reasons of optimisation of personal social and psychological outcomes.

Milgram did find in a variation on his experiment that distance from the victim enhanced compliance with immoral commands and that proximity diminished compliance. The variation that elicited the lowest incidence of compliance was that in which the participant was required to apply the electric shock to the 'victim' physically, though even then as many as thirty per cent of participants were prepared to continue to shock to the highest level, and the variation that elicited the highest incidence of compliance was that in which the participant had the least direct evidence of the consequences of his actions. In another variation Milgram found that if participants could use a teammate to administer the shocks compliance rose to ninety-two per cent being prepared to shock to the maximum. One explanation for these findings is that distance from the victim diminished the sense of personal responsibility, for when participants who refused to go on were reminded that the authority figure was responsible they continued, whereas when participants were told that they were responsible for their actions and their consequences there was far less compliance, the inference being participant concern to avoid consequential responsibility for harm, an indication of concern for their own welfare, not for the welfare of their 'victims'.[10]

The 'agentic state' with its exportation of responsibility by the participant to the authority figure may have been perceived to be optimal in that it avoided having to confront and defy the authority figure and avoided too being regarded as having failed by that authority figure, whilst not being responsible for, and whilst avoiding blame for, any harm done. This much to be desired 'agentic state' driven by motive to optimise personal social and psychological outcomes through avoidance of responsibility in social and psychological terms does though seem different from Milgram's conceptualisation of the 'agentic state'. For Lunt claims that Milgram's 'agentic state' referred to participants' being 'under the control of an external agent, in this case the experimenter', that it occurred naturally rather than from participants' motive to avoid responsibility, and that it was derived from a combination of socialisation in a 'social system of authority' 'supported by rewards for those who acquiesce and punishment against those who do not conform' (which meant that participants had experienced 'immersion in systems of social control all their lives' and that they were 'primed to look to see who is in charge in a given social context'), and legitimacy of authority derived from consonance with 'broader perceptions and expectations of authority' and 'lack of a competing authority'. Lunt adds that participants' having been 'volunteers' placed 'moral obligations on participants'.[11] Milgram also claimed an evolutionary explanation for participants acting 'agentically' where there is a hierarchy, because more hierarchically structured and better organised groups had better chances of survival than less hierarchal groups.[12]

Contrary to Milgram's conceptualisation of the 'agentic state', participants do seem to have experienced ambiguity over the locus of responsibility in the experiments, and to have been motivated to avoid responsibility for harm to 'victims' by obtaining reassurance that the authority figure was responsible for any harm to the 'victim', that is, to optimise their own outcomes. It is worth noting that Lunt refers to Milgram's 'agentic state' as being derived from antecedent experience in participants' socialisation, where the optimal outcome was compliance, for that does of course indicate the influence of primacy of pursuit of personal interest even if it is inadvertent and a response that occurs without intent or premeditated motive, as in Milgram's 'agentic state'. The evolutionary explanation only indicates the source of Milgram's 'agentic' behaviour at the group level of natural selection and does not preclude natural selection at the individual level of optimisation of outcomes through compliance, as has been indicated above.

Blass notes that 'defiant' participants did ascribe more responsibility to themselves (48.4 per cent) than 'obedient' participants did (36.3 per cent). Though that finding seems to support Milgram's 'agentic shift' explanation of compliance, 'obedient' participants did not ascribe more responsibility to the experimenter, the authority figure, than 'defiant' participants (for 'obedients' ascribed 38.4 per cent and 'defiants' ascribed 38.8 per cent of the responsibility to the experimenter), and the difference between 'obedients' and 'defiants' was in the attribution of responsibility to the 'victim', with 'obedients' ascribing 25.3 per cent and 'defiants' ascribing 12.8 per cent of the responsibility to 'victims'. The difference in compliance between 'obedients' and 'defiants' is then not explained by reference to more of an 'agentic shift' in 'obedients'.[13] On the contrary, it seems to reflect greater 'derogation of the victim' in 'obedients' than in 'defiants'.

Waller refers to Milgram's 'agentic state' as reducing 'inner conflict' by 'abrogation of personal responsibility' and comments that 'unable to defy the authority of the experimenter in Milgram's study, subjects attributed all responsibility to him', an indication of subjects' optimising their outcomes by ascribing responsibility to the experimenter, thus avoiding the embarrassment of having to refuse to go on to the experimenter and being seen to have failed at the task by the experimenter, and avoidance of responsibility for harm done to the 'victim'. Waller comments that Milgram's reference to the agentic state's resulting in a feeling of responsibility to the authority and none for actions prescribed by that authority is similar to Arendt's reference to Eichmann's being influenced by 'duty' over 'personal conscience'. Waller notes that the agentic state has been challenged by evidence of 'hesitation, tentative refusals, and extreme anxiety' in subjects and by 'virtually identical levels of responsibility' being attributed to the experimenter by 'both obedient and defiant subjects', when 'the agentic shift hypothesis would predict far more responsibility to be assigned to the experimenter by obedient subjects (looking to rationalize their obedience) than by defiant subjects', which corroborates Blass's findings. Waller also refers to the 1976 research of Mantell and Panzarella that found 'no relationship between the degree of obedience exhibited by subjects and the subjects' assignment of responsibility', with some who obeyed accepting responsibility and others not doing so, and some who obeyed and then disobeyed accepting responsibility and others not doing so for actions prior to their defiance. Waller concludes that 'the agentic shift is not essential to all acts of obedience' and that there is no direct correlation between 'the amount of responsibility attributed to the authority and the amount of obedience exhibited'. Waller postulates other possible reasons for compliance, citing 'an obligation to comply arising from a norm of reciprocity' or 'a norm of equity', neither of which derive 'from relative positions in a social hierarchy'. The agentic shift and the agentic state are then dismissed by both Blass and Waller as explanations for Milgram's findings of compliance with immoral authority.[14]

The preceding paragraphs indicate that Milgram's attribution of an 'agentic state' to the sixty-five per cent of participants who obeyed the experimenter throughout as an explanation for their compliance with immoral authority is not correct. On the contrary, the evidence seems to support my argument that participants optimised their social and psychological outcomes at the expense of 'victims'. For participants seem to have done so both in the sense of administering shocks that they believed caused great pain, distress and possible enduring harm to them, and in then blaming their 'victims' for their own misfortune. When questioned regarding their reasons for attributing so much responsibility to the 'learner' 'obedients' said that the 'learner' had 'volunteered for the experiment and did not learn very efficiently', a response indicative of the primacy of pursuit of their own interests at the expense of the 'victim' both during the experiment, by avoiding having to decline to continue to the authority figure, and thereafter, by exporting blame to their 'victims'.[15] The evidence indicates that 'obedients' ascribed responsibility for what they did to both the experimenter and the 'victim', optimising their social and psychological outcomes. It is worth adding that the reference to 'defiants' does not indicate participants who refused to administer any shocks or who refused at a low level of shock, just those who did not administer the maximum shock as directed and so defied the experimenter at some point. The voltages at which participants refused to continue to administer shocks and their numbers have been referred to above, with none refusing before 300 volts despite evidence of pain, distress and possible harm to 'victims'. Reference to the thirty-five per cent who did show defiance at some point before the maximum shock does then overstate the incidence of defiance and understate the extent of compliance Milgram found.

The 'agentic state' explanation Milgram proposed, that of an 'agentic state' that occurred naturally as a consequence of socialisation of obedience to authority figures, seems to be challenged also by the evidence of greater compliance when other people administered the shock, because in a naturally occurring 'agentic state' participants should have felt that the responsibility was with the authority figure, not them, and so should have had no need to pass it to someone else. Milgram's participants seem to have been uncertain as to who was responsible for inflicting pain and causing possible harm to 'victims'.

Milgram's 'agentic state' does then seem to be contradicted by evidence he himself cites, of distress in participants administering electric shocks and hearing their ostensible effect on the 'learner', of diminished compliance when the authority figure was not present, of greater compliance when instructing someone else to administer the shock, of participants' uncertainty as to their personal responsibility for their actions and their effect on 'learners', and of reduced compliance when another participant defied the authority figure. For none of these characteristics of participants' responses would have been found if participants had been in Milgram's conceptualised 'agentic state', as participants would have felt no personal responsibility for their actions, which they would have ascribed to the authority figure.

Milgram's reference to evolutionary selection of an adaptive trait of compliance with the orders of those of greater status in natural hierarchies to support his claim of an 'agentic state' in participants does then not seem plausible, and an inherited trait of hierarchical compliance seems to be evidence of inheritance of pursuit of personal interest because it is the trait that most aids survival to reproductive age for those not equipped to dominate.[16] Pursuit of personal interest as the primary influence on behaviour also of course explains the incidence of compliance despite distress at the task in Milgram's participants, to avoid the embarrassment of having to confront the authority figure and being seen to have failed at the task they had undertaken by that authority figure, their avoidance of the task when not observed by the authority figure, that is, when they had nothing to lose by not complying with the instruction of the authority figure, greater compliance when instructing someone else to administer the shocks, which would have diminished their visceral involvement and distress, and greater defiance when another participant defied the authority figure, for in that circumstance there would not have been the deterrent effect of being the only one who failed to complete the task. The seeking of reassurance from the authority figure that he was responsible, not the participant, is also consistent with optimisation of psychological outcomes for the participant and inconsistent with the 'agentic state' attribution in that in the 'agentic state' participants were supposed to have been conditioned by socialisation to obey authority figures and so would not have had to ask for reassurance over who was responsible.

Milgram's findings are relevant to an explanation of Eichmann's perpetrator behaviour in a number of ways. Eichmann's lack of distress is explained by his distance, in arranging transportation of Jews to extermination centres, from the actual extermination process, which appalled him when he did witness it. This is similar to the effect of distance from the victim in enhancing compliance in the Milgram experiments. Eichmann's compliance with the requirements of his role as a senior SS officer whose task it was to transport Jews to extermination camps is reflective of his optimisation of personal psychological, social and material outcomes in the form of SS identity, career, status and the approbation of his peers and bosses and avoidance of informal and formal sanctions for failure. This is similar to the avoidance of embarrassment and being seen to have failed by the authority figure on the part of Milgram's participants. Eichmann would as an SS officer have known that his bosses in the SS would have been aware of his meeting or not meeting the requirements of his role as transportation officer and so would have felt himself to have been in a similar position to participants in the Milgram experiments who knew they were being observed by the authority figure. Of course in the SS the proximity was one of a system of information that informed Eichmann's SS bosses regarding his compliance with orders rather than one necessitating the physical presence of Eichmann's SS bosses, and one in which Eichmann knew that he would have to answer for the extent of his compliance. For Eichmann there was no visceral involvement in the extermination of Jews, which is similar to the participants in the Milgram experiments who could instruct someone else to administer the shocks and so defied the authority figure less. And in the SS there was a universality of compliance and no prevalence of defiance of orders or of not meeting the requirements of role.

Milgram claimed that his experiments indicated 'the extreme willingness of adults to go to almost any length on the command of an authority', though in fact the term 'command' is not an adequate description of the authority of the experimenter, who exhorted participants to continue and told them that they had no choice but to continue, though he had no means of coercion of participants or real-life sanctions to threaten them with. Relating his study to the Holocaust, Milgram claims that 'the Nazi extermination of the Jews is the most extreme instance of abhorrent immoral acts carried out by thousands of people in the name of obedience' and that 'the most fundamental lesson of our study' is that 'ordinary people, simply doing their jobs, and without any particular hostility on their part, can become agents in a terrible destructive process'. Though Milgram notes that in his experiments, unlike Nazi Germany, there was 'no intense devaluation of the victim prior to action against him', he argues that any such devaluation would only have rendered compliance easier, which seems obvious.[17]

Relating his findings to Arendt's *Eichmann in Jerusalem*, Milgram concludes, 'Arendt's conception of the banality of evil comes closer to the truth than one might dare imagine. The ordinary person who shocked the victim did so out of a sense of obligation – a conception of his duties as subject – and not from peculiarly aggressive tendencies.' He continues, 'even the force mustered in a psychology experiment will go a long way to removing the individual from moral controls. Moral factors can be shunted aside with relative ease by a calculated restructuring of the informational and social field.'[18] Milgram seems, in referring to the 'duties' of the 'subject', to be using the term to refer to participants in the experiment and to their 'obligation' to the experimenter in the sense of having volunteered, having undertaken to perform the task, having taken the small sum offered just for turning up (regardless of participation), and having been aware that those 'randomly' assigned to the role of 'learner' also volunteered and undertook to enact their role.[19] Though Milgram refers to a 'tendency to obey those whom we perceive to be authorities', the replication of Milgram's findings in many different cultures and time periods seems to challenge the idea that the legitimacy of the authority figure is the explanation for the compliance observed in Milgram's participants. For different cultures and time periods have very different ideas of legitimacy of authority, and findings in more recent replications of the Milgram experiments of even greater compliance in liberal democratic countries with liberal freedoms and more challenging attitudes to conformity and authority indicate that legitimacy of authority may not be the only causal influence at work, that something more associated with the individual participant, for instance embarrassment at being seen to have failed at a task undertaken, may be an influence, though of course greater legitimacy of an authority figure would exacerbate the adverse experience of failure in the form of quitting the experiment and so act as a deterrent to doing so.[20]

It is not clear if the reference to participants' obedience out of a sense of obligation to the experimenter is associated with Milgram's 'agentic state' explanation for the findings of the Milgram experiments, for in the article in which reference to participants' sense of 'obligation' to the experimenter is made Milgram does not allude to the 'agentic state'. The inference is that the 'agentic state' indicates both a sense of obligation to the experimenter from participants and their being freed from responsibility for harm to victims. It is difficult to see the consonance between the 'agentic state' Milgram claims and the lack of capacity for moral reasoning that Arendt claims explains Eichmann's perpetrator behaviour. For the former removes an inhibitor to perpetrator behaviour and the latter alludes to a cognitive deficit in Eichmann.

In another indication of the causal influences on compliance, Milgram found that the refusal of other participants to continue to administer shocks resulted in a fall in compliance to a mere ten per cent prepared to continue to shock victims to the maximum,[21] which seems to indicate the influence of peer behaviour and norms and that the authority figure was not the only influence on participant behaviour in the Milgram experiments. For if obedience to authority were the dominant influence on behaviour there should have been no effect from numbers of others declining to continue, and the evidence of a fall in compliance where others resisted seems to indicate that the dominant influence on the behaviour of participants was avoidance of embarrassment or criticism either with the authority figure or with peers, or optimisation of social outcomes. What does seem to have been most punitive was resisting the authority figure alone, for then the experience of failure and embarrassment may have been enhanced. Milgram's attribution of an 'agentic state' to participants seems to be disproved by evidence of responsiveness to numbers of others resisting the authority figure, for in the 'agentic state' participants should have been immune to influence from others.

When the authority figure was not present and gave instructions by phone compliance fell to a mere 20.5 per cent prepared to administer the maximum shock and participants pretended to administer shocks, an indication that embarrassment in declining to continue to an authority figure and being seen to have failed by that figure, which could only have happened had the authority figure been present, was the most compelling influence on the behaviour of participants in the experiment. For if the participants had been in an 'agentic state' the presence of the authority figure should not have been necessary to continued compliance with the task.

Cesarani accuses Milgram of opportunism in linking his experiments with Arendt's assessment of Eichmann in Jerusalem. He claims that Milgram's participants were paid and that they suspected they would not be paid if they quit the experiment, though that would indicate that being paid mattered more to participants than continuing to inflict pain on an innocent victim, which in turn indicates a human tendency to serve the interests of the self regardless of the cost to others.

Cesarani also claims that almost half the participants believed the experiment was a 'set-up' and so not genuine, though the intensity of the distress evident in many participants argues against such a claim, and to the extent that there is evidence of what Cesarani claims it would of course have been self-exonerating for participants to make such a claim after the experiment to explain their shocking innocent 'victims', which challenges the veracity of any such claim by participants. Russell notes that Helm and Morelli, who are otherwise 'highly critical' of Milgram, concluded that 'the majority of subjects accept the experimental situation as genuine'.

Russell also alludes to the view of Mixon that participants in the Milgram experiments were confused by, and showed great stress and tension because of, the combination of personal experience that they were administering electric shocks that were causing the 'learner' genuine pain and the experimenter's assurance that the 'learner' would come to no serious harm. In fact the 'teachers' were told that the shocks would cause the 'learner' pain but that they would not cause him serious harm, so the experience of participants of administering shocks and the experimenter's assurances are not inconsistent with each other. What seems most plausible is that 'teachers' were influenced by their own personal 'experience' of administering shocks, as is indicated by their distress, in some cases extreme, in doing so, and motivated to avoid responsibility for having done so by assuring themselves that the experimenter would accept responsibility for any harm done. That is what is indicated by the evidence presented above regarding the thirty-five per cent who did refuse to administer shocks at some point, for they did not check on the welfare of the victim or insist that the experiment be stopped, the evidence of those who refused to continue then continuing to administer shocks when assured that the experimenter would take responsibility, and the evidence that when told they were responsible 'teachers" compliance fell. And of course exporting all responsibility to the experimenter permitted 'teachers' to 'succeed' at the task they had agreed to and to avoid being seen by the experimenter to have failed (and to avoid having to confront the experimenter).

Russell's article seems to take no account of any of this evidence, and his reference to the case of 'Carl', who is represented as having indicated that 'he trusted that the experimenter would not have allowed the learner to be hurt' and in regard to whom Russell includes the phrase 'if Carl was directly able to hear and see the consequences of the "harm" he was inflicting', when of course 'teachers' could hear very obvious sounds of pain, distress and refusal to continue from the 'learner' and were in no doubt that he had been 'hurt', is indicative of some confusion either of semantics or of the nature of the experiment itself in Russell's work. Russell's claim that 'Carl' did not entirely appreciate the consequences of his actions is not supported by the evidence of learners' audible responses or by that of 'teachers" distress. What seems to be missing in Russell and the researchers he refers to is any appreciation of the motivation of the 'teachers'. And there seems no appreciation that for 'teachers' the evidence of their own senses and experience of 'learner' distress, pain and pleas would have been far more compelling than general assurances from the experimenter that no serious harm would come to the 'learner'.[22]

Perry criticises Milgram on a number of grounds. One is that Milgram dramatised his findings by publicising the most dramatic of them, the sixty-five per cent of participants found to be prepared to shock a 'learner' with 'heart trouble' to the maximum 450 volts. Perry notes that there were many variations in the Milgram experiments and claims that 'in over half of all his variations Milgram found the opposite result – that more than 60 per cent of people disobeyed the experimenter's orders'. But Perry does not indicate at what point the participants disobeyed the experimenter's instruction to continue, and if she is claiming that over 60 per cent only refused to administer near the maximum level of shock in over half of Milgram's variations she is avoiding reference to the reality of preparedness to continue to administer lower levels of shock despite extensive evidence of genuine pain, distress and pleas from 'learners' for the experiment to be stopped. In fact, as has been indicated above, there were audible indications of pain, distress and pleas to stop from 'learners' from very early on in the administration of shocks, and a more compelling indication would be the incidence of those who refused to continue as soon as the 'learner' showed any signs of genuine pain or distress. Perry is aware of the escalation process of shocks, referring to thirty 'switches', and of participant awareness of their effect on the 'learner', referring to the fact that at 150 volts a 'learner' 'yelled to be released', and it does seem that her statements are deliberately vague regarding when participant resistance took place in the escalation of shocks because she wishes to optimise her criticism of Milgram.

Milgram did in his variations include the effect of greater proximity to the 'learner', which he found did diminish obedience to immoral authority, and the effect of another participant who refused to obey, which he also found diminished obedience. Perry cites the example of pairs of 'teachers' and 'learners' who were family members, friends or neighbours, claiming that only three were prepared to shock to the maximum, though that is hardly relevant to the general finding of participant preparedness to inflict significant pain, distress and even risk to health on innocent 'victims' or to any explanation of perpetrator behaviour, which is of course not characteristically inflicted on people known to the perpetrator. Here too Perry is vague, though the inference is that participants were prepared to administer multiple levels of shock to family members, friends and neighbours prior to the maximum level of shock despite extensive evidence of pain, distress and pleas to discontinue from them.

Perry also claims that the prompts from the experimenter, the authority figure, were misrepresented by Milgram as being more separate from each other than was the case in some instances, though it is worth noting that they were only prompts even in Perry's own account of them and so could have been disregarded. And Perry doubts the 'experimental realism' of the Milgram experiments, claiming that many participants felt that the experiments were not genuine, though as has been seen above the genuine distress and uncertainty of participants would tend to indicate that they did believe in the authenticity of the experiment, and claiming that they knew the experiment was not genuine would have been optimal for participants who had been obedient as it exonerated them from responsibility for having put their own interests in succeeding in the experiment before the welfare of the 'learner', which raises legitimate doubts over the veracity of such claims.

Perry's claim is in fact that Milgram was at fault for not excluding those who (claimed to have) had doubts regarding the experiment's authenticity, though that indicates that for Perry being prepared to take the risk of inflicting pain, harm and possible risk to health on 'learners' does not constitute a departure from ordinary expectations of human behaviour, not least given no compelling motive outside of the experiment for doing so (and as has been seen above, the claim that participants had doubts over the authenticity of the experiment is open to dispute given the motive to claim doubts regarding the genuineness of the experiment to exonerate themselves). If participants really did believe the experiment was a hoax it is difficult to see why they continued with it given that the remuneration was so small it could not have been sufficient to incentivise their continuing with a hoax.[23]

There are other sources that refer to the claims of participants in Milgram's experiments after the end of Milgram's research. Haslam and Reicher found that some months after the end of the experiments participants claimed that they had accepted the rationale of the experimenter, the authority figure, that the experiments were to assist the cause of science in being an investigation into learning and memory, and so believed in what they were doing as a social good in what Haslam and Reicher describe as 'engaged followership'. By contrast Hollander and Turowetz assessed the record of participants' interviews immediately after the end of Milgram's experiments and found that though sixty per cent mentioned obeying the experimenter's instructions the most common explanation, mentioned by seventy-two per cent, was that they believed that the 'learner' 'hadn't really been harmed'. This seems similar though not identical to Perry's claim of a significant incidence of disbelief in the genuineness of the experiments amongst Milgram's participants, for there is a difference between belief that the 'learner' had not been harmed, which leaves the possibility of participants' having knowingly inflicted pain and distress on 'learners', and Perry's claim that many participants believed that the entire experimental procedure was phoney, which indicates their disbelief in any pain or distress experienced by 'learners' too.

There may be a need for reconsideration of 'totalising' explanations, that is, explanations that attempt to account for the behaviour of all participants in all variations of Milgram's experiment. Even so a major commonality between the explanations claimed to have been given by many participants in Milgram's experiments after the research ended in the work of Haslam and Reicher, Hollander and Turowetz, and Perry is that all the explanations are self-serving and self-exonerating for participants in denying personal responsibility for inflicting pain and possible enduring harm on 'learners' for no legitimate reason, with participants' claiming to have believed that they were assisting the authority figure in the progress of science, that they were obeying authoritative instruction or that they believed no harm would come to the 'learner', and that they did not believe that the experiment was authentic respectively.[24] Another commonality is that all three explanations are challenged by the evidence of Milgram's experiments, for if participants genuinely believed that they were participating to help science and so were convinced that their actions were justified, if they felt they were merely obeying without any volition or that the 'learner' was not being harmed, or if they believed the experiment was not genuine, they should not have felt the intense distress many showed when continuing to obey the experimenter, there should not have been the observed significant difference in extent of obedience between participants' administering the electric shock themselves and instructing someone else to do it, and there should not have been the observed difference in obedience between participants who were told they were responsible and those who were assured the experimenter was responsible and they were not. As to Haslam and Reicher and the idea of 'engaged followership', participants' being told when distressed that 'the experiment requires you to continue' does not seem consonant with the idea of 'engaged followership'.

The indication from the Milgram experiments is then that participants inflicted what they perceived to be pain, distress and risk to health on 'learners' of whom they knew nothing adverse just to avoid having to defy an authority figure and be seen to have failed at a task they had undertaken before that authority figure and possibly peers who were also participants in the experiment, and then, after the research ended, demonstrated that their optimisation of their own outcomes extended to narratives that explained their behaviour in the experiments in ways that excused them from responsibility for having been prepared to inflict pain, distress and risk to health on an innocent victim just to avoid experience they perceived would be adverse even though there were no consequences outside the experiment. Though Hollander and Turowetz argue that participants' explanations of their behaviour in the experiments after they ended should not be dismissed as self-exonerating and evasive, it seems that the motive for self-exoneration and the variety of narratives presented by participants after the experiment, all of which are self-excusing, indicate that they are not true representations of the actual reasons for their obedience to immoral authority. That is not to say that in every case participants presented explanations that they knew to be untrue, for some participants may have managed to convince themselves that their administering shocks that inflicted pain, distress and possible harm on innocent 'learners' was not to avoid unpleasant embarrassment before the authority figure in the form of having to decline to continue with a task they had undertaken and of being seen to have failed at that task by the authority figure and possibly also by peers, but for the other, less reprehensible reasons they gave. The motive for such misrepresentation to the self is obvious, to avoid being compelled to acknowledge what they had been prepared to do and had done. In other cases the misrepresentation would have been to represent themselves in a positive manner to the interviewer or the recipient of reports and to their social audiences, to avoid the obloquy that would follow an admission that they had acted as perpetrators for some fleeting avoidance of discomfort to themselves without real-life adverse consequences (for the not inaccurate perception would have been that the members of their social audiences would never believe that they themselves would have done what Milgram's participants did). In both cases the motive would have been self-serving, to comfort the self and to avoid informal sanctions from the social universe. The likelihood is that both were present in most cases and that the misrepresentation was unreflective.[25]

There is a parallel with the behaviour of Nazi perpetrators, for they characteristically conformed to role requirements (as did Milgram's participants) for similar reasons of optimisation of personal outcome, in their case for reasons of careerism in the SS, the military or the Nazi state apparatus, avoidance of the perceived risk of demotion or maintaining the approbation of their bosses and peers. Then, after the war, Nazi perpetrators claimed that they were not responsible, referring to obedience to orders in the SS, military or state hierarchy, indicating that there had been no real choice but to obey, and to an ideological context that associated Jews with partisans and Bolsheviks and so the enemy in the east, indicating that they had been deceived into believing that the extermination of the Jews was a necessity for the Third Reich, to evade personal responsibility for what they had done.[26]

Perry does in fact seem to be guilty of precisely what she accuses Milgram of, misrepresentation of findings to dramatise them, and in her case to optimise the challenge she claims to present to Milgram's findings, when in fact her observations are trivial and do nothing to discredit the general inference from Milgram's experiments, that ordinary human beings drawn even from a liberal democratic society with a respect for individual rights and a culture of approved individualism are prepared to inflict pain, distress and harm to health on people of whom nothing adverse is known just to avoid having to defy or be seen to have failed at a task undertaken by them by an authority figure. And even if it were the case that Milgram did publicise the most dramatic variation of his experiments to optimise the impression made on fellow academics, it would not follow that his experiments in their entirety do not constitute an astonishing revelation regarding human behaviour and a profound refutation of the expectations of psychiatrists and psychologists of the extent of obedience to immoral authority by ordinary people.

Cesarani criticises Milgram's experiments on the odd basis that there was no reason for antipathy towards the 'learner', and though Cesarani acknowledges that 'prejudice might have increased the willingness to shock', he then argues that if participants had been told the 'learner' was a Jew or black that could have acted as a constraint. There is much wrong with such an assertion. To begin with a counterfactual cannot be assessed and so is safe from disproof, and in any case there seems to be no reason why the 'learners" being a Jew or black would have altered the findings without some knowledge of the racial attitudes of the participants. The point from the Milgram experiments is that even without 'victims' characterised by racial 'otherness' or who elicit racial antipathy individuals drawn at random from a population of ordinary people (and in a liberal democracy with a tradition of inalienable rights for the individual) were prepared to inflict extreme pain on and risk the health of a 'victim' of whom nothing adverse was known. What that seems to indicate is a German culture bereft of liberal democratic political traditions and with cultural antisemitism as a norm preceding the Nazis' rise to power in Germany, and Nazi and SS ideological eliminationist antisemitism, were not necessary conditions for SS perpetrator behaviour.

Cesarani concludes, 'a purely abstract and universal relationship cannot be used to explain another one that is shot through with history, politics and preconceptions'.[27]

Here it does seem that Cesarani is missing the point. For Milgram's experiments and their replications over time and in different cultures indicate a human tendency to compliance with authority, one that I have interpreted as indicating pursuit of personal interest as the primary motive in behaviour, in that conformity to authority optimises outcomes. The influence of the specific societal context to which Cesarani refers is in its defining what is rewarded and what is punished, and in Nazi Germany membership of the SS was advantageous in its being a recognised Nazi elite and in the status, privileges and influence it afforded.

Another argument against Cesarani's criticisms of the Milgram experiments is that the Milgram experiments' findings have been replicated over decades of time and in very different cultures, with very similar rates of participants being prepared to shock 'learners' to the end, for it is difficult to conceive of all such replications having the characteristics that Cesarani so criticises in Milgram's experiments, to the extent that such criticisms are in fact legitimate.

A final possible criticism of the Milgram experiments is that there is a very great difference between participants' inflicting pain on 'victims' and Eichmann's transporting Jews to known certain extermination and other SS perpetrator behaviour, and that as a consequence the Milgram experiments are not relevant to any explanation of Eichmann's or any other perpetrator behaviour.[28] Milgram claimed to have devised an experiment in which participants' 'responsibility is cast off' and they become 'agents of action', a reference to an 'agentic state' he sees as being common 'among soldier, party functionary, and obedient subject', who 'yield to authority' and employ 'identical mental mechanisms to reduce the strain of acting against a helpless victim'. Milgram seems to be claiming that his experiments were a legitimate means of replicating the position of perpetrators in the Holocaust and of identifying the psychological influences on obedience with immoral authority in general, which he explains by reference to the 'agentic state'. It is though odd that Milgram appears to refer to the 'agentic state' as a means of maintaining psychological equilibrium or averting distress following obedience to immoral commands when the 'agentic state' should have precluded such strain and many SS perpetrators do not seem to have experienced such distress, especially those, like the Einsatzgruppen commanders and Eichmann, who did not actually engage in genocide.

The relevance of the Milgram experiments to the explanation of Eichmann's perpetrator behaviour is then that ordinary, normal people were shown by Milgram to have optimised their own outcomes regardless of the perceived cost to someone of whom nothing adverse was known even though that perceived cost was extreme pain, distress and risk of harm to the health of the 'victim'. What seems to have mattered most to Milgram's participants was optimising their own outcomes, which dictated avoidance of responsibility for harm, avoidance of embarrassment and of a sense of failure before the authority figure, and avoidance of peer criticism. The implication for the explanation of Eichmann's perpetrator behaviour is that unless Eichmann was abnormal in terms of psychological motive the same optimisation of social and psychological outcomes would have been the dominant influence on his behaviour in his role in the transportation of the Jews of Europe to extermination camps. And it has been seen above that though Eichmann does seem to have been calmer than most would have been when on trial in Jerusalem, his psychiatric and psychological evaluations, when set in the context of what became known of the credibility of Szondi, indicate that he was normal, which makes the interpretation of the Milgram evidence presented above indicative of the probable decisive influence on Eichmann's perpetrator behaviour.

Zimbardo and the Stanford Prison Experiment

In what follows there is a detailed assessment of the Stanford Prison Experiment, its conduct by Zimbardo and his associates and his representation of the implications of the experiment, because of its relevance to the explanation of perpetrator behaviour in normal people and so in someone like Eichmann.

The objective of Zimbardo's notorious Stanford Prison Experiment, conducted in the summer of 1971, was to assess the power of social situation and role on human behaviour.

According to Zimbardo's account, the participants recruited were twenty-four male college students who were healthy, white and middle class. Psychological tests were conducted to exclude candidates with psychological problems. Of these twenty-four selected individuals nine were randomly assigned to be guards and nine to be prisoners. Zimbardo was prison superintendent and briefed the guards on their role, which was to 'maintain law and order' and 'command the respect of the prisoners'. Guards were given uniforms and wore sunglasses that optimised guard anonymity. The treatment of prisoners enhanced the credibility to the experiment for them, for they were compelled to wear dresses without underclothes and a stocking cap, had chains on their feet and were assigned a prisoner number. Prisoner conditions in the prison included confinement to small cells shared by three prisoners each and a small yard.

Zimbardo notes that the day after the experiment began there was a prisoner rebellion that took the form of prisoners discarding their prison uniforms, barricading themselves in their cells, and taunting the guards, who responded by a decision to use force, including fire extinguishers, stripping prisoners, taking their beds out, and consigning the leaders of the rebellion to 'the hole', solitary confinement, as punishment. The guards began harassment and humiliation of prisoners and decided to use psychological rather than physical tactics to deal with them. They separated the three prisoners who had been least involved in the prisoner rebellion and gave them privileges denied the rest of the prisoners, the result of which was a breaking down of any feeling of togetherness amongst prisoners, not least when there was an exchange of 'good' and 'bad' prisoners to receive privileged treatment, which isolated prisoners from each other. Guards became more of a group as a consequence and there was enhanced 'control, authority, surveillance, aggression' after the prisoner rebellion.

Zimbardo notes that guard mistreatment of prisoners continued, in the form of denial of decent toilet facilities and making prisoners do exhausting physical activities as punishment. Prisoner number 8612 then exhibited very distressed behaviour, but to begin with Zimbardo and his team believed he was 'trying to "con" us', before releasing him. Preparation for parental visits resulted in 'situational control' of parents and their becoming part of the 'prison drama', not least given

Zimbardo's being the 'authority I was unconsciously becoming – as superintendent of the Stanford County Jail'. There followed a rumour of an 'escape plot' with help from the outside, and Zimbardo recounts a meeting between the warden (an undergraduate student, Jaffe), the superintendent (Zimbardo) and 'one of the chief lieutenants' to 'plan our strategy', which was use of an informer and to dismantle the jail until the threat of outside help receded and prisoners could be returned to prison. Zimbardo notes that there was even consideration of 'luring' prisoner number 8612 back to prison because 'he was released on false pretenses'. Zimbardo recounts that it was then that an experimental psychologist colleague asked him what the independent variable in the experiment was and his, Zimbardo's, anger given he felt that he was dealing with the security of his men and the prison at the time, and his derogation of his colleague's liberal humanitarianism. When the rumour turned out to be false 'harassment' and 'humiliation' of prisoners was enhanced, and there was a growing confusion between 'role-playing and self-identity that was gradually taking place in all of us within the prison which we had created', with 'confusion' as to 'where role ends and identity begins'.

In another reference to the effect on prisoners, Zimbardo notes that when prisoner number 819 asked for a doctor and was sent to the rest and relaxation room, fellow prisoners chanted that he was a bad prisoner, for 'they were being punished because of him'. Zimbardo then relates the extraordinary identification with the prisoner role of prisoners before a parole board, at which all but four prisoners indicated they would forfeit their payment to be released and then accepted docilely being returned to their cells whilst a decision was being made, which Zimbardo sees as an indication that even when 'what we had made salient was the contract', prisoners did not resist, because 'their sense of reality had undergone a transformation'. Prisoner reactions over time were mixed, with four breaking down to escape the experiment, 'good prisoners' doing what the guards wanted them to do, and by the end of the experiment prisoners being 'just a bunch of isolated individuals', with the guards in 'total control'. Of the guards Zimbardo differentiates those who were 'tough but fair' and who did no more than follow the rules of the guard role from those 'who felt genuinely sorry for the prisoners', 'did little favors for them and never punished them' and from a third of guards who were 'extremely hostile, arbitrary, inventive in their forms of degradation and humiliation and appear to have thoroughly enjoyed the power they wielded' in a 'guard uniform'. Some guard behaviour was sadistic, and other guards were seen to feel helpless to stop it. The experiment was halted after six days, despite being scheduled to last two weeks.[29]

Le Texier, in an exhaustive investigation of the records of the Stanford Prison Experiment, provides evidence for a number of criticisms of what he obviously regards as Zimbardo's highly selective account of it. To begin with he notes Fromm's allegation that the psychological tests used were insufficient to exclude from the experiment individuals with sadistic tendencies. He points out too that the participants signed contracts under which they undertook to perform their roles as indicated by the experimenters, that the primary motive of participants was mercenary, that the pay was, even according to Zimbardo, good, that participants were paid after the experiment, not before, that some had been in other psychological experiments, and that most of the participants were drawn from local colleges or small universities and so would have found Zimbardo, as a professor at the prestigious Stanford University, especially authoritative.

Le Texier also notes that the 'guards were trained', 'knew what result the experiment was supposed to produce', did not act 'spontaneously to this pathogenic social environment' but were given 'clear instructions for how to create it', and 'during their orientation day' 'received instructions from the experimenters'. He continues, 'the experimenters intervened directly in the experiment, either to give precise instructions, to recall the purposes of the experiment, or to set a general direction', and 'Zimbardo intended to make the guards believe they were his research assistants', the result of which was that guards were 'conditioned', so negating the possibility of assessment of the autonomous effect of role and social situation on guard behaviour. As to intention, Le Texier produces evidence indicating Zimbardo's purpose from the outset, which was to establish that the relationships between guards and prisoners in real prisons were in need of reform because of the adverse effect on the welfare of prisoners. The indication is that Zimbardo's objective resulted in behaviour as superintendent that tended to produce the result he expected and wanted, in selective use of evidence and selective inferences and in misrepresentation to the media regarding the findings of the Stanford Prison Experiment.[30]

In another reassessment of the Stanford Prison Experiment and the claims made by Zimbardo regarding it, Haslam, Reicher and Van Bavel make a number of criticisms. They refer to the diversity of response between guards, with some robust or cruel in their treatment of prisoners and others far more lenient, and between prisoners, some of whom resisted the guards to the end of the experiment. This is in fact in Zimbardo's own account and would indicate some influence on the guard behaviour observed of individual personality differences, but Haslam, Reicher and Van Bavel propose a very different explanation for the record of Zimbardo's Stanford Prison Experiment. They share Le Texier's view that without the briefings from Zimbardo and Jaffe, the Warden, both of which were directive and the latter of which was extensive, the guards would not have acted as they did, and that role and social situation alone would not have elicited the guards' cruel behaviour. Their case is that Zimbardo as leader of the guard group and a respected university professor gave the guards a social identity and conferred on their behaviour a legitimacy it would otherwise not have had and without which it would not have been undertaken. They claim that new evidence from the Stanford Prison Experiment establishes that 'the traditional notion that guards became cruel of their own accord is very hard (if not impossible) to sustain', that 'the experimenters' leadership was a central feature of the study', and that 'experimenters engaged in identity leadership in an effort to encourage guard cruelty', from which they infer that 'identity leadership' was the decisive influence on the 'engaged followership' they claim resulted in the guard behaviour observed in the experiment.[31]

To be clear as to what is being claimed by Haslam, Reicher and Van Bavel in connection with the Stanford Prison Experiment, the identity leadership account has a number of components they identify – a 'common cause' and 'common group membership that links experimenters and guards', '"tough" or cruel behavior as necessary to advance the shared cause', and the 'group cause as worthy and noble' to justify the cruel behaviour to give effect to it. It is worth noting that this does not merely claim that guards identified with the experimenters for the social or psychological reward of such identification in the form of status but that they embraced the purpose of the experiment and regarded the means as legitimate to accomplish the objectives of the experiment.

Haslam, Reicher and Van Bavel refer to the evidence of research by Lovibond, Mithiran and Adams in 1979, in which guards were instructed to pursue 'authoritarian, democratic, or participatory approaches' and in which only the authoritarian instruction produced guard behaviour similar to that found in the Stanford Prison Experiment. They also refer to the BBC Prison Study undertaken by Haslam and Reicher, in which 'guards given no direct instruction about how to behave' 'showed no inclination to treat prisoners cruelly', which they claim indicates that 'few people spontaneously identify with rules that require them to be cruel to others' and that there is a need for 'identity entrepreneurship' to 'get others to identify with them and their group cause', to 'construe the group's goals as noble, virtuous and a source of pride', and to 'show how harmful acts are necessary to the achievement of those goals'.

Haslam, Reicher and Van Bavel do provide extensive evidence to the effect that the behaviour of the guards was preceded by directive leadership from Zimbardo and Jaffe, and argue that guard behaviour should not be ascribed to the influence of role and social situation alone but rather to the influence of authority figures. They claim that guard behaviour did not reflect 'prior societal learning of the meaning of prisons and the behavioral scripts associated with the oppositional roles of prisoner and Guard'. This does seem established by the extensive and specific nature of the briefing of guards as to their expected behaviour. They point to Zimbardo's indication to guards at his briefing of them, in which he told them, 'you can create in the prisoners feelings of boredom, a sense of fear to some degree, you can create a notion of arbitrariness that their life is totally controlled by us, by the system, you, me – and they'll have no privacy. They'll have no freedom of action, they can do nothing, say nothing that we don't permit. We're going to take away their individuality in various ways. In general what all this leads to is a sense of powerlessness.'[32]

Haslam, Reicher and Van Bavel also refer to attempts at identity leadership in Jaffe's extended briefing of guards at the beginning of the experiment in repeated references to 'we', in the fact that 'detailed instructions were not limited to orientation sessions but continued to the end of the study', and in evidence that 'multiple guards' reported 'direct, concrete, instructions from experimenters', which does indicate directive leadership on the part of the experimenters but does not indicate identity leadership and engaged followership as defined by Haslam, Reicher and Van Bavel.

Haslam, Reicher and Van Bavel also claim to provide evidence of identity leadership and engaged followership in the form of attempts by Zimbardo and Jaffe to legitimise the experiment and the cruelty of the guard role by reference to an objective of establishing the tendencies in real-life prison situations for prisoners. Yet there is just one instance of a guard, Guard 2, cited as indicating an appreciation of the objective of the experiment and the need for realistic guard behaviour, apart from a single instance of guard reluctance, from Guard 7, to meet the cruel requirements of his role, which elicited an intervention from Jaffe, who as warden 'made it clear at multiple points in the meeting that the experimenters expect (and require) him both to be more 'involved' in proceedings and to be more 'tough' and to 'embrace the role of the stereotype guard' and 'discard his personal identity'. In the face of continued opposition from Guard 7, 'the warden concluded the meeting with explicit and concrete instructions about the behavior expected of the Guard'. This evidence seems far more indicative of Jaffe's attempts to coerce Guard 7 to embrace a group identity and conform to the guard role than of some concerted attempt to persuade him of the legitimacy of the experiment, let alone any success in doing so. Jaffe does make reference to a shared aversion for the prison system but most of the evidence is of his exhorting Guard 7 to become a good guard and do his job as guard and to Jaffe's expectation that Guard 7 should become one of the guards and behave like them. The repeated use of 'we' by Jaffe is evidence of an attempt to elicit a group identity but not of identity leadership and engaged followership in the definition presented by Haslam, Reicher and Van Bavel, which involves acceptance of the legitimacy of the behaviour advocated. Here is an example of the difference between intention and outcome, for Guard 7 did not accept Jaffe's attempts to elicit engaged followership, so the one demonstration of an attempt to confirm the thesis presented by Haslam, Reicher and Van Bavel was a failure. There does seem to be some attention to establishing directive leadership in the Stanford Prison Experiment, which is not in dispute and has been established by Le Texier's work, which is referred to by Haslam, Reicher and Van Bavel, and to implicitly argue that directive leadership indicates identity leadership and engaged followership. That is not true.

What does seem indicated by Jaffe's interaction with Guard 7 and his exhortation to Guard 7 to behave like a guard and the other guards is that Zimbardo's claim that the experiment established the autonomous power of role and social situation on behaviour is invalidated, because the guard concerned was subjected to exhortation from an authority figure to conform to the requirements of the guard role, which would indicate that the guard's ensuing behaviour responded not to role and social situation but to the intervention of an authority figure, which makes the explanation for the guard's ensuing behaviour seem much more like the findings of Milgram's experiments on obedience to immoral authority referred to above.[33]

Haslam, Reicher and Van Bavel claim that the intention of Zimbardo and his fellow researchers was to elicit guard allegiance to the requirements of the guard role by identity leadership and a resulting engaged followership on the part of guards. They do not consider the possibility that guards behaved as they did because they found it difficult to resist Zimbardo and Jaffe as authority figures, did not want to be the one to defy an authority figure when others were not, and wanted to avoid the embarrassment and social awkwardness of having to confront and defy an authority figure, not because they endorsed the legitimacy of the guard role as defined by Zimbardo and Jaffe. This alternative explanation indicates individual optimisation of social and psychological outcomes rather than belief in the legitimacy of the role. And of course establishing the experimenters' intention is not evidence of outcome.

Another characteristic of the Haslam, Reicher and Van Bavel article is that they seem to disattend to evidence that does not support their attribution of cruel guard behaviour to identity leadership and engaged followership. For they do in the evidence they present include a reference to a guard being told 'it's your job', and an understanding indicated in a debriefing after the experiment by one guard (Guard 4) that 'it's the Professor who decides here', and in another case 'you're the Experimenter' and 'we're kind of like the employees'.

The evidence they present does seem to indicate hierarchy, control, appraisal and guards' having to account to Zimbardo and Jaffe for their behaviour, a situation more consonant with the explanation that guards behaved as they did to avoid being regarded as having failed in their role while others were seen to have been effective in the role, rather than any influence from perceived legitimacy of the experiment or any direct evidence of Jaffe's attempting to persuade guards of the legitimacy of the experiment from the outset (Jaffe's reference to 'we don't learn anything' is oblique and not the major focus of his role).

Both Le Texier and Haslam, Reicher and Van Bavel do take at face value statements made by guards after the end of the experiment. These included guards' claims that they had responded to directive leadership on the part of Zimbardo and his associates and so were not responsible, guards' claiming that they were only playing their part in an experiment that never distorted their sense of reality in the way Zimbardo claims it did, and guards' attributing their behaviour to having been persuaded by Zimbardo and his researchers of the legitimate purpose of the experiment. All these explanations do of course serve to exculpate guards and preclude their appearing so susceptible to role and situation that their behaviour was radically altered even though the experiment was ended on the sixth day, with all its implications for their personalities, yet there seems to be no concern that these explanations may be of dubious veracity because guards would be motivated to explain their cruel behaviour by such explanations of their behaviour.

Le Texier's claim that 'participants almost never lost touch with reality and were conscious of participating in an experiment' and that the 'concrete situation', including the 'decor', 'telephones ringing', 'photocopier noises', regular debriefings with the experimenters and completion of questionnaires, use of the new toilets in the Psychology Department, 'ridiculous gowns' and 'visits of photographers, cameramen, journalists, secretaries and Stanford colleagues' supports guards' claims that they never believed their situation to be anything more than entirely experimental and that they did not confuse role and reality during the experiment. And it indicates that it is implausible that there should have been so great an influence from role and social situation that role and reality became difficult to distinguish from each other. There is of course also the objective record of the conduct of the experiment, which is not reliant upon claims made by guards after its end, and does establish the directive leadership of Zimbardo and Jaffe, with Zimbardo being a professor at a respected university and so an authority figure of some prestige and influence. It also establishes that guards were paid well for their role as guards. The inference does seem to be that it was easier for the guards to do what was indicated to them by Zimbardo and Jaffe to avoid embarrassment and to secure the payment for which they had undertaken the role.

A more direct difficulty with Haslam's, Reicher's and Van Bavel's explanation is that

Zimbardo's and Jaffe's briefing of guards took place the day before they started the experiment, hardly long enough for Zimbardo or Jaffe to have cultivated the engaged followership and legitimacy that is being indicated by Haslam, Reicher and Van Bavel. It was of course long enough for them to appreciate Zimbardo's status and commitment to the experiment and to have wished to avoid being seen to have failed at a task they had undertaken to engage in and to have wanted to avoid the associated embarrassment.

There are other difficulties for the Haslam, Reicher and Van Bavel claim that guard behaviour in the Stanford Prison Experiment was motivated by identity leadership and engaged followership. One is that the diversity of individual responses, which would have to be attributed to personality differences, would seem to indicate that any generalising explanation is not adequate, for it is difficult to explain why their 'engaged followership' worked with some guards and not with others, even with very small numbers of guards being involved. Zimbardo's own behaviour and that of the Stanford Prison Experiment prisoners did not reflect the influence of identity leadership. And the fact that participants signed contracts and were paid to perform roles as indicated by the experimenters tends to argue against engaged followership and belief in the legitimacy of the experiment as the explanation for their guard behaviour. What the contractual nature of the relationship between the experimenters and guards does indicate is that evidence of guards' meeting the requirements of the guard role is explained by guards' being prepared to do the job they were hired to do to be paid and possibly some respect for Zimbardo and Stanford University.

The Haslam, Reicher and Van Bavel article does seem to commit the mistake it accuses Zimbardo of, that is, the imposition of a theoretical perspective to which they are attached on evidence which they use selectively to establish their case. The evidence of Zimbardo's intention of demonstrating the need for prison reform has been presented above. For Haslam, Reicher and Van Bavel their intention does seem apparent from their claim that the evidence of the Stanford Prison Experiment provides 'support for theoretical claims that were first made over a decade ago', indicating their interest in finding evidence that would confirm their social identity theory and their idea of identity leadership and engaged followership.

The consequences have been bias in approach and selectivity with evidence and with inferences. They couch their conclusions in guarded terms, noting 'at minimum, the results of our analysis are plainly more consistent with an identity leadership account than they are with the standard role account'. This does of course set the standard for their contribution very low given Le Texier's comprehensive discrediting of Zimbardo's conduct and representation of the indications of the Stanford Prison Experiment. They also refer to consistency with the identity leadership literature, which is not relevant to an analysis of the evidence of the Stanford Prison Experiment, which should be considered on its own merits, and to the BBC Prison Study by Haslam and Reicher in 2002 and Milgram's research, in further indications of the lack of direct evidence that supports their argument of identity leadership and engaged followership from the Stanford Prison Experiment on its own.

In an article on their BBC Prison Study Haslam and Reicher outline their 'social identity theory' and its claim that 'people do not automatically act in terms of group membership (or roles) ascribed by others, whether or not they do so depends upon whether they internalize such memberships as part of the self-concept'. The indication here does seem to be that acting in terms of group membership necessarily reflects individual endorsement of the attitudes and objectives of the group, as in their notion of 'engaged followership'. Haslam and Reicher do not appear to consider that there is another form of identification with a group, that is, identification because of its privileges and status without genuine ideological endorsement of the legitimacy of the group's purposes. In the Eichmann case his apparent endorsement of the extermination of the Jews does appear from the evidence to have been part of his presentation of self and seen by him to be necessary to the maintenance of his rank and elite SS status. Haslam's and Reicher's 'engaged followership' does then seem to be just one form of group identity and one explanation for group behaviour.[34]

The attribution of guard behaviour to engaged followership does seem to be part of a more general debate between those who argue for decisive influence from 'ideological' factors and those who argue for a primary role for pragmatic or instrumental factors in perpetrator behaviour. Haslam, Reicher and Van Bavel relate their claim regarding the Stanford Prison Experiment to Milgram's experiments, which they also explain by reference to identity leadership and engaged followership.[35] This claim is not credible because distance from the 'victim' in the Milgram experiments enhanced the preparedness of participants to inflict what they believed were electric shocks to 'victims' and proximity diminished such preparedness, because compliance was enhanced when someone else could be instructed to administer the shock, because participants were distressed by the task, because compliance was secured by reassuring participants that the authority figure was responsible, not them, because when the experimenter was not present compliance fell, and because when one other participant resisted compliance fell. None of these characteristics would have obtained had there been engaged followership.[36] The lack of any reference to possibilities of explaining guard behaviour other than by reference to engaged followership does seem to be a crucial omission in the Haslam, Reicher and Van Bavel case and one that follows from their theoretical lens of social identity research.

Haslam, Reicher and Van Bavel also refer, in their critique of the Stanford Prison Experiment, to Himmler's notorious Poznan speech on 6 October 1943, in which he exhorted SS officers to persevere with the extermination of the Jews of the occupied territories as a task necessary to the interests of the German people, without commenting that the extermination of the Jews in the east had been going on since June 1941 and by October 1943 had exterminated enormous numbers of Jews without any specific instruction from Himmler, which was a feature of the way in which decisions were made, communicated and implemented in the Nazi state hierarchy and the SS, that is, on the basis of understandings and expectations rather than specific written orders. This highly selective omission seems not untypical of their approach to the presentation of evidence to support their case of 'engaged followership'.

The alternative explanation has been referred to above, that the most decisive influence on guard behaviour was guards' motivation to optimise their material, social and psychological outcomes. This involved their following the instructions regarding the guard role given by Zimbardo as a respected university professor and

Jaffe as his warden to avoid disapprobation for failure to act as Zimbardo and Jaffe expected guards to act and the embarrassment that could cause, a form of pursuit of personal interest at the expense of others (in the Stanford Prison Experiment the prisoners) that was found also in Milgram's experiments on obedience to immoral authority. Added to this was of course the fact that guards were not paid until the end of the experiment and that they were paid well, indicating another form of optimising behaviour in explaining their preparedness to be guards as directed by Zimbardo and Jaffe. This explanation does not depend upon an argument that the guards deliberated over their decisions regarding their role, for the influence of motivation on behaviour may well be unreflective in most cases.

Zimbardo's own lack of duty of care to the prisoners and their welfare could also be explained by his having had a profound interest in establishing the effect of role and social situation on human behaviour that meant he was predisposed to continue with the experiment regardless of its human consequences.

What Zimbardo's Stanford Prison Experiment establishes remains controversial even decades after it ended. The conclusion Zimbardo drew, that there was an autonomous effect of role and social situation on human behaviour, has been credibly challenged by reference to his own behaviour as superintendent and the directive leadership as an authority figure he provided, which meant that the autonomous power of role and social situation on guard behaviour could not be inferred from the Stanford Prison Experiment.

The claim that guard behaviour reflected identity leadership on the part of Zimbardo and his associates and resulted in engaged followership on the part of guards with whom Zimbardo identified himself has also been challenged here, not least because the evidence is of experimenters' having attempted to establish identity leadership and engaged followership (and there is less evidence of that than of directive leadership in terms of demanding that guards perform their role as indicated by the experimenters) rather than an established reality in terms of authentic guard experience, because there was insufficient time to cultivate identity leadership and engaged followership between Zimbardo and his associates and the guards, and because of the alternative explanation that guards acted as they did to conform to Zimbardo's expectations not because they had been convinced of the experiment's legitimacy derived from its laudable intentions but because of the difficulty of defying authority figures observed in Milgram's experiments on obedience to authority, which indicate the influence of embarrassment and fear of being seen to have failed by an authority figure. There is also evidence of guards' having entered into contractual obligations with the experimenters and of their backgrounds' having been conducive to respect for Zimbardo as a Stanford University professor.

The conclusion drawn here, setting the Stanford Prison Experiment findings in the context of Milgram's experiments and Browning's finding that in wartime Germany 'ordinary men' murdered Jewish elderly people, women and children without extensive indoctrination (similar to engaged followership) to avoid being ridiculed or ostracised by peers and the context of conformity to role requirements in ordinary life to optimise outcomes, is that guard pursuit of personal interest does explain guard performance of the guard role as defined by Zimbardo and his associates. Identification as a guard with a collective or social identity does not seem to be indicated given the diversity of guard behaviour and the instruction from Zimbardo and Jaffe.

There does seem to have been some effect from role and social situation on prisoners' behaviour, for there was no leadership of the prisoners by Zimbardo or any of his associates and there seems to be no alternative explanation for the prisoners' behaviour, apart from reference to their pursuing their own interests as they saw them, with perception of what was optimal varying from prisoner to prisoner. The evidence of prisoner compliance with experimenters' returning them to prison pending a decision from the parole board on their application for release with an undertaking to forfeit their pay does seem evidence of the effect of role and social situation on prisoner behaviour. The case for which there is the least compelling evidence is that of identity leadership and engaged followership.

There has been reference to selective use of evidence and selective inference in Zimbardo's representation of the results of the Stanford Prison Experiment and in the inference of Haslam, Reicher and Van Bavel of engaged followerhsip amongst guards. The argument here is not of deliberate selection of evidence to support their case but rather inadvertent bias due to 'confirmation bias', the tendency to search for, find and accept evidence that confirms existing views and not to attend to disconfirming information and to refute its validity and relevance. Even so, the motive behind confirmation bias in this case does seem to be to demonstrate that their theories were valid and so protect their careers.

Milgram and Zimbardo

There are similarities between the Milgram and the Zimbardo findings. Both seem to be evidence of pursuit of personal interest in avoidance of embarrassment before an authority figure and avoidance too of failing compared to others, despite the significant cost to their 'victims' of their behaviour. In the Milgram case the authority figure was the experimenter and in the Zimbardo case it was Zimbardo himself as a respected university professor. Participants in both the Milgram and the Zimbardo research had some functional proximity to their 'victims', meaning they had evidence of the adverse effect their behaviour was having on them. One difference is that Milgram's participants believed they were harming their 'victims' in physical terms, whereas Zimbardo's guards had been prohibited from imposing physical punishment on prisoners. Having said that Zimbardo's guards did engage in various psychological techniques, including deindividuation in removing prisoners' personal possessions and assigning prisoners numbers to replace their names, intense control over the activities of prisoners in the form of random 'counts' of prisoners, and punitive isolation of prisoners for violations of rules, with calamitous psychological consequences for some prisoners who could not stand the treatment even for the limited number of days for which the experiment went on.

One significant difference is that a number of Milgram's participants experienced genuine distress at the inflicting of what they presumed was pain on, or risk to the health of, the 'victim', whereas there seems to be no evidence of Zimbardo's guards experiencing similar distress at their treatment of prisoners at any time. Another difference between the two experiments is that in the original experiment Milgram was dealing with participants on their own, whereas the guards in Zimbardo's experiment were part of a group. The lack of evidence of distress in guards could then be ascribed to the emergence of a norm of conduct for the guard role that precluded distress over mistreating prisoners. Milgram found that the presence of another person who escalated shocks resulted in the individual also escalating shocks, though that does not mean the individual did not experience distress in doing so, and what seems a majority of Christopher Browning's 'Ordinary Men' in Reserve Police Battalion 101, who were sent to Poland and required to participate in the Holocaust, did exhibit distress at their task despite the fact that the murders of Jewish elderly people, women and children were undertaken as a group. The explanation may be that the administration of what was presumed to be severe pain – given evidence of it for Milgram's participants and the shooting of Jewish old people, women and children – was extreme and could not be misrepresented as necessary to the maintenance of order, for instance (see Chapter Eight below).

Zimbardo had hypothesised that the power of the situation was greater than that of individual predisposition, and the study supported that hypothesis. What was odder was that the experiment was called off not by Zimbardo himself, despite evidence of warder sadism and adverse effects on prisoners even after just six days, but by the intervention of an associate, with Zimbardo himself acknowledging that he had even after so brief a period of time become a 'prison superintendent' and no longer a 'research psychologist', an indication of the power of the situation even in the case of an academic psychologist conducting an experiment on the power of role. Zimbardo's experiment is relevant to explanations of Eichmann's perpetrator behaviour because it indicates the influence on human behaviour of motive to secure the approbation of an authority figure and to avoid the embarrassment of not having completed tasks undertaken before such figures. The Zimbardo experiment with its dramatic exemplification of the effects of role and motive on human behaviour tends to indicate that Eichmann's conformity to the requirements of his SS roles was normal and that it reflected Eichmann's optimisation of personal outcomes through securing the continued approbation of his SS bosses and peers regardless of cost to others. Neither Milgram nor Zimbardo attributed their extraordinary findings to the human motive to optimise outcomes for the individual concerned, and this lack of reference to the centrality of motive in human behaviour does seem to be a consequential omission for the inferences they drew.

Notes

[1] See Harris, Peter R., 'Shyness and Embarrassment in Psychological Theory and Ordinary Language', in Crozier, W. Ray, *Shyness and Embarrassment: Perspectives from Social Psychology*, Cambridge University Press, 1990, p. 70 for reference to the extensive social psychological research indicating embarrassment to be a significant motive in human behaviour and for reference to Modigliani's view that the findings of Milgram on obedience to immoral authority and of Asch on conformity are to be 'understood in terms of the inhibition brought about by the fear of embarrassment'.
[2] See Milgram, Stanley, *Behavioral Study of Obedience, Journal of Abnormal and Social Psychology*, 67 (4), 1963, pp. 371–78.

[3] See Milgram, Stanley, *Behavioral Study of Obedience, Journal of Abnormal and Social Psychology*, 67 (4), 1963, pp. 371–78, for reference to all participants' preparedness to shock to 300 volts, at which point the 'victim kicks on the wall and no longer answers to the teacher's multiple-choice questions'. See Blass, Thomas, *The Roots of Stanley Milgram's Obedience Experiments and Their Relevance to the Holocaust, Analyse und Kritik 20 (1998)*, 2. 46–53, Westdeutscher Verlag, Opladen, for the observation that the experimenter 'had no coercive means to enforce his commands'. And see Milgram, Stanley, *Some Conditions of Obedience and Disobedience to Authority, Human Relations 18 (1)*, 1965, pp. 57–76, for Milgram's having consulted forty psychiatrists from the medical school and found that they predicted that at 300 volts only 3.73 per cent of participants would continue, with just over 0.1 per cent expected to shock to the maximum, compared to the 65 per cent Milgram found were prepared to shock to the maximum in his experiments. The Milgram findings were in fact a very great surprise to psychologists as well and to Milgram himself.

[4] See Waller, James, *Becoming Evil, How Ordinary People Commit Genocide and Mass Killing*, Oxford University Press, USA, 2007, p. 110.

[5] See ibid, pp. 107–11 for reference to the finding that information that the 'learner' had an existing heart condition had no effect whatever on the level of compliance.

[6] See ibid, pp. 107–11 for the assurance that participants received regarding there being no enduring harm to 'victims', see Milgram, Stanley, *Behavioral Study of Obedience, Journal of Abnormal and Social Psychology, 67 (4)*, 1963, pp. 371–78, and see Blass, Thomas, *The Roots of Stanley Milgram's Obedience Experiments and Their Relevance to the Holocaust, Analyse und Kritik 20 (1998)*, 2. 46–53, Westdeutscher Verlag, Opladen.

[7] See Milgram, Stanley, *Behavioral Study of Obedience, Journal of Abnormal and Social Psychology, 67 (4)*, 1963, pp. 371–78.

[8] See Gibson, Stephen, *Arguing, Obeying and Defying: A Rhetorical Perspective on Stanley MilgramE "Milgram, Stanley"'s Obedience Experiments*, Cambridge University Press, 2019, p. 18, for the figures of 20 per cent compliance when someone ordinary gave the orders and 47.5 per cent compliance when the institutional context was changed and diminished in prestige. Gibson also notes that two peers' rebelling reduced compliance to 10 per cent, that a peer administering the shock enhanced compliance to 92.5 per cent, and that an absent authority figure reduced compliance to 20.5 per cent.

[9] See ibid.

[10] See Alcock and Sadava, *An Introduction to Social Psychology*, op. cit., p. 189 for reference to the effect of proximity to the victim in reducing compliance and to the thirty per cent prepared to shock to the maximum even when applying the shock themselves. See Jonas, Klaus, *An Introduction to Social Psychology*, John Wiley and Sons, 2012, p. 267 for reference to the ninety-two per cent prepared to endorse the maximum shock if someone else administered it. See Perry, Gina, *Behind the Shock Machine: the untold story of the notorious Milgram experiments*, Scribe Publications, 2013, pp. 2, 3 and 4, for reference to a participant's refusal to 'take responsibility for him getting hurt in there' and asking, 'who's gonna take responsibility if anything happens to that gentleman?' (referring to the 'learner') in a context of evidence of severe pain, distress, refusal to continue, and reference to a heart condition from the 'learner', to which the experimenter responded, 'I'm responsible for anything that

happens', and for reference to the participant's ensuing compliance, administering shocks to the maximum of 450 volts despite continuing evidence of severe distress and even ominous silence from the 'victim'. And see Taylor, Shelley E., Peplau, Letitia Anne, and Sears, David O., *Social Psychology*, Prentice Hall, 2000, p. 225 for reference to reduced preparedness to administer shocks when participants were reminded of personal responsibility for their actions and their consequences.

[11] See Lunt, Peter, *Stanley Milgram: Understanding Obedience and Its Implications*, Macmillan International Higher Education, 2009, pp. 33 and 34.

[12] See Lawrence, Bruce B., and Karim, Aisha (eds.), *On Violence: A Reader*, Duke University Press, 2007, p. 301.

[13] See Blass, Thomas, 'Social Psychology of Stanley Milgram', in Zanna, Mark P. (ed.), *Advances in Experimental Social Psychology*, Volume 25, Elsevier, 1992, pp. 302 and 303.

[14] See Waller, *Becoming Evil*, op. cit., pp. 114 and 115.

[15] See Milgram, Stanley, *Obedience to Authority: An Experimental View*, Harper & Row, New York, 1974, p. 204.

[16] See Waller, *Becoming Evil*, op. cit., pp. 113 and 114 for his reference to Milgram's indication of evolutionary selection of compliance as an adaptive trait as evidence of a naturally inherited 'agentic state'. And see Alcock, James, and Sadava, Stan, *An Introduction to Social Psychology: Global Perspectives*, Sage, 2014, p. 189 for the 20.5 per cent prepared to shock to the maximum when instructed by the authority figure by telephone and for reference to participants who in that circumstance pretended to shock victims.

[17] See Milgram, *Obedience to Authority*, op. cit., pp. 5, 2, 6 and 9.

[18] See Milgram, Stanley, *Obedience to Authority: An Experimental View*, HarperCollins, New York, 1975, p. 6.

[19] See Milgram, Stanley, 'Behavioral Study of Obedience', *Journal of Abnormal and Social Psychology, 67 (4)*, 1963, pp. 371–78.

[20] See ibid.

[21] See Alcock and Sadava, *An Introduction to Social Psychology*, op. cit., p. 191, for the reference to the mere ten per cent prepared to shock to the maximum where others resisted the authority figure, compared to the sixty-five per cent prepared to administer the maximum shock when alone, and to the finding that when participants were given a free choice most delivered low voltages, with less than three per cent administering the maximum shock. What that indicates is that there was no malevolence involved, just protection of personal interest and the dominant influence on participant behaviour of a small cost with no real-life consequence even when the perceived cost to someone of whom nothing adverse was known was great.

[22] See Rattansi, Ali, *Bauman and Contemporary Sociology: A Critical Analysis*, Oxford University Press, pp. 73 and 74, citing Cesarani, *Eichmann*, op. cit., pp. 353 and 355, and Russell, Nestar, 'Stanley Milgram's Obedience to Authority "Relationship" Condition: Some Methodological and Theoretical Considerations', in *Social Sciences, 2014, 3*, pp. 200 and 201.

[23] See Perry, *Behind the Shock Machine*, op. cit., pp. 9 and 10, and Andersson, Tanetta, Review of 'Behind the Shock Machine: The Untold Story of Milgram's Notorious

Experiments', in *International Social Science Review*, Volume 89, 2014, Issue 1, Article 16.

[24] See Hollander, Matthew M., and Turowetz, Jason, *British Journal of Social Psychology*, Volume 56, Issue 4, 2017. Hollander and Turowetz assessed ninety-one participant reports obtained just after the end of the experiment and focussed on the forty-six 'obedient' subjects rather than the forty-five who are claimed to have defied the experimenter, though at what stage in the process of escalation of shocks is not specified, so it would not be appropriate to describe the latter as having resisted the experimenter without some specific reference to just when refusal to continue to obey began, that is, to just how many times they obeyed the authority figure. See also Gibson, *Arguing, Obeying and Defying*, op.cit., pp. 59, 60 and 61 for reference to Haslam and Reicher and their 'engaged followership' explanation for Milgram's findings.

[25] See Gibson, *Arguing, Obeying and Defying*, op.cit., p. 91 for reference to the view of Hollander and Turowetz that participants' claims after the experiments should not be dismissed as self-justifying and evasive.

[26] See Bazyler, Michael E., and Tuerkheimer, Frank M., *Forgotten Trials of the Holocaust*, NYU Press, 2015, pp. 176–79.

[27] See Cesarani, *Eichmann*, op. cit., p. 355 for Cesarani's criticism of the Milgram experiments.

[28] See Milgram, *Obedience to Authority*, op. cit., pp. 175 and 176.

[29] See Zimbardo, Philip G., The Stanford Prison Experiment: A Simulation Study of the Psychology of Imprisonment, on http://web.stanford.edu.

[30] See Le Texier, Thibault, 'Debunking the Stanford Prison Experiment', *American Psychologist 74 (7)*, 2019.

[31] See Haslam, S. Alexander, Reicher, Stephen D., and Van Bavel, Jay J., 'Rethinking the nature of cruelty: The role of identity leadership in the Stanford Prison Experiment', *American Psychologist 74 (7)*, 2019.

[32] See Reicher, Stephen, and Haslam, S. Alexander, 'Rethinking the Psychology of Tyranny: the BBC Prison Study', in *British Journal of Social Psychology*, 2006, 45. See Howarth, Caroline, and Andreouli, Eleni (eds.), *The Social Psychology of Everyday Politics*, Taylor and Francis, 2016, p. 105. See Rector, John M., *The Objectification Spectrum: Understanding and Transcending Our Diminishment and Dehumanization Of Others*, Oxford University Press, 2014, p. 169, for a slightly different account of what Zimbardo told guards at what seems to be the same briefing, in the added comments, attributed to Zimbardo, that 'what all this should create is a sense of powerlessness. We have total power in this situation. They have none', an indication of Zimbardo's role, intentions and instruction to those selected as guards.

[33] See ibid.

[34] See Reicher, Stephen, and Haslam, S. Alexander, 'Rethinking the Psychology of Tyranny: the BBC Prison Study', in *British Journal of Social Psychology*, 2006, 45.

[35] See Haslam, S. Alexander, and Reicher, Stephen D., Contesting the "Nature" of Conformity: What Milgram and Zimbardo's Studies Really Show, PLoS Biol 10 (11): e1001426 http://doi.org/10.1371/journal.pbio.1001426, November 2012. The article reiterates their claim that there was directive leadership from Zimbardo in the

Stanford Prison Experiment and argues that Milgram's participants were engaged 'followers' who identified with the experimenter and believed that they were administering shocks for the benefit of science. It also refers to Cesarani's work on Eichmann and claims that it supports their claim that Eichmann was motivated by eliminationist antisemitism rather than compliance with orders, which does seem a selective interpretation of Cesarani's case, for Cesarani also notes that the evidence of Eichmann's eliminationist antisemitism is to be found only when transportation of Jews to extermination centres became his role in the SS, and notes too evidence of Eichmann's careerism and attachment to SS rank and status, which indicates that Eichmann's identification was with his SS rank and status rather than elimnationist antisemitism and that his desire to maintain his SS rank and status resulted in his eliminationist antisemitic statements and behaviour once the extermination of the Jews of the occupied territories became the task of the SS.

[36] See Milgram, Stanley, 'Behavioral Study of Obedience', *Journal of Abnormal and Social Psychology*, 1963, 67, and Milgram, Stanley, 'Some Conditions of Obedience and Disobedience to Authority', *Human Relations*, 1965, 18.

Chapter Eight

The evidence of other German perpetrators. Browning's 'Ordinary Men' and the Einsatzgruppen commanders

Browning's 'Ordinary Men'

Browning's research is relevant to understanding Eichmann's perpetrator behaviour because of its finding of an extraordinary incidence of perpetrator behaviour from 'ordinary' German men and because of Browning's inferences regarding the causes of such compliance with the requirements of role.

Browning's research was based on the records of the 'postwar judicial interrogations' of members of Reserve Police Battalion 101 of the German Order Police, a unit from Hamburg, which executed 1,500 Jews (the assignment was to murder women, children and the elderly) in Józefów in Poland on 13 July 1942. Browning's 'ordinary men' were middle-aged working or lower middle-class reservists from a city known to be one of the least Nazified in Germany, had not been socialised under Nazi rule and had no intensive indoctrination that would account for preparedness to commit such murders of Jews. Even so, of nearly 500 men Browning notes that a mere 12 took advantage of Major Trapp's willingness as commanding officer to permit those of his men who wished not to participate in the murders to decline to participate in them, that some of those later volunteered for execution squads, and that eighty per cent to ninety per cent of the men engaged in shooting Jews.[1]

Such an extraordinary incidence of preparedness to murder Jewish elderly people, women and children occurred despite the fact that Major Trapp had displayed genuine distress at the task assigned the battalion and was generally a non-authoritarian authority figure, though he does seem to have told the men that the order had come from the 'highest authorities', that bombs were falling on German women and children, that some Jews in Józefów were involved with partisans, and that the Jews had been in part responsible for the American boycott of Germany, all it seems in an effort to make the task easier for the men.[2]

Browning dismisses the idea that the men in the battalion who perpetrated atrocities in Józefów were the result of selection of certain personality types, and disputes too the defence of compliance with orders for fear of sanctions and that of 'putative duress', the idea that the men did not know there were no sanctions for not participating, because Major Trapp had made it clear that men could excuse themselves without sanctions and had then protected the first man to take advantage of the offer.[3] Browning concludes, 'there are many societies afflicted by traditions of racism and caught in the siege mentality of war or threat of war. Everywhere society conditions people to respect and defer to authority,' and 'everywhere people seek career advancement. In every modern society, the complexity of life and the resulting bureaucratization and specialization attenuate the sense of personal responsibility of those implementing official policy. Within virtually every social collective, the peer group exerts tremendous pressure on behavior and sets moral norms. If the men of Police Battalion 101 could become killers under such circumstances, what group of men cannot?'[4]

Here Browning is referring to the social psychological context for ordinary people in many societies, but in the case of the massacre at Józefów many of the circumstances he refers to did not obtain. Taking them in turn, Browning notes (as has been indicated above) that the men's indoctrination was quite insufficient to legitimise the murder of Jewish elderly people, women and children, that Hamburg was one of the least Nazified cities in Germany, and that the men were middle-aged and so not socialised under the Nazi regime. Browning refers to a general Nazi indoctrination having elicited a 'Germanic racial superiority and "a certain aversion" towards the Jews' but concludes regarding the men of Reserve Battalion 101 that 'explicitly prepared for the task of killing Jews they were most certainly not'.[5]

As to obedience to orders and deference to authority, Browning notes (again as has been indicated above) that Major Trapp, the commanding officer, was non-authoritarian, showed revulsion and distress at the task the battalion had been given, and offered the men of the battalion the chance to decline to participate in the shooting of Jews without sanction. The explanation of compliance with direct orders from a chain of command that attenuated Browning's men's sense of personal responsibility is then diminished in credibility by the fact that their commanding officer left them with the possibility of excusing themselves from participation in the shooting of Jews without adverse consequence, which made them more responsible for the choice they made than they would otherwise have been. And the task at Józefów was viscerally immediate rather than bureaucratic (unlike the situation of Eichmann), and without any division of labour, which enhanced the sense of personal responsibility in Browning's men.

Browning notes too that there was no brutalisation effect from experience of irregular warfare or previous committing of atrocities for the men who were assigned the task of murdering the Jews of Józefów on 13 July 1942, for the battalion was involved in the massacre less than three weeks after arrival in Poland.

What is left is the reference to the influence of careerism and peer group norms, both reflecting pursuit of personal interest. Browning observes that 'to break ranks and step out, to adopt nonconformist behaviour, was simply beyond most of the men. It was easier for them to shoot,' and that refusing to shoot was exempting oneself from 'an unpleasant collective obligation' and leaving comrades to do one's part in it. Such nonconformity 'risked isolation, rejection and ostracism' far from any other form of 'support and social contact' and so would have been more punishing than it would have been in ordinary life. Browning notes that the result was that nonconformists attributed their avoidance of murdering Jews to weakness rather than to moral reservations and that such an attribution 'legitimized and upheld "toughness"'. He also notes that most men avoided being regarded as weak by participating in the murder of Jews.[6]

Browning does acknowledge the judgement involved in the historian's assessment of the veracity of testimonies, the limited number of them (210) and the even more limited number of men (125) for whom there was 'substantive' information from the 'judicial interrogations'. He also notes that under interrogation in post-war Germany some 'feared the judicial consequences of telling the truth' and 'lied', and that there were 'differing perspectives', 'repression', 'distortion' and 'conscious mendacity' in the testimonies of the men of Order Police Battalion 101.[7]

Browning notes that most of the men 'denied that they had any choice', claiming that they had not heard the commanding officer's speech or the part of it in which he offered to exempt men who did not feel they could participate in the shooting of the Jews. This is the characteristic Nazi perpetrator defence of obedience to orders, and so is the other defence Browning finds, that the experiential context was so dissimilar to that of post-war Germany as to be incomprehensible. Another defence Browning found was that the Jews would have been murdered anyway, an obvious rationalisation, and a more bizarre one was of a man would have murdered only children, that they could not do without their murdered mothers. Browning found that there was no reference to antisemitism, which was to be expected given that it would have indicated personal responsibility and criminal intent to murder Jews. Concluding, Browning notes that 'the men's concern for their standing in the eyes of their comrades was not matched by any sense of human ties to their victims. The Jews stood outside the circle of human obligation and responsibility.' While this does seem to have been true, one does wonder if the sense of Jewish 'otherness' was a necessary condition to the perpetrator behaviour of the men of Order Police Battalion 101, for if approbation and avoidance of denigration by peers were the primary influences on the men's perpetrator behaviour, a sense of the 'otherness' of their victims would seem to be no more than facilitative. The presumption is that Browning dismissed testimony claiming compliance with orders as it was obviously false (given that Major Trapp had indicated that men could exempt themselves without sanction from him) and concentrated upon testimony that had some credibility.

The credibility of the men who testified to the influence on their perpetrator behaviour of career considerations or peer group pressure is enhanced by the fact that such explanations do not lend themselves to post-war exoneration of their perpetrator behaviour, for reference to participating in perpetrator behaviour because of concerns over career or peer group antipathy were hardly likely to be regarded as legitimate excuses for shooting helpless elderly Jewish people or Jewish women and children and so does have some authenticity from the absence of ulterior motive. Other references on the part of Browning's men, for instance to reservations, severe distress, shooting wide deliberately or not engaging in shooting when unobserved, may be more subject to the criticism that they would have been expedient to the men's exoneration of perpetrator behaviour after the war. Even so the testimony of the great majority of the men is that they participated in the shooting of Jews rather than denial that they did so, which would seem to have been the optimal response to elicit exoneration of perpetrator behaviour, and that enhances the authenticity of the evidence.

In the battalion's ensuing massacre of Jews at Łomazy the situation facing the men of Reserve Police Battalion 101 was quite different to that at Józefów. To begin with the men were given no choice but to participate in the massacre, diminishing their sense of personal responsibility, and the primary task of the battalion was to round up the Jews, for most of the shooting of Jews was done by Eastern European 'volunteers' or Hiwis. There were circumstances in which the men of the battalion were required to shoot Jews but there was a combination of 'depersonalization' that was unlike the situation at Józefów, and 'habituation' to the role and to the realities of the east that facilitated the men's complicit behaviour. The battalion's ensuing involvement in ghetto clearing, even knowing that the Jews were being transported to Treblinka, had similar characteristics to those at Łomazy. By contrast at Józefów there was no influence on the men's behaviour from such factors because the battalion had only just arrived in Poland, because it was assigned the task of murdering Jews on its own, and because the men could excuse themselves from participation without sanction from Trapp. Such differences make the Józefów massacre the most significant for identifying sufficient conditions for perpetrator behaviour and isolating them from other factors that may have facilitated the battalion's ensuing complicity in or commission of genocide.[8]

Browning notes reference to 'Jewish passivity' that made it seem that 'the Jews were complicit in their own deaths' and no admission of the 'political and ideological dimension'.[9] Browning claims that the credible testimonies of the men of the battalion explained their participation by reference to the influence of the peer group on conformity, which is unlike the Milgram finding of compliance with authority, which Milgram astutely notes is generally preferred in that it seems to absolve the individual from responsibility. Even so, Browning notes that in variations Milgram conducted on his basic experiment resistance to conformity from other participants enhanced individual resistance, and that the example of others escalating shocks enhanced individual compliance with immoral authority. Browning concludes that 'the mutual reinforcement of authority and conformity seems to have been clearly demonstrated by Milgram', and points out that the men in Poland were comrades rather than mere participants in an experiment, which, with their isolation in Poland, would have made comrades' influence more decisive.[10] Neither Browning nor Milgram seems to interrogate such evidence for some common motive that would explain both deference to authority and conformity, such as individual optimisation of outcomes in social and psychological terms.

Browning did then find something similar to Milgram in the mass murder of Jewish old people, women and children by 'ordinary men' not long after arrival in Poland despite having no extensive Nazi indoctrination, apparently to be seen to have accomplished an assigned task known to be difficult or to avoid peer group sanctions for declining to participate, despite evidence of repugnance for and distress over the task that indicates the sort of moral awareness that Arendt claims was missing in Eichmann and the lack of which she claims explains Eichmann's perpetrator behaviour. In other words most of those who felt distress over the task took part in the murders of Jews to avoid informal sanctions from the peer group, and their capacity for moral reasoning did not exert decisive influence on their behaviour, for a relatively small perceived cost to the self exerted more influence on behaviour than being agent to suffering and loss of life for others despite the moral awareness implicit in the distress of the men. Moral awareness does then seem to be less compelling in terms of influence on behaviour than pursuit of personal interest even where there is little to be lost as a consequence of refraining from perpetrator behaviour.[11]

There seems to be some congruity between the causes of Eichmann's perpetrator behaviour and Milgram's and Browning's findings. In the Milgram experiments there was the difficulty participants found in resisting authority because of their desire to avoid the embarrassment of having to confront an authority figure and to avoid being seen to have failed by the authority figure, and in the Browning case there was avoidance of ridicule and ostracism from peers through conformity even when it required the murder of helpless Jews. Such evidence indicates the primacy of pursuit of personal interest and overriding concern with individual outcomes even at the expense of others because conformity to role requirements optimised personal outcomes. Given the evidence presented above that Eichmann was normal in psychological terms the inference is that he would have been motivated by similar concerns, and the evidence does indicate that Eichmann was concerned to maintain the regard of Müller and Kaltenbrunner and his SS rank and identity.

Browning's 'Ordinary Men' and its conclusions have been criticised by Daniel Goldhagen, in his 'Hitler's Willing Executioners', written four years after the initial appearance of 'Ordinary Men' in 1992. Goldhagen claims that 'eliminationist anti-semitism' was a characteristic of ordinary Germans long before the Nazis' assumption of power and that Hitler had only to release the desire of ordinary Germans to exterminate the Jews. Goldhagen uses the same evidence, that of Reserve Police Battalion 101, to support his case. Browning's 'Afterword' at the end of 'Ordinary Men' addresses Goldhagen's claims, which were very controversial and received a scathing reception from historians in general. Browning agrees with Goldhagen that ordinary Germans were involved in the extermination of Europe's Jews but points out that Hilberg, whom Goldhagen criticises, had noted as early as 1961, in his 'The Destruction of the European Jews', that German perpetrators 'were not different in moral makeup from the rest of the population. The German perpetrator was not a special kind of German'.

Browning acknowledges the existence of cultural antisemitism in Germany and its association with German conservatism, nationalism, dislike of democracy and modernity, and generally reactionary tendencies but notes the existence of a variety of different antisemitisms that Goldhagen claims all eventuated in eliminationist antisemitism, which Browning disputes. Browning notes that a new form of antisemitism, 'chimeric' or 'redemptive' antisemitism, materialised in the interwar years, following German surrender in the First World War, the Treaty of Versailles with its punitive terms, the colossal reparations demanded under it and their deleterious effect on the German economy, but claims that even as late as Kristallnacht in November 1938 'the general population' was not 'mobilised around strident and violent anti-Semitism'. He does acknowledge that Germans were 'increasingly "apathetic", "passive", and "indifferent" to the fate' of the Jews, but claims that 'most "ordinary Germans"' would not 'approve of, much less participate in, the mass murder of European Jewry'.

Browning quotes a number of distinguished Holocaust historians whose expertise is in the attitudes of ordinary Germans towards Nazi policy regarding the Jews. For Bankier 'ordinary Germans' differentiated 'an acceptable discrimination' from the 'unacceptable horror of genocide', Kulka claims that 'abysmal indifference to the fate of the Jews as human beings' facilitated the Holocaust, and Kershaw notes that 'the road to Auschwitz was built by hatred, but paved with indifference'. All these views indicate no popular endorsement of the extermination of the Jews from ordinary Germans, with debate limited to controversy over terminology, such as over Kulka's use of 'passive complicity' to describe the attitude and role of ordinary Germans. By contrast Goldhagen claims that 'indifference' is 'psychologically impossible', which is of course untrue, that the German population was 'pitiless', 'unsympathetic' and 'callous', and that its silence indicated approval, which is also untrue. For just in ordinary life indifference is common, and silence indicates nothing in the way of approval. Goldhagen's claim that eliminationist antisemitism was characteristic of ordinary Germans during the war has then been discredited by historians whose expertise is in German public opinion during the war.[12]

Ideological influences do seem from the evidence of Browning's 'Ordinary Men' to be no more than facilitative, as for instance in the form of the Führerprinzip that exonerated SS officers from all responsibility for their perpetrator behaviour and Nazi propaganda that enhanced Jewish 'otherness' and that claimed that the Jews were enemies of the German state and race in time of war.

The relevance of this evidence to explaining Eichmann's perpetrator behaviour is that Eichmann was found to be an ordinary German, so the motive behind his behaviour would be expected to be similar to the careerism and desire to meet the requirements of role found in Browning's 'Ordinary Men', that is, to optimise personal outcomes and avoid adverse ones. The evidence here also indicates that antisemitism would not have been a plausible motive for an ordinary German like Eichmann.

The Einsatzgruppen Commanders

The evidence on Einsatzgruppen commanders challenges Arendt's claim that Eichmann's perpetrator behaviour is to be attributed to his lack of capacity for moral reasoning and lack of appreciation of the consequences of his behaviour, and indicates the extent of conformity to role requirements in the middle to more senior ranks of the SS. It does then set a context for Eichmann's compliance with role requirements and 'normalises' it as well as being indicative of its probable causal influences.

The evidence is similar to that of Milgram and Browning in contradicting Arendt's attribution of Eichmann's perpetrator behaviour to a lack of capacity for moral reasoning, for Einsatzgruppen commanders clearly had a capacity for moral reasoning that did not preclude their participation in the Holocaust, and in pointing to optimisation of personal outcomes being the decisive influence on complicity in perpetrator behaviour in the middle to senior echelons of the SS.

The Einsatzgruppen were SS battalions that followed the German military advance eastwards. In Poland in 1939 they were tasked with the elimination of Poland's leadership, including its intelligentsia, and in the Soviet Union following the German invasion in the summer of 1941 they were tasked with the elimination of partisans and Bolsheviks to secure the German rear, and with the extermination of Jews. Here the concentration is on the perpetrator behaviour and motives of the commanders of Einsatzgruppen units in the Soviet Union from the summer of 1941 onwards, for though Jews were murdered by the Einsatzgruppen in Poland in 1939 extermination of the Jews of the east was not an SS objective then – destruction of the Polish leadership was. The Einsatzgruppen role in regard to the Jews in Poland in 1939 was ghettoisation. That means that the evidence of Einsatzgruppen units in Poland in 1939 is not directly relevant to inferences regarding the reasons for Eichmann's perpetrator behaviour in transporting Jews to extermination centres.

The orders issued to Einsatzgruppen commanders regarding their task in the Soviet Union following the advance of the German army under Operation Barbarossa are indicated by Heydrich's letter to the Higher SS and Police Commanders of 2 July 1941, when he referred to the 'most important instructions given by me to the Einsatzgruppen and Einsatzkommandos of the Security Police and the SD', for he indicated that

> Those to be executed are all
> Functionaries of the Comintern (and all professional Communist politicians of
>   any kind)
> People's Commissars
> Jews in Party and State posts
> All radical elements (saboteurs, propagandists, snipers, assassins, agitators, etc.).

Einsatzgruppen were also to support and encourage anticommunist and anti-Jewish sentiment and action in the local populations of the east. Longerich notes that Heydrich made it clear in meetings with Einsatzgruppen commanders before Operation Barbarossa that 'Soviet Jews and Bolshevism represented a closely linked collection of enemies, leaving them to shoot the Jews under one pretext or another', and that the list does 'not expressly forbid the murder of women and children'. Longerich does refer to there having been some 'latitude for initiative' for Einsatzgruppen commanders and to a vagueness of orders characteristic of the workings of the Nazi state, but also to an understanding on the part of Einsatzgruppen commanders regarding their task and its nature predicated upon their having been recruited from the SS and the police and awareness of the SS orthodoxy of there being a 'Jewish-Bolshevist complex'. Longerich notes that 'this degree of uncertainty on the part of the commandos explains their readiness to adjust to the new and far more radical approach to Jewish persecution in the East that had been pursued by the SS leadership since July' and that 'the Einsatzkommandos, now considerably strengthened in terms of personnel, started to expand the range of their executions by murdering women and children'. He concludes that Einsatzgruppen commanders had 'a degree of room for manoeuvre, but only within the framework established by the SS leadership', and that the activities of the Einsatzgruppen 'corresponded to the orders that the Einsatzgruppen had received at the beginning of the campaign' and were consistent with the policy 'propagated by the leadership of the SS: a policy of systematic ethnic annihilation'.[13]

It is then clear that Einsatzgruppen, Einsatzkommando and Sonderkommando commanders were in their perpetrator behaviour obeying both the explicit and the implicit nature of the orders they had received from Heydrich and the understandings he had conveyed to them regarding the nature of their role behind the German advance, rather than acting on their own initiative in accordance with preferences derived from an attitudinal disposition towards extermination of the Jews of the occupied territories, for instance. On the contrary, as shall be shown below, there is significant evidence of careerism and aspiration to maintain or enhance personal status that does seem to have resulted in concern to be seen to have succeeded or at least not to have failed when compared to peers amongst the commanders of Einsatzgruppen, Einsatzkommandos and Sonderkommandos, and no evidence of the sort of eliminationist antisemitism necessary to explain extensive executions of Jews on its own.

Einsatzkommandos and Sonderkommandos were subordinate units that composed the Einsatzgruppen, and for the Einsatzgruppen, Einsaztkommando and Sonderkommando commanders in the Soviet Union MacLean's evidence indicates that as many as thirty-nine out of seventy-eight commanders (or fifty per cent) were educated to degree level in law, that twenty-six (or a third) held doctorates in law, that those with law degrees were lawyers before becoming Einsatzgruppen, Einsatzkommando or Sonderkommando commanders, that a total of fifty-seven (or seventy-three per cent) had university degrees, and that there were amongst the commanders two who had been physicians and one who had been a Protestant pastor. Such evidence challenges Arendt's claim that Eichmann's perpetrator behaviour is to be explained by a lack of capacity for moral reasoning, for the extraordinary preponderance of lawyers, whose training would have involved some appreciation of the law as reflecting the norms and morality of society, indicates that having the capacity for moral reasoning and in fact training involving such reasoning did not constrain Einsatzgruppen, Einsatzkommando and Sonderkommando commanders from participation in genocide.

It cannot be argued that the capacity for 'moral reasoning' of those who were to become Einsatzgruppen, Einsatzkommando and Sonderkommando commanders had been degraded by socialisation and education as lawyers under the Nazi regime with its distorted ideas of morality and legitimacy, for the commanders had been socialised and educated, including their training in the law, before the Nazis assumed power in 1933. Ernst Kaltenbrunner, who replaced Heydrich as Himmler's deputy in the SS hierarchy on 30 January 1943, following Heydrich's assassination in Czechoslovakia on 4 June 1942, and Hans Frank, who became Governor-General of the General Government in occupied Poland, are two more instances of lawyers intimately involved in the genocide of the Jews. And as has been seen, even theological study and Protestant ministry, both of which would indicate capacity for and training in moral reasoning, did not exert a decisive constraining influence on one Einsatzkommando commander.[14]

The extraordinary incidence of lawyers amongst Einsatzgruppen, Einsatzkommando and Sonderkommando commanders is explained by their having been drawn in significant numbers from the SS leadership school at Berlin-Charlottenburg, from the SS criminal and security police and from the more senior echelons of the Reich Security Main Office, and their having been selected by Heydrich and Himmler, an indication of the importance attached to the role of the Einsatzgruppen in Operation Barbarossa, the invasion of the Soviet Union from the summer of 1941.[15]

The explanation that the incidence of lawyers reflects the sources of recruitment does though introduce the question of why so many lawyers, and other very educated men, joined the SS and the Reich Security Main Office in the first place. One plausible answer seems to be optimisation of career and outcomes in a state in which everything was politicised and in which the SS represented an elite engaged in what was seen as one of the objectives of the Nazi state, elimination of racial and political enemies, so that relatively senior rank in the SS represented a form of accomplishment in career terms and in terms of privilege, status, elite identity and participation in major Nazi objectives.

Einsatzgruppen commanders' ensuing preparedness to commit mass murder of Jews and eastern Europeans in compliance with the changing dictates of Nazi racial policy and their roles in one of the major enterprises of the Nazi state indicates that careerism and status are the most probable explanation of their perpetrator behaviour. For though there does seem to have been an incremental process, from joining the SS as one of the optimal careers in Nazi Germany, followed by various roles in the Reich Security Main Office, the Security Police (the SD), the Gestapo, the Kripo or the Waffen-SS and only eventually by roles involving the mass murder of Jews and others in eastern Europe in a war in which the Jews were claimed to be enemies of the German race and state, Einsatzgruppen commanders' compliance with the very different requirements of the role of Einsatzgruppen commander did of course optimise outcomes for them. Pursuit of personal interest in the form of an SS career does then seem to have been the major influence on their committing genocide.

Though there is no evidence that the men involved had been eliminationist antisemites on joining the SS or in roles in the SS which did not involve mass murder of Jews, an argument could be made that they became eliminationist antisemites through embracing Nazi ideology concerning Jews as threats to the German race and state in time of war and associated with Bolshevism and communist partisans, though that would have to have been coincidentally only when it became Nazi policy, the major task of the SS and their role as Einsatzgruppen commanders. That is not plausible.

That is not to say that Einsatzgruppen, Einsatzkommando and Sonderkommando commanders were not ideologically attached to Nazism, for there was the influence of right-wing nationalist sentiment in German universities and elsewhere in the interwar period.[16] Evidence of ideological attachment to Nazism to the extent required for SS membership seems to have included a sense of German racial superiority and entitlement in relation to other races, militarism, nationalism, anticommunism, and antipathy for socialism, capitalism and liberal democracy as exemplified by the Weimar Republic (all of which were characteristics of the German middle-classes). Exhibiting evidence of these attributes could of course have reflected both genuine ideological leanings and careerist considerations given the politicisation of life in the Nazi state, but ideological affiliation for Nazism did not involve commitment to eliminationist antisemitism, not least because before 1941 it had not been Nazi policy towards the Jews or the major assignment of the SS.

Earl notes the high educational level of many in the Nazi hierarchy, observing that 'over forty percent of those indicted at Nuremberg in 1947 had earned doctoral degrees' and that 'of the sixty-nine leaders of the Einsatzkommandos (the sub units of the Einsatzgruppen) twenty-three percent held doctoral degrees and the remainder had some university training'. Earl notes the combination of intellect and aspiration, 'of intelligence and ambition', in the Einsatzgruppen, Einsatzkommando and Sonderkommando commanders and continues, 'in any other setting this group would surely have been considered the elite of their society. As it turned out, they were the young elite of the Nazi Party who, given the opportunities provided by the Third Reich, carried out their tasks with verve and conviction'.[17] There is here some confusion as to attribution of decisive influence on the perpetrator behaviour of Einsatzgruppen, Einsatzkommando and Sonderkommando commanders, for Earl indicates both aspiration and ideological commitment as influences.

A similar confusion is apparent in Earl's 'The SS-Einsatzgruppen Trial', where she claims that 'this group of perpetrators believed in the principles of National Socialism so much that they made its ideology the very basis of their behaviour', not having been 'born with an eliminationist-type antisemitism' but having 'adopted a form of national chauvinism that germinated in the aftermath of Germany's defeat in the First World War', though even in the context of claiming that 'some joined the Party out of conviction' she also claims of Einsatzgruppen, Einsatzkommando and Sonderkommando commanders that 'their trajectories show that they were career-oriented go-getters, social climbers, and actual leaders like Ohlendorf'.[18]

The attribution of Einsatzgruppen, Einsatzkommando and Sonderkommando leaders' perpetrator behaviour to opportunism and aspiration is more convincing than the attribution to ideological conviction regarding extermination of the Jews in the east, for as has been indicated there is no direct evidence of the latter before it became Nazi policy and the task of Einsatzgruppen, Einsatzkommando and Sonderkommando commanders. The inference of decisive influence from the ideological commitment seems to rely on the testimony of Einsatzgruppen, Einsatzkommando and Sonderkommando commanders at their post-war trial, hardly a source without bias, not least as they could have perceived it to be optimal to attribute their perpetrator behaviour to the experience of World War One, to the sense of 'unrealistic expectations' or 'nationalism' to which Earl refers, and to Nazi association of Jews with Bolshevism in the east rather than to something as banal as optimising outcomes for the self.[19]

The point being made here is that there was a significant difference between the generalised nationalistic right-wing sentiment in German universities and elsewhere in Germany between the wars that Earl refers to and desire or preparedness to murder great numbers of Jews in the east in the most visceral manner, for the former relates to a general right-wing rhetoric of cultural antisemitism and the latter to personal involvement in the eliminationist antisemitism of the Holocaust. It is possible that Earl's inference regarding perpetrator conviction is predicated upon her concentration on Ohlendorf, though she notes that even he displayed a 'careerist sensibility' when the Nazi Party assumed power in 1933 in abandoning a career in the law for one in economics to be part of the enterprise of the Nazi state, and that he joined in the Security Police (the SD) following disagreements with Nazi officials in his previous work rather than having gravitated to the SD out of ideological preference.[20]

The evidence presented above indicates that Einsatzgruppen commanders engaged in perpetrator activity because it optimised their careers, social status and identity in a Third Reich in which all elite careers were politicised. It is of course common for people to affect to believe in what they perceive is optimal for them to appear to believe, so one would not expect major Nazi perpetrators such as Einsatzgruppen commanders to have expressed any reservation regarding tasks assigned to them. The same is of course true of Eichmann. On the contrary, the expectation would be expressions indicative of attitudinal conformity to a rhetoric and a narrative that endorses and legitimises the task concerned as part of behavioural conformity to the normative order of the Nazi state apparatus and the SS.

Commenting on the attributes of Einsatzgruppen commanders, Browning notes that 'of the four Einsatzgruppen commanders, three held a total of four doctorates', that 'of the seventeen SK, EK and Vorkommando chiefs, a further seven held the doctorate', and that with recruitment from the Security Police (the SD), the Reich Security Main Office and the Gestapo and with most recruits having come through Heydrich's SD, 'they virtually all shared the same ideological outlook concerning Jews, Bolsheviks, and Slavs and Germany's imperial future in the east as well as attributes and dispositions of "energetic ruthlessness", initiative, and activism that were the common characteristics of the SS intellectual elite'.[21] What Browning's commentary does not address is the evidence that the most plausible decisive influence on such men's perpetrator behaviour and expressed attitudes as Einsatzgruppen, Einsatzkommando and Sonderkommando commanders seems to have been careerism and a desire to be part of an elite SS historical enterprise in the east of Europe, for there is no evidence that any of them had expressed eliminationist antisemitic sentiments in their other roles in the Nazi state, before the annihilation of the Jews of Europe became Nazi policy, the major task of the SS and their own role.

Browning notes a sense of German historic mission in the east of Europe in a context of a belief in German racial entitlement, racial derogation of Jews and Slavs, and ideological loathing of Bolshevism. Even so the primary influence on Einsatzgruppen commanders and their perpetrator behaviour does seem to have been the career, social and psychological rewards of conformity to the SS code and identity of compliance with orders, discipline and ruthlessness, and concern over possible loss of reputation or status compared to peers or of SS rank with its privileges, status and involvement in one of the major enterprises of the Nazi state. These inferences are in fact consonant with the ones Browning himself draws regarding the causes of the behaviour of the 'Ordinary Men' of Police Battalion 101.

The evidence on the majority of Germans indicates unreflective compliance with the dictates of the Nazi state and avoidance of political matters to optimise outcomes, and the evidence on perpetrator behaviour in the SS indicates that orders received through the SS hierarchy were carried out, without moral anguish, to maintain or enhance careers and status or to avoid the disdain of peers. A German sense of racial superiority and entitlement cultivated by Nazi propaganda would have appealed to Germans in that it would have been rewarding and would have been seen as conferring upon them rights not accorded other races, for instance to Lebensraum, though it seems unlikely to have been a necessary condition to perpetrator behaviour, and the most probable inference is that Einsatzgruppen men did what they conceived to be best for them, that is, compliance with orders. It is though possible that in some cases, where some form of legitimation was felt to be necessary, the commanders of the Einsatzgruppen, the Einsatzkommando and the Sonderkommando came to believe what was optimal for them to believe in terms of psychological outcomes.

There was of course Nazi propaganda portraying Jews as racial and political enemies of the German Reich before the Einsatzgruppen operations in the Soviet Union from the summer of 1941, when there was association of Jews with Bolshevism and partisan activity. Despite such a context of antisemitic indoctrination there is no evidence of eliminationist antisemitism in individuals who became Einsatzgruppen, Einsatzkommando or Sonderkommando commanders in SS roles prior to their assignment to murder Jews in the east. Though it could be argued that such evidence would not exist given the code of discipline within the SS and its task of giving effect to Nazi policy rather than commenting on what it should be or formulating it, the case of the outspoken Ohlendorf, who had it seems major disagreements with Nazi officials in roles prior to joining the SD, is indicative, in that there is no evidence of his being an eliminationist antisemite (as opposed to a national socialist) before becoming the notorious commander of Einsatzgruppe D.

Another argument against the idea that ideological eliminationist antisemitism rather than conformity to role requirements to optimise personal outcomes explains the preparedness to commit mass murder of Jews in the east of Einsatzgruppen commanders is that given their educational level they could not have accepted the crude idea that Jewish elderly people, women and children had to be exterminated to secure the German rear against Bolshevik or partisan activity, or the explanation that the entire Jewish race had to be exterminated to preclude Jewish vengeance, unless there was some compelling motive dictating acceptance. In other words, the likelihood is that Einsatzgruppen commanders accepted what was conceived to be in their interests to accept at the time.

Taken with the Milgram research the German evidence indicates that ordinary people engage in perpetrator behaviour, even if distressed by it and despite a capacity for moral reasoning, because of the primacy of pursuit of personal interest in human motivation and behaviour. That seems to be apparent in Milgram's experimental setting, in the immediacy of commitment of atrocities in the war in the east noted by Browning and in the careerism of men like the Einsatzgruppen, Einsatzkommando and Sonderkommando commanders, who aspired to maintain their status in Nazi Germany, where advancement and status were politicised in a totalitarian state and the SS constituted an occupational and social elite. Though there are exceptional cases in which moral principle, which may not be the same as the moral reasoning to which Arendt refers, informed resistance to immorality despite severe adverse consequences, these seem to be very isolated.

The evidence of the Einsatzgruppen does admittedly relate to individuals who were different in class background in some cases and in educational attainment to Eichmann. Nor was Eichmann in the position of most participants in the Milgram experiments, the men in Browning's research, or the Einsatzgruppen commanders, all of whom had far greater proximity to their victims than Eichmann had given that he had no more than a limited number of visits to extermination centres and could have felt that he was not responsible for what happened to the Jews there, just for their transport and under orders in that role too.

Differences in proximity to victims may explain the significant moral anguish experienced by Milgram's participants and Browning's men (which may not be the same as Arendt's moral reasoning, which may have had greater sophistication of understanding) and the apparent lack of moral anguish in Einsatzgruppen, Einsatzkommando and Sonderkommando commanders and Eichmann, for Eichmann was not proximate to the Jews he sent to the extermination camps, and though the Einsatzgruppen, Einsatzkommando and Sonderkommando commanders were more proximate to their victims they did not it seems actually murder Jews themselves. There would also have been some influence from the SS code of obedience to orders and of personal toughness in carrying out unpleasant tasks in the cases of Einsatzgruppen, Einsatzkommando and Sonderkommando commanders because of their desire to establish themselves as efficient and ruthless, both SS values, to secure the approbation of their SS bosses and peers.[22]

Despite the dissimilarities between Eichmann and the Einsatzgruppen commanders referred to above, Eichmann was aspiring and orthodox within the SS, reflecting a desire for elite identity, privilege and status in the SS, and the evidence of the relationship between education, aspiration and optimisation of outcomes through compliance with the dictates and purposes of the Nazi state of Einsatzgruppen, Einsatzkommando and Sonderkommando commanders is also evidence of the causal relationship between occupational and social aspiration to optimise outcomes and active rather than passive conformity in the more opportunistic part of the conforming German population under Nazi rule, of which Eichmann seems to have been a part. Education was for some a means to achieve career aspirations, whereas in others aspiration was present and pursued through similar political and ideological orthodoxy and being of use as a functionary in the Nazi state apparatus. The common point is the decisive influence on behaviour of conformity to achieve personal aspirations or to avoid loss of rank and status regardless of cost to others, for there seems to have been no ideological commitment to exterminate Jews in those who became Einsatzgruppen commanders prior to their transfer to the task of shooting great numbers of Jews.

One very direct similarity between the Einsatzgruppen commanders and Eichmann is that the Einsatzgruppen commanders were moved from ordinary Gestapo, Kripo or SD work to command Einsatzgruppen in the eradication of Jews, partisans and Bolsheviks, and that Eichmann's role changed from being a Jewish specialist planning Jewish emigration to arranging the transportation of Jews to extermination centres. In both cases there seems to have been a natural compliance with the transition of role despite its nature, and it is not plausible to attribute to Einsatzgruppen commanders or Eichmann a sudden conversion to eliminationist antisemitism just when it became the task assigned them by the SS hierarchy, for that would be to postulate an extraordinary coincidence. The Einsatzgruppen evidence is then of special relevance to inferences regarding the causes of Eichmann's perpetrator behaviour given the similar change of role for the Einsatzgruppen commanders and Eichmann, and does support the case being made here that Eichmann was motivated by similar considerations of pursuit of personal interest in the form of optimising career and status in the SS rather than by eliminationist antisemitism in undertaking perpetrator behaviour. Such contextual evidence also indicates that to be dissimilar in the motives that decisively influenced his behaviour to his fellow Nazis and Germans and to ordinary people in many cultures at different times Eichmann would have had to have been decidedly abnormal in personality or much more antisemitic than the norm in the SS. There is no evidence to either effect and in fact much to the contrary. And the contextual evidence presented above does establish that capacity for the moral reasoning to which Arendt refers does not preclude perpetrator behaviour.

The improbability that Eichmann should have become an eliminationist antisemite just when transportation of Jews to extermination centres became his role in the SS, his previous role as Jewish specialist and expert on Jewish emigration having been eliminated by the change in Nazi policy and by the new task assigned to the SS in regard to the Jews, indicates that Eichmann's perpetrator behaviour did not reflect eliminationist antisemitism. For the Einsatzgruppen, Einsatzkommando and Sonderkommando commanders there is a similar implausibility of an extraordinary coincidence between change of role and causally significant change of attitude (to the extermination of the Jews).

Festinger's Theory of Cognitive Dissonance (1957) claims that discomfort is caused by 'holding two inconsistent ideas at the same time' and that it 'causes one or both of the ideas to be modified in order to reduce "cognitive dissonance". One implication of this principle is that changing behaviour will also change attitudes when they are inconsistent with each other'.[23] Applying this principle to the situation of men appointed as Einsatzgruppen commanders in the east, given no evidence that they were eliminationist antisemites before being appointed to the role, the expectation would be attitude change following behavioural changes undertaken by them to conform to the role requirements of being an Einsatzgruppen commander. Genuine attitude change (beyond mere conformity to a rhetoric of eliminationist antisemitism in the east amongst SS officers there) to eliminationist antisemitism would then be predicted for men for whom compliance with orders was an insufficient justification for their engaging in perpetrator behaviour for the first time. The objective would have been reduction in the discomfort of dissonance between new behaviour and previously existing attitudes, a form of optimisation of psychological outcomes, so Festinger's theory does support the argument that conformity to new role requirements (which in turn of course reflects pursuit of personal interest to optimise outcomes in the new role) explains Eichmann's perpetrator behaviour and that of Einsatzgruppen, Einsatzkommando and Sonderkommando commanders.

Notes

[1] See Browning, Christopher, *Ordinary Men, Reserve Police Battalion 101 and the Final Solution in Poland*, Penguin, London, 2001, pp. 176 to 185 for the nature of the 'indoctrination' the men of Reserve Police Battalion 101 received prior to their perpetrator behaviour in Poland in July 1942 and for Browning's view that it does not explain the perpetrator behaviour of his 'ordinary men', not least because it did not prepare the men for or dictate extermination of Jews. See p. 71 for the numbers taking advantage of Trapp's offer and p. 184 for the percentages of the men who engaged in the shooting of Jews.

[2] See ibid, p. 2.

[3] See ibid, p. 171 for Browning's reference to 'putative duress' and to Trapp's offer to excuse those 'not up to it', though see p. 2 for Browning's reference to Trapp's offer having been made to 'older men'. The inference is that the effect was that any man who requested it would be excused regardless of age. And see Russell, *Stanley Milgram's Obedience to Authority "Relationship" Condition*, op. cit., pp. 211 and 212 for Russell's conjecturing that Browning's 'Ordinary Men' were compliant with the terrible task assigned them because of their close relationship with and fondness for Major Trapp and because of his offer to exempt men who could not participate, which meant that their participation was voluntary, though Browning does not refer to this possibility from the evidence he gathered and Trapp exempted himself from the shootings and was a non-authoritarian authority figure, so the idea is implausible. The reasoning derived from Russell's argument that the nature of the relationship between participant and authority figure could be as significant for behaviour as that between participant and victim.

[4] Ibid, pp. 188 and 189.

[5] Ibid, p. 184.

[6] See ibid, pp. 184 and 185, and p. 72 for the claim that 'bonds of military comradeship were not yet fully developed' in the battalion at the time and that even so a major reason given by the men for shooting the Jews was that they did not wish to 'lose face' and be regarded as a coward by their peers. See also Westermann, '"Ordinary Drinkers" and Ordinary "Males"? Alcohol, Masculinity, and Atrocity in the Holocaust', in Kaplan, Matthäus and Homburg (eds.), *Beyond Ordinary Men*, op. cit., pp. 30 to 38 for reference to social science findings that alcohol use is linked to aggression and that there is also influence from 'social and psychological predispositions related to conceptions of masculinity, including qualities such as toughness, brutality, and the readiness to engage in violent acts' (p. 32), for the claim that alcohol use 'promoted psychological disinhibition' (p. 35) and so 'facilitated acts

of murder and atrocity' (p. 33), that it had a 'desensitizing effect' (p. 34) after perpetrator behaviour, and that the influence of alcohol on perpetrator behaviour was associated with 'a National Socialist conception of masculinity' (p. 35) and a National Socialist ideal of 'hypermasculinity especially within the SS and the police complex that helped to promote and catalyse extreme manifestations of male aggression' (p. 38). But see also Browning, *Ordinary Men*, op. cit., p. 61 for Browning's claim that it was not until 'some point in the afternoon' that there was a 'supply of alcohol for the shooters' at Józefów, indicating that there had been none throughout the entire morning's shootings and that alcohol use was not a necessary condition for the shooting of Jewish old people, women and children (Westermann acknowledges that alcohol use was not a necessary or sufficient condition for perpetrator behaviour). Both Browning's and Westermann's findings do in fact indicate perpetrator pursuit of personal interest through conformity to avoid peer group sanctions, for as has been seen there was conformity in Browning's men to a peer group norm of participation in murders of Jews, and there was a similar conformity in Westermann's normative male drinking sessions with their disinhibiting effect on violence and in the influence of a Nazi ideal of 'hypermasculinity' that dictated ruthlessness and violence and that could have been a normative influence on the members of Reserve Police Battalion 101 who were the decisive influences on a norm of participation in murders of Jews at Józefów and on the general conformity within the battalion that ensued. A disinhibiting effect of alcohol could of course have been to render the individual even more susceptible to the norms of the peer group than before alcohol use, in that awareness of the self and of the principles of one's background could have been diminished and the influence of the immediacy of peer group conformity enhanced.

[7] See Browning, *Ordinary Men*, op.cit., pp. xv and xvi.

[8] See ibid, pp. 80, 85 and 88. See p. 87 for Browning's observation that 'at Łomazy following orders reinforced the natural tendency to conform to the behaviour of one's comrades', and p. 90 for Browning's reference to the lack of distress amongst the men over the deportations of Jews to Treblinka even though it was known that they were to be exterminated. Here there is another indication of the effect of diminished immediacy upon a sense of personal responsibility and of the lack of genuine German interest in what happened to Jews in Poland.

[9] Ibid, p. 152.

[10] Ibid, pp. 174 and 175.

[11] See Browning, *Ordinary Men*, op. cit., p. 74 for his observation that those who quit the shootings of Jews at some point cited 'sheer physical revulsion' rather than 'ethical or political principles behind this reaction' but that such lack of reference to principle could be explained by the educational level of most of the men.

[12] See ibid, pp. 200 and 201. See also Browning, Christopher R., 'Ordinary Germans or Ordinary Men? A Reply to the Critics', in Berenbaum, Michael and Peck, Abraham J. (eds.), *The Holocaust and History: The Known, the Unknown, the Disputed, and the Reexamined*, United States Holocaust Memorial Museum, Indiana University Press, 1998, pp. 253–55 for Kershaw's reference to 'retreat into the private sphere' and 'widespread indifference and apathy toward Nazi Jewish policy', for Kulka's reference to SD reports in which there was an 'almost total absence of any

reference to the existence, persecution and extermination of the Jews – a kind of national conspiracy of silence', and for Bankier's noting that 'the more the news of mass murder filtered through, the less the public wanted to be involved in the final solution of the Jewish question'.

[13] See Longerich, *Holocaust*, op. cit., pp. 189, 190, 191, 204, 205, 206, 208 and 212. See also Longerich, Peter, *Heinrich Himmler: A Life*, Oxford University Press, 2012, p. 539 for reference to Himmler's extensive travelling through the Soviet Union between the end of July and the end of September or the beginning of October 1941, for Longerich's view that 'in all the territories where his Einsatzgruppen were operating the decisive impetus to move to more systematic murder of the Jewish civilian population came in every case from him personally', and for Longerich's reference to a conversation on 6 October 1943 in which Himmler said he could not justify sparing Jewish children given the risk of their perpetrating vengeance against Germans as adults, an indication of his endorsement of the murder of Jewish children in the east.

[14] See MacLean, French L., *The Field Men: The SS Officers Who Led the Einsatzkommandos – The Nazi Mobile Killing Units*, Schiffer Military History, 1999, pp. 36–130 for information on individual officers and for reference to commanders in Poland in 1939 many of whom had similar educational backgrounds. The percentages relating to educational attainment quoted are different to those found in MacLean on p. 132, because MacLean includes Einsatzkommandos in the earlier campaign in Poland and in the Balkans, for instance, and all officers rather than just commanders. MacLean uses the term 'Einsatzkommandos' to refer to both Einsatzkommandos and Sonderkommandos. See Fritz, Stephen G., *Ostkrieg: Hitler's War of Extermination in the East*, The University Press of Kentucky, 2011, for reference to the comment, in regard to the Einsatzgruppen, Einsatzkommando and Sonderkommando, that 'for the most part, the commanders of these units came from educated backgrounds, with academics, lawyers, economists, civil servants, an opera singer, and even a Protestant minister among them; three of the four Einsatzgruppen commanders, in fact, totalled four doctorates between them'. And see Bartov, Omer, *The Eastern Front, 1941–45, German Troops and the Barbarisation of Warfare*, Springer, 1986, p. 50, for reference to thirty-five per cent of Einsatzgruppen commanders' having held doctoral degrees.

[15] See Headland, Ronald, *Messages of Murder: A Study of the Reports of the Einsatzgruppen of the Security Police and the Security Service, 1941–1943*, Fairleigh Dickinson University Press, 1992, p. 25, for reference to many Einsatzgruppen and Einsatzkommando commanders having been in leadership roles in the Reich Security Main Office prior to being sent 'directly' to the east. Such roles would not have prepared them for mass murder of Jews in the east.

[16] See Bartov, *The Eastern Front*, op.cit., p. 50, for reference to historians' finding an 'enormous degree of support in German universities for the Nazis even before they came to power'.

[17] See Berghahn, Volker Rolf, and Lassig, Simone, *Biography between Structure and Agency: Central European Lives in International Historiography*, Berghahn Books, 2008, p. 173.

[18] See Earl, Hilary, *The Nuremberg SS-Einsatzgruppen Trial, 1945–1958: Atrocity, Law and History*, Cambridge University Press, 2009, pp. 101 and 297. Though it could be argued that the right-wing climate of German universities represented a form of 'moral reasoning', it was not one that Arendt would have recognised as such given her liberal democratic context and does not diminish the reality that the young men who were to become Einsatzgruppen, Einsatzkommando and Sonderkommando commanders who had experience of the nationalism of German universities in the interwar period did have a capacity for moral reasoning that training in the law would have cultivated. They would not then have been unreflective in the manner Arendt accuses Eichmann of being in *Eichmann in Jerusalem*.

[19] See ibid, pp. 106 and 201.

[20] See Berghahn and Lassig, *Biography between Structure and Agency*, op. cit., p. 168.

[21] See Browning, *The Origins of the Final Solution*, op.cit., pp. 225 and 226.

[22] See MacLean, *The Field Men*, op. cit., pp. 148 to 150, for reference to negative appraisals of Einsatzkommando commanders, indicating that such men were being assessed and would have known that was so.

[23] See H. Skipton Leonard, Rachel Lewis, Arthur M. Freedman and Jonathan Passmore (eds.), *The Wiley-Blackwell Handbook of the Psychology of Leadership, Change, and Organizational Development*, John Wiley & Sons, 2013, p. 249.

Chapter Nine

Discussion of the historiographical, experimental and historical evidence and an alternative explanation of Eichmann's behaviour

Though the evidence of Milgram, Zimbardo, Browning and the Einsatzgruppen commanders does no more than indicate the primacy of pursuit of personal interest in human behaviour, the inference is that it is probable that Eichmann, who seems from the evidence of the Israeli psychiatrist and psychologist above to have been normal, was motivated by a similar interest in optimising his own outcomes. It is acknowledged that such evidence does not on its own establish Eichmann's motives, but the argument here is that, with the more detailed historical evidence on his background and career presented above, the social psychological evidence indicates Eichmann's normality and lends credibility to the inference that the decisive influence on Eichmann's perpetrator behaviour was personal optimisation of outcomes in the form of careerist considerations and desire to secure or to maintain the approbation of his bosses and peers in the SS.

The argument here is that it was optimal for Eichmann to engage in perpetrator behaviour as an SS officer because the SS afforded him the order, belonging, elite identity, status, sense of participation in a major enterprise of the Nazi state and the major task of the SS, experience of power and influence that would have been alien to him before joining the SS and achieving status and rank as a Jewish expert, and the approbation of SS bosses and peers. It would have been similarly optimal for him to assimilate a vocabulary of eliminationist antisemitism once the task of eliminating the Jews of Europe had been assigned to the SS, so that he could maintain an SS identity and rank he found rewarding in material, social and psychological terms, enhance his reputation in the Nazi hierarchy and secure the approval of SS bosses such as Müller and Kaltenbrunner.

Fulbrook argues that totalitarian dictatorships and other forms of political regime should be understood not in terms of 'distinctive combinations of terror and obedience, or congruence of interests and commitment to ideology, or social backgrounds and personal motives' but in terms of 'how people adopted and learned how to play new roles; and how they developed the newly appropriate "manners of speaking and acting" required of them under the new circumstances'. Fulbrook, an expert on the GDR (the German Democratic Republic or East Germany), seems here to be indicating the primacy of human adaptation to changed reinforcement contingencies in behavioural responses to totalitarianism (and in fact to any political regime), which could only be to optimise personal outcomes (though she does not say so), and the assimilation of new vocabularies and behavioural norms to that end. Such commentary is of course relevant both to Eichmann's adopting an eliminationist antisemitic vocabulary and behavioural norms following the change of his role from expert in Jewish emigration to transporting Jews to extermination centres, and indicates that Eichmann's assimilation of the norms relating to his new role would have been normal.[1]

When on trial in Jerusalem Eichmann defended himself and his role by reference to obedience to orders, a form of 'agentic state' argument of no responsibility for having made the decision to annihilate the Jews of Europe and of having been no more than a functionary in the SS task of exterminating them, another indication of Eichmann's optimising his outcomes by various strategies.

Such a combination of natural, possibly inadvertent pursuit of personal interest and lack of concern for the welfare of others seems to be different only in context and outcome from the conformity to role requirements to optimise personal outcomes in ordinary life that is approved of and entirely normal in the competitive individualistic incentive societies of the liberal democratic west, not in process or motive. And in the more immediate context of Nazi Germany attributing self-interest and careerist motives to Eichmann would not single him out from the majority response to Nazi totalitarianism, which in the German population as a whole was compliance either of a minimal kind, in turning away to the private sphere, or one of opportunism, using the Nazi hierarchy to enhance career and personal outcomes (the relative numbers of those who minimally conformed and those who regarded Nazism as presenting opportunities are unknown).

The evidence of Gellately on the significant incidence of entirely voluntary denunciations to the Gestapo, many of which were anonymous, is indicative of opportunism rather than defensive pursuit of personal interest in the German population under Nazi rule, for Gellately found that the great majority of denunciations were motivated by 'selfish interests' and that denunciation for ideological motives was 'rare'.[2] And as has been seen above, Goldhagen has pointed out that a great many ordinary Germans would have had to have been involved in the extermination of the Jews in various capacities. Though such evidence on the ordinary German public does not on its own preclude Eichmann's having been motivated by eliminationist antisemitism in transporting Jews to extermination centres, not least given the greater indoctrination of SS personnel than of the ordinary German public in Nazi Germany, it does, taken with the other evidence on Eichmann, Milgram's and Zimbardo's participants, Browning's men and the Einsatzgruppen commanders presented above, indicate that the most plausible inference is that Eichmann's perpetrator behaviour resulted from careerism and desired social and psychological rewards derived from SS rank and membership rather than from eliminationist antisemitism as an autonomous influence, and that Eichmann was entirely normal in being so motivated.

The argument presented here is that Eichmann's self-interested motives are to be found in the majority of people in all cultures at all times and that they are the dominant influence on human behaviour. In another context Eichmann would have behaved differently to optimise his outcomes, and though that does attribute influence to the reinforcement contingencies of the Nazi state it does so only because of Eichmann's pursuit of optimal outcomes for himself and indifference to the consequences for others. Eichmann's apparent eliminationist antisemitism was then just part of his conformity in the SS and reflected pursuit of personal interest and indifference to others. What seems to be missing in attributions of Eichmann's perpetrator behaviour to eliminationist antisemitism is an appreciation of human motivation and its influence on behaviour and reaction to circumstance and context.

The evidence is that Eichmann was not an eliminationist antisemite when he was told that the decision had been made to exterminate the Jews, and it is implausible that he should by coincidence have become one just before or at exactly the same time as the shift in Nazi policy from Jewish emigration or expulsion to the east as slave labour to extermination of the Jews. The timing is relevant, because for eliminationist antisemitism to have been the decisive causal influence on Eichmann's role in the Holocaust Eichmann would have had to have embraced eliminationist antisemitism before he was directed to change policy towards the Jews to transportation to extermination centres or at the same time and independently of that change in role. And it would have to be established that it was Eichmann's eliminationist antisemitism rather than the change in the role requirements of Eichmann's SS career from arranging Jewish emigration to transportation to extermination centres that resulted in his compliance with the role requirements of his new task.

Eichmann's past both before joining the SS and in his earlier SS career as a Jewish specialist content in arranging for Jewish emigration indicates that Eichmann's actions in the war are not explained by reference to eliminationist antisemitism and that Eichmann would have with the same efficiency and lack of moral reservation transported Soviet POWs, partisans and Bolsheviks to extermination centres had that become his job in the SS. The evidence indicates that Eichmann's behaviour in the war reflected his desire to be approved of by the senior echelons of the SS, to retain his elite SS identity, status and privilege and to preserve the sense of belonging, purpose and power the SS gave him, and that eliminationist antisemitic behaviour and expressions followed as a consequence and represent a form of conformity and identification with the code and task of the SS because of the psychological, social and material rewards of SS membership and rank to Eichmann. Eichmann could have remained indifferent to what happened to the Jews throughout, or he could have assimilated eliminationist antisemitism when it became expedient for him to do so to maintain his position in the SS hierarchy or to avoid the consequences of dissenting for him. In either case Eichmann would have been acting to enhance or protect his own material, social and psychological interests, with ideological commitment either never present or a means to that end.

The case being made here is that Eichmann's banality and ordinariness were of motive, and his attitude towards the Jews seems to have been one of indifference, which would mean that it would not have had to have altered to diminish dissonance with behaviour undertaken to optimise his personal outcomes in material, social and psychological terms. Arendt's emphasis on conceptualisation of moral choice does not seem to be part of ordinary experience, for much of human behaviour appears to be in the nature of inadvertent pursuit of personal interest at the expense of others to whom people are indifferent, with attitude change to reduce dissonance between conforming, optimising behaviour and attitude taking place without any deliberation or awareness on the part of the individual concerned where such attitude change is in fact needed.

The nature of Eichmann's identification with his role as an SS officer of some rank and status has been alluded to above in reference to the work of Haslam and Reicher on 'identity leadership' and 'engaged followership', which they presented as the cause of the perpetrator behaviour in Milgram's experiments and in the Zimbardo Stanford Prison Experiment, an explanation that has been rejected here because it is inconsistent with the evidence of the behaviour of participants in the Milgram experiments and the Stanford Prison Experiment. For it has been commented that Haslam and Reicher do not refer to two, quite different forms of identification, one being their 'engaged followership', which is similar to ideological conviction in, for instance, eliminationist antisemitism, and the other being motivated to secure and retain a desired identity because of its privileges, status and power but without any ideological conviction and with ideological attitudes being affected to maintain the desired identity and status. This latter is the nature of Eichmann's attachment to his SS rank and identity, one indicated by optimisation of personal outcomes and by Eichmann's own desire for belonging, for an elite identity, and for authority figures he would obey and who would remove from him any need to make autonomous decisions or to accept responsibility for them.

Arendt claims Eichmann was banal in that he failed to see the moral choice presented to him, without reference to the fact that perception is a motivated activity and that Eichmann conceived of the Jewish question in the manner optimal to his maintaining his SS career, identity and reputation. It does seem that Arendt is right in one respect, that is that Eichmann was ordinary in personality, though his ordinariness seems to have been of motive in putting himself and his interests first and regardless of cost to other people against whom he initially had nothing apart from the general European antisemitism of the time, not of the lack of understanding of the consequences of his actions or the lack of capacity for moral reasoning to which Arendt refers.

Arendt observes that Eichmann would have preferred 'to be hanged as Obersturmbannführer' than to have lived out his life 'quietly and normally as a traveling salesman', an indication that even Arendt understood that Eichmann was motivated by the status and elite identity of SS membership and rank, though were Arendt's statement to be literally true Eichmann would have surrendered himself to be tried for war crimes at Nuremberg. Eichmann's own reflection after the war ended in 1945 that he would have 'a leaderless and difficult individual life, I would receive no directives from anybody, no orders and commands would any longer be issued to me, no pertinent ordinances would be there to consult' is indicative in its tone of regret and loss of Eichmann's own appreciation of his need for belonging to an organisation the leadership of which decided upon ultimate purpose and for an identity supported and reaffirmed by a hierarchy like that of the SS, quite apart from the social status and privilege of elite SS membership.[3] Of course membership, belonging and identity that were not elite and were without privilege and social status would have been much less attractive regardless of Eichmann's need for external authority, identity and purpose.

The most compelling evidence of eliminationist antisemitism in Eichmann is, as has been seen, in his continuing to transport Jews from Hungary to Auschwitz in defiance of an order from Himmler to stop the transports, and in what he said in the Sassen interviews. Both have been contextualised and the inference drawn has been that they are to be explained by Eichmann's attachment to his SS identity and to the task given him with Hitler's authority, and to Eichmann's susceptibility to the most proximate audience in the form of Müller and Kaltenbrunner in the SS in Hungary and Sassen and other Nazis in Argentina. Any eliminationist antisemitic action or expression of views then seems to reflect Eichmann's attachment to his SS identity and desire for the approval of bosses or those he considered to be Nazi peers rather than eliminationist antisemitism's being a cause of Eichmann's participation in the destruction of the Jews.

The difference between Cesarani and Arendt is that she does not believe that Eichmann's treatment of the Jews and involvement in their transportation to extermination centres is explained by eliminationist antisemitism at any stage, for she claims that Eichmann's perpetrator behaviour is explained by lack of capacity for moral reasoning and lack of appreciation of the consequences of his actions for the Jews. She does not seem to appreciate the centrality of motivation in human behaviour and ignores the evidence of Eichmann's visits to extermination centres that prove that he knew very well what the consequences of his work were for the Jews he was transporting.

Cesarani notes 'it is not necessary to be abnormal to become a practitioner of genocide', and as has been seen seems to endorse the view that Eichmann 'adopted anti-Semitism as a career' and that 'he was not personally anti-Semitic'.[4] That is very similar to the case being made here, in fact, that Eichmann was motivated by pursuit of personal interest in his role in the destruction of Europe's Jews, though Cesarani does not seem to conclude that the decisive cause of Eichmann's eliminationist antisemitic behaviour and utterances after 'physical annihilation' became part of Nazi racial policy was Eichmann's pursuit of his SS career and cultivation of approval from his bosses in the SS and the SS identity he seems to have found so rewarding given its prestige in Nazi Germany. That may be because Cesarani's meticulous tracing of Eichmann's background, career and 'radicalization' as he moved from expertise on Jewish emigration to deportation to ghettoes and from there to transportation to extermination centres results in a concentration on the attitudinal context rather than on motive.

Eichmann seems to have been an individual for whom belonging and membership, and approval and regard it seems especially from bosses, mattered a great deal, and that would have meant that for him membership of and relatively senior rank in the elite SS would have had psychological benefits in addition to those of enhanced social status and power. The attachment to the SS and to the Führerprinzip does then seem for Eichmann to reflect optimisation of outcomes in the form of avoidance of the low economic and social status, lack of involvement and influence, and social isolation that Eichmann seems to have abhorred, and avoidance too of responsibility for difficult decisions. In other words, Eichmann's eliminationist antisemitic rhetoric and actions did not reflect an autonomous eliminationist antisemitism in Eichmann, for his attitude to the Jews seems to have remained throughout one of indifference, and the motive was to secure the approbation of his peers and bosses in the SS, in part to maintain the status of SS membership and rank.

Eichmann then optimised his returns in much the same manner that human beings in general do, regardless of the cost to other people, and that was the nature of his banality and normality. Moral reflection of the sort alluded to by Arendt would have made no difference to his primary motivation to optimise his own outcomes in his behaviour, and his lack of reflection or concern even given his firsthand knowledge of the genocidal consequences of his transportation of Jews to extermination centres was itself indicative of there being no incentive for such reflection or concern. That is what makes Eichmann so little different from the majority in the middle of the normal distribution of human traits, for the evidence in the communist east is that people in general respond to totalitarianism by manipulating the reinforcement contingencies to optimise their outcomes, often at the expense of associates and intimates. And the legitimacy in the liberal democratic west of economic and social inequality seems indicative of a general acceptance of a need for individual material incentives to optimise economic prosperity through competitiveness between individuals, and of an acceptance that individuals pursue their own interests and compete with each other in economic and social life.

To elaborate on Eichmann's 'normality' or 'banality' further, it is possible that Eichmann should be located, within the population of entirely ordinary individuals who conform to optimise their outcomes and who constitute the great majority of any human population, at the maximising or opportunistic end rather than at the satisficing or minimally conforming end, where conformity is less for personal advantage than to avoid punishment or loss of the status quo. Eichmann is then seen to be entirely 'normal' in the maximising part of the conforming population that constitutes the great majority of human responses, though not at the extreme end, in that minority of ideologically motivated zealots who embraced Nazism before it offered any material or social advantages. Of course it is possible to argue that Eichmann in adapting to the change in his role from Jewish expert concentrating on Jewish emigration to transportation of Jews to extermination centres was safeguarding his SS career rather than advancing it and that he was attempting to retain rather than enhance his reputation with his SS bosses and peers, a more defensive rather than opportunistic form of conformity.

Arendt chose to concentrate on the existence of and capacity for moral choice rather than what is natural for the great majority of people, and seems to have disregarded the motive to pursue reward and avoid punishment that is part of human nature, and its consequences for perception and behaviour. For even perception is a motivated activity. What links the much replicated Milgram experiments that found an astonishing incidence of obedience to immoral commands and the finding of

Browning's research that ordinary men were prepared to murder Jewish men, women and children on arrival in Poland despite having had no specific Nazi indoctrination is the dominant influence of self-interest on human behaviour and the fact that a small perceived cost to the self is more influential on behaviour than a massive cost to someone else against whom nothing specific is known. Eichmann's reaction to his assignments is in such a context, and that of the Einsatzgruppen, ordinary, what most people would do to avoid being seen to have failed, to avoid demotion and the obloquy of failure, or to secure the good regard of peers and bosses and a valued identity in the elite SS.

Eichmann's claimed lack of reflectiveness is in fact to be attributed not to the banality Arendt refers to but to a lack of motivation to engage in such reflection regarding the consequences of his involvement for the Jews and to indifference. For Eichmann did reflect on his task of transporting the Jews to extermination centres to optimise the efficiency and comprehensiveness of the transportations because of the incentive to impress his bosses and enhance his reputation in the SS.

Eichmann does seem to have had a number of forms of authority that served to legitimise or normalise his part in the annihilation of the Jews. There was to begin with the authority of the Nazi hierarchy of which he was a part, there was the authority of Nazi racial ideology, there was the authority of the SS code of discipline and compliance with orders, and there was the authority of universality in Nazi Germany, where opposition was almost unknown and regarded as treachery to the German race and state in a context of ideologically defined racial and political enemies (in the association of Jews and Bolsheviks), and of an even greater universality in the SS, where long chains of command implicated everyone at Eichmann's level and above in the Holocaust.

There was also the authority of normality, the authority of the process, of task, of role, of dehumanised Jews in great numbers (the result of Nazi persecution, ghettoisation, theft, starvation and disease over many months), and the contextual authority of a background of no tradition of individual rights of the sort guaranteed in liberal democratic societies. Such a context facilitated compliance driven by optimisation of outcomes in material, social and psychological terms for Eichmann and would have meant that even conceiving of declining to endorse the shift from a policy of emigration for Jews to one of ghettoisation and slave labour in the east and then to extermination would have been difficult. And of course Eichmann would have had no motive to consider such resistance.

The inadvertent as well as deliberate optimisation of outcomes is a characteristic of normal human behaviour in all societies, including those in the liberal democratic west, in which there is a tradition of individual rights and freedoms, and as has been seen in such societies individualistic competitiveness, that is, pursuit of personal interest at the expense of others, is normative, part of the incentive society. Though such optimisation of outcomes may be primarily material, in terms of affluence and lifestyle, there is also optimisation of status, a zero sum attribute implying relative well-being and competition with others within one's social horizon, to which career is for the majority of people central, and of psychological outcomes such as belonging, legitimised purpose and involvement, as in the assimilation of corporate 'values' by zealots or even ordinary employees, for it is expedient, in fact optimal, to embrace such 'values'. Human drives from natural selection and the influence of societal norms that enhance the effect of genetic inheritance do then reinforce each other in the thriving incentive societies of the capitalist west, whereas in the failing economies of the communist east of the Cold War period human drives for personal optimisation of outcomes were dissonant with communist appeals to the common good and there were no individual material incentives. As in the west, the people of the communist east optimised their outcomes by minimal conformity or opportunism.

Any challenge to societal norms and conventions requires a motive, and given that in ordinary life there is a compelling motive to conform in terms of behaviour and attitude, and to refrain from non-conformist behaviour and attitudes, to optimise personal outcomes, there is no motive to engage in moral or other reflection on the definition of morality as it has been defined by the state or normality, and the state or normative definition of what is worthwhile and what is reproved seems likely to be accepted without reflection. That is an attribute of free and totalitarian societies because it seems to be a characteristic of the great majority of human beings, with a very small minority of people reflecting upon or rejecting conformity in an overt manner and prepared to suffer the consequences. What does seem to have happened in the communist east is not reflection upon the morality of the ideological exhortation of the state but rather compliance with its dictates to avoid sanctions whilst optimising personal outcomes through individualistic opportunism either within the confines of the communist state, through denunciations or slavish political orthodoxy, for instance, or by covert attempts to optimise personal outcomes, for instance in the extra effort devoted to private plots in communist Poland, from which only the individual benefited. Even in the latter case and in the great majority of similar cases the process seems to have been unreflective and to have been predicated upon genetic inheritance of a drive to optimise personal experience.

In such a context Eichmann's attitudes to the Führerprinzip and to the oath of loyalty of the SS, and compliant behaviour, do seem a normal response, not least given their correlation with privilege, status, power and elite identity. In fact the Führerprinzip does seem functionally similar to Milgram's 'agentic state' in being optimal for perpetrators, for it facilitates avoidance of the adverse material, social and psychological consequences of defiance of immoral authority and at the same time absolves the perpetrator from any responsibility for perpetrator behaviour both in terms of liability and adverse consequences and in terms of some sense of responsibility that could trouble the perpetrator.

Eichmann acted in a manner that indicated that his own efficient accomplishment of a set task as an SS officer was his sole concern, and that given that Hitler had decided that the Jews were a racial and political threat to the German race and state and should be exterminated, that was not Eichmann's responsibility. In fact, Eichmann seems to have felt that his role was to follow the dictates of the Führerprinzip, obey and do whatever was given to him as a duty, though that did of course optimise Eichmann's outcomes in material, social and psychological terms as a member of the elite SS of some rank and involvement, power and prerogatives.

There is the possibility of some influence on Eichmann's compliance with the changed requirements of his role in the SS from his immediate context, for Eichmann joined the SS and then the SD without any trace of eliminationist antisemitism and then moved from arranging the emigration of Jews to deporting them to the east and then to transporting them to their extermination in the camps of the east. For it is difficult to imagine how Eichmann would have declined to participate in the altered policy towards the Jews given the hierarchy and code of the SS and the apparent legitimacy of the order from Hitler and Himmler to Heydrich, not least when everyone else at Wannsee seemed to be altogether compliant despite the nature of the change of policy towards the Jews, including Eichmann's boss, Müller, and when there was no trace of dissent or reluctance from any of Eichmann's bosses or peers within the SS.

Given Eichmann's desire to belong, to be accepted and to maintain the approval of bosses in the SS and his elite SS identity, and his sense of Hitler as the ultimate arbiter and the person responsible for policy in the Third Reich, Eichmann's compliance seems to be the consequence of a normal process of adaptation to optimise returns to the self. Just how Eichmann or most entirely normal people would have declined to continue to do as ordered in a totalitarian military hierarchy in time of war and in an SS culture of universal compliance is difficult to imagine. For he would have either had to challenge the authoritarian and ruthless Heydrich or his immediate bosses in the SS, Müller and Kaltenbrunner, or to plead that he did not have the 'character' for participation in the task assigned to the SS even as a 'desk murderer', which would have been very punishing for Eichmann given his desire for approval and involvement, for elite status and identity in the SS. Given the compliance found in Milgram's participants, where there were no real-life consequences, the compliance of perpetrators like Eichmann seems unsurprising.

As a context, the record of most totalitarian societies is of minimal or no resistance to the dictates of the state, and especially not from functionaries of that state. Eichmann's reaction of continued compliance when his role changed dramatically would then seem normal given the circumstances. And as has been seen above, the Einsatzgruppen commanders had been compliant in the radical change of their role to the eradication of Jews.

In the case of Eichmann the decision to exterminate the Jews was one made above him and he was in fact a mere functionary though an agent of the destruction of the Jews for whom he arranged transportation to extermination centres. During the war he seems to have exulted in the role and its importance to the annihilation of the Jews as part of the SS objective and SS identity, though after the war in Jerusalem he did resort to the defence of not being responsible for the decision to murder the Jews and of being the recipient of orders in a military hierarchy in time of war. Had he been assigned a different task with or without ideological justification he would have conformed to the role requirements in a similar way.

The argument here has been that Eichmann's role in the transportation of Jews to extermination centres is explained by his pursuit of personal interest at the expense of the Jews of Europe, that is, a placing of his own interests before those of others that is normal for people in general and especially for maximisers, who are opportunistic in optimising their outcomes, as opposed to satisficers, who aspire to less and attempt to avoid loss rather than to compete for status, though even the latter would in Eichmann's situation have been motivated to protect their status.

Notes

[1] See Fulbrook, Mary, *Dissonant Lives: Generations and Violence through the German Dictatorships*, OUP, 2011, p. 98.

[2] See Gellately, Robert, *Backing Hitler: Consent and Coercion in Nazi Germany*, OUP, 2002.

[3] See Arendt, *Eichmann in Jerusalem*, op. cit., pp. 34 and 32.

[4] See Cesarani, *Eichmann*, op.cit., pp. 17 and 360.

Chapter Ten
Conclusion

Arendt's intellectual conceit and disdain for Eichmann resulted in her judging him by the standards of a liberal moral and intellectual elite of which she conceived herself to be a member. Using the concepts of social philosophy to explain Eichmann's perpetrator behaviour, she seems to have been unsighted by her intellectual, moral and class arrogance in relation to Eichmann.[1]

Arendt seems not to have understood that most people do not conceive of issues in a reflective way to assess the moral choices inherent in them because there is no incentive for them to do so. Nor does she seem to have any appreciation of the decisive role of motivation and of pursuit of personal interest at the expense of others in normal human behaviour, of the fact that pursuit of personal interest is often unreflective, of the reality that perception is itself a motivated activity and that people do not attend to what they do not want to experience, and that following changes to behaviour to optimise outcomes attitudes may change to remain consonant with new behaviour if there is dissonance, that is, to optimise psychological outcomes. In such a context of research on human motivation evidence of eliminationist antisemitism in Eichmann's utterances and actions after a certain date seems to reflect his having assimilated the SS vocabulary of genocide to maintain the good regard of his peers and bosses in the SS and to retain his elite SS identity and rank as well as involvement in the major task assigned to the senior echelons of the SS, not least as before it became the elimination of the Jews Eichmann had pursued Jewish emigration with similar fervour. Arendt's intellectual conceit did in fact extend beyond Eichmann to disparagement and dismissal of psychiatry and psychology as means of understanding human behaviour, an extraordinary arrogance that resulted in her lack of appreciation of the primary role of human motivation in human attitudes, cognition and behaviour, including Eichmann's.[2] For Eichmann had a capacity for consideration of matters that concerned his own welfare, as in his presentation of self before different audiences, which indicates concern for consequences for himself. Eichmann participated in the Holocaust because involvement optimised material, social and psychological outcomes for him, not because he could not reason through the consequences.

Eichmann's banality was then one not of lack of moral reasoning or understanding of the consequences of his actions but of pursuit of personal interest regardless of cost to other people. It was not the case that had Eichmann engaged in moral reasoning or had greater understanding of the consequences of his actions he would not have done what he did as part of the process of extermination of the Jews of Europe, for his own psychological, social and material interests would have remained the decisive influence on his behaviour. Eichmann's lack of moral reasoning did in fact reflect his optimisation of outcomes and indifference to the adverse consequences for others, and, as has been seen, Eichmann was aware of the consequences for the Jews of his arranging for them to be transported to what he knew were extermination centres. And, given the primacy of self-interest as a motive in human behaviour, had Arendt been in Eichmann's position she could have done just what he did, despite the moral reasoning from which she judges Eichmann.

Cesarani's assessment of Eichmann seems more compelling, in that he acknowledges the lack of evidence of anything more than cultural antisemitism in Eichmann's background and the evidence of pursuit of personal interest and careerism in Eichmann in a meticulous consideration of Eichmann's background and career as an SS officer, though he does not seem to conclude that it was just such optimisation of outcomes that explains Eichmann's having assimilated an eliminationist antisemitism rhetoric when extermination of the Jews of the occupied territories became Nazi policy and an SS objective. For Eichmann never had an ideological conviction that the Jews should be exterminated but rather an identity as an SS officer of some seniority of rank that he identified with and sought to retain by his perpetrator behaviour, an instrumental orientation to his role as an SS officer for the privileges and status it conferred upon him.

Eichmann's perpetrator behaviour is then not explained by reference to a lack of capacity for moral reasoning (Arendt's explanation), by obedience to orders despite moral anguish and out of powerlessness (Eichmann's explanation in his memoir and the nature of the defence at Eichmann's trial in Jerusalem) or by eliminationist antisemitism (Stangneth's and Cesarani's attribution). On the contrary, Eichmann transported Jews to extermination centres to optimise his material, social and psychological outcomes regardless of the cost to the Jews he transported, to whom he seems to have been entirely indifferent.

Eichmann does seem to have been normal in terms of motivation, for most people pursue personal optimisation of outcome at the expense of others, and many are opportunists like Eichmann. What was different in the Eichmann case was context and outcome, not process and motive. It is possible that Eichmann had a greater desire than most people for belonging, elite identity, approval, involvement and power, though many maximisers have similar drives.

Notes
[1] See Arendt, *Eichmann in Jerusalem*, op. cit., pp. 48 and 49. And see pp. 54 and 55 for Arendt's reference to Eichmann's not being a monster, though he could be a 'clown', and for Eichmann's taking the high moral ground in reference to having sworn an oath.
[2] See Brunner, *Eichmann's Mind*, op. cit., p. 444.

Post-war Justice for Nazi War Criminals

War Criminals

Context, Culpability and Legitimacy

Introduction

The nature and extent of the post-war justice meted out to Nazi perpetrators has been debated, but a consensus has emerged in the liberal democratic west that the punishment of Nazi perpetrators has been wholly inadequate. One enduring issue is semantic, the definition of perpetrator behaviour and complicity. This issue is associated with that of appreciation of the experiential context of those who committed perpetrator behaviour in the Third Reich. Another issue has been the proper function of post-war trials, their objectives, standards of proof for conviction and the legitimacy of the 'justice' that has emerged. The case argued here is that liberal democratic bias has interfered with impartial appreciation of the influence of experiential context on Nazi perpetrators and has imposed on behaviour in the Third Reich expectations of behaviour derived from peacetime in modern western liberal democratic societies, where the consequences for non- conformity are far less adverse than those believed to have been the case in Nazi Germany. Applying a moral liberal democratic and humanitarian standard to behaviour in the Third Reich does not, it is argued, have any psychological legitimacy because it does not reflect the reality that in all societies and cultures at all times people optimise their outcomes by conformity that is either minimal, to avoid sanctions, or opportunistic, to take optimal advantage of the possibilities of their situation. This conformity is seen in the great majority of cases as being not deliberative and calculated but rather inadvertent and unreflective, that is, it is argued that people in all societies and cultures act in ways that optimise their outcomes and in particular avoid adverse consequences such as sanctions whether formal, from the state, or informal, from the peer group, without rational assessment of choices and their respective consequences, and that this tendency reflects evolutionary selection of those who adapt to changing circumstances by such optimisation of personal outcomes. There is also reference to the decisive influence of the experiential context on human behaviour, for it is perception rather than reality that dictates human behaviour, and there is consideration of the relationship between concepts of ascribed culpability and views regarding the legitimacy of post-war 'justice'. The work does then address the influence of various perspectives on conceptualisations of post-war justice.

The first chapter is an overview of the context of post-war West Germany and its effect on the West German public's perception of the validity of the post-war trials, and addresses the influence of German and Allied optimisation of outcomes in the aftermath of the war on attributed complicity and criminality, the nature of justice for perpetrator behaviour and the appropriate function of courts. The focus here is on West Germany, for which there is so much more evidence than for East Germany, though there is reference to the East German policy on Nazi perpetrators. A number of perspectives are considered, not least that of Mary Fulbrook, in her monumental study of post-war justice, *Reckonings*, but also the views of other historians the great majority of whom share Fulbrook's liberal democratic humanitarian perspective and insistence upon individual responsibility for perpetrator behaviour.

The following chapters address specific instances of perpetrator behaviour and reflect those for which there is sufficient evidence to form a considered view. These are the cases of perpetrators who survived the end of the war and underwent some form of psychological assessment and trial, for they permit some appraisal of the motivations, perceptions and experience of the perpetrators concerned, the arguments presented in their defence and the court's treatment of the defence cases. The second chapter is concerned with the particular case of the trial of the Einsatzgruppen commanders, the nature of their defences and their psychological legitimacy. The Einsatzgruppen commanders were tried before a US Military Tribunal, as were many other specific groups of alleged Nazi perpetrators following the Nuremberg Tribunal, and the approach of the court to legal procedure, admissible evidence and standards of proof reflected the difference between its practices and those under West German criminal law.

The third chapter deals with the case of an individual Nazi perpetrator, Rudolf Höss, the commandant of Auschwitz, who was tried before a court in Warsaw, in Poland, under communist rule and whose trial was then influenced by Soviet preferences and Stalin's agenda in Eastern Europe, having given evidence to the Nuremberg trial of the major Nazi war criminals, and is compared to the case of Adolf Eichmann, who arranged the transportation of Jews to extermination camps, who was abducted from post-war refuge in Argentina and who was then tried before an Israeli court in Jerusalem. The focus in this chapter is on the nature of Höss's personality and perpetrator behaviour, on the experiential context for it, compared to Eichmann's personality, motives and experiential context, and on the evidence of the court proceedings against Eichmann in Jerusalem. In both cases the concepts of 'justice' and legality may be seen to reflect the agenda of the power conducting the trials.

The fourth chapter addresses the evidence of Gitta Sereny on Franz Stangl, the commandant at two extermination camps, Sobibor and Treblinka, and Albert Speer, the Nazi armaments minister. Sereny's consideration of the nature of their responsibility, guilt and experience is an implicit commentary on the post-war justice they received, for judgments regarding the nature of perpetrators' responsibility, guilt and experience are inextricably linked with conceptualisations of justice, as are the perspectives of commentators such as Sereny.

Sereny's work is an indication of the decisive influence on judgments of Nazi perpetrators of inadvertent but distorting bias not just from a post-war liberal democratic humanitarian perspective but also from attachment to a certain psychological theory, in this case psychoanalysis, which presumes the existence of conscience, and of the accompanying influence of a certain objective, in this case cultivation of a therapeutic and revelatory encounter. It is also indicative of the influence of the commentator's sense of self on the judgement made of the responsibility, guilt and experience of former Nazis, in Sereny's over-confidence in her own ability to psychoanalyse and so understand Stangl and Speer and in her assumption of intellectual and moral superiority over Stangl and moral superiority over Speer. Sereny's judgment of the post-war justice meted out to Stangl and Speer reflects her emphasis on individual responsibility for behaviour, a liberal concept that disregards the experiential context and psychological experience of Nazi perpetrators. The influence of Sereny's books on Stangl and Speer, based on her interviews of both men and correspondence with Speer, is indicative of the reliance on rare sources for information relevant to the motives and perceptions of individual Nazi perpetrators.

Chapter One

Post-war justice. The case of Nazi war criminals in the Federal Republic of Germany (West Germany)

At the Nuremberg International Military Tribunal there were just twenty-one defendants, representing the most senior echelon of surviving Nazis (Hitler, Goebbels, Himmler and Ley having taken their own lives and Bormann missing). At this trial of major Nazi war criminals and at ensuing trials conducted at Nuremberg by US military courts, of 'industrialists, lawyers, bureaucrats – as well as the military, the SS, and the Einsatzgruppen',[1] the nature of the 'justice' meted out was exemplary in nature, the object apparently being to demonstrate that those who commit war crimes would be punished and so to deter war crimes and crimes against humanity. There seems also to have been an intention in these post-war trials of Nazis to express general and profound disgust at the crimes against humanity committed by the Nazis and to give effect to a natural desire for retribution for them.

Mary Fulbrook has though pointed to the singular lack of enthusiasm in the Federal Republic of Germany (hereafter referred to as West Germany) for the prosecution of Nazi war criminals and those complicit in the perpetrator behaviour of the Nazi regime, especially for those of some occupational and social status, and to the very low numbers of investigations undertaken, the even fewer prosecutions and convictions, and West German influence on the leniency indicated by reductions in the sentences imposed by US military trials in West Germany, despite West Germany's having cultivated a reputation for addressing Nazi war crimes, which Fulbrook claims is undeserved.

In a scathing indictment of West Germany's record in punishing Nazi perpetrators, Fulbrook notes that 'perhaps two hundred thousand people, and possibly closer to a million, were at one point or another actively involved in killing Jewish civilians. And the ranks of those that made this possible were far wider.'[2] This extraordinary range of possible active perpetrators and Fulbrook's reference to many more Germans involved less actively in the Holocaust do raise doubts regarding the definition of Nazi perpetrator that appear to remain unresolved in Fulbrook's *Reckonings*, the result of which is that it is difficult to assess in exact terms the numerical relationship between those she claims were Nazi perpetrators and those who were after the war punished for their perpetrator behaviour. What is apparent is that very few Nazi perpetrators were punished.

Another question is of course adequacy of punishment for various types of perpetrator behaviour. Fulbrook claims that in West Germany and United Germany between 1946 and 2005 36,393 cases involving 140,000 individuals resulted in a mere 6,656 convictions and 5,184 acquittals, with just 16 death sentences and 166 sentences to life imprisonment, many of which were not served in their entirety.[3] She continues, 'the vast majority of sentences – just under 5,000 (4,993) – were relatively lenient, with terms of imprisonment up to two years', and 'of those perpetrators actually brought to court in the Federal Republic of Germany before the end of the twentieth century, only 164 individuals were eventually sentenced as perpetrators of murder, rather than for lesser crimes. In view of the hundreds of thousands of individuals who had been involved in the making of mass murder and the six million people who had died in what we now call the Holocaust, 164 convictions for murder is not an impressive total.'[4] McKale endorses Fulbrook's view, quoting with apparent approval Hilberg's assessment—

'For the great bulk of perpetrators', the acclaimed historian Raul Hilberg wrote in his monumental history of the Holocaust, 'most were simply by-passed (by the Allied and later German authorities). By the law they had not lived. By the law they did not die.'

Hilberg's claim that the great majority of Nazi perpetrators were not punished is not disputed, but his claim that Nazi perpetrators had lived outside the law is manifestly untrue, for the law in any country is a reflection of political power, a truth indicated by Hans Frank's references to Nazi law's being in the service of the racial Volksgemeinschaft, and for Germans the wartime experiential context was one in which Nazi ideology was central in all aspects of life and dominated by the Führerprinzip, under which the preferences of the Führer had the legitimacy of the law and were supported by sanctions such as incarceration in a concentration camp before the war and belief in the existence of even more punitive sanctions during the war. In other words Nazi perpetrators and others complicit in Nazi perpetrator behaviour were acting in compliance with Nazi law, not outside it except in the very small minority of cases of sadistic treatment of Jews and other camp inmates not required by their roles as camp guards. It is of course possible that Hilberg was referring to some concept of international, natural or religious law that forbade the perpetrator behaviour legitimised by Nazi law reflective of Nazi ideology and totalitarianism, but any law outside that of Nazi Germany would have been irrelevant to the experiential context of Nazi ideology, state power, legality and punitive sanctions of ordinary Germans in the Third Reich and so to any characterisation of German perpetrator behaviour and complicity in the Holocaust.[5]

McKale also claims that 'the overwhelming majority of perpetrators acted after the war with impunity, and enjoyed post-war lives of comfort, free of consequences or guilt'.[6] The reference to post-war impunity is the lack of West German and Allied desire to identify and prosecute Nazi war criminals. The reference to Nazi perpetrators' freedom from guilt is indicative of the influence of the experiential context of ordinary Germans in the Third Reich on their lack of guilt and responsibility for their part in the Holocaust and other Nazi perpetrator behaviour.

That is of course an expedient attribution for Nazi perpetrators, and is consistent with the case being argued here that human behaviour reflects human motivation to optimise personal material, social and psychological outcomes, in this case psychological ones, by adapting to the circumstances facing them.

Even so, it does not follow from Nazi perpetrators' ascribing their perpetrator behaviour or complicity to the totalitarianism of Nazi Germany that the attribution is not genuine, for it is possible for an attribution to be both expedient and true. Nor does it indicate that ordinary Germans were different to what other people would have done in their position, for there is no known instance of popular resistance to totalitarianism and the dictates of totalitarian power. In the Soviet Union the end of the Stalinist period and the denunciation of Stalin and Stalinism in the Khrushchev thaw, during which the NKVD was diminished in numbers, influence and power, did not result in any trials of those responsible for denunciations, arrests, interrogations, prosecutions, sentences and conditions in the labour camps under Stalin, and the Soviet people do not appear to have expected any such accounting for collaboration at the expense of others to take place. On the contrary, various forms of collaboration were expected and accepted.[7] The indication is that post-war justice is an instrument of policy for the victors and serves their ends in being adjusted to ensure it is expedient when circumstances change, as in the emerging context of the Cold War in Europe.

Fulbrook points to the difference between the justice meted out by the Nuremberg trials of major Nazi war criminals, which addressed criminality through ideas of complicity and 'collective responsibility', and that of West German courts under the 'ordinary criminal charge of murder', in which 'personal brutality' and 'subjective mentality' were considered and which do seem to have required behaviour that indicated exceeding the requirements of one's role, and criminal intent, neither of which were considerations in the Nuremberg trials. Fulbrook also notes the West German public's view of the Nuremberg trials, despite Allied pressure on the press to endorse it, claiming that 'most people seemed to have simply lost interest' and quoting the view that 'by far the greatest majority' felt that it was unjust that German war crimes should be prosecuted whilst Allied war crimes, such as the bombing of Dresden, were not, and correspondingly unjust that those below the leadership who were doing no more than meeting the requirements of their roles should be indicted. Fulbrook claims that 'vested political and economic interests ensured that some areas received greater prominence and attention, while others were quietly excluded from the spotlight'.[8]

Fulbrook notes the criticality of the 'West German legal system', a reference to the German Penal Code, for the prosecution of Nazi perpetrators in West Germany, for its terms stipulated that 'justice should not be retroactive, that people should not be tried for acts that, at the time they committed them, had not actually been criminal – one of the major criticisms of the Nuremberg trials'. She continues, 'in practice, the West German legal system proved problematic. It meant using the charge of murder,' and 'to prove someone guilty of murder (Mord) or the lesser charge of "aiding and abetting" murder (Beihilfe zum Mord) rather than merely manslaughter (Totschlag), meant fulfilling exacting requirements regarding subjective states of mind,' and 'the accused must have personally taken the initiative rather than merely followed orders; acted for "base motives" (niedrige Beweggründe) with particular sadism, cruelty or ferocity, as an "excess perpetrator" (Exzesstäter); and have been aware of wrongdoing at the time.' Fulbrook notes that defences could then refer to defendants' 'subjectivities and include arguments that the defendant had "killed only on orders", that there was "no sadism or personal pleasure" involved, that there was "reluctance to kill", that the defendant was "unaware that the act was unlawful" or, if aware of the illegality of the act, afraid that disobeying an order would result in adverse consequences.' The result was that most defendants were charged with being 'accomplices', and Fulbrook notes that sixty-one per cent of defendants in the 1960s were charged only with being 'accessories to murder' and received lenient sentences of between three and five years, with thirty-one per cent receiving between six and ten years, which Fulbrook regards as wholly inadequate, not least in the case of defendants from the Belzec extermination camp, who she claims 'had killed thousands of innocent people' but 'could, under West German law, be found not guilty by claiming that they were only following orders'.[9] Fulbrook's reference to individuals' having killed innocent Jews is in fact inaccurate, for the process was one in which the terrible work was broken down into parts, so that no one was personally responsible. Fulbrook's reference here does seem indicative of the distortion that results from a liberal humanitarian narrative and emotional outrage rather than one informed by psychological realities.

Fulbrook concludes that 'legal systems, political considerations and social practices that were simply not up to the task of dealing with state-sponsored acts of violence on the scale committed by the Nazis' were responsible for the lack of post-war justice and that 'in effect, if not in intention, West German law condoned obedience to a deadly regime and condemned only those who had individually stepped beyond Nazism's already murderous limits'.[10] Fulbrook claims that the effect of German criminal law in exonerating Nazi perpetrators by a defence of 'following orders' was enhanced by a context of bias Fulbrook sees as having pervaded a West German judiciary in which Nazi perpetrators were reinstated after the war and in which there was sympathy for the experience of Nazi perpetrators in the Third Reich.

Taylor notes that in the US zone the feeling was that 'denazification should be about rehabilitation, not just punishment' and, in an indication of what was to come under West German law, that anyone accused should have the 'opportunity to vindicate himself on the basis of a "just consideration of his individual responsibility and his actual conduct, taken as a whole"', which seemed a 'licence to acquit'.[11] He also notes that 'within months of the end of the war' denazification 'had lost a lot of public support' in Germany and claims that 'Germans soon began to see themselves as victims and to reject the notion of indiscriminate 'collective guilt' – he notes that in the US zone approval of denazification had fallen to a mere seventeen per cent by 1949 and that the idea of collective guilt seemed to preclude that of individual guilt.[12]

Frei points to a policy under Adenauer of 'amnestying and integrating former supporters of the Third Reich' whilst 'completing a normative separation from Nazism'. Frei claims that 'those damaged by denazification' regarded the '"liquidation" of the hated political purging as a touchstone of the new state's sovereignty' and a test of 'the state's very legitimacy'. Of course such a specious argument was what would be expected from former Nazis wishing to be exonerated and to resume normal life in West Germany. Even so, there was widespread German public support for such sentiment and the consequence was, Frei claims, 'the amnesty law already initiated in the first days of Adenauer's government' and a policy of 'extensive amnesty for Nazi criminals' that resulted in 'limiting the blame for Nazi crimes to the narrow band of top Nazi leaders', a policy of 'amnesty and integration' Frei notes was a necessity for the Social Democrats to retain popularity in West Germany.[13]

On 31 December 1949 the West German government passed an amnesty law that 'conveniently obscured the distinction between' minor offences such as profiting from the black market after the war and 'often violent criminal acts committed under Nazi auspices', and another West German amnesty law in 1954 covered 'sentences of up to three years if in the period of the "collapse" from October 1944 onward and involving what was called a "collision of duties". The law 'emphasized the significance of having obeyed orders for fear of adverse consequences, even if in a period of confusion during the "final phase" many might have been mistaken in their beliefs'. The narrative of people having been 'under immense pressure to obey orders' became 'ever more current'.[14]

The other narrative was, as has been seen, that former Nazis had been 'blinded' by Nazi ideology and propaganda. The result was that 'while a few Nazis were demonised, the rest were effectively exculpated', so much so that on 11 May 1951 the law facilitated the reinstatement of former Nazis who had lost their jobs in the denazification process, with the consequence that two fifths of the Foreign Ministry and the Interior Ministry were former Nazis. Even those actively complicit in the 'ghettoization and deportation' of Jews to the camps in Poland blamed the SS and claimed to have been no more than administrators, and Fulbrook notes that those of 'bourgeois social status', including 'professional groups' who had been involved in violent perpetrator behaviour, tended to be exonerated by West German courts that 'often showed sympathy with the perpetrators and far less often with their victims' as 'the notion of perpetrator' became one of 'thugs' of low social status, though not those who had 'only been following orders', just those who had 'exceeded' the requirements of their murderous roles. Fulbrook refers to a '"renazification" of the West German legal profession in the 1950s', with a possible three quarters of West German judges and lawyers having 'served during the Third Reich' exonerated by reference to their 'professional obligation to uphold the law', so that those involved in decisions regarding investigations and prosecutions of former Nazis would themselves have had Nazi pasts and very little desire to prosecute fellow former Nazis.[15]

Referring to the sentences imposed by US military trials, Bazyler and Tuerkheimer note a 'perceived need for West Germany to serve as a bulwark against an expansionist Soviet Union' and its corollary, a 'need to placate growing sentiment in West Germany that all of the trials were unjust and simply the imposition of victor's justice'. They claim that 'while the Cold War did not come in time to save Goring, it did lead to the wholesale release of all Einsatzgruppen defendants, excepting the four whose death sentences were not reduced'. This is a reference to the reconsideration of the sentences imposed in the Nuremberg trials, including that of the Einsatzgruppen commanders, by the US High Commissioner to West Germany from 1949 to 1952, McCloy, in January 1951. For, cognisant of the need for West Germany to be 'an effective buffer to Soviet expansionism' and under pressure from the West German government and public opinion for clemency and leniency, McCloy's amnesty included all those with sentences 'of less than fifteen years', and 'other sentences were commuted or shortened'. Bazyler and Tuerkheimer regard the intervention as 'one of the largest failures of justice' given the undisputed evidence of the nature and scale of Einsatzgruppen murders of Jews in the east, and as an instance of politics adversely influencing the administration of law. The result was that by 1958, 'most of the people convicted at Nuremberg had been released'.[16] Pendas refers to a post-war emphasis on German divergence, a version of the Sonderweg view of German history, at the International Military Tribunal at Nuremberg and to an emerging emphasis on German 'individual pathology' at the ensuing US military tribunals of specific classes of Nazi perpetrator, and refers to Priemel's assessment that the 'path to German democracy' was derived from a 'convergence' in the form of German '(re)Westernization' as the imposition of post-war justice moved from an emphasis upon prosecution to clemency and from there to amnesty to facilitate West German 'rehabilitation' because of its attractions in its 'economic liberalism' and 'anti-communist credentials' in a European Cold War context indicated by the Sovietisation of East Germany and of other countries in eastern Europe.[17] The western attitude is indicative of the general thesis here, that all parties in the post-war period pursed policies that they perceived would be optimal for them. For the western powers the objective was a liberal democratic and capitalist West Germany to provide a bulwark against communism and Soviet influence in central Europe, for West Germans it was obtaining a restoration of their economic and political status to optimise their standard of living and security against communism and the spread of Soviet domination from eastern Europe, and for the Soviet Union the objective was to Sovietise the economy and political structure of East Germany and the rest of eastern Europe. And concepts of legality and legitimacy were contingent and subordinated to the objectives of political power.

The context of West Germany after the war does seem to have had significant influence on its government's reluctance to prosecute those complicit in Nazi war crimes and crimes against humanity and on the leniency shown regarding sentences imposed on convicted Nazi war criminals such as the Einsatzgruppen commanders. For there was a combination of wartime devastation and the threat to the western zones that became the Federal Republic of Germany or West Germany in 1949 of Soviet expansionism and opportunism and communism known to thrive in conditions of chaos and impoverishment, both of which were to be found in western Germany, not least because the western zones received so many displaced persons and so many ethnic Germans who had fled or had been deported from elsewhere in Europe. Another consequence of the very adverse conditions of life in western Germany after the war ended was of course that most West Germans had 'other priorities'.[18]

In such circumstances former Nazis were needed for their expertise and experience in the civil service, the law, and the professions, for under the bureaucratic totalitarianism of the Nazi regime education and aspiration meant working for or in the Nazi state apparatus, so most of those most needed for government and imposition of law in West Germany were former Nazis with that extent of complicity at least. And of course former Nazis were profoundly anticommunist and so in the emerging Cold War context were seen to be people on whom the state could depend in political terms. The West German government approach was then pragmatic and designed to optimise West German economic and social recovery and security in the context of the Cold War. Fulbrook notes that 'once the Cold War took precedence over dealing with Nazism and denazification proceedings were handed over to the Germans themselves, treatment of offenders was even more lenient'.[19] There was also the enormity of the task of denazification given that affiliation with the Nazi Party or its associated organisations had been so widespread in Nazi Germany, and the difficulty of finding 'untainted' law officers (that is, people without involvement or complicity in, or sympathy for perpetrators under, the Nazi regime) to investigate and prosecute cases.[20]

The other agenda of West German governments seems to have been to enhance social cohesion rather than division and to look to the future rather than to the past, for there was, as has been seen, a general aversion in the West German public for what was regarded as victor's justice, combined with a lack of interest in prosecuting former Nazis and far more compelling immediate concerns such as the standard of living in West Germany. It could of course be argued that the policies pursued by successive West German governments reflected a continuing sense of Jewish 'otherness' and indifference to what happened to Jews in the part of Europe occupied by the Nazis during the war apart from to the extent that it embarrassed the West German government. The consequence seems to have been a West German government policy that implicitly explained Nazi perpetrator behaviour by reference to perpetrators' having had a professional obligation or their having had to obey orders in a psychological and social universe in the Third Reich that was very different to that of West Germany, and that regarded issues of criminality and responsibility for complicity and perpetrator behaviour as having been accordingly complex. West German policy was then avoidance of prosecution of Nazi war criminals whose expertise was needed by West Germany and leniency regarding those convicted, not least because of West German public opinion. The Ulm Einsatzkommando trial in 1958 was the first major trial of Nazi war criminals conducted under West German criminal law and was for war crimes committed by the Einsatzkommando known as Tilsit in Lithuania in 1941.[21] All the defendants were found guilty and sentenced to terms of imprisonment, which seems to be a departure from the preceding period of avoidance of prosecuting Nazi war criminals, who were, as has been seen, reintegrated into West German society, though Fulbrook claims that poll data shows a trend in German public attitudes from a majority wanting an end to post-war trials of former Nazis in the beginning of the 1950s through to just thirty-four per cent wanting an end to such trials in 1958 to fifty-three per cent wanting the trials to end at the time of the Eichmann trial, and records references to victors' justice, to low numbers of war criminals and to Allied war crimes such as Dresden in April 1961. For Fulbrook 'changes in public reactions in West Germany' came 'in the 1960s'. The Ulm Einsatzkommando trial had been brought by a survivor of Einsatzkommando activities in Tilsit and resulted in Adenauer's creation of the Central Office of the State Justice Administrations for the Investigation of National Socialist Crimes as a government response.[22] Even so the results were limited. In the Frankfurt Auschwitz trial, held between 1963 and 1965, just seventeen people were sentenced and the sentencing was generally lenient, and though the young were engaged the older generation that had lived through the period wanted to forget. There was a general sense amongst West German judges that witnesses were poor sources given the vagueness of their testimony and the period of time that had elapsed since the war and the need for specific charges, and in the Operation Reinhard trials, between 1963 and 1970, the West German criminal justice system meant that cruelty beyond the requirements of role had to be established, as had some indication of criminal intent and agency rather than mere compliance with orders.[23] Weinschenk has a very different appreciation of the record of the West German judicial system in dealing with Nazi war criminals. He refers to West German public aversion to pursuit of Nazi perpetrators but with a change around 1955, when he claims there was an alteration in attitude from indifference and rehabilitation of Nazi perpetrators to resolve to prosecute them, with the creation of the Central Office for the Investigation of Nazi Crimes on 6 November 1958. Weinschenk refers to the numbers of proceedings between 1968 and 1970 and claims that 'the core of the Nazi criminals has been prosecuted', for 'after the responsible actors in command positions, the judicial apparatus reached up to the "desk-murderers", the Eichmann-type bureaucrats, and down to the "squad-leaders"', with only the 'ideologists' and 'foreign helpers' having 'escaped prosecution'.

Weinschenk points out that West German criminal procedure placed much less reliance upon oral testimony than documentation and that such a tendency was enhanced by the understanding that whilst SS personnel had an 'obvious motive to minimise', victims had problems remembering traumatic events many years earlier, and that there were genuine 'difficulties of proof' in West German trials with 'no "neutral" witnesses'. Weinschenk points out that Section 211 of the German Penal Code required the establishment of 'base motives' such as 'racial hatred, or sadistic perversion' and evidence that the defendants were 'actors, not mere conduits or transmitters', so that the defence of 'I only followed orders' resulted in dismissals of cases against defendants who 'only passed on and followed orders without themselves engaging in heinous acts' (see similar reference in Fulbrook above).

He notes that 'followers of orders' would have been guilty as accessories but that the statute of limitations precluded that possibility for prosecutors, and notes the defence of 'duress' in a context of the 'iron discipline' of the SS, despite the fact that not a single instance of actual punishment has been found, which of course of itself does not mean that defendants did not have the impression of dire adverse consequences for non-compliance with orders.[24] One does wonder whether under the German Penal Code to which Weinschenk refers Eichmann would have been convicted given that he received his orders from and had to account to Müller as his immediate superior in the SS and Kaltenbrunner, Heydrich's successor, above him. In other words, when was an SS officer more than a conduit? At Heydrich's level or

Himmler's, given Himmler's exterminatory antisemitism? A tentative answer would be at Heydrich's level given his zealous initiation of the Holocaust at the Wannsee Conference, albeit implementing a decision made above him, at Goering's and Himmler's level.

One difference between Fulbrook and Weinschenk appears to be that Fulbrook judges the West German legal system by consequence and attributed motive given her conviction that the legal system reflected political decisions, whereas Weinschenk addresses the West German legal process and its difficulties given the laws concerned and the standard of proof needed to convict and the efforts made to investigate Nazi war criminals.

Fulbrook claims that 'the West German justice system showed more sympathy for the perpetrator than for the victims', and that there was more 'judicial empathy' with perpetrators 'under orders' than with victims 'desperate for justice',[25] though she seems to be inferring West German prejudice in part from judicial insistence upon interrogating witnesses for evidence that could be regarded as credible and relevant to the issue of guilt or innocence under the criminal justice system in West Germany. Dealing with emotional and possibly chaotic witnesses could have been difficult for West German courts, and understanding of the psychological context and experience of those charged as perpetrators was required to establish guilt under West German law given that inferences of guilt could only be made if there was evidence of going beyond the requirements of role in cruelty and beyond compliance with orders. West German judicial bias in favour of perpetrators of a certain socioeconomic class does seem to have been apparent more in the lack of investigations of former Nazis of a certain class status and in sentencing and in commutation of sentences, for West German criminal law and its requirements for establishing guilt could not have influenced the extent of investigation of former Nazis or consideration of sentences unless the sentences were mandatory under the law. In the early to middle of the 1960s the constraint of West German criminal law with its requirement for credible evidence in the form of identification and proof of criminal intent and behaviour beyond the requirement of role was seen in the investigation of Belzec camp personnel, for all the defendants except one were acquitted on grounds of 'putative duress', a reference to experience of threat on the part of the alleged perpetrators concerned, which was regarded as not obtaining for the remaining defendant because of his relationship with his superior officer in the SS. In the Treblinka and Sobibor trials there were more surviving witnesses and convictions and fewer lenient sentences, but the numbers prosecuted were very limited, with just twelve defendants at the Sobibor trial and eleven at the Treblinka trial, and only one defendant in any of the trials was a commissioned SS officer.

Fulbrook notes that 'time made a major difference to the likely fate of Nazi perpetrators, to the ways in which witness testimony was received and evaluated and to what sorts of evidence were seen to count' in what was a 'change in legal practice' in West Germany and as a 'younger generation' took an interest in justice for the Holocaust after unification in 1990. The change meant that there was to be no continuing reliance on eyewitness testimony, which, given the lack of survivors and concerns regarding the veracity of their testimonies, had resulted in acquittals in previous cases, and that all that was necessary to secure a conviction was 'documentary evidence of a particular role and presence in a place of mass murder'. No evidence regarding defendants' actions or intentions was needed. Fulbrook claims that for most Nazi perpetrators the change came far too late, and the ensuing trials were isolated and addressed to the 'wrong targets' in West Germany.[26]

Fulbrook claims that guilt has been greater amongst survivors than perpetrators, that perpetrators have engaged in 'self-distancing' in the form of exaggerating geographical distance or cultivating moral distance from perpetrator behaviour and have excused their perpetrator behaviour by alluding to 'relative powerlessness' and being 'blinded by ideology', and that 'perpetrators even see themselves as "victims" because of the difficulty of the task they had to undertake'.[27] Exculpatory attributions are though normal means of evading responsibility for behaviour not normatively approved. And the greater guilt experienced by survivors may be explained by their having survived when their families perished, and some having done so through various forms of collaboration, whereas perpetrators were not related to each other and most perpetrators also survived and evaded punishment.

In terms of identification of the actual motives behind the perpetrator behaviour and complicity of ordinary Germans, Fulbrook claims that 'various combinations of careerism, cowardice, conformity, fear, lust, brutalisation, hopelessness, desire for reward, choosing the lesser of two evils (for whom, one wonders), simply "doing one's duty" or "obeying orders", or fitting in with what others were doing would all play a role.' Though Fulbrook elaborates on the effect of ideology in references to talk of combatting 'partisans' and of a need to 'terrorize troublesome populations' that she claims would have legitimised murder as part of warfare in the east, she does not differentiate between the most plausible decisive influence or influences on German perpetrator behaviour and complicity of various kinds and those that may have been merely facilitative or even insignificant in most cases.

From Browning's evidence of the effect of peer group pressure on the perpetrator behaviour of the men of Police Battalion 101, which Fulbrook refers to herself, from Kershaw's claim that the attitude of ordinary Germans to the Jews during the Nazi period was one of 'indifference', from the way in which expressed attitudes towards the Jews altered with roles and their requirements on what seems an expedient basis, from the ordinary conformity to role requirements and societal norms that is characteristic of all societies, cultures and time periods, and from the combination of perpetrator self-exoneration and the antipathy of ordinary Germans for war crimes trials and justice for the Jews and attention to their own futures after the end of the war, the inference is that optimisation of personal outcomes was the decisive influence on the behaviour of ordinary Germans in all roles and circumstances during and after the war.[28]

Fulbrook notes that the generation from which perpetrators were drawn and that had some complicity in the Holocaust remained silent and avoidant when the succeeding generation began to show an interest in prosecuting the crimes of the Nazi period, which is exactly what would be expected given the desire of the complicit generation of Germans not to incriminate themselves and for the entire Nazi period to be dismissed from discourse. The anguish over the Nazi past and the 'representational justice' (see below) of the relatively recent show trials of Demjanjuk and Gröning under altered West German criminal procedures do seem indicative of a younger generation of Germans with no complicity in the criminality of the Nazi regime being able to affect 'continuing unease and heightened moral responsibility' and 'guilt' without any of the adverse consequences that would have ensued for the adult generation of the Third Reich had they manifested similar guilt and responsibility for Nazi crimes against humanity. The younger, post-war generation of Germans does then seem to have condemned their parents' generation on moral grounds when they themselves have been fortunate enough to have had no experience of Nazi totalitarianism with its combination of authoritarianism, repression and state violence or of the perceptual world of their parents. The implication is that they, the generation of the children of Nazi perpetrators who had in many cases done no more than meeting the requirements of their roles in the military and the SS, would have both reflected upon the morality of what they were being ordered to do or what they were complicit in, and then, having appreciated the immorality of it all, have had the moral courage to defy the Nazi state, military or SS hierarchy in time of war and declined to meet role requirements in the treatment of Jews in the east. There is no evidence of any kind that they would have done either.[29]

What the evidence does seem to indicate is that the generation of ordinary Germans of the Third Reich, both those who became perpetrators to meet the requirements of their roles and those who were complicit in Nazi criminality through passivity or involvement in the Nazi bureaucracy, optimised personal outcomes before the war, when they turned away when Jews were ostracised and discriminated against, during it, when they conformed to the requirements of roles involving perpetrator behaviour or engaged in various forms of passive or active complicity, and after it, when they sought to evade detection and punishment and to resume ordinary lives in West Germany. The same motive of optimisation of personal outcomes seems to have been present in the succeeding generation with its attempt to establish its liberal and humanitarian credentials in the form of show trials of men convicted of perpetrator behaviour by virtue of their roles even though there was no proof of their having committed any perpetrator behaviour beyond their role requirements or of criminal intent.

The case of John (Ivan) Demjanjuk was indicative of the new West German approach. In April 1988 Demjanjuk had been convicted in an Israeli court of being Ivan the Terrible, a notoriously brutal guard at Treblinka who exceeded the requirements of his role, on the basis of eyewitness testimony from former prisoners at Treblinka and of a Trawniki ID card that was then discredited on a number of grounds.[30] Demjanjuk's trial in an Israeli court was in fact a demonstration of agendas other than pursuit of justice for the accused, for, despite previous Israeli experience of a show trial in the case of Eichmann, in which there was endless testimony from countless witnesses as to their terrible experiences in the Holocaust that did not bear upon the issue of the guilt or innocence of Eichmann, the Demjanjuk trial was a similar pantomime of theatre or therapy, in this case for former prisoners at the Treblinka extermination camp whose emotional testimony culminated in misidentification of Demjanjuk as Ivan the Terrible.

The witnesses were of course elderly by the time of the Demjanjuk trial and there may have been a desire to identify and punish someone responsible for Ivan the Terrible's gratuitous malice, though certitude is different from certainty, and in the case of one, particularly accusatory and emotional witness, evidence emerged that he had asserted in an earlier document that Ivan the Terrible had been murdered in a camp revolt during the war. There was in fact no credible evidence that Demjanjuk had ever been at Treblinka. The humiliating consequence of the discrediting of earlier evidence and witness testimony and of the emergence of new evidence indicating that Ivan the Terrible's name was Marchenko, not Demjanjuk, was that Demjanjuk's conviction had to be quashed by the Israeli court.

With so obvious a lesson in the perils of reliance on witness testimony so long after the events being recalled and from elderly and emotional witnesses motivated to identify someone for the suffering they experienced or witnessed, when Demjanjuk was charged in a West German court, between 2009 and 2011, with being a guard at Sobibor extermination camp, the prosecution relied on documentary evidence of his having had a Trawniki ID card and on expert testimony to the effect that Trawniki men were used as camp guards in extermination camps like Sobibor, that the choice for Trawniki men was guard duty at such camps or forced labour rather than execution, and that Demjanjuk had chosen to become a guard at an extermination camp, Sobibor. Douglas does mention Demjanjuk's defence's reference to the mistreatment, neglect and malnourishment of Soviet POWs, whose prospects of survival were poor, but only to point out that such reference could only be part of a defence for collaboration with the Nazis as a camp guard, not one that argued that Demjanjuk had not been a camp guard at Sobibor but that had he been he would have been exonerated by the adverse circumstances facing Soviet POWs. The context was that by the time of the Demjanjuk trial there was no need for proof that Demjanjuk had exceeded his role as camp guard at Sobibor, for 'accessory to murder' was by then established by mere presence in a camp the sole purpose of which was the extermination of Jews. The attribution of causation to the unique circumstances of the Third Reich that was accepted to exonerate former Nazis of some occupational and social status in previous decades does not seem to have obtained in the case of Demjanjuk.[31] For though 'after World War II, the West German legal system stubbornly refused to confront the distinctive quality of Nazi criminality and apply "crimes against humanity" against alleged Nazi war criminals, and so imposed a "very high bar of proof" on cases in which there was "participation of defendants in a collective enterprise in mass murder in which their roles in individual acts of murder and their motives were far from transparent", "in 2010, a German court in Munich accepted prosecutors" novel "collective participation" theory in the trial of John (Ivan) Demjanjuk', who was 'convicted as an accessory to murder' because the prosecution had proved that he had been a voluntary guard at Sobibor when 27,000 Jews were exterminated.[32]

Issues of complicity, criminality and responsibility, and the intended and advocated function of post-war trials and 'justice'

The claimed injustice of West Germany's pragmatic policy and its exoneration of the great majority of former Nazis on the basis of professional obligation, obeying orders or the effect of Nazi propaganda calls into question the nature of complicity, criminality and responsibility in the Third Reich.

Fulbrook does acknowledge the difficulties in assigning semantic categories such as 'perpetrator', 'victim' and 'bystander', pointing to the reality that individuals could be both victims and perpetrators. The instance she cites is of Poles who were mistreated by their German occupiers but who collaborated with them in the apprehension of Jews.[33] Other instances would include those victims in what Primo Levi has characterised as 'the gray zone', which challenges the binary distinction between 'victims and perpetrators' by reference to victims who collaborated in some form or other, though Levi does emphasise the existence of perpetrators and victims. Levi refers to a heterogeneous group of victims of the Holocaust who became privileged prisoners in the camps through being Kapos in the work squads, clerks in the camp administrations, other functionaries in the camps or Jewish council members in the ghettoes of Poland.[34] And there were former Soviet POWs who became extermination camp personnel, moving from Slav victims of the Nazi advance east to perpetrators of genocide against the Jews in Poland. Fulbrook also indicates the inherent ambiguity of 'bystanders', and points to narrowing definitions of 'perpetrators', with those complicit in the Holocaust representing themselves as mere 'bystanders' and excoriating others after the war for direct complicity, and to a similar narrowing of the definition of 'victims', but emphasises the fundamental difference between perpetrators (and those who collaborated with them) and the victims of the Nazi regime.[35]

Noting that the Nazi 'system' required the involvement of great multitudes of Germans, Fulbrook acknowledges that 'the system was willed by the few, sustained through the conformity and mobilization of the many, and backed up by the repression of those who opposed', and notes that 'the rapid shift of many Germans into acquiescence, even enthusiasm, was accompanied by draconian repression of the rest through fear, imprisonment and exile', which permitted Germans to represent themselves as 'having been forced or constrained to act in the ways they did, bearing no personal responsibility for their actions'. Fulbrook elaborates upon the extent of ordinary German involvement in Nazi atrocities in referring to the complicity not just of 'those who gave the orders and the most prominent men at the top of the hierarchy' but also those who exploited slave labour, professional people and the 'highly educated', who also descended into 'inhumanity', and notes the 'apparatus of terror' and the 'conflicting priorities of their own welfare and that of their families', though she does indicate a 'spectrum' of responses to Nazi totalitarianism in differentiating 'willing complicity' from 'unwilling capitulation or miserable accommodation', even if without indicating the numbers in different degrees of complicity with the Nazi regime.[36]

Elaborating on Fulbrook's reference to circumstantial factors and to the experiential context of Germans in the Third Reich, one issue is just how an individual could have conceived of refusing to undertake a task assigned in a totalitarian context characterised by a number of compelling factors. There was something approaching a universality of compliance that may have meant that ordinary Germans did not even conceive of resistance, and the fact that dissenters, a tiny minority, were regarded as enemies of the state and consigned to concentration camps following arbitrary arrest conducted with impunity by the state. For SS members there was the SS code of discipline, obedience, toughness and ruthlessness that dictated what was regarded as normatively approved behaviour and what was derogated for members of the SS. There was the ultimate source of legitimacy in the Führerprinzip, under which any directive (or in fact indication or inference of a preference) from Hitler as the ultimate source of authority in the Third Reich had the force of law. There was the reality that in Nazi Germany the state was intensely bureaucratic and controlled the great majority of careers that afforded privilege and status, and so attracted the aspirational middle classes and the educated to work for the Nazi state. And there was the Jews' quality of 'otherness' from a history of German cultural antisemitism, exacerbated by Nazi propaganda vilifying Jews as enemies of the German race and state, and similar racial derogation of Slavs. It is then possible that defiance of an order or refusal to meet role requirements did not occur to the great majority of Nazi perpetrators or those complicit in Nazi criminality in the war.

The preceding paragraph concentrates on the perceptions of Nazi perpetrators, but there was also the issue of motive and the influence of motivation on perception. For compliance with role requirements in the Nazi hierarchy and the SS optimised career prospects and approbation and avoided perceived sanctions for not meeting role requirements or violating norms of conduct. This is what would be expected given the primacy of optimisation of personal outcomes in human behaviour in all societies at all times and its being the reason for conformity to societal norms. For in ordinary life in all societies the great majority of people conform to the requirements of their roles to maximise reward and minimise adverse experience without reflecting on the nature of their roles or their consequences and without feeling any responsibility for the consequences of their meeting their role requirements.

In such a context the complicity of Nazi perpetrators and of those otherwise complicit in Nazi war crimes seems little different to the sort of compliance to optimise personal outcomes found in the great majority of people in all societies. Though there is no known case of punitive measures for refusal to obey an order or failure to meet role requirements in the Nazi state apparatus or the SS, that may be the difference between the actuality and the perception of those involved at the time, and in the Third Reich the threat of punitive formal sanctions such as loss of SS or other career or transfer to the eastern front was accompanied by that of informal sanctions such as gossip, ridicule, disapproval and ostracism. And of course one reason for there being no instance of punitive measures for refusal to comply with role requirements may be that so few ever refused because of the perceived threat.

The argument that Nazi perpetrators did not conceive of disobeying orders or disregarding role requirements because of their pursuit of their own interests is supported by imagining what would have happened if such perpetrators had been given a compelling motive to violate rather than to conform to role requirements, for in that eventuality the expectation would be that such perpetrators would have conceived of defiance of role requirements. What is being argued here is that Nazi perpetrators who did not exceed the requirements of their roles were being ordinary human beings in not reflecting on the requirements of their roles and in putting their own interests before those of others, in this case the Jews.

The personalisation of responsibility implicit in arraigning before courts those held to have been responsible for or complicit in the Holocaust is comprehensible given the impossibility of trying a system rather than individuals in court, the desire for some accounting for heinous acts, and the need, apparently felt especially by the Americans after the war, to demonstrate that perpetrator behaviour would be punished and so deter it in the future, but the reality is that ordinary Germans behaved in much the same way people in general behave and for the same motives. Concepts such as 'justice', 'criminality' and 'responsibility' in the Third Reich seem more problematic in the context of the evidence on ordinary human motivation and conforming responses in all societies.

Fulbrook's conclusion that the trials reflected post-war priorities, that is, 'contemporary social and political considerations' that resulted in 'selective prosecution of particular sorts of perpetrator' and confined prosecutions to 'physical thugs' and the 'few giving orders in high places', with the 'vast majority' evading 'justice' and very few Nazi perpetrators even investigated as 'rehabilitation of former Nazis took precedence', does seem borne out by the evidence, as does her reference to the extent of complicity in its various forms, including benefiting from the crimes of the Nazi regime. Having said that, though the extent of ordinary German complicity in the crimes of the Third Reich is very much understated by the low incidence of prosecutions in such post-war trials, it does not follow that the policy of selective prosecutions was an injustice given the evidence of the social and political context faced by ordinary Germans of all classes and the wider evidence of conformity being the norm for the great majority in all societies, who conform to optimise personal outcomes (this inference is supported by social psychological and historical evidence on perpetrator behaviour from Milgram and Browning respectively).

The requirements of West German criminal law also meant that establishing guilt required evidence of cruelty in excess of role requirements and of agency beyond compliance with orders, as has been seen. Fulbrook herself refers extensively to the exigencies of the social and political context facing ordinary Germans during the war, though also claiming that post-war West German governments failed to prosecute and convict former Nazis out of greater sympathy for perpetrators than victims (see above).[37] West German prosecution of those who in their brutality exceeded the requirements of their roles, endorsement of the prosecution of the senior Nazis who directed Nazi policy towards the Jews, and reintegration of all other ordinary Germans, including perpetrators in roles of various sorts, does then seem to represent an appreciation of not just pragmatic and criminal law considerations but also the psychological context facing ordinary Germans in the Third Reich and the realities of human motivation in all societies.

Given the experiential context for Nazi perpetrators, the primacy of optimisation of personal outcomes in almost all human behaviour and the fact that under the Führerprinzip Hitler as Führer had ultimate responsibility and was the sole source of legitimacy in the Third Reich, it does seem that the Nuremberg trial of major Nazi war criminals was more justified than those that ensued. For some of these senior Nazis competed with each other to enhance or protect their careers through eliciting Hitler's approval for radical policies they knew he preferred, though some, for instance Goebbels and Bormann, were intensely antisemitic. These very senior Nazis, who were involved in meetings with Hitler to decide Nazi policy in the east, including towards the Jews and the Slavs, had far greater complicity in and responsibility for the Holocaust and the losses of Soviet POWs than others arraigned at the Nuremberg trial of major war criminals, such as Speer, for instance, for it is difficult to see how he could have declined to use slave labour to optimise German productivity, though he could have resigned without any draconian sanction, it seems. And there were functionaries such as the Einsatzgruppen commanders, extermination camp commandants such as Höss at Auschwitz and Stangl at Sobibor and then Treblinka, and Eichmann, who implemented decisions made above them in the Nazi hierarchy, doing no more than meeting the requirements of their roles, appalling though the consequences were. Though at the meetings of the most senior Nazis with Hitler the decisive influence came from Hitler himself, there remains possible influence on Nazi racial policy and Nazi policy in the east from these very senior Nazis' proposed schemes designed to secure his approbation and from possible misrepresentation of the extent of Führer approval of policies by members of that echelon to each other to enhance their domains of responsibility and power.

Some of the Nuremberg defendants, for instance the military men, Keitel and Jodl, appear to have been prosecuted for their seniority in the German military, and with that responsibility for activities in the east, including complicity in the Einsatzgruppen murders of Jews, which they took no action to stop, though according to Otto Ohlendorf, the notorious commander of Einsatzgruppe D, they were under an order from Hitler to identify enemies of the Reich and pass them on to the Einsatzgruppen. Nor do these military commanders seem to have been complicit in the systematic ghettoisation and transfer of Jews to camps and their extermination there. Others who were arraigned at Nuremberg seem to have had their responsibility for the extermination of the Jews established through reference to their being part of the most senior echelon of the Nazi state, not through reference to any direct compelling evidence. On the contrary, it seems at Nuremberg to have been enough to establish that such individuals knew of the Holocaust to find them guilty of crimes against humanity, a radical departure from the normal rules of criminal procedure.

Though there is no record of the decisive meeting between Hitler, Himmler, Goebbels, Bormann, Frank and some other unidentified Reich leaders and Gauleiters on 12 December 1941 at the Reich Chancellery, where Hitler is claimed to have given his approval to the extermination of the Jews, it is possible, especially given the motive amongst his immediate acolytes to ingratiate themselves with him, that the systematic extermination of all Jews in territories occupied by the Nazis was proposed by one of the acolytes present as a means of resolving the 'Jewish problem' and received tacit approval from Hitler, for that seems consonant with the way in which decisions were made in the Third Reich, given the concentration of power in Hitler as Führer and his known indolence, preference for radical solutions and lack of interest in or attention to detail. For though there is evidence that Hitler had made it plain that he wanted to be rid of the Jews in the Third Reich, there seems to be no direct evidence of Hitler's intentions as to the means by which that objective was to be accomplished.

What seems to follow is that it was appropriate that some senior Nazis were prosecuted, not just because someone had to be held responsible for the purpose of exemplary justice but also because some of that senior echelon of Nazis seem to have been intimately involved in the discussions that preceded the decision to exterminate the Jews, may have been instrumental in that decision by the manner in which the issue was presented and in possible radical solutions proposed, and may also have interpreted Hitler's wishes in a liberal way in the systematic extermination of the Jews of Europe in centres designed for that exclusive purpose.

For the other trials conducted by US military courts and under West German criminal law referred to above, unless there was evidence of perpetrators' having acted in cruel ways not dictated by their role requirements, it does seem that defendants were found guilty in a form of 'victors' justice', for the nature of the experiential context of such lesser Nazi perpetrators who obeyed orders received from above them in the Nazi state apparatus in meeting the requirements of the roles assigned to them was such that resistance to compliance may not even have been conceived of by them. For though such lesser Nazi perpetrators conformed to role requirements for reasons of inadvertent or deliberate optimisation of personal outcomes in the form of careerism and maintenance or enhancement of status and the approbation of their bosses and peers, or in instinctive, unreflective or deliberate avoidance of loss of privilege and status, they were in that respect no different to the great majority of ordinary people at any time and in any culture in terms of motive, as has been argued above.

Even so, there is a moral difference between corporate callousness that results in exploitation of labour, low pay or unemployment for other people for instance, and engaging in work that results in genocide, for though the motive may be the same the difference in context results in a colossal difference in outcome known to perpetrators at the time of their perpetrator behaviour. It could not be argued that there was a record of draconian punishments for declining to participate in Nazi crimes against humanity in the treatment of the Jews, because there seems to be no record of anyone being severely punished or executed for such failure to meet role requirements, but there was as has been seen a perception of possible sanctions from the state in the event of declining to participate in genocide. Even so, avoiding becoming a perpetrator was possible, as is apparent from Police Battalion 101 in Poland, some of whose members shot wide or went missing when the shooting was due to begin, or acknowledged weakness as the explanation for their not participating in a group task, and another possibility was resignation on various grounds.

Browning indicates that the commanding officer told his men that anyone who did not feel they could participate could decline without fear of sanctions from him, and the evidence on Einsatzgruppe D under Otto Ohlendorf is that not participating in genocide even when that was the implicit purpose of the unit did not elicit draconian sanctions in the SS.[38] The explanation may then be that despite there being no great objective cost to avoidance of compliance with orders to murder Jews, the great majority of perpetrators did so because of a combination of lack of reflection or exclusive pursuit of their own optimal social outcomes in the form of the views of superiors and peers and relative indifference to the Jews. The process is the same as that in ordinary life in the liberal democratic west, of course, and indicates that in similar circumstances the citizenry of modern western states would have engaged in compliance with role requirements for the same objective.

To reiterate a point made earlier, the lack of any trials of those who could have been regarded as being responsible for the colossal loss of life under Stalinism in the Soviet Union is indicative, for though in the Soviet Union the political system remained unchanged, unlike the dramatic contrast between the racist and militaristic totalitarianism of the Nazi regime and liberal democratic post-war West Germany, in the Soviet Union there could have been prosecutions of those responsible for the conditions and loss of life in the slave labour camps under Stalinism given that the Stalinist period came to be regarded as an aberration of communism. Yet, as has been seen, in the Soviet Union collaboration and perpetrator behaviour within the state apparatus seem to have been regarded as to be expected from people under the conditions of Stalinist totalitarianism, for purposes of personal advancement or security against arrest themselves. Though there seems to be a distinction between the Nazis' systematic murder of all Jews in the occupied territories and Stalinist labour camps, the combination of Stalinist slave labour and malnutrition continued regardless of appreciation of the consequences for the countless numbers who perished, so the difference does seem to be one of form rather than of ultimate intention or outcome.

The concern of the people and government of West Germany to optimise their own future outcomes and aversion for prosecutions for complicity in Nazi extermination of Jews, which they attributed to the circumstances of the Third Reich, may be seen to reflect the popular German 'indifference' to what happened to the Jews during the war to which Kershaw refers.[39] At the very least one would have to infer relative indifference in the West German general public to the Holocaust after the war, compared, that is, to what seems to have been a manifest concern with their own immediate prospects in post-war West Germany.

The West Germans of the decades after the war were though not alone in their attitude to the Holocaust. For indifference to the Holocaust and hostility or antipathy towards Jews who had survived seem to have been not uncommon in Europe after the war, for instance in Poland and Slovakia, where antisemitism seems to have endured despite what happened to the Jews in the occupied east during the war. And communist bloc punishment of those complicit in Nazi crimes seems to have been harsher because of communist ideological antipathy for Nazism and for Nazi war crimes perpetrated against Soviet POWs, partisans, commissars and Bolsheviks rather than from greater outrage over the Holocaust.

West German policy towards Nazi war criminals was in fact not dissonant with a context of general relative indifference to the Jews of Europe on the part of most European nations and the US before, during and after the war. In the US in the 1930s popular antipathy for immigration resulted in there being no legislation to facilitate the immigration of Jewish refugees from Nazi Germany and in July 1941 immigration by anyone with relatives in Europe under Nazi occupation was banned and US consulates in such countries were closed, resulting in an end to Jewish immigration to the US. Even in 1945, with news of the Holocaust in visceral images, a mere five per cent of Americans were prepared to receive more European immigrants than before the war.

The centrality of the concept of justice and the nature of attributed guilt

I have alluded above to the nature of the concept of guilt under West German criminal law with its requirement there should be identified acts of cruelty beyond the requirements of role and beyond mere compliance with orders in the Nazi hierarchy. That does of course place any ascribed criminality within the experiential context of Nazi Germany. Here I shall elaborate upon the difference between that concept and its implications for the establishing of guilt and the standard set for the establishing of guilt at the International Military Tribunal at Nuremberg.

The attitudes towards the idea of a war crimes trial of the Allied leaders is indicative of their view of the status of any tribunal. At a Cabinet meeting as early as 6 July 1942 Churchill had said, 'if Hitler falls into our hands we shall certainly put him to death,' and on 12 April 1945, with the prospect of a war crimes trial, he is noted as having said, 'agree the trial will be a farce. Indictment: facilities for counsel. All sorts of complications ensue as soon as you admit a fair trial. I would take no responsibility for a trial – even though U.S. wants to do it. Execute principal criminals as outlaws – if no Ally wants them.' Even more indicative is the record of his having said, on 30 July 1946, in a context of having changed his view regarding the value of a trial because he had 'no idea German atrocities had been on the scale that the Nuremberg evidence had shown them to be', that if he had been in the dock he would have said, 'I do not recognise the competency of your court,' and 'you have won the war; take your vengeance in whatever way you like,' and there is Lord Ismay's reference to Churchill's having told him, when the results of the Nuremberg Tribunal were known, that they indicated 'that if you get into a war, it is supremely important to win it. You and I would be in a pretty pickle if we had lost.' These statements are the clearest possible indication of Churchill's appreciation that the Nuremberg Tribunal constituted victors' justice and that Allied war crimes had been committed and would have been prosecuted in a similar fashion had Germany won the war.[40]

Stalin's initial preference had been for the execution of 50,000 German officers, but was 'keen on holding a didactic trial to expose the enormity of the Nazi enterprise, foster Soviet unity, highlight the sacrifices made by the Soviets to defeat the Nazis, indicate the national suffering, establish a legal claim for 'reparations in kind' from Germany, and 'position the Soviet Union as a post-war international power'. Stalin's agenda for the Nuremberg trial was then propagandistic in nature. This conceptualisation of a 'show trial with pre-determined outcomes' was of course very different to the 'legalistic traditions of the other allies', for they included admission that defendants were entitled to a fair trial, a defence, and observance of 'strict due process'.[41]

The US objective at the International Military Tribunal of major Nazis at Nuremberg was indicated by the opening speech of the US Chief Prosecutor, Robert Jackson, who proclaimed that Nazi crimes were so appalling that 'civilization cannot tolerate their being ignored because it cannot survive their being repeated', and that the preparedness of the Allies to 'stay the hand of vengeance and voluntarily submit their captive enemies to the judgement of the law is one of the most significant tributes that power has ever paid to reason'.[42]

There are several observations to be made regarding this statement. It was to begin with untrue, for Churchill had, as has been indicated, favoured executing the most senior Nazis, and had been opposed by Roosevelt, who argued that the US public would want a trial, and Stalin, who believed it would have propaganda value. And it was not the case that 'civilization' could not 'survive' another experience of appalling war crimes and crimes against humanity, for it has, as more recent instances of genocide have shown, and US 'civilization' had survived its own genocide of Native Americans relatively well. The statement also extols the law as the ultimate expression of reason, legitimacy and it seems morality and indicates conviction that the Nuremberg defendants would receive a fair trial. It is then self-regarding and is more in the nature of rhetoric than reason or objective truth. The intended coverage of the Nuremberg trial of major Nazis was impressive, with four major counts, waging aggressive war, crimes against the peace, war crimes and crimes against humanity.

The fact that the Nuremberg trial was followed by other trials of Nazi war criminals conducted by US Military Tribunals does appear to confirm that the US was the prime mover in the Nuremberg Tribunal, and the quote from Churchill above confirms that this was his experience at the time. The US introduced the 'concept of conspiracy' to the justice meted out to those accused of Nazi criminality, and the opening statement by the US Chief Prosecutor indicates assumption of the moral high ground of principle and judgment by the US.

There does in fact seem to have been attention to observance of form over context at the Nuremberg Tribunal, with its conduct appearing to conform to the protocols of fair trials in the liberal democratic west whilst having far less interest in imposing justice than in appearing to do so and really reflecting the objectives of the powers that had won the war. Concepts of responsibility, legality, legitimacy and appropriate legal procedure, not least standards of proof, also reflected these objectives. And when the exigencies of the emerging Cold War dictated abandonment of pursuit of Nazi war criminals to appease the anticommunist West German public there was a leniency to the sentencing and an amnesty that freed many convicted of serious war crimes and crimes against humanity in West Germany in the 1950s.

One indication of the victor's justice of the Nuremberg Tribunal would appear to be the fact that it denied the defence the right to the *tu quoque* defence, that is, the argument that those bringing the prosecutions were guilty of the very crimes the defendants were being charged with. In other words a form of 'justice' expedient to the victorious Allies was decided upon before the trial began, for the defence could not argue that the British had fire bombed Hamburg with colossal and intended loss of civilian life and terror, that they had with the US bombed Berlin and Dresden with similar intentions and outcomes, or that the US had dropped atom bombs on Hiroshima and Nagasaki, both civilian targets intended to elicit a Japanese surrender, to say nothing of the crimes against humanity committed over the years of Stalinist rule.

Referring to the Nuremberg trials, Douglas notes that for 'statesponsored atrocities, guilt is not to be measured by acts of cruelty or savagery alone; guilt follows function. Such was the simple, terrible, and great insight of these courts.'[43] Douglas's approval of this development in international 'justice' seems to applaud it on moral grounds, without any reference to the experiential context facing those who found themselves in roles in the German military, the SS or elsewhere in the Nazi state apparatus during the war or reference to the reality that the great majority of people in all societies in all times act to optimise their own material, social and psychological outcomes and to avoid punishment or discomfort. That includes people like Douglas himself in the liberal democratic west, not least in his aggrandisement of the role and influence of the law and the legal profession (he is a professor of law) and in his occupying the moral high ground from which to pass judgement on those complicit in Nazi criminality and those who engaged in perpetrator behaviour because of their roles from a safe distance from the experiential context of Nazi Germany.

For a liberal lawyer Douglas does seem to have scant regard for alleged perpetrators' civil and legal rights, not least to a fair trial, to a presumption of innocence, and to the right to acquittal unless the case against them were proved by evidence to be beyond all reasonable doubt. Douglas's case is that 'numerous prosecutors (in Nazi war criminals' trials) defended the proceedings as didactic or pedagogic exercises'. Douglas notes the reference by Hausner, the Israeli prosecutor at the trial of Adolf Eichmann in Jerusalem, to the 'enormity of the crime', but does not comment that given the weakness of the evidence against many Nazi war criminals it was expedient for prosecutors to justify proceedings against them as 'a means of teaching history, creating narratives from which political lessons may be teased'. Nor does Douglas refer to the reality that testimony from numerous survivors of the Holocaust would have had some effect on the judges as human beings and could have altered their judgements.

Douglas differentiates the didactic trial from the 'corrupt show trials staged in the Soviet Union under Stalin' but does not elaborate upon the difference in terms of the 'justice' meted out to the defendant. On the contrary, he claims that 'the atrocity trial would continue to perform the conventional function of ascertaining guilt and assigning punishment'. Douglas does refer to Arendt's criticism of the Eichmann trial and of 'Hausner's prosecutorial tactics' and to her comment that 'the purpose of the trial is to render justice', by which she appears to have meant that rendering justice should have been the objective of the trial but seemed to her not to have been. Douglas acknowledges that the Israeli trial of Eichmann was an example of 'legal didactics' but justifies it by claiming that it provided a 'gripping account of the Holocaust' that 'galvanised attention around the world'. Douglas argues for 'transitional justice' in the form of a 'judicial reckoning' with a previous regime for a country emerging into democracy in the case of the Federal Republic of Germany but does note that Demjanjuk's misidentification in his trial in Israel made 'clear the limits of didactic legality'. Even so, he endorses the ensuing West German conviction of Demjanjuk as a guard at Sobibor, because 'guilt follows function'.[44] Douglas does not seem to address just what is intended shall ensue from courts' 'didactic' objective in atrocity trials or why not all atrocities, for instance those committed by victorious countries in wars, are prosecuted at all, let alone in similar ways. It may be his intention that liberal democratic societies should learn from 'didactic' trials and then object to state behaviour that involves similar atrocities. If that is the case he does not indicate how that could occur.

In terms of deterrence to future acts of genocide the exemplary justice of the post-war trials of Nazi war criminals Douglas so approves of seems to have failed, as the Khmer Rouge, the Balkans War and Rwanda indicate. The explanation seems to be that what motivates most people is what seems optimal to their interests at the time, such as the perceived threat of more or less immediate formal or informal sanctions or the attractions of career and approbation from peers, rather than, in the case of perpetrators, the possibility of punishment for perpetrator behaviour should their country lose the war concerned. What is left is the moral rectitude of international justice, which seems then to be of some advantage only to those issuing the verdicts and endorsing them in what seem to be attempts to establish liberal moral and humanitarian credentials, for the insight to which Douglas refers is certainly not psychological in nature.

The explanation of Nazi perpetrator behaviour and of the complicity of others in the Nazi state apparatus does seem to be unreflective pursuit of personal interest rather than the moral or legal imperative of the Führerprinzip. The latter seems to have been less a cause of perpetrator behaviour at the time than an attribution after the war in an attempt to evade responsibility for perpetrator behaviour by Nazis. It is of course entirely comprehensible that Germans complicit in Nazi crimes against humanity should try to exonerate themselves by reference to the political and ideological environment of the Third Reich rather than by claiming that everyone, including their accusers, would have done precisely as they did, and would have met the requirements of their roles, regardless of consequences for the Jews, to optimise their own material, social and psychological outcomes. For that would not have enhanced their prospects of avoidance of exemplary punishment after the war.

In addition to arguing that guilt should be attributed from nothing more than roles, Douglas does then argue that the unprecedented nature of the Holocaust required the practice of law to perform, in addition to its traditional administration of justice to the accused, a function of 'didactic legality', to demonstrate the nature, magnitude and terrible human consequences of the Nazis' crimes in not just legal or statistical but also experiential terms. Douglas argues for a new function for the justice system and the courtroom in asking 'did the trial do justice to the testimony of the survivors?' and asking not 'whether the law has succeeded in doing formal justice to the perpetrators of the Holocaust, but whether the law has succeeded in doing representational justice to the Holocaust qua event', indicating that one role for the court should be to 'satisfy the need of those who have survived to bear witness'. Douglas notes that at the Nuremberg, Eichmann and Demjanjuk trials the normal rules of evidence were 'relaxed', though he claims that permissiveness over witness testimony 'did not upset the overall fairness of the proceedings'.[45] There is something rather odd here, in that Douglas argues for appreciation of the experience of Holocaust victims whilst not even considering the experience of perpetrators.

The claim that permitting extensive eyewitness testimony did not affect the 'fairness' of the 'proceedings' is controversial, for it is difficult to see how in such circumstances the accused could possibly have received a fair trial. For the courtrooms were intense forums of witness after witness recounting terrible personal experiences many of which did not bear on the guilt or innocence in evidential terms of those accused but could have resulted in verdicts or sentences to appease very emotional courtrooms and witnesses or ones that reflected the judges' emotional reaction to, or disgust with the perpetrator behaviour indicated by, the witness evidence, with implicit reasoning that for such appalling crimes against humanity someone must be held responsible and anyone remotely complicit should be punished (and of course there was no one else on trial except the accused). Another motive in the judges' verdicts and sentences could have been a conviction that public policy, the administration of justice, and the logic of deterrence necessitated exemplary punishment of anyone complicit in such ghastly crimes and that someone had to be seen to be held responsible, and that with long chains of command in a totalitarian system the risk was that no one would ever be held responsible.

Douglas's case may be that the verdicts reflected documentary rather than unreliable eyewitness testimony and so were predetermined by the objective evidence rather than influenced by the emotional nature of the courtroom given the distress and terrible experiences of Holocaust survivors, though that would leave the severity of the sentences to be affected by what had been witnessed in the courtroom, unless that too was dictated by the verdict, that is, unless the sentence followed from the guilty verdict in a mandatory way. That does not seem to have been the case at Nuremberg, as while some were executed others were given more lenient prison sentences.

If the verdicts and sentences were not dictated by objective evidence it is difficult to see how Douglas concludes that the trials were unaffected by the 'representational' justice they offered, in that it would not be possible to be sure that the emotional and distressing courtroom experience had not influenced the verdicts and sentences. The guilty verdict in the Demjanjuk trial in Israel may have been influenced by the terrible experiences recounted by Holocaust survivors from Treblinka, for as has been seen the miscarriage of justice there was overturned because of evidence invalidating the verdict and discrediting the testimony of witnesses who recounted with great outrage their experience of the Holocaust at Treblinka and then misidentified Demjanjuk as Ivan the Terrible.

The fact that Demjanjuk was found guilty by a court in West Germany even though his complicity seems to have been no more than presence and role as a guard at Sobibor at a time at which exterminations were taking place is incongruous when considered in the context of avoidance of investigation of former Nazis for decades in West Germany, leniency for those who were prosecuted, and the West German public's aversion during the 1950s and 1960s to prosecution of individuals who did no more than conform to role requirements. The trial does seem to have been a forum for the 'representational' justice Douglas advocates for Jewish victims whose need to share their experiences and to implicate and derogate those they identify as having been responsible in some way seems to have been undiminished.

Though the West German policy of leniency towards Nazi war criminals over many decades was pragmatic and rational, its legitimacy would seem to derive not from reference to professional obligation or duty to obey orders in the Third Reich but from the reality that human behaviour is motivated by optimisation of personal interest regardless of circumstance, with the latter affecting consequence. In that regard Nazi perpetrators and those complicit in the Nazi state apparatus seem no different in motive from the majority of people in the liberal democratic west. In a different societal context Nazi perpetrators and those complicit in the Holocaust would have cultivated careers in corporate life, in bureaucracies or the professions, or become minor functionaries, for there is no evidence of former Nazis engaging in perpetrator behaviour after the war, when there was no longer any advantage to be derived from such behaviour. It would not have been possible for West Germany to prosecute all Nazi perpetrators and those complicit in Nazi war crimes and crimes against humanity because of their numbers, given the bureaucratic totalitarianism of the Nazi regime, and as a democratic government that of West Germany would have been influenced by popular disenchantment with the pursuit of former Nazis.

What does then seem inappropriate in West German 'justice' is the much more recent prosecution of a very small number of 'war criminals' such as Demjanjuk, for whom there seems to be no evidence whatever of his exceeding the requirements of his role as camp guard at Sobibor. For the other recent notorious case, of Oskar Gröning, who was responsible for the currency and property of Jews at Auschwitz and who admitted to pilfering some possessions of Jews there, the evidence is of minor acts of squalid opportunism rather than sadism or inflicting harm on Jews.

Fulbrook's criticism of the Demjanjuk trial does seem valid given the exemption of former Nazis of greater social and occupational status in the earlier decades of West Germany. Fulbrook's more general criticism of the lack of justice in West Germany in regard to the great majority of Nazi war criminals and those complicit in Nazi war crimes and crimes against humanity does though seem to disregard the influence of context and the reality of human optimisation of outcomes in all social contexts. For evidence from other historical contexts indicates that the great majority of people would, in the context faced by ordinary Germans under the Nazi regime, have behaved as ordinary Germans did, with a combination of minimal and more opportunistic conformity to the dictates of the Third Reich even where that included perpetrator behaviour. Of course it could be argued that there was some latitude for Nazi perpetrators and those complicit in Nazi perpetrator behaviour, that they could have evaded formal and informal sanctions by the sort of evasion employed by Browning's 'Ordinary Men' (referred to above), for instance by being less zealous in the accomplishment of what their roles required of them, and it is possible that some complied minimally with the requirements of their roles. But such methods were dangerous and risked denunciation in a Nazi society in which the practice was common, and for the aspirational and opportunistic optimising their outcomes necessitated optimal achievement of tasks assigned them. And in the climate of fear and the perceived universality of compliance, any form of evasion or lack of preparedness to accomplish the task, regardless of its nature, risked adverse comparison with peers by superiors and peers and the imposition of sanctions whether formal or informal.

The passive and active complicity in Nazi criminality of the overwhelming majority of ordinary Germans in various capacities and forms during the war was followed by similarly widespread self-exoneration on the part of Nazi perpetrators in their references to obedience to orders and to the influence of Nazi ideology and by a general West German aversion to war crimes trials and to action to give effect to any form of justice to Europe's Jews when the war ended. The commonality between the wartime and the post-war period is that for the great majority of ordinary Germans optimisation of their own outcomes in the form of exclusive pursuit of their own interests took precedence over any consideration for others, not least the Jews.

The exclusive concern with their own outcomes of the great majority of ordinary Germans seems to have been entirely unreflective and so almost inadvertent in nature both during and after the war. In fact ordinary Germans seem to have regarded themselves as victims after the war, because of the devastation caused by Allied bombing, most notably in the notorious instances of Hamburg, Dresden and Berlin, and to have felt that the enactment of post-war 'justice' was 'victors' justice' imposed by show trials.

Germans made reference to the influence of the very different social and political context of the Third Reich as a means of exonerating them and their complicity, though the evidence on ordinary Germans does not seem to differentiate them from ordinary people in all historical and social contexts, for the great majority of people in all cultures and times have prioritised their own interests over those of others, with some doing so to maintain status and standard of living and others for more opportunistic and careerist reasons.

Avoidance of responsibility through claims of obedience to orders and role requirements is of course commonplace in ordinary life, as is actual compliance with role requirements to keep one's job, attending selectively to one's own circumstances, and avoidance of blame. The reason for such selectivity may be that it is natural to sympathise with oneself and one's own problems and to disregard or excuse one's involvement in or responsibility for the plight of others in an entirely unreflective process of optimising economic, social and psychological outcomes for the self.

The evaluation of perpetrators and of post-war 'justice' by historians and other academics may be a reflection of a number of factors. A significant influence on the moral condemnation that is so prevalent seems to be an unrealistic view of human motivation and behaviour. That view may in turn reflect the distorting influence of social protocols that dictate avoidance of reference to the primacy of competitive self-interest and of the motive to optimise personal outcomes, including that of relative well-being (that is, rank, status and privilege in relation to others within one's social horizon), in human behaviour.

That primacy is indicated by various strands of evidence, including the pioneering work of Asch on conformity to group norms, of Milgram on obedience to immoral authority, and of Zimbardo on the influence of assigned role, all of whose results may be interpreted to indicate the primacy of pursuit of personal interest. There is also the fact that all legal systems are supported by sanctions to elicit compliance, and the reality that the conditioning that occurs in the socialisation process results in conforming behaviour that is undertaken to optimise rewards and to avoid punishment, with emulation of behaviour observed to elicit reward and avoidance of that seen to be punished, so that even what may be regarded as behaviour reflective of normative attachment derives from optimisation of personal outcomes. And there is the observation that evolution has selected in those who survive to reproduction age through either social dominance or compliance within hierarchies imposed on them. Open acknowledgement of human motivation and behaviour being fundamentally self-interested is avoided because reference to the reality of human motivation and behaviour would itself be punished by informal social sanctions such as gossip, ridicule, disapproval and ostracism. The reality of human alienation is then avoided.

There is one other possible significant influence on judgements of complicity in the Nazi regime, a tendency on the part of those making judgements regarding Nazi complicity and responsibility and post-war 'justice' not just to reflect the liberal humanitarian perspective and standards of their socialisation and upbringing in liberal democratic societies that respect human rights, but also to conform, albeit possibly inadvertently, to a norm of expression of (entirely understandable) revulsion for the Nazi regimes' crimes against humanity to avoid disapproval and criticism from academic peers. The consequence has been liberal humanitarian condemnation of those involved in Nazi perpetrator behaviour and in some cases the entire German population. This is understandable but does not address the reality of human motivation and the primacy of pursuit of personal interest in human behaviour, but historians cannot be expected to be psychologists too (this is the reason why Christopher Browning's 'Ordinary Men' was so pioneering, in that it did refer to the social psychological experiments of Milgram and Zimbardo and so addressed the causes of human behaviour).

For the Allies after the war there was the American motive to assume the moral high ground and impose on Germany a number of publicised show trials to establish the legitimacy of American justice and to dictate international behaviour thenceforth, and Stalin's agenda at Nuremberg to use the court as propaganda. These tribunals did of course exonerate by implication the Allies and their conduct of the war, including the atom bombing of Hiroshima and Nagasaki and the colossal bombing of German cities such as Berlin, Hamburg and Dresden. For the Germans the narrative was different, of course, one of pointing to Allied violations of the rules of war, to the devastation of Germany, and to the social and ideological context of Nazi Germany in mitigation of their complicity in German war crimes. What is common to all these postures is that they were perceived to be optimal for those assuming them at the time.

The preceding paragraphs are not intended to establish that there is any moral equivalence between Nazi and Allied war crimes, for there is not. Nor are they intended to exonerate perpetrators. They do though indicate that the entirely normal human motive of optimising personal social and psychological outcomes does explain the behaviour of ordinary Germans of the wartime generation during and after the war; the post-war quest for 'justice' by the Allies and the use of the post-war asymmetry of power in their favour to dictate what was and was not a war crime to be considered by the various tribunals; the appreciations of academics from various disciplines who seem to have exceeded their remits in moral judgements regarding the behaviour of ordinary Germans during and after the war and regarding the adequacy of the 'justice' imposed by the Allies and West German governments over time; and the moral outrage of a generation of West Germans with no experience of, or complicity in the crimes of, the Third Reich and so nothing to lose by advocating prosecution and punishment of anyone present when violations of human rights were committed, regardless of the role of the person concerned, which seems intended to establish their liberal and humanitarian credentials before liberal democratic audiences of approving peers and to indicate that they would have behaved differently from the previous generation in similar circumstances. It is of course expedient that such implications are counterfactual and cannot be proved, or disproved. Having said that, it is acknowledged that it is not a legitimate argument against punishment for a crime that in similar circumstances any human being could or would have done the same. What the realisation of the contingency involved, and the power of the situation over so much of human behaviour, given the ubiquity of the motivation to optimise personal outcomes, does counsel is less sanctimony and moral rectitude on the part of those delivering judgements. Of course even if it is the behaviour that is being punished for exemplary purposes, it is the actor of that behaviour who receives the punishment. That returns one to the experiential context of the Third Reich and the war in the east for Nazi perpetrators and the possibility that they too were victims of the Third Reich.

There is one final indication of the influence of the asymmetry of power at the end of the war. For the 'justice' meted out by the victors rejected the defence of reference to the experiential context of the Third Reich, with its combination of the Führerprinzip, which conferred on any 'decision' attributed to Hitler the legitimacy of the law, the SS code of obedience and discipline and the universality of compliance both within the SS and in the Nazi hierarchy and Nazi society in general (the latter supported by widely known evidence of summary arrest and incarceration in concentration camps for any form of dissent from early on in the Nazi period), and the prevalence of Nazi propaganda vilifying Jews and SS indoctrination portraying them as enemies of the German race and state and associated with Bolshevism and partisan activity behind the German lines in the east. The implication is that Nazi perpetrators who did no more than meet the requirements of their roles in the SS and elsewhere in the Nazi state apparatus were, despite the context described here, expected to have reflected upon and to have challenged the requirements of their roles and ultimately to have declined to meet them. It is difficult not to observe that there was no similar expectation that the British RAF bomber pilots assigned to perpetrate bombing of civilian targets in Hamburg, Dresden and Berlin, and the US pilots who bombed Hiroshima and Nagasaki, should have challenged and refused to meet the requirements of their roles. Of course the argument would be that the objectives were different, in the Nazi case the extermination of innocent Jews who objectively posed no threat to Germany and in the case of British and US bomber pilots the objective of bringing to an end as quickly as possible a war started by Nazi Germany, but the experience of the perpetrators in each case would have been similar in the process involved, conformity to optimise personal outcomes and especially to preclude adverse ones, and in the perceptions of justification and necessity because of the effect of propaganda in both cases.

Notes

[1] See Fulbrook, Mary, *Reckonings: Legacies of Nazi Persecution and the Quest for Justice*, Oxford University Press, 2018, p. 212.

[2] See ibid, p. 104.

[3] See ibid, p. 356. There is no apparent explanation of the missing 11,840 cases (the total number of cases minus the convictions and acquittals).

[4] See ibid. The loose reference to 'hundreds of thousands' of perpetrators does make calculation of the percentage sentenced for murder problematic. See below for Fulbrook's acknowledgement of the difficulties in assigning the category of 'perpetrator'. And see p. 356 for Fulbrook's assessment of the situation in East Germany, where she claims that there were as many as 12,890 guilty verdicts between 1945 and 1989, far more than in a West Germany in which post-war devastation and fear of communist expansionism were regarded as the priorities and in which the public rejected a prioritisation of pursuit of Nazi war criminals. In East Germany public opinion was hardly an influence and there were harsher sentences for the guilty. Even so the majority, 7,732 sentences, were for prison terms of under three years. Unlike the Federal Republic of Germany, where the priority was reconstruction and the standard of living in a context of fear of the spread of communism, in East Germany it was derogation of the capitalist west as the threat to the communist east and ideological reference to the extent of Soviet sacrifice in the war.

[5] See McKale, Donald M., *Nazis After Hitler: How Perpetrators of the Holocaust Cheated Justice and Truth*, Roman & Littlefield, 2012, p. x.

[6] See ibid.

[7] See Walker, Shaun, 'Stalin's secret police finally named but killings not seen as crimes', *The Guardian*, 6 February 2017, for reference to the finding of the names of 40,000 NKVD officers involved in state security in the Great Purge of 1937 and 1938, which does of course exclude Stalin's more general use of NKVD terror before and after that time, not least in the Ukrainian Famine of 1932 and the deportation of entire nationalities during and after the war. There is also reference to the view of Petrov, a historian involved with Memorial, an organisation that has been documenting 'Stalin-era crimes', that in the poverty and hunger of the early 1930s those obtaining a prestigious job in the NKVD could not have anticipated their being responsible for thousands of sentences of death in a matter of years. Of the 40,000 NKVD officers identified an estimated ten per cent were executed or jailed and some of the latter were released to participate in operations during the war. The report indicates that no Soviet or post-Soviet government in Russia has prosecuted those involved in Stalinist state terror, possibly because there has been continuing state repression using the NKVD's successor organisation, the KGB, and because of reluctance to discredit state security in Russia given its continuing influence. The narrative in Russian school textbooks is one of 'mistakes' rather than 'crimes'. The other point is that there appears to have been no popular clamour for an accounting with the NKVD for the use of terror or with collaborators for their complicity in terror, indicating broad acceptance of popular collaboration and even of perpetrator behaviour under Stalinist terror and totalitarianism.

[8] See ibid, pp. 213, 216, 217 and 265. See also p. 313 for reference to the difficulties of securing convictions of former Nazis under West German criminal law and to the resulting failure of the system to 'bring the vast majority of those who were guilty of mass murder and collective violence to any form of adequate justice'. And see p. 252

for the note taken under West German criminal law of the 'subjective state of defendants "blinded by Nazi ideology and propaganda"' or having 'acted unwillingly, obeying orders without really wanting to act as they did'. Though the two defences are incompatible with each other, for the defence of belief from experiential context does mean that a defence of compliance with orders under duress is not plausible, both defences could have been legitimate, just not in the same case. There is then here no indication of bias in West German criminal law in favour of exoneration of Nazi perpetrators, just of an ordinary standard of proof in a criminal case in the need to establish criminal intent to prove murder.

[9] See ibid, pp. 245 and 246.

[10] See ibid, pp. 355 and 356.

[11] Taylor, Frederick, *Exorcising Hitler: The Occupation and Denazification of Germany*, Bloomsbury Publishing, 2012, p. 282.

[12] See ibid, p. 286.

[13] See Frei, Norbert, *Adenauer's Germany and the Nazi Past: The Politics of Amnesty and Integration*, Columbia University Press, 2002, pp. 303 and 304.

[14] See Fulbrook, *Reckonings*, op. cit., pp. 249 and 250. Fulbrook also notes that for some crimes the statute of limitations precluded prosecution by 1950.

[15] See ibid, pp. 249–53. And see pp. 355 and 356 for her reference to the very low numbers of Nazi perpetrators investigated and the even lower numbers brought to trial and convicted.

[16] See Bazyler, Michael E., and Tuerkheimer, Frank M., *Forgotten Trials of the Holocaust*, NYU Press, 2015, pp. 189–93. See also Kay, Alex J., Review of Earl, Hilary, 'The SS-Einsatzgruppen Trial', in *Journal of Contemporary History, Volume 46, No 2*, April 2011, for reference to the protests against the sentences in the Einsatzgruppen trial by Protestant and Catholic clergymen and to McCloy's having 'drastically' reduced the sentences, with nine of the thirteen death sentences commuted to life imprisonment on 31 January 1951 even though there was no evidence of a sense of guilt on the part of the Einsatzgruppen commanders concerned, and with the last convicted Einsatzgruppen commander released on 9 May 1958. See also Earl, Hilary, *The Nuremberg SS-Einsatzgruppen Trial, 1945–1958: Atrocity, Law and History*, Cambridge University Press, 2009, p. 299 for Earl's view that the 'worst outrage' was the early release of Einsatzgruppen commanders who had been responsible for the murders of 1,000,000 people, a policy of commutation of sentences she sees as reflecting the perceived political priorities of the Cold War. And see Fulbrook, *Reckonings*, op. cit., p. 248 for the terms of McCloy's 1951 amnesty and for reference to the outcome by 1958.

[17] See Pendas, Devin O., *Democracy, Nazi Trials, and Transitional Justice in Germany, 1945–1950*, Cambridge University Press, 2020, p. 2, and Priemel, Kim Christian, *The Betrayal: The Nuremberg Trials and German Divergence*, Oxford University Press, 2016, p. 402.

[18] See Fulbrook, *Reckonings*, op. cit., p. 216.

[19] See ibid, p. 212.

[20] See Taylor, *Exorcising Hitler*, op. cit., p. 282.

[21] See ibid, p. 280.

[22] See ibid, p. 286. See also p. 287 for reference to the effect of the Eichmann trial in

drawing attention to genocide and to the testimonies and experiences of the victims of the Nazis.

[23] See ibid, p. 252 for Fulbrook's observation that 'in the 1960s and early 1970s very few individuals were actually brought to trial, and slightly more than half were acquitted,' and p. 248 for her note that a West German law passed in 1968 meant that 'prosecution as an accomplice to a Nazi crime could no longer be pursued after 1960' and that 'the legal system was itself the consequence of political decisions.'

[24] See Weinschenk, Fritz, 'Nazis Before German Courts: The West German War Crimes Trials', in *International Lawyer, Vol.10, No.3,* Summer 1976.

[25] See Fulbrook, *Reckonings*, op. cit., pp. 290–98 and 310–15. See also pp. 322 and 323 for the claim that West German judges had 'more sympathy with former Nazis than with their victims' and the influence on sentencing of a defendant's middle class status even as late as 1966. And see Frei, *Adenauer's Germany and the Nazi Past*, op. cit., p. 67 for the attribution of a decrease in prosecutions of former Nazis from the beginning of the 1950s to the 'degree of personal continuity in the judicial system' and a resulting reluctance to apply the law, though such avoidance of prosecutions was consonant with the 'public mood', and for reference to a more general amnesty in 1954 than the initial one, in 1949, one that resulted in another decrease in prosecutions of former Nazis.

[26] See ibid, pp. 336, 337, 347, 348 and 349.

[27] See ibid, pp. 405–08 for Fulbrook's references to perpetrators' means of exculpating themselves. And see p. 107 for Fulbrook's reference to perpetrators' seeing themselves as 'victims'.

[28] See ibid, p. 107. Fulbrook does not seem to attempt to isolate the effect of one possible causal factor from another, and her use of instances does not of course establish incidence.

[29] See ibid, p. 456 for reference to the 'unease and heightened moral responsibility' of the younger generation in West Germany. Responsibility does seem to be more readily assumed when there are no adverse consequences for doing so.

[30] Trawnikis were Soviet POWs who 'volunteered' to collaborate with the SS in the east and were used as auxiliaries to the Einsatzgruppen in shooting Bolsheviks, partisans and Jews behind the German lines and as extermination camp guards.

[31] See ibid, p. 348 for Fulbrook's noting that Demjanjuk was convicted despite the absence of any evidence of intention or actual participation in murder on his part, unlike previous prosecutions for war crimes. And see Douglas, Lawrence, *The Right Wrong Man: John Demjanjuk and the Last Great Nazi War Crimes Trial*, Princeton University Press, 2018, pp. 130, 157, 219, 227 and 240.

[32] See Hilton, Laura, and Pratt, Avinoam (eds.), *Understanding and Teaching the Holocaust*, University of Wisconsin Press, 2020, p. 179.

[33] See ibid, pp. 8–10.

[34] See Levi, Primo, *The Drowned and the Saved*, Simon and Schuster, 2017, pp. 25–57.

[35] See Fulbrook, *Reckonings*, op. cit., pp. 8–10. See also p. 139 for reference to perpetrators' complicity in the 'collective violence' yet lack of any sense of responsibility 'for the murderous outcome' as 'the division of labor was accompanied by a corresponding diminution of any sense of personal guilt.'

[36] See ibid, pp. 521–26.

[37] See Fulbrook, *Reckonings*, op. cit., pp. 526–29. Fulbrook rejects the argument that Nazis were needed for governments in post-war states, pointing to the 'emergent dynamics of the Cold War'.

[38] See Browning, Christopher, *Ordinary Men, Reserve Police Battalion 101 and the Final Solution in Poland*, Penguin, London, 2001, pp. 184 and 185, and Earl, *The Nuremberg SS-Einsatzgruppen Trial*, op. cit., p. 244.

[39] See Kershaw, Ian, *Hitler, the Germans and the Final Solution*, Yale University Press, 2008, pp. 198 and 229.

[40] See McGuinness, Peggy, 'Churchill on War Crimes Trials', opinio.juris.org, 23 January 2006, for reference to the wartime quotations from 1942 and 1945, and Gilbert, Martin, *Winston S. Churchill, Never Despair, 1945–1965*, Rosetta Books, 2015, for the 1946 quotation and Ismay's reference.

[41] See van Shaak, Beth, 'Setting the Record Straight on the Soviets at Nuremberg', 17 June 2020, Commentary on Francine Hirsch, *Soviet Judgment and Nuremberg: A New History of the International Military Tribunal After World War II*, Oxford University Press, 2020, on warontherocks.com.

[42] See Bassiouni, M. Cherif, 'The "Nuremberg Legacy"', in Mettraux, Guénaël (ed.), *Perspectives on the Nuremberg Trial*, Oxford University Press, 2008, p. 577.

[43] See Douglas, *The Right Wrong Man*, op. cit., p. 260.

[44] See Douglas, *The Right Wrong Man*, op. cit., pp. 6–12 and 260.

[45] See Douglas, Lawrence, 'The Memory of Judgment: Making Law and History' in the *Trials of the Holocaust*, Yale University Press, 2001, pp. 113, 126 and 257.

Chapter Two
The Einsatzgruppen trial

The Einsatzgruppen trial was the ninth trial conducted by the US military authorities in West Germany and took place between September 1947 and April 1948. Amongst the US military trials that followed the arraignment of the senior echelon of surviving Nazis the Einsatzgruppen trial was especially significant in that the defendants, Einsatzgruppen, Einsatzkommando and Sonderkommando commanders, were charged with having been directly responsible for mass murder in the east and with the visceral immediacy of shooting Jews in many cases. The Einsatzgruppen and their sub-units, the Einsatzkommandos and Sonderkommandos, were SS units tasked with eradicating, from the rear of the German advance into Poland in September 1939 and the Soviet Union from June 1941, 'the political and racial enemies of the Reich'.[1]

The Einsatzgruppen trial was predicated upon the discovery by US military investigators of Einsatzgruppen field reports detailing numbers of Jews eliminated in the Soviet Union behind the German advance. These had been sent to various parts of the Nazi state apparatus. The Einsatzgruppen trial discussed here does then relate to Einsatzgruppen operating in the German rear following the Wehrmacht advance into the Soviet Union from June 1941 rather than the Einsatzgruppen that followed the Wehrmacht invasion of Poland in 1939 (there was also the 1958 Ulm Einsatzgruppen trial of members of the Einsatzkommando Tilsit for atrocities committed in Lithuania in 1941, the first major war crimes trial conducted by the West German state rather than involving US military courts).

There were four Einsatzgruppen behind the Wehrmacht advance into the Soviet Union, Einsatzgruppen A, B, C and D, each assigned to an army group and region in the Soviet Union. Einsatzgruppe A covered Latvia, Lithuania and Estonia and regions to their east, Einsatzgruppe B covered the central region to the south of Einsatzgruppe A, Einsatzgruppe C covered most of the Ukraine, and Einsatzgruppe D covered the south of the Ukraine, Crimea and the Caucasus. During the years in the Soviet Union Earl claims that there were eighty-four Einsatzgruppen, Einsatzkommando and Sonderkommando commanders, of whom fifteen were Einsatzgruppen commanders, and that four of the fifteen and twenty of the sixty-nine Einsatzkommando and Sonderkommando commanders were indicted in 1947, which she regards as a significant percentage of the Einsatzgruppen leadership.[2] This is open to controversy, for the percentage of Einsatzgruppen commanders especially does seem low. The defendants at the Einsatzgruppen trial pleaded 'not guilty, in the sense of the indictment'.[3]

A major influence on the Einsatzgruppen trial was Otto Ohlendorf, the commander of Einsatzgruppe D, who had admitted under interrogation associated with the Nuremberg trial of major Nazi war criminals that his Einsatzgruppe D had been responsible for the mass murder of 90,000 Soviet citizens whilst under his command between May 1941 and May 1942.[4] Ohlendorf was 'voluble' in his preparedness to provide 'shocking detail' regarding the activities of the Einsatzgruppen and their links with the German High Command, and his 'uncompromising disposition and colossal arrogance' were apparent in his belief that he could be seen to be of use in creating an underground intelligence organisation with the western allies. When that was rejected by the British he altered his strategy to offer to provide information on those from whom he received his orders, being a witness at the trial of Ernst Kaltenbrunner, Heydrich's successor as the head of the Reich Security Main Office (the RSHA) of the SS.

Though Ohlendorf stood out in his urbanity, being at trial 'the epitome of composure',[5] he was not unrepresentative of his cohort of Einsatzgruppen, Einsatzkommando and Sonderkommando commanders, for in his level of education and careerist aspiration he was similar to a generation of young university educated Germans (Wildt's 'Uncompromising Generation')[6] for whom tradition elicited disdain in a radical shift to the right and to an ethos of translating ideology into action and who became the 'leadership corps of Heydrich's RSHA' and then Einsatzgruppen, Einsatzkommando or Sonderkommando commanders.[7] Earl claims that such commanders were a 'highly-educated elite group' that would have attained important positions in any society.[8]

Ohlendorf's open acknowledgement of his involvement in the murder of 90,000 people was an error of some consequence, given that Musmanno, the trial judge, who found Ohlendorf 'erudite and profound', imposed the death penalty only on defendants who confessed.[9] An unrepentant Ohlendorf was executed on 7 June 1951. The other Einsatzgruppen, Einsatzkommando and Sonderkommando commanders who were executed were Blobel, commander of Sonderkommando 4a and responsible for the notorious Babi Yar massacre, Braune, commander of Sonderkommando 4b, and Naumann, commander of Einsatzgruppe B. Though Musmanno had sentenced fourteen of the defendants to death the rest of the sentences were commuted, in a changed political landscape informed by the Cold War, recovered West German political confidence and resurgent German nationalism, by McCloy, the US High Commissioner to Germany, who also reduced prison sentences on other defendants.[10]

While the prosecution case rested on Einsatzgruppen reports of mass murders of Jews in the Soviet Union, the defence employed a variety of arguments. These included claims that the defendant concerned was absent at the time of the atrocities being cited and other challenges to the validity of the prosecution evidence, including Blobel's absurd defence that the numbers of Jews claimed to have been murdered by his Sonderkommando 4a of Einsatzgruppe C were an 'exaggeration', as if having murdered rather fewer Jews than the enormous numbers that had been claimed was a defence, and that his tenure as commander of Sonderkommando 4a had been only between June 1941 and January 1942, when he claimed to have been 'removed for disciplinary reasons', with other interruptions due to periods in hospital, the argument being that he was not the only commander of Sonderkommando 4a and so not the only officer responsible for its extermination of Jews.

Of the 'broader conceptual defences' there was the claim that the perpetrator behaviour of the Einsatzgruppen was not criminal under the law of any country and certainly not at the time of its commission, a claim that had been dismissed at the Nuremberg trial of major Nazi war criminals on the basis that the perpetrator behaviour concerned involved murder, which was of course regarded as criminal under all legal systems. Another defence was the 'tu quoque' (or 'you too') defence, employed especially by Naumann, commander of Einsatzgruppe B, and Ohlendorf, which pointed to Allied war crimes committed especially by the Soviets (though the western Allies' bombing of Dresden and the US bombing of Hiroshima and Nagasaki were mentioned). That too had been rejected in the trial of major Nazi war criminals as a defence, and the point was made at the Einsatzgruppen trial that there was a significant difference between Allied bombings to bring to an end as quickly as possible a war that had been started by Nazi Germany and Nazi war crimes and crimes against humanity that gave the Nazis no wartime advantage (though in fact Soviet POW and Jewish slave labour did assist the German war effort). That left defences that claimed 'self- defense and necessity' in an ideological context of Jews' being regarded as enemies of Germany in time of war, collaborators with the Soviets and associated with Bolshevism, the argument that there was no difference between Bolsheviks, partisans and Jews or that it was impossible to differentiate them from each other, and the defence of following 'superior orders'.[11]

According to the trial transcript the case for the defence sought to contextualise the perpetrator behaviour of the Einsatzgruppen by locating their task within the framework of the Nazi organisation and experience of the war in the east. The defence claimed that the Einsatzgruppen were under the command of the army and that Einsatzgruppen activities reflected the 'express will' or 'tacit consent' of army commanders in the east. The defence also attempted to show 'how difficult the position of each man was to disobey the order of the Fuehrer', pointing to the defendants' conception of 'the East European Jewish problem as part of the problem of bolshevism', and to their regarding it as a 'national emergency' central to the resolution of which was resolving the 'Jewish problem', which required 'unreserved execution of the Fuehrer order'. In other words the defence was that the organisational, ideological and psychological context of Nazi rule, the SS and the war in the east made it virtually impossible for Einsatzgruppen, Einsatzkommando and Sonderkommando commanders to conceive of challenging the legitimacy of the Führer Order regarding their task in the east.[12]

Ohlendorf's testimony in an affidavit dated 2 April 1947, on which Ohlendorf testified in court on 9 October 1947, was as follows—

'On the basis of orders which were given by former Brigadefuehrer Streckenbach, Chief of Amt 1 of the RSHA, by order of the head of the RSHA, to the Chiefs of the Einsatzgruppen and the Kommandofuehrer at the time of the formation of the Einsatzgruppen in Pretzsch (in Saxony) and which were given by the Reich Leader SS to the leaders and men of the Einsatzgruppen and

Einsatzkommandos who assembled in Nikolaev in September 1941, a number of undesirable elements composed of Russians, gypsies, and Jews and others were executed in the area detailed to me. All Jews who were arrested as such were to be executed within my area'.[13]

Here Ohlendorf seems to be claiming a defence of obedience to orders received from Himmler as Reich Leader SS. Ohlendorf further testified, on 24 April 1947, that the Einsatzgruppen had been created as a result of an agreement between the Chief of the Security Police and a representative of the German High Command to be responsible for 'political security tasks' in the German rear and 'clearing the area of Jews, Communist officials, and agents by killing all racially and politically undesirable elements seized who were considered dangerous to the security'. Ohlendorf claimed that 'orders concerning undesirable elements went directly to the Einsatzkommandos and came from the Reich Leader SS himself or by transmission through Heydrich', and 'commanders in chief were ordered by Hitler to support the execution of these orders. Through the so-called Commissar Order, army units had to sort out political commissars and other undesirable elements and hand them over to the Einsatzkommandos' to be eradicated.[14] Ohlendorf does then seem to be claiming a defence of obedience to orders received directly from Himmler and indirectly from Hitler himself. Ohlendorf's statements should be interpreted in the context of the defence argument regarding the nature of the experience of Einsatzgruppen commanders in the east, and in the context of the Führerprinzip, the oath of obedience and of personal loyalty to Hitler sworn by SS officers, and the code of discipline of the SS.

Earl addresses the timing of the Führer Order, the Führerbefehl, that dictated the extermination of all Soviet Jews, noting that Ohlendorf's claim to have received the order in June 1941, before the German invasion, has been disputed by other historians, with a possible early August or September date proposed. The significance of the date is that if there were such a Führer Order prior to mass murders of Jews in the east then an obedience-to-orders defence could mitigate the guilt of perpetrators giving effect to that order, though Earl notes that Ohlendorf's claim as to the date of the order was before the prospect of mitigation was introduced (and so was credible) and that the date was not significant for the Einsatzgruppen trial itself because the court did not consider the motivation of defendants. Earl does note that the order was specific in its instruction to murder all Soviet Jewry, not just communists or threats to the Reich.[15]

Though the defence argued that account should be taken of the experiential context in which the perpetrator behaviour of the Einsatzgruppen, Einsatzkommando and Sonderkommando commanders occurred, the court seems to have considered each defence argument separately. On the 'self-defense and necessity' argument the observation was made that there was no evidence of actual association of Jews with Bolshevism or of an inherent threat posed by Bolshevism to Nazi Germany, and that the 'self-defense' argument was not credible because it required only conviction that there was such a threat, not reason or actuality of threat, so that 'an obsession became a valid defense'. It was also observed that if Bolshevism was the legitimising threat every Russian would have to be murdered, which did not happen, and that only Jews who were members of the Communist Party should have been murdered, when in fact all Jews were eradicated. On the 'superior orders' defence the court ruled that there would have to be evidence of no awareness of the illegality of the order and evidence of duress for it to be credible.[16]

Earl claims that the Einsatzgruppen, Einsatzkommando and Sonderkommando commanders murdered Jews, Bolsheviks and partisans for ideological reasons, that is, because of their ideological attachment to Nazism and its association of Jews with Bolshevism seen to represent a threat to the Reich as enemies of the German race and state, though she also refers to the careerist motives of the Einsatzgruppen, Einsatzkommando and Sonderkommando commanders.[17] The Führerprinzip dictated obedience to orders that ultimately came from Hitler and would seem to be part of the ideological commitment and experiential context of these commanders, and Earl claims that 'according to Ohlendorf, Hitler, Himmler and Heydrich were at the center of the decision-making process, and the members of the killing units had little or no agency. They were, as Ohlendorf told his captors, simply following orders. His co-defendants reiterated his obedience to superior orders defense' and claimed they had 'no choice but to obey'. Earl does not accept this case for the defence. She differentiates the defence of obedience to orders from the influence of ideological commitment on the perpetrator behaviour of the Einsatzgruppen, Einsatzkommando and Sonderkommando commanders, and claims that ideological conviction was the decisive influence.[18]

According to Earl, 'with few exceptions, the defendants at Nuremberg refused to acknowledge they had done anything wrong. To do so would have betrayed Hitler, the Party, the SS, and Germany.' Yet Earl's observation that almost all the defendants did not admit to having done anything wrong is hardly surprising given that admission of guilt may have been seen to enhance their risks of execution. Earl's claim that most defendants did not admit having done anything wrong because to do so would have 'betrayed Hitler, the Party, the SS, and Germany' is an inference for which Earl provides no evidence, and the far more plausible explanation is that their defence required a combination of no admission of having done anything wrong and attribution of their perpetrator behaviour to the experiential context of Nazi Germany, including Nazi ideological association of Jews with Bolshevism and threat to the German state and race, the exigencies of a war with irregular partisan warfare behind the lines in the east, the SS code of discipline and obedience and the Führerprinzip, which conferred on any Führer Order the force of law in Nazi Germany. The fact that such a defence was a form of evasion of responsibility does not of itself prove that it was not true, but the legitimacy of the extermination of the Jews for Einsatzgruppen defendants, inferred from Earl's observation that defendants did not feel they had done anything wrong in their perpetrator behaviour, may reflect the legitimacy for them of meeting role requirements regardless of ideological commitment and personal attitudes.

Earl goes on to enumerate the defences proffered by the defendants. She refers to the 'superior orders defense', which is consistent with the SS code of compliance and discipline, to 'military necessity' to defend the Reich in a war without norms in the east and to the legality of their actions given the claimed criminal activities of the victims, both of which are consistent with loyalty to Hitler, the SS and Germany. But she also notes defences that referred to the threat of punishment for disobedience to orders and to appreciation that refusal to obey orders would not have saved the Jews as someone else would have murdered them.[19]

The reference to defences of 'superior orders' under threat of punishment and belief that their abstaining would not save the Jews do not seem to be consonant with Earl's claim that the Einsatzgruppen, Einsatzkommando and Sonderkommando commanders murdered Jews because of ideological commitment or her claim of defendant loyalty to the Nazi regime. For decisive influence from an experiential context of SS propaganda claiming that Jews were associated with Bolshevism and partisans behind the German lines and that Jews were a threat to the German race and state would indicate belief in the extermination of the Jews as a matter of national survival in the war in the east. This is of course not consistent with a defence that argued that Nazi defendants were reluctant to murder the Jews on moral grounds and only did so under orders in time of war out of fear of punishment for failing to do so, for that argument would mean that they were not that influenced by Nazi and SS propaganda that sought to legitimise the extermination of the Jews. What they could have argued is that they regarded the elimination of the Jews as legitimised by their being a threat to the German race and state and associated with Bolshevism and the partisans because of the effect on them of Nazi propaganda, and that not meeting role requirements that involved the murder of the Jews of the occupied territories was not conceived of because of the SS code of discipline and the universality of conformity in the SS, not least given the Führerprinzip. That does of course not argue compliance with 'superior orders' under 'duress'.[20]

The very existence of so many forms of exoneration, some of them inconsistent with each other, does seem to diminish the credibility of any one of them and leave the impression that any form of self-exculpation believed to be even remotely plausible was going to be presented, though the general defence case does seem to have been that the experiential context was such that a combination of normative obedience to orders in the German military and SS (and universality of compliance), the exigencies and savagery of the war in the east with its irregular warfare behind the German lines (and possible difficulty of identifying partisans) and the ideological association of Jews, commissars, Bolsheviks and partisans meant that resistance to compliance with role requirements was not even conceived of by Einsatzgruppen, Einsatzkommando and Sonderkommando commanders.

Though Earl refers to concerns with career in the Einsatzgruppen, Einsatzkommando and Sonderkommando commanders she does not consider the possibility that they engaged in perpetrator behaviour because they aspired to enhance their careers and status within the SS or did not feel they could fail at a task assigned them when other Einsatzgruppen, Einsatzkommando and Sonderkommando commanders were meeting their role requirements. Nor does she consider that they may also have been motivated to avoid public humiliation before their peer group as a consequence of demotion for failure as Einsatzgruppen, Einsatzkommando or Sonderkommando commanders, indicating a defensive orientation as an explanation for their perpetrator behaviour.

Earl does not then consider the possibility that what motivated the Einsatzgruppen, Einsatzkommando and Sonderkommando commanders and that what explains their wartime perpetrator behaviour and their defences at trial was their optimisation of personal outcomes in the form of avoidance of being seen to have failed by SS peers and bosses during the war and in the form of attempts to evade the gallows at their post-war trial. This is despite extensive evidence on the prevalence of conformity to group norms and on the influence of role on human behaviour in the social psychology literature, not least that of Asch, Milgram, and Zimbardo, and despite evidence too of the ubiquity of pursuit of personal interest in ordinary life. The Einsatzgruppen, Einsatzkommando and Sonderkommando commanders' motive to exculpate themselves at their trial does of course raise obvious questions regarding the veracity of their accounts, including the defence of obedience to superior orders and that of claiming a decisive effect from ideological context.

Earl does not seem to appreciate that evidence that 'even under intense cross-examination, these defendants remained certain about their ideological commitment to Nazism and its world view' may be interpreted in more than one way. She sees it as evidence of the decisive influence of Nazi ideology on Einsatzgruppen, Einsatzkommando and Sonderkommando commanders, though the evidence also indicates that attachment to Nazi ideology seems to have been separate from and not to have resulted in immediate preparedness in the defendants to participate in the mass murder of Jews in the east. It had after all not been Nazi policy towards the Jews before the invasion of the Soviet Union in Operation Barbarossa. It was then perfectly possible to be a committed Nazi in ideological terms and be averse to mass murder of Jewish men, women and children, not least by such visceral means as shooting with its immediacy of experience of what was being done to the Jews.

Earl does note that Ohlendorf was aspiring and concerned to optimise outcomes in the form of career and status in her references to him but does not take account of such a motive in assessing the reasons for his perpetrator behaviour as commander of Einsatzgruppe D, which she attributes to ideological commitment. Her position then seems to be that Ohlendorf was aspiring before the war, was not so during the war as Einsatzgruppe D commander, when he is claimed to have been motivated by ideological commitment, and returned to being influenced by his own interests after the war, at trial, when he invoked the defence of obedience to orders to evade execution for the murder of Jews.

Earl does acknowledge that 'none of the individuals took any responsibility for his actions' and that such lack of acceptance of responsibility 'seems out of character for ideologically motivated individuals', but offers the explanation 'that they were in a court, fighting for their lives', an indication that she acknowledges self-interest as a motive in the defendants. She then expresses surprise at the lack of any indication of regret from defendants to exculpate themselves, though that is what would be expected for those who claimed to be obeying orders and who wished to avoid any acknowledgment of personal responsibility for their perpetrator behaviour. For any admission of regret could have been in their view an indication of guilt and so not conducive to their best interests at their trial, where their objective was to minimise the sentences imposed on them by Musmanno.[21]

On the question of what motivated the Einsatzgruppen, Einsatzkommando and

Sonderkommando commanders to the mass murder of Jews, in a review of Earl's 'The SS-Einsatzgruppen Trial', Steinweis notes that the Einstazgruppen, Einsatzkommando and Sonderkommando commanders were 'an exceedingly well-educated group of men, but, like many of their generational cohort, saw their professional opportunities restricted by the economic conditions of the postwar period. As a consequence, they drifted into the orbit of the Nazi movement.' He also notes that 'Earl points out that they did not join the SD with the intention of becoming mass murderers.'

Steinweis seems to be indicating the influence of optimisation of personal outcomes in terms of career and status on the part of highly educated young men in circumstances in which they assimilated the right-wing ideology of the Nazi movement during university education to the extent of embracing a combination of nationalism, militarism, German racial superiority and a disdain for liberal democratic politics, for the pursuit of personal interest for such aspiring young men of some education in the Third Reich from 1933 onwards would have been optimised by work somewhere within the colossal bureaucratic apparatus of the Nazi state and possibly by a career in the SS as the elite of the Nazi movement. The influence of aspiration is indicated by Steinweis and so is that of the general zeitgeist of right-wing ideology in German universities in the interwar period, though the latter did not include any reference to extermination of the Jews of Europe, let alone visceral involvement in it. Even from a generally approving review then there is a challenge to Earl's attribution of mass murder to ideological commitment on the part of Einsatzgruppen, Einsatzkommando and Sonderkommando commanders and an indication of the role of pursuit of personal interest in the form of cultivating their careers and their status within the SS and the cohort of Einsatzgruppen commanders.[22]

Earl refers to Judge Musmanno's comment that if Blume, commander of Sonderkommando 7a of Einsatzgruppe B under Nebe, had been as opposed to the exterminations as he claimed to be he should have 'falsified reports' to his superiors, and claims that 'Blume's consciousness had become so nazified that he believed it was more nefarious to falsify reports to his superiors than to shoot innocent people'. That is one inference. The rather more obvious one might be that Blume was apprehensive that any falsification of reports would be found out and severely punished.

In the case of Sandberger, commander of Sonderkommando 1a of Einsatzgruppen A, Earl explains his avoidance of any admission of guilt by the claim that 'to admit guilt would have been tantamount to questioning the convictions he had nurtured since his youth', though she notes that he claimed to have objected to the Führerbefehl, to have asked for a transfer to the Wehrmacht, and to have requested to be released 'from his duties in Russia' as many as seven times, which, if true, would indicate his having had serious reservations regarding the Nazi racial policy of exterminating Jews in the east even though it was the logical consequence of Nazi ideological association of Jews with the threat to the Reich of Bolshevism. In other words it is possible that Sandberger had already 'questioned' the ideological context of the SS, and his not admitting guilt may have been intended to evade being executed.

Earl claims that ideology 'ensures a level of certainty that can only come when one relinquishes one's own moral choice in favour of the prevailing one the ideology embraces' and that a form of 'cognitive dissonance' facilitated the defendants' conviction that the murder of Jews was justified. Earl's reference to relinquishing personal choice and subordinating oneself to the ideology of the social context seems to be similar to Milgram's 'agentic state', in which Milgram claimed that participants in his experiments on obedience to immoral authority felt they were no more than 'agents' of the authority figure and so felt no responsibility for their actions. Earl's reference to 'cognitive dissonance' is difficult to understand given that her argument is that Einsatzgruppen, Einsatzkommando and Sonderkommando commanders carried out their perpetrator behaviour because of ideological conviction resulting from assimilation of Nazi and SS propaganda, for Festinger's 'cognitive dissonance' refers to behaviour that is undertaken for instrumental reasons, for instance enhancement or maintenance of career or status, that is dissonant with existing attitudes and results in attitude change to eliminate the discomfort caused by the dissonance between behaviour and attitude.[23]

Festinger's 'cognitive dissonance' would then indicate that Einsatzgruppen, Einsatzkommando and Sonderkommando commanders, far from engaging in genocide because of Nazi ideological attachment, did so for careerist reasons or to avoid failure relative to peers, and that SS propaganda that associated Jews with Bolshevism and partisans and claimed that they represented a threat to the German race and state in time of war appealed to Einsatzgruppen, Einsatzkommando and Sonderkommando commanders because it justified perpetrator behaviour undertaken for pragmatic reasons.

What that means is that even in those cases in which there was belief that the mass murder of the Jews of the east was necessary to combat the threat of Bolshevism with which Jews were associated in Nazi and SS ideology and propaganda, the decisive influence on the perpetrator behaviour of Einsatzgruppen, Einsatzkommando and Sonderkommando commanders was meeting role requirements and accomplishing the assignment given them by their bosses in the SS hierarchy to avoid being seen to have failed where others were succeeding through demonstrating the necessary 'toughness'. The belief that the Jews of the east had to be eradicated to resist Bolshevism would then be an attitude change to reduce the dissonance between previously existing attitudes, for instance against murder of civilians or the murder of women and children, and behaviour undertaken to meet the requirements of role for reasons of maintenance of career in the SS and status amongst peers.

Of course the experience of Einsatzgruppen, Einsatzkommando and Sonderkommando commanders would have been a combination of the Führerprinzip, the SS code and identity that obligated SS officers to compliance with orders that had the ultimate legitimacy of the Führer, the universality of disciplined conformity to role requirements in the SS, and Nazi and SS propaganda that claimed Jews to be associated with Bolshevism and partisans in the east and a threat to the German race and state in time of war, in a context of desire to enhance their careers and status within the SS and to avoid disapprobation from SS peers and bosses for failure to succeed at the task of the Einsatzgruppen, the Einsatzkommando and Sonderkommando. There would not have been deliberate calculation to optimise material, social and psychological outcomes, for the process would have been unreflective.

When addressing individual defendants Earl differentiates between those who claimed an ideological defence, that is, reference to the ideological context, 'deniers' who claimed not to have been responsible for any murders of Jews despite documentary evidence, and those she regards as having been 'conflicted', an inference drawn from evidence of alcoholism and erratic behaviour. The case of Blobel, the notorious commander of Sonderkommando 4a of Einsatzgruppe C under Rasch, seems to be one without resort to ideological justification as an exculpating defence strategy for his infamous perpetrator behaviour at Babi Yar. Earl interprets Blobel's resort to drink as evidence that he knew what he was doing was wrong, that he could not rationalise his perpetrator behaviour by reference to ideological or military context, and that he could not 'bring himself to deny his horrible misdeeds at trial'. His lack of 'coping mechanisms caused him such physical and mental torment that he had to find some way to cope'. Yet the use of alcohol to facilitate mass murder was common in the east, as Browning indicates for his reserve police battalion in its own murder of Jews in Poland, and could be interpreted as indicating that it was the visceral nature and immediacy of the task that was horrifying, rather than the idea of the extermination of the Jews of the east.[24] In other words Earl's interpretation is conjectural, and in fact Milgram's experiments on obedience to immoral authority found that greater immediacy dramatically diminished the preparedness of participants to inflict pain and possible harm on an innocent 'victim', whereas distance enhanced compliance with immoral authority. The inference is indifference to outcomes for others but some reservations regarding personal involvement because of the possibility of being held responsible for perpetrator behaviour, and aversion to the visceral immediacy of some perpetrator behaviour, for those participants in Milgram's experiments who did at some point refuse to continue to administer electric shocks to 'victims' did not check on the welfare of 'victims' or insist that the experiment be halted to prevent further harm to 'victims', indicating that their concern was their own experience of visceral unpleasantness or responsibility rather than the welfare of the 'victim'.

In conclusion, Earl seems to infer from the educated and elite background of Einsatzgruppen, Einsatzkommando and Sonderkommando commanders in the right-wing, nationalistic, militaristic culture of German universities, with their disdain for liberal democracy and capitalism, that is, in Wildt's 'uncompromising generation', susceptibility to the sort of ideological commitment that would justify the extermination of the Jews of the east. Earl then claims that evidence of continued attachment to Nazi ideology on the part of the defendants at their trial is indicative of such ideological commitment. As has been indicated, though, there is a decisive difference between the sort of general attachment to right-wing, nationalistic or even Nazi ideology of German universities in the interwar period and preparedness to murder Jewish men, women and children in the east because of an ideological association of Jews with Bolshevism. Earl does refer to careerist motives but does not infer that optimisation of personal material, social and psychological outcomes was the decisive causal influence on defendants' wartime perpetrator behaviour undertaken by them to enhance or maintain their rank and status in the SS, to avoid being seen to have failed by their bosses and their peer group of other Einsatzgruppen, Einsatzkommando and Sonderkommando commanders, and to conform to the SS code and identity of compliance, toughness and ruthlessness to avoid ridicule or ostracism from their peer group in the SS.

The most plausible explanation is that the combination of orders from Himmler as Reichsführer-SS, Hitler's implicit endorsement of such orders with the legitimacy of the Führerprinzip that conferred on Hitler's preferences the authority of law in Germany, the code of compliance with orders and discipline in the SS that resulted in a universality of meeting of role requirements in the SS, the natural desire to secure status within the SS and to avoid ridicule and ostracism from bosses and peers, and indoctrination that claimed that the Jews were associated with Bolshevism and partisan activity in the German rear and so represented a threat to the German state as well as the German race, meant that resistance to orders was impossible to conceive of, not least because the tendency to conform does seem to be unreflective, a measure of psychological economy and so optimal for the men concerned.

The preceding paragraph does not of course isolate the causal influences referred to from each other in terms of their respective causal contributions to the perpetrator behaviour of Einsatzgruppen, Einsatzkommando and Sonderkommando commanders. Attribution of specific causal influence to any one factor is problematic because they were all part of the experiential context of the east. Even so, the decisive influence on Einsatzgruppen, Einsatzkommando and Sonderkommando commanders' extermination of the Jews of the occupied territories of the east does seem to have been their pursuit of personal interest by conforming to the requirements of their role (and so to the SS code of discipline, toughness and ruthlessness) so as to retain their rank and status within the SS and to avoid disapprobation from or removal from post and demotion by their bosses in the SS, and to preclude gossip, ridicule and ostracism from fellow SS officers. That conclusion is indicated by the minimal case of Browning's 'Ordinary Men', who murdered Jewish old people, women and children despite having had little Nazi indoctrination prior to their initial massacre of Jews in Poland, the motive apparently being to optimise career prospects in the SS by securing the approbation of SS echelons above them in the SS hierarchy in the case of relatively few men, and to avoid peer group ridicule and ostracism for failure to meet the requirements of role and to do their part in what was regarded as an unpleasant task in the case of many of the men. The influence of SS indoctrination that claimed Jews to be associated with Bolshevism and partisan activity and to be an ideological and political as well as a racial threat to Germany and the Reich was that it provided a justification for the perpetrator behaviour of the Einsatzgruppen, Einsatzkommando and Sonderkommando commanders, as did reference to the Führerprinzip and the legality and legitimacy of Führer orders, both during the war, to the extent that the men did experience the 'cognitive dissonance' referred to above, for much conformity does seem to be unreflective rather than following consideration of moral issues, and after the war, when it was of course expedient to claim influence from ideological context and orders to exonerate themselves.

Notes

[1] Earl, Hilary, 'A Judge, A Prosecutor, and a Mass Murderer, Courtroom Dynamics in the SS-Einsatzgruppen Trial', in Priemel, Kim C., and Stiller, Alexa, *Reassessing the Nuremberg Military Tribunals: Transitional Justice, Trial Narratives, and Historiography*, Berghahn Books, 2012, p. 50.

[2] See Earl, Hilary, *The Nuremberg SS-Einsatzgruppen Trial, 1945–1958: atrocity, law and history*, Cambridge University Press, 2009, p. 97.

[3] See *Trials of War Criminals Before The Nuernberg Military Tribunals under Control Council Law No.10, Volume IV*, 'The Einsatzgruppen Case', Nuernberg, October 1946–April 1949, U.S. Government Printing Office, Washington D.C., pp. 25 and 26.

[4] See Bazyler, Michael E., and Tuerkheimer, Frank M., *Forgotten Trials of the Holocaust*, NYU Press, 2015, p. 165 for the claim that Ohlendorf calmly admitted 'his responsibility for the murder of ninety thousand civilians' and for reference to Einsatzgruppe A reports that mentioned Jewish resistance, collaboration with the Red Army and association with Bolshevism.

[5] See Earl in *Reassessing the Nuremberg Military Tribunals*, op. cit., pp. 51 and 52.

[6] See ibid, p. 51.

[7] See ibid, p. 50.

[8] See Earl, *The Nuremberg SS-Einsatzgruppen Trial*, op. cit., pp. 120 and 134.

[9] See Earl in *Reassessing the Nuremberg Military Tribunals*, op. cit., p. 64, and ibid, p. 252.

[10] See Earl, *The Nuremberg SS-Einsatzgruppen Trial*, op. cit., pp. 266 and 287.

[11] See Bazyler and Tuerkheimer, *Forgotten Trials of the Holocaust*, op. cit., pp. 176–79.

[12] See *Trials of War Criminals Before The Nuernberg Military Tribunals under Control Council Law No.10, Volume IV*, 'The Einsatzgruppen Case', op. cit., pp. 63 and 65.

[13] See ibid, pp. 133 and 134.

[14] See ibid, pp. 92–94.

[15] See Earl, *The Nuremberg SS-Einsatzgruppen Trial*, op. cit., pp. 182–85 and 210.

[16] See *Trials of War Criminals Before The Nuernberg Military Tribunals under Control Council Law No.10, Volume IV*, 'The Einsatzgruppen Case', op. cit., pp. 462, 463 and 464.

[17] See ibid, p. 101. And see pp. 244 and 245 for Musmanno's interrogation of Braune regarding the inconsistency between Braune's claiming that he was opposed to the order dictating the mass murder of Jews in the east and his endorsing the claim of Nazi propaganda that 'the Jews were the bearers of bolshevism'.

[18] See Earl, Hilary C., *Legacies of the Nuremberg SS-Einsatzgruppen Trial after 70 years*, 39 Loy. L.A. Int'l. and Comp. L. Review 95 (2017), p. 99. See p. 100 for Earl's noting that Ohlendorf had admitted in January 1946, when used by the US to provide evidence against Kaltenbrunner, who had replaced Heydrich, that his Einsatzgruppe D had murdered 90,000 people, mostly 'Soviet Jews'.

[19] See Earl, *The SS-Einsatzgruppen Trial*, op. cit., pp. 142–44.

[20] See Review by Christopher R. Browning of 'The Nuremberg SS-Einsatzgruppen Trial, 1945–1958: Atrocity, Law, and History', by Hilary Earl, in the *Canadian Journal of History*, Vol. 45, No. 2, for reference to the 'two-pronged, but ultimately contradictory, defense argument' of 'duress in having to obey superior orders' and 'militarily necessary and justifiable self-defense in a total war against Jewish Bolshevism that threatened to destroy Germany if not destroyed first', and to the Einsatzgruppen commanders as 'ideological soldiers who consistently clung to their belief in the rightness of what they had done and showed no remorse whatsoever'. Browning also notes their good education.

[21] See ibid, pp. 158–60.

[22] See Steinweis, review of Earl, Hilary, *The SS-Einsatzgruppen Trial*, on H-net.

[23] See ibid, p. 160 for Earl's claim regarding the effect of attitude on behaviour through 'cognitive dissonance', though see p. 177 for her contradictory understanding that cognitive dissonance is normally reduced by changes of attitude to 'conform to behavior' or by derogation of the victim, a form of justification that eliminates dissonance between behaviour undertaken and dissonant attitudes. The existence of Milgram's 'agentic state' has been challenged by evidence that participants in his experiments did experience distress when inflicting pain on 'victims' and so did not regard themselves as just agents of an authority figure who was responsible for the pain and harm experienced by 'victims'. For this and other references to the research of Milgram in this paper see Milgram, Stanley, 'Behavioral Study of Obedience', *Journal of Abnormal and Social Psychology, 67 (4)*, 1963, pp. 371–78.

[24] See Earl, *The SS-Einsatzgruppen Trial*, op. cit., p. 166.

Chapter Three
The case of Rudolf Höss and the trial of Adolf Eichmann

Rudolf Höss was commandant of Auschwitz between 1 May 1940 and the end of November 1943 and again from 8 May 1944, when he returned to Auschwitz to supervise the annihilation of Hungary's Jews. Höss appeared before the Nuremberg Tribunal as a defence witness for Ernest Kaltenbrunner on 15 April 1946, and his affidavit dated 5 April 1946, prior to his being a witness at the Nuremberg trial, was used at the trial of Oswald Pohl of the Main Economic and Administrative Office and at the IG Farben trial, by which time Höss had been sent to Warsaw (he was passed to the Polish authorities on 25 May 1946) to be tried by the Polish Supreme National Tribunal. There he was found guilty, and he was hanged at Auschwitz on 16 April 1947.

For Höss there is more information than there is for most Nazi perpetrators. For the major Nazi war criminals at Nuremberg there are the assessments of the US military psychiatrists, Drs Kelley and Goldensohn, and the US military psychologist, Dr. Gilbert; for the cases of Franz Stangl and Albert Speer there are the books written after extensive interviews by Gitta Sereny (Speer had of course also been one of the major Nazi war criminals tried at Nuremberg) and Speer's own self-exonerating books and interviews after his release from a twenty-year sentence in Spandau prison; and for Eichmann there are psychiatric and psychological assessments related to his trial in Jerusalem and the evidence of his memoir and of his behaviour in an Israeli courtroom.

The evidence on Höss comes from assessments of him by Goldensohn and Gilbert at Nuremberg, an assessment by Dr Batawia related to Höss's trial in Warsaw, Höss's affidavit of 5 April 1946 and the record of his witness before the Nuremberg Tribunal on 15 April 1946, his demeanour and testimony at his trial by the Polish Supreme National Tribunal in Warsaw, and Höss's own autobiography and letters to his wife and children not long before his execution at Auschwitz. The purpose here is to interrogate the various assessments of Höss to establish the nature of Höss's personality and the reasons for his perpetrator behaviour to assess the legitimacy of the justice meted out to him.

Höss was brought up in a 'very strict Catholic tradition' with an emphasis on morality, sin, guilt and atonement, and military discipline under a father who had been an army officer, who became a businessman, who had taken a vow that Höss would enter the priesthood, and whom Höss regarded as a 'higher being'. Höss apparently had a very poor academic record. His father died in 1914 and Höss claimed to have joined the German Army aged 15, in 1916, and to have served during the First World War in the Middle East and been wounded and decorated, but Koop claims that the evidence challenges that and many other contentions made by Höss regarding his life.[1]

Following Germany's defeat in the First World War Höss joined the Freikorps, right-wing militias composed of ex-soldiers in Weimar Germany, and in 1922 he left the Catholic Church of his upbringing and joined the Nazi Party, making him one of the earliest members of the party, joining long before it could have been advantageous in material or social terms for him to do so. The time of Höss's membership does seem to indicate either genuine ideological attachment or the meeting of some psychological need or desire to belong, especially to an organisation committed to views and strategies he endorsed. Höss took part in paramilitary activity and in 1923 was involved in the beating to death of a member of another right-wing party, the German Völkisch Freedom Party, who was believed to have denounced a Nazi Party member to the French.

Höss was sentenced to ten years in prison but was released in 1928, when he joined the Artaman League, a back-to-the-land movement. In his autobiography, composed in prison in Poland, he wrote, 'during the long years of seclusion in my cell I had come to the conclusion that there was for me only one object for which it was worth working and fighting, namely, a farm run by myself, on which I should live with a large and healthy family', an indication of Höss's priorities upon release from prison.[2]

On 1 April 1934 Höss joined the SS and became block leader at Dachau in December of that year. In 1938 he became adjutant at Sachsenhausen and in 1939 he was in the Waffen-SS in Poland. On 1 May 1940 he was appointed as commandant at Auschwitz. The initial prisoners were Soviet POWs and Poles. In June 1941, according to Höss's testimony on 15 April 1946 at Nuremberg, he was summoned to see Himmler personally and was told of the decision to effect a 'Final Solution' of the Jewish question by extermination, a decision that was to remain secret. The date does not seem credible, for the Reich Chancellery meeting on 12 December 1941 appears to be when the extermination of the Jews was indicated by Hitler, months later than Höss claims, but there seems to be no dispute over Höss's having met Himmler in Berlin in the summer of 1941, and as commandant of Auschwitz at the time the purpose of the meeting must have been related to the camp.[3] The timing of the order to exterminate the Jews is relevant to Höss's claim that he only obeyed orders in what he did at Auschwitz, but there is no doubt that the order to exterminate Jews at Auschwitz was issued. As shall be argued below, it is implausible that a personality like that of Höss should have undertaken policies not previously ordered by Himmler. What is known is that Höss developed ever more 'efficient' means of annihilation of immense numbers of Jews. At the end of the war Höss attempted to evade apprehension and punishment for war crimes but was captured by the British on 11 March 1946 and brutally interrogated.

As a defence witness at the Nuremberg trial of Kaltenbrunner Höss appalled the courtroom with his calm, apathetic recitation of his experimentation with various means of optimising the rate of murder of Jews at Auschwitz and his indifference to the process and its effects on the Jews. He exhibited no desire to exculpate himself or to minimise his own role.

Höss's affidavit of 5 April 1946, which was selectively quoted to him as a witness before the Nuremberg Tribunal, is similar to his appearance at Nuremberg in its preparedness to divulge details of the horrors of Auschwitz without any emotional or moral inflexion, as is indicated by the following passage—

'I commanded Auschwitz until 1 December 1943, and estimate that at least 2,500,000 victims were executed and exterminated there by gassing and burning, and at least another half million succumbed to starvation and disease, making a total of about 3,000,000 dead. This figure represents about 70 per cent or 80 per cent of all persons sent to Auschwitz as prisoners, the remainder having been selected and used for slave labor in the concentration camp industries. Included among the executed and burnt were approximately 20,000 Russian prisoners of war (previously screened out of Prisoner of War cages by the Gestapo) who were delivered at Auschwitz in Wehrmacht transports operated by regular Wehrmacht officers and men. The remainder of the total number of victims included about 100,000 German Jews, and great numbers of citizens (mostly Jewish) from The Netherlands, France, Belgium, Poland, Hungary, Czechoslovakia, Greece, or other countries. We executed about 400,000 Hungarian Jews alone at Auschwitz in the summer of 1944.'[4]

At Nuremberg Gilbert asked Höss how it was possible to exterminate 2.5 million prisoners at Auschwitz. He recorded that Höss asked if he meant technically and that Höss then said, 'that wasn't so hard – it would not have been hard to exterminate even greater numbers'. Höss continued, as if having to explain the process to someone who had no experience of the mechanics and arithmetic of mass execution, 'the killing itself took the least time. You could dispose of 2,000 head in half an hour, but it was the burning that took all the time. The killing was easy; you didn't even need guards to drive them into the chambers; they just went in expecting to take showers and, instead of water, we turned on poison gas. The whole thing went very quickly.'

Gilbert noted that Höss 'insisted disobedience of the order (from Himmler) was not an option', and Primomo notes that Höss did not need to 'worry about responsibility or consequences because, under the prevailing view in Germany at the time, the man who gave the orders was responsible'. When Gilbert referred to the 'human', Höss interrupted him and said 'that just didn't come into it'.

Gilbert concluded, 'in all of the discussions, Höss is quite matter-of-fact and apathetic, shows some belated interest in the enormity of his crime, but gives the impression that it never would have occurred to him if somebody hadn't asked him. There is too much apathy to leave any suggestion of remorse and even the prospect of hanging does not unduly stress him. One gets the general impression of a man who is intellectually normal, but with the schizoid apathy, insensitivity and lack of empathy that could hardly be more extreme in a frank psychotic.'[5]

From some of the evidence presented to Gilbert by Höss, Gilbert's assessment of Höss as manifesting 'schizoid apathy' does seem justified, not least as Höss had told Gilbert that he, Höss, had been brought up in a 'very strict Catholic tradition' by a father who 'was really a bigot', that he had never had a relationship of any genuine intimacy or warmth, and that even his marriage had been characterised by a certain 'estrangement' and lack of 'a real spiritual union', but that 'I am entirely normal'.[6]

It is worth noting that Gilbert claims that Höss exhibited 'schizoid apathy, insensitivity and lack of empathy', but does not claim that Höss was a schizoid personality. For the diagnostic criteria for 'schizoid' personality include not only the detached demeanour and experience and apathy exhibited by Höss, but also a lack of interest in relationships and a preference for a solitary life, and Höss had all his adult life joined organisations that involved significant interaction with other people, from his time in the German Army in the First World War, active membership of the Freikorps and in the early years of the Nazi Party, his joining the Artaman League, to his becoming an SS officer in 1934, contrary to the preference for a solitary life that is one of the diagnostic criteria for a schizoid personality.

What is inconsistent with Höss's extensive record of joining organisations that involved him in multiple relationships is his claim to Gilbert that he had 'always preferred to be alone', that he had 'never had close relationships to anybody', not even his wife, and that he 'never had a truly trusting relationship with my parents – and to my sisters, either'.[7] For if Höss really was that solitary by preference he could have chosen a quiet rural life in Germany before the war and remained a German nationalist, and then have become an anonymous German soldier if he were required to serve in the war. He would in doing so have avoided the intense interaction with other people that his military, paramilitary, and SS career involved, exacerbated by his promotion to leadership roles, and would have been a schizoid personality.

Gilbert's reference to 'schizoid' attributes but not schizoid personality disorder in Höss does then seem to be accurate, for it is consonant with Höss's behavioural record and does not depend exclusively upon Höss's claims as to his experience of life, other people and relationships. In fact, even Gilbert's finding of schizoid apathy is open to challenge, in that Höss displayed a degree of animation indicative of desire to demonstrate his experience and expertise to Gilbert rather than apathy, though he did appear apathetic regarding the Jews he exterminated. That indicates that Höss's apathy was reserved for people other than himself. The evidence of Höss's claims with Gilbert does call into question Höss's veracity when compared to the evidence of his behaviour.

In conversation with Goldensohn, also at Nuremberg, Höss estimated that he had organised the annihilation of around 2.5 million Jews, including women and children. When asked for his view of 'what happened at Auschwitz' Höss looked 'blank and apathetic', and when asked if he approved of what went on at Auschwitz, Höss responded, 'I had personal orders from Himmler', claiming he could not protest but had to accept the reasons that Himmler gave him. Höss said that Himmler had told him that, 'if the Jews were not exterminated at that time, then the German people would be exterminated for all time by the Jews', and that 'when Himmler told us something, it was so correct and so natural we just blindly obeyed it'.

When Goldensohn pursued Höss regarding his 'personal feelings' and asked him directly 'do you feel guilty, or merely a soldier who has done his duty?', Höss responded, 'up to the capitulation of Germany I believed I carried out orders correctly in the right manner.' He added that he then understood, after the end of the war, that what had happened was 'not right', and that he was guilty. This appears to indicate Höss's being very responsive to the most proximate influence. In another insight into Höss's mentality, Goldensohn noted that when he asked Höss what he was reflecting upon when he had seemed pensive Höss had looked at him with a 'puzzled, apathetic expression' and said he had not been reflecting upon anything at all.[8]

The relationship between Höss's need for order and correctness from his strict Catholic upbringing and his compliance with Himmler's orders and belief in Himmler's explanation for them is less consistent than expected. Höss claimed that he was 'firm and often harsh' but denied 'any acts of ill-treatment or cruelty', but Levi claims that Höss 'had an affair with an Auschwitz prisoner and extricated himself by sending her to her death' and that Höss's memoirs 'expressed Höss's wholly merciless and deceitful nature.[9] Primomo by contrast claims that Levi found Höss's autobiography to be 'substantially truthful', adding that 'if there is deception, it occurs in his attempts to convince posterity he pitied his victims and was helpless to control his subordinates in the barbaric treatment of Auschwitz prisoners.' Even so Primomo notes that Höss 'said he was "guilty", an indication of acceptance of post-war judgement, not that he felt guilt or shame.[10]

Primomo claims that Dr Batawia, in his assessment of Höss in Poland, found 'nothing abnormal in Höss's psychological make-up', and that Batawia believed that Höss was 'not an unfeeling psychopath nor was he a human being who ever showed criminal inclinations or sadistic tendencies'. According to Primomo Batawia believed that Höss 'tended, from childhood, to subordinate himself to every kind of authority', that he was 'sensitive' but 'did not show his feelings', that he was serious and conscientious regarding duty and that the 'sociological' and 'historical' context were responsible for Höss's becoming 'more of a robot than a human being, the ideal citizen of the Third Reich and of an SS man". Primomo also indicates that Batawia concluded that Höss only reflected on 'what was right and wrong outside of the context of the SS' at the end of his life.[11]

The evidence of Höss's demeanour in Warsaw is similar to that at Nuremberg. Primomo notes, 'through most of the trial, Höss remained stoic. As he had done at Nuremberg, Höss answered all questions in a brief, precise manner, without emotions.' Höss 'acknowledged his entire responsibility for everything that occurred in the camp whether he personally knew it at the time or not', and 'his whole defense rested on the submission that he was only carrying out orders received from his superiors.'

Primomo also notes that Dr Cyprian, the state prosecutor at the Warsaw trial, said that Höss reacted to 'everything with an iron expression and an almost legendary calm. He has no pity for these people; the most horrible descriptions do not move him,' and that Cyprian continued, 'the accused explained constantly that he executed the orders from above without a word of protest and submitted to them because he trusted his superiors blindly,' and referred to Höss's concentration on correctness and exactitude, becoming animated only over such matters and acting as if he were addressing a Nazi audience. The difference here is that whereas Primomo claims that Höss enacted orders from above, leaving open the possibility of his having done so out of fear of punishment of some sort, a characteristic Nazi war criminal defence and one employed by Stangl, the commandant of Sobibor and Treblinka, Cyprian indicates that the reason was implicit trust in the orders and their source on the part of Höss, a defence that indicated no moral qualms because of the faith Höss had in Himmler.[12]

Gutman and Berenbaum support and elaborate upon Primomo's view of Höss's demeanour at his trial in Warsaw. They note—

'Höss behaved as he had at the Nuremberg trial. He replied briefly, precisely, and impassively to every question posed to him. He did not deny the charges' and 'explained details without emotion. He did not display any servility or attempt to draw a lighter sentence by admitting guilt. He never entertained any illusions about his sentence. His last words restated his responsibility for all that had happened at Auschwitz. He did not appeal for clemency.'

They continue, in more evidence of Höss's demeanour—

'While the sentence and its grounds were read out, Höss stood stiffly at attention with a stony face that betrayed no emotion. After he was sentenced, he made a statement thanking his defense counsel for the effort invested in his case, and declared he would not ask for clemency.'

They conclude—

'In contrast to many other Nazi defendants, his behaviour during the proceedings against him revealed a man capable of assuming responsibility for his deeds without begging for his life or trying to shift the blame onto others. He was what he appeared to be: no ideological fanatic but obedient and devoted to the slogans of German nationalism and a fairly gifted organizer and bureaucrat.' He could have demonstrated 'equal diligence' in ordinary working life under different circumstances.[13]

Primomo cites the evidence of Höss's letters to his wife and children days before his execution at Auschwitz. These letters are very long, very sentimental and almost embarrassingly affectionate, and self-exculpating regarding his responsibility for mass murder. On 11 April 1947 he wrote to his wife as follows—

'Fate has worked out a truly sad ending for me. How fortunate were the comrades who were allowed to die an honest soldier's death.' Even so, he told her, 'calmly and composed I look towards the end.'

He went on, 'it is tragic that, although I was by nature gentle, good-natured and very helpful, I became the greatest destroyer of human beings who carried out every order to exterminate people no matter what. The goal of the many years of SS training was to make each SS soldier a tool without his own will who would carry out blindly all of Himmler's plans. That is the reason why I became a blind, obedient robot who carried out every order.'

Höss may be seen here to be exculpating himself by reference to Himmler's responsibility for the Holocaust and the influence of SS training on his, Höss's, compliance with Himmler's orders, and he goes on in the same manner, 'my fanatic patriotism and my most exaggerated sense of duty were good prerequisites for this training.' Höss does in the same letter acknowledge his responsibility for what happened at Auschwitz but these passages indicate his belief that he was not really responsible, just a victim of his own good intentions and Himmler's dominance and objectives, and he denies responsibility for some of what happened at Auschwitz, deploring 'how I was deceived, how my directives were twisted'.

The fact that the narrative Höss uses in this letter to his wife attributes his perpetrator behaviour to patriotism, belief in Himmler, and SS training does not mean that it is not the truth in terms of causation of Höss's behaviour as commandant at Auschwitz. Primomo notes that 'Hitler and Himmler had repeatedly warned Germans that the Jews would destroy Germany if they did not first destroy the Jews. Because Hitler said it, it must be true, according to Höss. Besides, an order from the Reichsführer-SS, in the name of the Führer, was sacred.' Even so, as is indicated by the excerpts above, Höss does expatiate at great length on his own reserved nature, his serving an ideology he had come to believe was wrong, and his own moral anguish (he refers to it as a 'hard struggle'). The concentration on his own experience is indicative of self-absorption and relative indifference to the suffering of the Jews at Auschwitz and his responsibility for it. And there is a romanticisation of his own life as a form of tragedy, as if Höss were a victim of Nazism too.

For Primomo the 'apathy and lack of emotion' in Höss witnessed by Goldensohn and Gilbert do seem to have been replaced by evidence of genuine and intense affection for his family, from which Primomo infers that Höss had an 'outward appearance of insensitivity and apathy' behind which there was intense emotion felt for his family. Primomo concludes, 'the two driving principles in Höss's life were love of country and love of family'.[14]

The intense affection for his wife and children that is so apparent in his letters does seem all the more indicative of profound affiliation in Höss as it appears that he was in fact given away by his wife after the war when in hiding on a farm. According to Goldensohn Höss believed that his oldest son had given the British authorities his address and so caused his apprehension and arrest, but that did not prevent Höss from addressing him specifically in the most affectionate terms in his letter to his children dated 11 April 1947.

The evidence of Höss's relationship with his wife seems contradictory. For Goldensohn notes, from an interview apparently on 8 April 1946, that 'he (Höss) states that he was happily married during his four years at Auschwitz' and that Höss claimed to have 'had no marital difficulties as a result of his work'.[15] By contrast Koop notes that in Höss's conversation with Gilbert on 12 April 1946, just four days later and also at Nuremberg, Höss claimed that after his wife found out what was happening at Auschwitz there was no sexual contact between them, that he 'always preferred to be alone', 'never had any friends or close relationships', and that his tendency towards solitude meant 'there was an estrangement' between him and his wife', though Höss claimed to be 'completely normal' and that 'even when I carried out the extermination task, I was leading a normal family life and so on.'[16] This corroborates the account referred to by McKale above (and may in fact be drawn from the same source), and Höss's inconsistency tends to support the reservations Levi had regarding the veracity of Höss's testimony, an issue of concern also over the dissonance between Höss's presentation of self as solitary by nature and his propensity for joining organisations all his life.

The apparent inconsistency between the record of Höss's relationship with his wife, of his believing that his eldest son had given his location away after the war, resulting in his capture by the British, and of his earlier statements regarding his relationships, and the evidence of Höss's letters to his wife and children on 11 April 1947, may be explained by Höss's reversion to Catholicism and the imminence of execution at Auschwitz. For Catholicism would have provided Höss with a very different source of authority to obey than Himmler and the SS, which after the end of the war was of course no longer that of a dominant or elite group. The timing of Höss's reversion to Catholicism could explain the dissonance between Höss's attempt to save himself when on the run in the British zone after the end of the war and his preparedness to accept execution for his crimes in Poland, for Höss first asked to see a priest on 4 April 1947, indicating reversion to the Catholicism of his childhood prior to that time, in his period in prison in Poland prior to his trial in Warsaw.

There are a number of issues with Batawia's and Primomo's psychological assessment of Höss. To begin with there is the issue of what is 'normal'. There is the evidence of Höss's participation in the brutal beating to death of a man who was believed to have denounced a fellow Nazi at Bormann's instigation, which does seem indicative of 'criminal tendencies' as well as of Höss's responsiveness to authority figures or those who assumed authority, in that case Bormann. Another issue is that the sociological and historical context of upbringing in an authoritarian and militaristic German society, followed by military experience in the First World War and then liberal democracy in the Weimar Republic that to many Germans on the right and the left had no legitimacy whatever, and the emergence following the Great Depression of the Nazi Party to national prominence and then to power, was shared by an entire generation of Germans, and very few became perpetrators in the immediate and visceral manner Höss did, indicating that some other causal factor must have been present. In the case of Höss it does seem to have been a combination of personality and responsiveness to authority figures and chance and circumstance, for other ordinary Germans conformed to the dictates of the Nazi state in other ways, defined by their respective roles.

The reason behind Höss's abandoning the rural lifestyle he claims in his memoir to have desired and valued above all else when he joined the SS in 1934 does seem to be a decisive causal factor in Höss's perpetrator behaviour as an SS officer if that perpetrator behaviour is to be attributed to Höss's having found it impossible to refuse to accept an assignment from Himmler and to Höss's having wished to avoid being seen to have failed in any assigned task by Himmler given Höss's regard for him as an authority figure. The inference of decisive influence on Höss's perpetrator behaviour from Himmler's authority as Reichsführer-SS is consistent with Höss's own reference to having trusted Himmler in his letter to his wife and with the findings of Milgram on obedience to immoral authority even in a liberal democratic culture that valued individualism and even when there were no real life consequences for refusal to comply with the authority figure's directives. It is also consistent with the finding in other social psychological research on conformity within groups that peer group norms exert great influence on individual members' behaviour. For the SS with its code and identity would be very much an example of a group that would exert such influence given the universality of compliance with orders, a culture of discipline and ruthlessness, the elite nature of an SS identity in Nazi Germany and the circumstances of war in the east against Bolshevism.

The reason for Höss's joining the SS in 1934 does in fact seem to be the influence of Himmler himself even at that time, for the Artaman League was not just an agrarian movement extolling the attractions of a rural lifestyle but also a political movement associated with German racial regeneration and racial exclusivity by removal from the corrupting modernity of urban life, and was antisemitic and anti-Slav in nature. It was also an organisation of which Himmler was an early member, reflecting his concept of a racially pure German peasantry exempt from the corrupting effect of urban life, and Höss had contact with Himmler in the Artaman League. Höss claims in his memoir that in the Artaman League, 'soon our land would be allotted to us.'

But it was not to be!

In June 1934 came Himmler's call to join the ranks of the active SS'.

And elsewhere in the memoir he notes that in 'June 1934, during an inspection of the Pomeranian SS, Himmler asked me whether I would like to join the active SS in a concentration camp'.[17]

There does seem to be a combination of influences on Höss here. One point is that his claimed desire to run a farm on his release from prison in 1928 was not quite what it appeared to be, in that the Artaman League was very politicised in nature, and the other is the influence on Höss of the authority figure of Himmler even before Höss joined the SS. For it does not seem to have occurred to Höss to have declined Himmler's offer. And Höss knew what sort of work he would be doing in the SS, as Himmler appears to have indicated concentration camp work, and Höss would have known of the purpose of and practices in concentration camps. At the time Höss could not have known he would be appointed by Himmler as commandant of an extermination camp, but by June 1941 Höss's experience at Dachau and at Sachsenhausen would have habituated him to the violence and mistreatment of concentration camp inmates and, with his admiration for Himmler and Himmler's status in the SS and Höss's tendency to follow orders in hierarchies, would have made refusal difficult to conceive of, let alone enact.

One commonality between the Nazi war criminals tried after the war is their surprisingly calm demeanour in contexts of near certainty and imminence of execution, which seems to indicate an extraordinary calmness or self-control in adverse circumstances (their lack of emotion when presented with evidence of the Jews' terrible suffering could be explained by genuine indifference to, or lack of acceptance of their responsibility for, the persecution and annihilation of Europe's Jews). This calmness seems to have been true of the Nuremberg defendants as a generality (more so for some than others) and of Eichmann, whose calmness, even apparent boredom, before a hostile prosecutor and audience in an Israeli court and with certainty of impending execution, does appear extraordinary. The evidence indicates that Höss exhibited a similar calmness and detachment at Nuremberg and at his trial in Poland when he knew his execution was a certainty and made no effort to avert it.

Another commonality is one of narrative, the characteristic 'obedience to orders' defence combined with one that alludes to the experiential context of the Third Reich and the SS with its code of obedience, toughness, discipline and ruthlessness as virtues, and the universality of compliance with that code, the argument being that its uniqueness makes fair judgement by those not subject to it impossible. The slight dissonance between the two explanations has been noted above, for the 'obedience to orders' defence indicates that there was reluctant compliance for fear of draconian sanctions for non-compliance with orders, that is, that the defendants knew the policies were wrong but had to carry them out nevertheless because of the coercive nature of the Nazi state apparatus and the SS, as evidenced by Hitler's exterminatory orders in relation to Jews, Bolsheviks and partisans and the history of incarceration in concentration camps of political opponents from the very start of the Third Reich. The reference to the experiential context of the Nazi state argues something rather different and possibly incompatible with the 'obedience to orders' defence, that is, that Nazi conditioning and indoctrination were so influential that perpetrators were convinced that the Jews were associated with Bolshevism and partisan activity and with international capitalism and so had to be exterminated as enemies of the German race and state, a legitimate and defensive policy. In that case there would be no need for implicit threats accompanying orders as perpetrators believed the policies were necessary.

This combination of apparently incompatible exculpations was apparent at the Einsatzgruppen trial and appears to have been presented by Höss in conversation with Goldensohn, as indicated above. At his trial in Warsaw Höss, as has been seen, presented a defence of obedience to orders but also made it very clear that he accepted personal responsibility for what happened at Auschwitz, which does, as Gutman and Berenbaum have pointed out, differentiate Höss from most other Nazi defendants. Having said that Höss did, in his letter to his wife, claim to have followed Himmler's orders because he trusted him.

It may of course be that the experiential context for Nazi perpetrators was in fact composed of three factors. For there may have been a perception of possible draconian punishments for failure to obey orders, for instance being sent to combat on the eastern front, propaganda that argued that the Jews had to be exterminated to preserve the German race and state, and universal compliance with the requirements of tasks assigned the SS that reflected conformity to an SS code and identity of obedience, ruthlessness and discipline, predicated upon attachment to the SS as an elite in Nazi Germany and to SS rank, and upon the prohibitive nature of being the one to resist and so be the object of peer ridicule and ostracism. Sanctions do not have to be a threat to life such as combat on the eastern front to be effective, as social psychological evidence has established.

Of these three components of the gestalt of influences on Nazi perpetrators apprehension of the sort of draconian punishment indicated by transfer to a combat unit on the eastern front may not be the most plausible in Höss's case, not because there appears to be no known instance of its having occurred, for there remains the possibility of a perception of serious adverse consequences for non-compliance with orders, but because it seems more plausible that conformity to the requirements of role and task and the motive to avoid being seen to have failed by authority figures in the Third Reich, in Höss's case Himmler, was the decisive influence on Höss. For there may have been influence from the adverse prospect of the embarrassment of declining an assignment from Himmler as Reichsführer-SS, the Auschwitz assignment, and, once there, being seen by Himmler to have failed at a task he, Höss, had accepted. Höss may in fact have found it impossible to conceive of declining to obey an order from Himmler or to conceive of failing to do what the assignment required of him. The experiential context and its reference to the Jews as enemies of the German race and state and associated with partisans would have been insufficient to justify murdering helpless Jewish elderly people, women and children whose condition made it clear that they represented no threat whatever without the influence from Himmler as an authority figure in the Third Reich and the susceptibility to authority figures in Höss's case, for he seems less an instance of genuine ideological conviction than of susceptibility to proximate authority figures who would take responsibility for defining what he should do. What made Himmler proximate was of course Höss's leaning to the right of interwar German politics and his affiliation for German nationalism and militarism.

To return to differences and similarities between Höss and Eichmann, there is no evidence that Eichmann engaged in violence, whereas as has been seen Höss had been involved in the brutal murder of a man believed to have betrayed a Nazi Party member in 1923. This would seem to indicate a certain autonomous voluntarism in Höss that was not to be seen in Eichmann. Combined with the fact that Höss joined the Nazi Party as early as 1922, when it had no popularity at all and was just another right-wing nationalist fringe group, whereas Eichmann did not join the party until 1932, by which time the Nazi Party was the largest right-wing party in the country, the evidence of the murder does seem to indicate greater ideological commitment in Höss than Eichmann, as does the evidence of Eichmann's careerism. But the murder in 1923 was instigated by Martin Bormann, indicating that Höss did not show initiative or autonomy over the murder but was responding to a form of authority and so was not an autonomous initiator of the murder.

Both Höss and Eichmann appear to have been very much influenced by authority figures, Höss apparently first by Bormann and then by Himmler, and Eichmann by Kaltenbrunner and Müller, in both cases the most proximate authority figures. Both men seem to have been drawn to membership of organisations in which they would receive orders to carry out that absolved them from responsibility but permitted them rank and an identity they could not find for themselves but seem to have needed. Like Höss Eichmann was fond enough of his wife and children to send for them, with all the attendant risks, from his hiding place in Argentina, and in fact it was that decision that resulted in his being apprehended, abducted, tried and executed in Israel, because of the indiscretion of one of his sons. And Eichmann too could have been a middle-ranking functionary in ordinary life in different circumstances.

One contrast is between Eichmann's appealing his guilty verdict and then appealing for clemency and Höss's acceptance of his sentence to be executed. Another is that there is no evidence of Höss's bragging of his SS career to fellow Nazis, unlike the evidence of the Sassen tapes of Eichmann's boasting of his SS career to an audience of Nazis and Nazi sympathisers in Argentina after the war, but that may be due to the fact that Höss was apprehended in Germany in 1946 and never had a chance to reflect upon his SS career before an approving, in fact admiring, audience in the manner Eichmann had.

There are partial parallels between Höss and other relatively senior Nazis. For Höss's demeanour under interrogation appears to be similar to that of Ohlendorf, who openly admitted to the extraordinary extent of murders of Jews by his Einsatzgruppe, argued that it was a military necessity, compared the annihilation of the Jews to the use of the atom bomb on Japan, and exhibited no remorse. The unnaturally calm demeanour under interrogation and open admission of the numbers of Jews for whose murders they were responsible do seem to be noteworthy commonalities, but unlike the arrogant and unrepentant Ohlendorf, Höss did, very late on and just before his execution, show some repentance.

In that regard there is some similarity to the case of Hans Frank, the notorious Nazi sycophant who was the Governor of the General Government in Poland, who reverted to Catholicism and repented during the Nuremberg trial, and was hanged for war crimes. Having said that, the US prison psychiatrist at Nuremberg, Kelley, challenged the view of the US prison psychologist, Gilbert, that Frank's conversion was genuine, for Kelley believed that Frank's claimed reversion to Catholicism was a narrative in which Frank was the tragic hero.[18]

A commonality shared by many Nazi perpetrators does seem to be exclusive concentration on their own experience rather than any genuine concern for the great numbers of Jews they were instrumental in exterminating in their various capacities, and Höss certainly gives evidence of this tendency in his letter to his wife in April 1947, in which he appears to present himself as a victim of circumstance. Similar concentration on personal experience may be found in the cases of Franz Stangl, the notorious commandant of Sobibor and Treblinka, Albert Speer, Hitler's Armaments Minister, who used slave labour, and Hans Frank himself.

The search for commonalities and contrasts between Nazi war criminals who survived the war and for whom there is some evidence does seem to be of limited use in explaining Nazi perpetrator behaviour. For the reality is that the great majority of ordinary people in all cultures and time periods have conformed to, and continue to conform to, the norms of their societies to optimise their outcomes in terms of occupational prospects in careers and social outcomes in maximising approbation and acceptance and avoiding obloquy and ostracism. What that means is that Nazi perpetrators did not need to be pathological personalities to do what they did, and in fact research has established that Nazi war criminals were in general entirely normal, for it was an altogether normal response for a normal person to meet the requirements of assigned roles at work to optimise their careers and avoid demotion and failure relative to peers or to preclude ridicule and ostracism from peers for not participating in unpleasant tasks. What was different was circumstance, in the form of a violently antisemitic Nazi totalitarianism, and consequence for the Jews, who were exterminated by multitudes of entirely ordinary and psychologically normal Germans.

Höss does appear from the evidence of his calm, detached and matter-of-fact demeanour with Goldensohn and Gilbert and as a witness at Nuremberg and at his trial in Warsaw, when relating details of the atrocities committed under his command at Auschwitz, to have exhibited 'schizoid' apathy, insensitivity and lack of empathy. Even so, and despite Höss's telling Gilbert of his preference for being alone and of his never having had 'close relationships to anybody', Höss does not appear to have been a schizoid personality, because the evidence of his joining one organisation after another, with the extent of social interaction involved, tends to indicate a desire to belong and for an identity as part of a group, and possibly a desire to be told what to do and why by someone who would be responsible for decisions he would then not have to consider. The evidence of Höss's letters to his wife and children not long before his execution also indicates that Höss was not a schizoid personality, for they seem to indicate that Höss did have experience of closeness and love for his family at the end of his life. It is possible that the evidence of Höss's letters is explained by his reversion to Catholicism.

Another issue is the relevance of any psychological diagnosis to an explanation of Höss's perpetrator behaviour, for apathy, insensitivity and lack of empathy would have been facilitating factors but would not explain why Höss presided over the extermination of Jews at Auschwitz. For the traits Gilbert found would be permissive rather than directive for behaviour.

The most plausible explanation of Höss's perpetrator behaviour is that there was a combination of factors. To begin with, Höss does seem to have found membership of groups in which he was not required to make decisions optimal for the belonging and identity they offered, and for the avoidance of responsibility for decisions he does not appear to have wanted to make. There was also Höss's intense nationalism and militarism, which predisposed him to right-wing groups in interwar Germany, where the context included a threat from communism. And Höss's respect for authority, hierarchy and order, and acceptance of the authority of Hitler as Führer and the arbiter of what was true and legitimate and of Himmler as his appointed representative in the SS, meant that declining an assignment was impossible to conceive of and that failure to meet the requirements of the role was similarly beyond what Höss could contemplate. Höss's apparent need to demonstrate his efficiency as commandant at Auschwitz that was in evidence when he spoke to Gilbert and in his affidavit to the Nuremberg Tribunal, his evidence as witness at Nuremberg and as defendant at his own trial in Warsaw, may be explained by his desire or need for order, purpose, objectives and the optimal accomplishment of them. That desire for order and authority may have been met after the war by Höss's reversion to Catholicism.

One characteristic of Höss that has been noted above was his calm and detached divulging of the detail of the annihilation of Jews at Auschwitz and his commentary to the effect that the murder process was not a problem, as if he were unaware of the effect on his audiences, which included Goldensohn, Gilbert, and the Nuremberg and Warsaw Tribunals, for all of them were hostile and must have manifested some horror at what Höss was indicating happened at Auschwitz, at his responsibility for it and his undisguised indifference. The only evidence of animation in Höss appears to have been in relating the detail of Auschwitz and in his seemingly uncharacteristic letters to his wife and children before he was executed.

The emphasis here on Höss's personality attributes does explain his journey to perpetrator behaviour and his attitude to it, but they do not seem to have been necessary conditions to such behaviour, for as indicated above situational rather than individual factors seem to explain perpetrator behaviour, which appears to be undertaken by normal people just to avoid adverse career and social outcomes.

Eichmann was relatively unknown at the time of the International Military Tribunal that tried the cases of the major Nazi war criminals, but was mentioned by a number of defendants. He was the organiser of the transports that took Jews to the extermination camps and so central to the Holocaust of Europe's Jews. He was apprehended in Argentina in 1960 and abducted to Israel with the intention of conducting a public trial to apprise world opinion of the nature and extent of the suffering of Jews in occupied Europe, which does mean that the trial should be regarded as a show trial. Certainly the conduct of Hausner, the Israeli Attorney General and state prosecutor, was flamboyant and played to the audience in the courtroom and the cameras from various countries covering the trial. The consequence was that rhetoric interfered with the presentation of evidence germane to Eichmann's guilt, not least given the number of Holocaust survivors who testified as to the terrible suffering they had experienced and witnessed but whose testimony had little to do with Eichmann's own guilt or innocence. Reference has been made above to Arendt's scathing criticism of Hausner's conduct and the nature of the trial. She notes Judge Landau's attempts to stop the trial from becoming 'a show trial under the influence of the prosecutor's love of showmanship' and refers to the trial as 'the show trial' Ben-Gurion, the Prime Minister of Israel', had intended when he authorised the abduction of Eichmann from Argentina to face a public trial in Israel. Arendt sees Ben-Gurion as 'the invisible stage manager of the proceedings' and as speaking through Hausner, for whom Arendt has only contempt. She portrays Eichmann as an anonymous, pathetic figure in the dock and has the following compelling account of the prerequisites of 'justice'—

'Justice demands that the accused be prosecuted, defended, and judged, and that all other questions of seemingly greater import – of "How could it happen?" and "Why did it happen?" of "Why the Jews?" and "What was the extent of co-responsibility on the side of the Allies?", of "How could the Jews through their own leaders cooperate in their own destruction?" and "Why did they go to their deaths like lambs to the slaughter?" – be left in abeyance. Justice insists on the importance of Adolf Eichmann.'

For 'on trial are his deeds, not the sufferings of the Jews, not the German people or mankind, not even anti-Semitism or racism.'

Even so, Arendt does believe that Eichmann was guilty and that his conviction and execution were justified, her criticism being related to the process and the theatre of the court rather than the final judgement on Eichmann. For Arendt Eichmann's perpetrator behaviour is to be explained by reference to banality Arendt defines as lack of reflection and moral reasoning, even though she does refer to Eichmann's careerism, of which there is evidence over his SS career that is indicative of a motive to avoid disapprobation from superiors and peers in the SS and to enhance his career prospects and reputation as a senior SS officer. Eichmann's defence that he was a functionary who implemented orders received from superior SS officers was the common defence of Nazi perpetrators and was not accepted by the court.[19]

Lipstadt endorses much of Arendt's criticism of the conduct of the Eichmann trial, noting Hausner's view 'that the survivors had the perfect right to be "irrelevant" regarding Eichmann's specific crimes', so 'their testimony did not have to directly relate to what he did'. 'Some observers considered this evidence to be highly prejudicial', according to Lipstadt, which is very much the view expressed here in connection with Douglas's advocacy of 'didactic' trials, that is, that such permissiveness interfered with the right of any defendant to a fair trial on relevant evidence. Lipstadt concludes that 'the criticisms of Hausner's courtroom tactics were not unjustified' and that 'he seemed intent on trying to extract that unambiguous confession', an indication of Hausner's orientation to Israeli and world audiences and his cultivation of drama rather than an organised presentation of the evidence against Eichmann specifically to establish his guilt before the judges.[20]

Even so, Eichmann's complicity in the Holocaust as the SS officer who arranged the transportation of Jews to extermination camps was never in doubt, and there was never any possibility of his being acquitted by an Israeli court. The proceedings were then just there to give the appearance of a fair trial in Israel, an observance of protocol rather than any detailed consideration of the evidence presented that did actually relate to Eichmann's guilt or innocence and of his position in the SS hierarchy with its culture of compliance and discipline and the chaos of the war in the east, that is, of Eichmann's experiential context. Eichmann was represented as the architect of the Final Solution but was no more than an SS officer intimately involved with the persecution and extermination of Jews in the occupied territories under orders from Müller and Kaltenbrunner, as has been noted. That could have saved him in the Federal Republic of Germany before the more recent change noted above, but there was no likelihood of its doing so in Israel in 1960. Eichmann was found to be psychologically normal by an Israeli assessment and does seem to have shared with Höss a susceptibility to influence from authority figures and their objectives. Like Höss, Eichmann appears to have had a desire to be part of an enterprise in which he would have no responsibility for decisions and would be the efficient functionary who would implement them. Unlike Höss, Eichmann seems to have been careerist and to have aspired to senior SS rank, and to have taken some pleasure in his power over the Jews.[21]

Notes

[1] See Koop, Volker, *The Commandant of Auschwitz: Rudolf Höss*, Frontline Books, 2021, pp. 2–4.

[2] See Hoess, Rudolf, *Commandant of Auschwitz: The Autobiography of Rudolf Hoess*, Pan Books Limited, 1974, p. 64.

[3] See Longerich, Peter, *Holocaust: The Nazi Persecution and Murder of the Jews*, OUP, 2010, p. 260 for the claim that Goering's written authorisation to Heydrich on 31 July 1941 was only for 'all the necessary preparations from an organizational, functional and material point of view for a total solution to the Jewish Question within the German sphere of influence in Europe', not an authorisation to proceed to annihilate Jews. See also Winkler, Heinrich August, *Germany: The Long Road West: Volume 2: 1933-1990*, OUP, 2007, pp. 87 and 88, for Goebbels' diary reference to the Reich Chancellery meeting with Hitler on 12 December in Berlin, where Goebbels recorded that Hitler was resolved upon the extermination of the Jews, having promised that if the Jews started another world war they would be destroyed, and for Hans Frank's speech on 16 December 1941, in which he referred to the Berlin meeting and claimed that the message had been that the Jews should be exterminated. See Primomo, John W., *Architect of Death at Auschwitz: A Biography of Rudolf Höss*, McFarland , 2020, p. 112 for reference to Höss's having indicated in affidavits dated 14 March and 5 April 1946 that he had been summoned to meet Himmler in Berlin in June 1941, and see Gutman, Israel, and Berenbaum. Michael, *Anatomy of the Auschwitz Death Camp*, Indiana University Press, 1998, p. 213 for the view that Höss confused June 1941 with a real date of June 1942 for when he was summoned to meet Himmler in Berlin.

[4] See Barnes, Thomas Garden, and Feldman, Gerald D. (eds.), *Breakdown and Rebirth, 1914 to the present: A Documentary History of Modern Europe, Volume IV*, University Press of America, 1972, p. 142.

[5] See Primomo, *Architect of Death at Auschwitz*, op. cit., 2020, pp. 184 and 185.

[6] See McKale, Donald M., *Nazis After Hitler: How Perpetrators of the Holocaust Cheated Justice and Truth*, Rowman & Littlefield, 2012, p. 205.

[7] See Koop, *The Commandant of Auschwitz*, op. cit., p. 56.

[8] See Goldensohn, Leon, *The Nuremberg Interviews: Conversations with the Defendants and Witnesses*, Random House, 2010, pp. 296, 300, 308 and 310.

[9] See McKale, *Nazis After Hitler*, op. cit., p. 207.

[10] See Primomo, *Architect of Death*, op. cit., pp. 10, 90, and 189–92.

[11] See ibid.

[12] See Primomo, *Architect of Death*, op. cit., p. 167.

[13] See Gutman and Berenbaum, *Anatomy of the Auschwitz Death Camp*, op. cit., pp. 297 and 298.

[14] See Primomo, *Architect of Death*, op. cit., pp. 112, 189–92, 193 and 194.

[15] See Goldensohn, *The Nuremberg Interviews*, op. cit., pp. 295 and 307.

[16] See Koop, *The Commandant of Auschwitz*, op. cit., p. 56.

[17] See Hoess, *Commandant of Auschwitz*, op. cit., pp. 66 and 228.

[18] See Housden, M., *Hans Frank: Lebensraum and the Holocaust*, Springer, 2003, p. 221. See also p. 234 for reference to Kelley's view that Frank was 'one of Nazism's "businessmen"', and for Gilbert's view that Frank was one of Hitler's 'revolutionists'

who found himself torn between his 'better judgement and pathological impulses'. The contrast in interpretation between the US prison psychiatrist and the US prison psychologist does seem indicative of the difficulties of assessing the personalities of Nazi war criminals after the war.

[19] See Arendt, Hannah, *Eichmann in Jerusalem: A Report on the Banality of Evil*, Penguin, 2006.

[20] See Lipstadt, Deborah E., *The Eichmann Trial*, Knopf Doubleday Publishing Group, 2011.

[21] See Cesarani, David, *Eichmann: His Life and Crimes*, Vintage Books, 2005, pp. 357–68 for reference to Eichmann's careerism and enjoyment in his power over Jews. Cesarani does though also claim that Eichmann became an ideological and zealous antisemite, not having been one until it became his role in the SS to organise the transportation of Jews to extermination camps when a primary task of the SS became the extermination of the Jews of the occupied territories. This is implausible, for it could not have been coincidence that Eichmann had not been an eliminationist antisemite before it became Nazi policy towards the Jews. The more plausible inference is that Eichmann was, as Cesarani points out, relieved to have a continuing role in the SS when Nazi policy changed from Jewish emigration to their extermination and that his expressed attitudes altered to indicate approval of the new task of the SS.

Chapter Four
Gitta Sereny on Franz Stangl and Albert Speer

Gitta Sereny was an Austrian historian, biographer and investigative journalist who took a particular interest in Nazi war criminals and wrote two books on them, one on Franz Stangl, the camp commandant at the extermination camps at Sobibor and Treblinka, and the other on Albert Speer, Hitler's architect and Armaments Minister, who evaded execution at Nuremberg by an ingenious defence that acknowledged that as part of the Nazi elite he should and could have known of the Holocaust but claimed that he had not known of it.

Here the objective is to identify the influences on Sereny's approach to, and objectives in, her assessments of Stangl and Speer, and to demonstrate the commonalities in her treatments of them in an indication of the decisive influence of perspective on perception and inferences regarding personality and experience. The relevance to a consideration of the 'justice' meted out to the two men as Nazi perpetrators after the war is in the extent to which they were responsible for what they did, rather than individuals without volition or intent who committed perpetrator behaviour as a result of roles to which they were appointed by those above them in the Nazi hierarchy and who never went beyond the behaviour indicated by their roles in the Nazi regime.

Sereny on Stangl

Sereny's *Into That Darkness: From Mercy Killing to Mass Murder* (Random House, 2013) had a previous title, *Into That Darkness: an examination of conscience* (1983), which seems to indicate her being engaged in a search for conscience in Stangl's personality. Stangl, an Austrian, had been involved as an SS police superintendent in the T4 euthanasia programme before becoming SS camp commandant at Sobibor and then at Treblinka, where he introduced changes to the extermination process to rectify the chaotic situation that his predecessor had allowed to develop. After the war Stangl escaped to Syria and then to Brazil, where he was finally apprehended and extradited to Germany. There he was tried, entered a plea of obedience to orders, was convicted and sentenced to life imprisonment.

Sereny interviewed Stangl in a German prison for seventy hours in two one-week periods between 2 April and 27 June 1971. Her objective was to humanise Stangl and so avoid a characterisation of him as just another Nazi 'monster', by understanding him as a human being. To that end she investigated his family life, which seems to have been entirely normal, in fact affectionate, not least in Stangl's manifest fondness for his wife. Sereny then attempted to explain Stangl's perpetrator behaviour by setting it in the context of his life and experience, and by interrogating his explanation of his role in the Holocaust after having cultivated an understanding relationship with him to facilitate his speaking with freedom. Sereny's challenging of Stangl's account used evidence she had found in her research on his record and questioning the reasoning in his account.

Sereny prefaces her book by claiming that it was inspired by the fact that no Nazi war criminal had 'found the strength to change, or to reveal their past and their feelings about it to their children. On the contrary, they did their utmost to suppress – to 'block' – their experiences and deeds'.[1] Sereny claims that Stangl was different, that he became 'profoundly involved in his effort at self-knowledge', indicating what seems to be a therapeutic approach in Sereny's interviews with Stangl.

Sereny does not consider the possibility that Nazi war criminals in general were not tormented by what they had done during the war and that they either did not reflect on it at all because it was not salient to them in their post-war lives or that they genuinely felt that they were not responsible, attributing their wartime behaviour and experience to the political and ideological context of the time, to Germany's war without normative restraint on either side against Bolshevism in the east, to association of Jews with Bolshevism and partisans behind the German lines, to the Führerprinzip, to an SS identity and code that dictated obedience and toughness, and to a universality of conformity to role requirements in the SS.

Sereny's presumption of the existence of conscience in Stangl seems to indicate her having assumed the position of psychologist or psychiatrist, even though she had no expertise in either profession. Her attitude to Stangl is reminiscent of Arendt's contemptuous attitude towards Eichmann, for Sereny describes Stangl as 'an intellectually limited but morally certainly troubled man, who frequently revealed extraordinary manifestations of a dual personality', and notes that her interest in Stangl derived from her impression that at his trial he 'seemed less primitive, more open, serious and sad: the only man with such a horrific record who manifested a semblance of conscience'. These were intuitive, impressionistic personal inferences in which Sereny seems to have had great confidence, despite her lack of psychological or psychiatric expertise.[2]

The conversational context in *Into That Darkness* begins with Stangl's childhood and upbringing, not least his relationship with his father, of whom he was apparently terrified and who died when he was young, and his joining the police in Austria before moving on to his work as police superintendent in the T4 euthanasia programme and when it closed his being told to report to Berlin for new orders. Stangl claimed that he chose to go to Lublin rather than return to Linz and Prohaska, a man Stangl loathed, on the understanding that in Lublin he would be there to 'fight partisans'. He was directed to report to SS Gruppenführer Globocnik in Lublin. Globocnik was in charge of the extermination of Jews in Poland and instructed Stangl to report to Wirth at Sobibor, which Stangl claimed to have understood to be a 'supply camp for the army'. Wirth was '"Inspector" of the three major extermination camps, Belzec, Sobibor and Treblinka', had been involved in the T4 euthanasia programme at Hartheim, and was known by Stangl there to be crude, brutal, ruthless and callous in speech and behaviour. Wirth did in fact have a reputation for such attributes and was then a credible threat to Stangl when he told him and assembled others that at Sobibor 'any Jews who didn't work properly'…'would be "eliminated"' and that 'if any of you don't like that'…'you can leave, but under the earth.' This is of course according to Stangl, who claimed he told Wirth that he 'couldn't do it' but was told that his response would be passed to HQ and to return to Sobibor. Stangl then claims to have made various attempts to obtain a transfer, including one that sought to bypass Wirth by obtaining agreement from Globocnik, but to have received no response. Sereny makes a number of references to Stangl's claims of desire for and attempts to obtain a transfer but cites no evidence to confirm or disconfirm them.[3]

Stangl's tenure at Sobibor was relatively brief, and Sereny concentrates on his time at Treblinka, to which he was sent by Globocnik, ostensibly to find out why no money or materials had been received from the 100,000 Jews who had been sent there. Sereny claims that Stangl 'admired Globocnik' and denounced Eberl and Wirth to Globocnik, claiming that they were planning to send 'Treblinka valuables to Berlin instead of to the HQ in Poland'. Sereny claims that 'from then on Globocnik considered him "one of his men"', on whose loyalty he relied completely'. Sereny's account continues—

"'But if you made this offer to Globocnik," I said, "it means you actually volunteered your collaboration, doesn't it?"

"'All I was doing," he replied sharply, his face again undergoing that now familiar change, "was to confirm that I would be carrying out this assignment as a police officer under his command."'

Sereny goes on to note that Stangl claimed accepting the posting to Treblinka was 'a matter of survival', and that he told her that he coped with the role by a process of 'compartmentalizing' that involved reference to what he had been taught as a police officer, that 'the definition of a crime must meet four requirements: there has to be a subject, an object, an action and intent', and that 'if the "subject" was the government, the "object" the Jews'…'intent' (he called it 'free will') 'was missing'.[4]

The idea that Stangl had moral qualms during the war that he resolved as he claims does not seem to be plausible as a representation of Stangl's experience in the Third Reich in any of the capacities he had as an SS officer and does not seem consistent with his reference to regarding the Jews as 'cargo' within two weeks of arrival at Treblinka, for he told Sereny that he had come to regard the Jews as 'cargo' when standing next to Wirth at the Totenlager, when Wirth looked at the 'pits' of 'corpses' and referred to them as 'garbage'. For Wirth only remained at Treblinka for two weeks after Stangl's arrival there, and the terrible piles of corpses were part of the chaos at Treblinka that Stangl had been transferred to Treblinka to resolve. The inference from Sereny's evidence is that Stangl's moral anguish lasted less than two weeks after arrival at Treblinka. It is worth adding that if Stangl did regard the Jews as 'cargo' there would have been no need for him to ascribe responsibility for their treatment to the Nazi state rather than to himself, for regarding the Jews as 'cargo' indicates detachment from the process of their extermination rather than having needed to resolve his moral anguish by 'compartmentalizing' and reference to the police definition of criminality he had received in his training to exculpate himself. The inference of detachment is supported by Stangl's comment that 'I rarely saw them as individuals.' The claim that he compartmentalised his role in the process seems much more like one Stangl devised to minimise or eradicate his own responsibility for what he presided over at Sobibor and Treblinka, after he had been arrested or in conversation with Sereny.[5] And even if one accepts Stangl's claim of 'compartmentalizing', it only indicates his capacity for optimisation of his own personal outcomes by meeting the requirements of the role of camp commandant at Sobibor and Treblinka and so preserving or enhancing his material and social outcomes in terms of privileges and status and his psychological outcomes by precluding any resulting discomfort.

Sereny notes that Stangl did not feel he had to answer for what he did for that 'was a question of survival'. She records that, in response to her interrogation of him as to why he did not decline the assignment at Treblinka, Stangl told her, 'I knew it could happen that they wouldn't shoot someone. But I also knew that more often they did shoot them, or could send them to concentration camps. How could I know which would apply to me?'.[6] Sereny indicates that Stangl also claimed he could not have altered anything of the horror or the brutality of the process of extermination itself, because 'this was the system. Wirth had invented it. It worked. And because it worked, it was irreversible.'[7]

Kekes infers careerism and apprehension of sanctions as motives for Stangl's acceptance of the role of camp commandant at Treblinka, noting that during his exchanges with Globocnik 'the prospect of promotion and other rewards for his loyalty and efficient service were dangled before him and threats for disloyalty were implied'. Stangl then accepted.[8] There is other evidence of Stangl's aspiration to succeed, in his concern at what he regarded as a 'demotion', in his wife's reference to his aspiration to Sereny, and in the testimony of a survivor of Sobibor, Szmajzner, who Sereny found 'fair and tolerant' and who said that he 'never saw Stangl hurt anyone' but that what made him special was his 'arrogance' and an 'obvious pleasure in his work' no other Sobibor camp personnel showed to the same extent, with a 'perpetual smile' that indicated to Szmajzner that Stangl was 'happy'. Stangl was also found to be the '"best camp commander" in Poland'. And there is the evidence of Erich Bauer, an Oberscharführer at Sobibor, who claimed that he had overheard a conversation between Frenzel, Stangl and Wagner comparing the 'numbers of victims of the extermination camps of Belzec, Treblinka and Sobibor and expressed their regret that Sobibor 'came last' in the competition'.[9]

Stangl's narrative here refers to the experiential context of Nazi perpetrators and is reminiscent of the reference to context of the defence of the Einsatzgruppen commanders at the Einsatzgruppen trial, though in the Einsatzgruppen case there was more emphasis upon the ideological and social context rather than on threat to personal survival. Though it is possible that Stangl did in fact fear for his life or was apprehensive regarding draconian punishment in the event of any refusal to accept an assignment as an SS officer during the war in the east, the far greater likelihood is that the experiential context was such that refusal to accept an assignment was impossible to conceive of given the universality of compliance in the SS and the SS identity and code of discipline, acceptance of orders and toughness, and that a system of extermination that had been introduced by a senior SS officer and had worked would have been experientially very difficult to conceive of challenging in the context of the extermination camps of the east and the recent history of chaos at Treblinka. Behind such difficulties of conception of resistance would of course have been Stangl's desire to secure the approbation of peers and bosses in the SS and avoid punishing sanctions such as demotion or dismissal and ridicule or ostracism from peers, for motivation influences cognition. Had it been in Stangl's interests as he perceived them to conceive of declining to accept the assignment of camp commandant at Treblinka or to amend the extermination process he would have done so.

Sereny refers with contempt to Stangl's use of a narrative characteristic of Nazi war criminals in general after the end of the war, that 'he had never done anything but obey orders', but she does not address the possibility that its very reiteration could indicate that the narrative is in fact a true reflection of the experiential context of the Third Reich, in which declining to meet role requirements or to undertake a role could have been impossible to conceive of given the nature of the regime, the wartime context and the universality of compliance in the SS referred to above.[10]

In an indication of the influence of Sereny's psychodynamic perspective and reliance on her own intuitive impressions, her view was that Stangl 'had manipulated events, or his memory of events, to suit his need to rationalize his guilt, his awareness of his guilt or (at that point in our talks) his need to avoid facing it'.[11]

Sereny comments on Stangl's reference to his 'guilt' over what he seems to have felt was his complicity with Germans who had mistreated an Austrian he had greatly respected. Sereny's inference is that Stangl accepted guilt for 'comparatively harmless failings' because 'he wanted to and needed to say "I am guilty" but could not pronounce the words when speaking of the murder of 400,000, 750,000, 900,000 or 1,200,000 people.' She continues, 'except for a monster, no man who actually participated in such events (rather than "merely" organised them from far away) can concede guilt and yet, as the young prison officer in Dusseldorf put it, "consent to remain alive".[12]

This sentimentalisation of what is to be inferred takes no account of evidence that Nazi war criminals did not feel guilty or responsible for what they did in their perpetrator roles because they were a natural and unreflective response to what was required of them in the SS. It was not that they needed to exonerate themselves but rather that they did not even reflect on issues of responsibility before being interrogated, which, as has been indicated above, is not dissimilar to the lack of sense of responsibility for meeting role requirements amongst the great majority of normal people in ordinary circumstances. And Sereny's extraordinary inference regarding Stangl's intentions in his having recounted an anecdote is nothing more than conjecture informed by her overconfidence in her judgement of Stangl and assumption of psychological insight she did not possess because of her lack of experience.

The final 'confession' Sereny obtained from Stangl began with an insistence that 'my conscience is clear about what I did, myself' and that 'I have never intentionally hurt anyone, myself.' He went on—

"'But I was there", he said then, in a curiously dry and tired tone of resignation. These few sentences had taken him almost half an hour to pronounce. "So yes," he said finally, very quietly, "in reality I share the guilt…. Because my guilt…my guilt…only now in these talks…now that I have talked about it all, for the first time." He stopped.'

'He had pronounced the words "my guilt": but more than words, the finality of it was in the sagging body, and on his face.'
Sereny claims that Stangl then said, 'in a dull voice', 'my guilt'…'is that I am still here. That is my guilt'…'I should have died. That was my guilt.'[13]
Van Voren refers to Stangl's having said *'my guilt' 'is that I am still here, that is my guilt'…'I should have died. That was my guilt,'* in what he regards as the 'closest to admission of his guilt'.[14]
Eaglestone refers to the same interlude in Sereny's last interview with Stangl and claims that as a consequence of Sereny's conduct of their interviews Stangl 'moves past his courtroom words, "my conscience is clear about what I did myself", through to "I never intentionally hurt anyone" to "in reality I share the guilt…my guilt…only now in these talks…my guilt is that I am still here". Eaglestone notes that Sereny infers that Stangl died just nineteen hours later because he had at last 'faced himself and told himself the truth: it was a monumental effort to reach that fleeting moment when he became the man he should have been'.[15] Yet this is a *post hoc, ergo propter hoc* fallacy that attributes great significance to Sereny's having obtained, in her own account through judicious use of silence, a therapeutic breakthrough with Stangl.

Sereny did then infer that she had through her interviews brought Stangl to a realisation of his responsibility and guilt after many hours of the sort of rationalisation and evasion she refers to as characteristic of Nazi war criminals. There are though some troubling concerns regarding what Sereny seems to see as a therapeutic breakthrough. For Sereny's claim of its having been an admission of guilt and responsibility to be ascribed to her own astute interviewing technique is just one possible interpretation of what Stangl said.

One issue is the extent to which Sereny's record of the specifics of the interview is accurate, not least given her tendency to dramatise, to draw impressionistic inferences and to attributions that reflect her conceit and agenda of a therapeutic breakthrough. Did she for instance write down exactly what Stangl was saying whilst he was unburdening himself in so emotional a manner, or did she write down the way she recalled it afterwards, which could have been influenced by what she wanted to hear? Why did she reject Stangl's credibility when he claimed compliance with orders as a defence of his perpetrator behaviour but accept that he was credible when he made his alleged 'confession'? The indication here is of 'confirmation bias', the tendency to interrogate, derogate or dismiss evidence that is dissonant with one's attitude and counter to one's agenda and to accept without challenge or interrogation evidence that supports one's attitudes and agenda.

Even if one accepts that Sereny's account of what Stangl said at their final interview is accurate, Sereny concentrates on the later parts of the quotation and disregards the significance of Stangl's initial statement that 'my conscience is clear about what I did, myself' and that 'I have never intentionally hurt anyone, myself', which are a reiteration of his claim that he was not responsible in any personal way. And even in the later part of the statement she quotes the actual words Stangl is claimed to have said, 'but I was there', 'in reality I share the guilt…. Because my guilt…my guilt…only now in these talks…now that I have talked about it all, for the first time'…'my guilt is that I am still here. That is my guilt', and 'I should have died. That was my guilt', may in fact indicate no more than the guilt of the survivor of a war in the east that had no normative restraint and a reference to the enormous suffering and loss of life for Germans too. There is for instance no admission of agency or volition and so personal responsibility in what Stangl said, and what he said in these later quotations was vague enough to be not inconsistent with the defence of reference to the objective and experiential context of the war in the east. It is also consistent with his claim to Sereny that he had not wanted to be involved in the extermination of Jews but that he had no choice. That is quite different to Sereny's inference that Stangl admitted personal guilt. It is also possible that Stangl hoped, even in this late interview (Sereny claims she intended just one more interview), to elicit Sereny's assistance in an appeal against his sentence, a motive Sereny acknowledged, though she claimed that even when she made clear that the purpose of her interviews was to uncover Stangl's past, his experience of life and his personality, and then provide an account of it as a journalist he indicated a desire to continue. As has been indicated, Stangl's desire to perpetuate Sereny's visits is comprehensible given that their discussions centred upon Stangl's experience.[16]

There is also the possibility that Sereny has got the causation the wrong way round, that rather than Stangl's weary, broken demeanour and 'confession' causing his death just hours later, his exhausted demeanour and 'confession' were the consequence of his feeling very unwell at the time. She does mention that Stangl had been unwell but claims he felt better by the time of the statements above as a result of her having brought him some soup, and does not consider the possibility of Stangl's health having been poor as an explanation of what he said because it does not lend itself to her agenda of a therapeutic breakthrough.

Eaglestone alludes to concern regarding interpretation of Stangl's final 'confession' in asking, 'how much of this is real and how much shaped by the genre demands of "accusatory biography"?' and says it is possible to regard Sereny's book as a form of 'Arendtian moral therapy', returning Stangl 'to selfhood'.[17]

Another possible explanation is that Stangl was influenced by the dynamic of the interaction, that the 'confession' reflected Stangl's desire for approval from Sereny. In an interview conducted for the Web of Stories online collection of autobiographical interviews and entitled 'Gitta Sereny – Who Was Franz Stangl?' Sereny claimed that her view of Stangl was 'very, very important to him', that 'he really was a very limited man, you know', an 'Austrian provincial man' (followed by her disparaging laughter) who tried to speak to her in High German rather than his native Austrian, an indication both of her disdain for Stangl and of the possible validity of the view that Stangl's final 'confession' of guilt was in fact designed to please or impress her. There may also have been some influence from Stangl's 'depression', to which Sereny refers and which may have made him susceptible, over time, to her agenda of extracting some form of 'confession' from him.[18]

In a presentation thirty years after *Into That Darkness*, Sereny claimed that Stangl was 'an essentially subservient personality' dependent upon and afraid of his bosses in the SS, especially Wirth, which seems to indicate that careerism and desire to be approved of by his bosses through cultivation of a reputation for competence as a camp commandant explain Stangl's perpetrator behaviour. Sereny also claimed that 'in a normal bourgeois life, such as he had always planned and started before the Nazis took over in Austria in 1938, with a wife he adored, he would have been a perfectly decent man.' Sereny's ensuing inference is more problematic, for she claims that 'a violent childhood and a despotic government, or even authoritarian environment (as against a democratic one) brings out in men'...'hidden tendencies toward force and often brutality,' but she does not explain why everyone in the generations born in the 1930s and earlier, all of whom would have had authoritarian patriarchal upbringings, did not display violent tendencies and predisposition towards perpetrator behaviour. Sereny does not identify responsiveness to perceived role requirements to be the dominant influence on human behaviour, it seems because of her lack of knowledge of psychological realities that would have been known to psychiatrists and psychologists.

In the same presentation Sereny claims that under Nazi rule Stangl revealed the extent to which he was susceptible to corruption in regarding the Jews he arranged to exterminate as 'cargo', in his implicit claims of virtue in taking action against 'cheating', and in his recounting having permitted a relative of a Jew a last meal as a virtue. What the anecdote does indicate is the extent of Stangl's regard for himself and concentration upon his own experience in having the temerity to relate an anecdote intended to show his humanity and the gratitude it elicited. Sereny concludes her presentation by claiming that Stangl implicitly denied responsibility for the extermination of Jews at Sobibor and Treblinka by indicating that God was responsible for what happened. That is of course not consistent with Sereny's claim in *Into That Darkness* to have obtained from Stangl an admission of guilt, for if Stangl did not feel responsible for what happened at Sobibor and Treblinka he would not have felt that any guilt should be attributed to him.

Sereny's moral and intellectual disdain for Stangl in her presentation thirty years on from *Into That Darkness* is undiminished, and so is her sense of entitlement to pronounce upon his psychological nature.[19] What is missing is any appreciation that normal human beings conform without reflection to role requirements to optimise their own outcomes by avoiding formal sanctions, for instance loss of career or demotion, and avoiding too being the object of informal sanctions of gossip, ostracism, ridicule and disapproval from peers and bosses, some understanding of which could have diminished Sereny's moral and intellectual arrogance in regard to Stangl and could have precluded the bias inherent in her search for a moment of moral transformation in him.

Sereny's *Into That Darkness* is compromised as a historical source by Sereny's amateur psychoanalytic perspective, by her failure to consider other possible interpretations of what Stangl said to her, by her impressionistic concentration on her own experience of the encounter with Stangl and on his experience of his life, by her apparent desire for a therapeutic breakthrough as a consequence of her astute interviewing technique, by her tendency to sentimentalise and dramatise, by her moral and intellectual arrogance, and by her assumption of a position of moral rectitude that precluded genuine appreciation of the influence on Stangl's behaviour of his experiential context in the SS.

The influence of Sereny's psychoanalytic perspective on her appraisal of Stangl does seem to have been enhanced by her intuitive and impressionistic approach, her personal confidence in her conjectural inferences regarding Stangl, and her thera-peutic objective. Hughes sees a difference between Arendt, a philosopher and polit-ical theorist whose judgement was that there was no possibility of experience of guilt in Eichmann, and Sereny, who believed that 'Stangl was capable of experiencing guilt'. Hughes' own view is that Sereny's 'firm yet tactful policy enabled Stangl to reach – for a fleeting moment in that final interview – a part of himself that could feel guilt'.[20] This is a remarkable endorsement of Sereny's impressionistic judgement of Stangl and one which Sereny was, according to Hughes' own account, predisposed to find from the outset, indicating that Sereny's inferences reflected her impressionistic conviction that Stangl could feel guilt, her resulting predisposition to find guilt in Stangl, and her arrogant assumption that she could through her sophisticated interviewing technique and personal attributes elicit a therapeutic breakthrough with Stangl.

This does not seem good scientific procedure. The fact that Hughes does not com-ment adversely on these attributes in Sereny's work may be explained by Hughes' own disciplinary background as a historian specialising in the history of psycho-analysis and trained as a psychoanalyst, which may have predisposed her to endorse Sereny's psychoanalytic inferences despite the fact that Sereny had no psychoana-lytic training or expertise, which means of course that Sereny's inferences regarding Stangl were no more than impressionistic conjecture.

There are a number of reservations regarding psychoanalysis. To begin with, psycho-analytic theory seems to be predicated upon a series of presumptions that define them-selves by reference to other abstractions, as in the dynamics between the superego or conscience, the rational ego and the primal desires of the id, and references to defence mechanisms to protect the self. There is no established therapeutic validity for psycho-analysis that could validate the theory from established therapeutic effectiveness. And there is the suggestibility of patients susceptible to the inferences of the psychoanalytic ther-apist over the characteristically long periods under which psychoanalytic therapy is under-gone, in which a relationship develops between the psychoanalytic therapist and the patient, and the assumption by the psychoanalyst of a status that means that psychoana-lytic inferences cannot be challenged.

Psychoanalytic theory does then seem to depend upon plausibility posturing as certainty and truth and on the assumed authority of the psychoanalyst. It is worth noting that psychoanalysis is now considered unscientific and lacking in empirical support by psychiatry and psychology faculties in universities and is no longer regarded as of use there. It is to be found in other academic faculties, including literature and history, where its lack of scientific and empirical validation appears not to have precluded reference to it. The inference is of course that psychoanalytic inferences are no better than plausible conjecture.

In an indication of the effect of the psychoanalytic bias on assessments of personality, Hughes claims that Arendt had no interest in contact with Eichmann because she regarded him as a man who had long ago 'divested himself of any guilt', for the implicit assumption that Eichmann did feel guilt at some time is one without any evidence to support it but one that follows from psychodynamic theory and its presumptions regarding the dynamics of an ordinary personality referred to above. In further evidence of the psychoanalytic bias in Arendt, Sereny and Hughes, Hughes notes that Sereny 'assumed that Stangl might be able to recover the guilt that had gone missing – provided she 'approached' him 'as a human being', and that Sereny claimed that Stangl had 'voluntarily but unwittingly revealed' how 'he had lived – and was still living – on two levels of consciousness and conscience'. These attributions indicate that psychoanalytic theory tends to impose itself on the evidence and to distort inferences to its own ends in a psychoanalytic narrative that does not attempt to validate its inferences by reference to objective, that is, behavioural, evidence.[21]

In Stangl's case the consequence was Sereny's presumption that Stangl had a conscience and felt some form of guilt that genuinely tormented him, rather than his having had a post-war experience of attention to ordinary life and inattention to the past, or, when interrogated on his wartime behaviour, genuine belief in the validity of his reference to the experiential context of the war, to his having done no more than conform to the requirements of the roles he was assigned in the SS, and to the responsibility of those above him in the SS and the Nazi state hierarchy who formulated and decided upon Nazi policy towards the Jews.

Stangl's attribution of responsibility for the Holocaust to his superiors in the SS and to the Nazi state hierarchy was of course optimal for him both during and after the war, for it legitimised perpetrator behaviour undertaken by him to maintain his SS rank and the approbation of his peers and bosses in the SS, and excused him afterwards. Here Stangl appears to be reflecting motivation to optimise his psychological outcomes, an entirely normal human process that obtains in ordinary life, in the same manner in which he optimised his objective and career outcomes during the war. For Stangl continued as an SS camp commandant, at Treblinka, after his experience at Sobibor, was a conspicuous success in reorganising the extermination process at Treblinka, and lived a normal family life in Syria and Brazil after the war, indications that he was not afflicted by guilt over his wartime perpetrator behaviour during the war or after it.

Sereny's psychoanalytic bias and her overconfidence in her own intuitive inferences preclude consideration of other possible explanations of Stangl's behaviour, in Stangl's case his reference to obedience to orders and to the perceived possibility of draconian sanctions for declining to accept an SS assignment, a reference to the experiential context of the SS, which Sereny derogated in inferences that validated her initial presumption of Stangl's being susceptible to an admission of guilt to himself and to Sereny given her sophisticated interviewing technique.

Sereny and Arendt seem to presume that their status as liberal intellectuals entitled them to appraise from a position of moral and intellectual superiority the personalities of Nazi war criminals, even though they did not have the expertise to make an accurate assessment. Neither asks what they themselves would have done in Stangl's situation. The implication is that they believed that their moral and intellectual qualities would have precluded their conforming to role requirements in the manner that Stangl did. That indicates their belief that intellectual and moral attributes are correlated with each other, and it is expedient for them that their implicit claims regarding what they would have done cannot be disproved.

These comments are not intended to legitimise perpetrator behaviour but rather to address the possibility of its being an entirely normal response to the circumstances of an SS officer in Nazi Germany during the war. The idea that moral reasoning and intellect would preclude commission of acts of genocide has been comprehensively discredited by the visceral immediacy of the perpetrator behaviour of Einsatzgruppen, Einsatzkommando and Sonderkommando commanders, many of whom had law degrees (some had doctorates) and so had been trained in moral reasoning. German universities of the interwar period may not have trained law students in a liberal humanitarian morality of individual rights and freedoms, but the evidence of the Milgram experiments in the US in the 1960s establishes that even in liberal democratic societies that emphasise human freedom and individual rights conformity to immoral authority was the norm, to optimise personal outcomes.

Sereny does note that 'no one's actions can be judged in isolation from the external elements which shape and influence his life,' but does not then draw the inference that Stangl became a perpetrator because it was the job he was given in the SS and because he wanted to be seen to succeed or at least not to fail at it to preserve or enhance his reputation as an SS officer and to secure the approbation of his bosses and peers.[22] For these are entirely normal motives that exert great influence on ordinary human behaviour in all cultures and societies at all times.

Sereny's apparent purpose, to elicit from Stangl some admission of guilt and responsibility for his role in the Holocaust through a therapeutic breakthrough with him, is of course quite different from an attempt to identify the actual causes of his perpetrator behaviour in the war. Van Voren refers to Stangl's telling Sereny that he had during the war regarded the Nazi state as having intended and directed the extermination of the Jews, and that as a consequence he regarded himself as having no immoral intent and so no responsibility or guilt. This sounds like Milgram's 'agentic state', in which he claimed individuals feel no responsibility because they regard themselves as mere agents of authority rather than acting with volition and intent, but also like an expedient attribution for Stangl in prison for life for his perpetrator behaviour in its claim of obedience to orders and responsibility being with the Nazi hierarchy and state, not him.[23] For Stangl the evidence does tend to indicate careerism and identification with the role of a senior SS officer as camp commandant as the causes of his perpetrator behaviour.

Sereny on Speer

Of the senior Nazis arraigned at Nuremberg as major war criminals maybe the most intriguing was Albert Speer, Hitler's architect and then, from February 1942 to the end of the war, his Armaments Minister, who evaded the gallows by devising a defence in which he exhibited contrition, claimed that like many others in Nazi Germany he had been initially beguiled by Hitler (and by the opportunities being Hitler's architect offered him), accepted collective guilt as part of the Nazi leadership but disclaimed knowledge of the Holocaust and so individual guilt for it. In doing so he ingratiated himself with the western Nuremberg judges as a senior Nazi prepared to admit some sort of responsibility even though he at the same time denied personal responsibility. In fact Speer's defence at Nuremberg was to export blame for the treatment of Jews associated with his work to other Nazi ministers, not least the unfortunate Sauckel, the Minister for Labour who procured the slave labour used in Speer's armaments production, and to claim that as a senior Nazi minister he (Speer) could and should have known of the Holocaust but that he did not. Speer's case does then seem to have been one of selective attention to the requirements of his role as Armaments Minister and inattention to the means by which armaments were being produced, that is, to Jewish slave labour. Goda notes that Speer presented himself as 'a young apolitical architect' attracted by 'the national renaissance that Nazism provided', and that Speer claimed that, as Armaments Minister, he had been focused on optimising the war effort rather than on the treatment of Jews. Goda concludes that Speer 'had saved his skin through a staged repentance before the Tribunal', a '*faux penitence*'.[24] The consequence appears to have been that, despite an unaltered Russian desire to execute him, Speer's upper-middle-class manners, urbane demeanour, his having provided the western Allies with extensive information on Nazi war production with great openness, and his apparent preparedness to consider his own culpability with similar frankness, had so engaged the British and the Americans at Nuremberg that he received a twenty-year prison sentence in Spandau. Goda notes that while Sauckel was hanged for providing slave labour 'Speer, who had demanded the slave labor, received but twenty years'.[25]

Gitta Sereny spent years researching Speer and cultivated a close personal friendship with him, conducting many interviews and obtaining access to personal documentation from him. Her technique was the same as that she had employed in her assessment of Stangl, cultivating a personal relationship with Speer to facilitate his being open with her, then interrogating his account by use of evidence obtained through her research on him. Her assessment of Speer was informed by the same precepts of psychoanalysis that had presumed the existence of conscience in Stangl, and by the same intuitive, impressionistic, emotional and personally involved technique, indicating a similar possibility of loss of impartiality because of selective attention to confirming information and inattention to or dismissal of disconfirming information and possible alternative explanations of evidence. Sereny's obvious predispositions meant it was in the interests of Stangl and Speer to present an anguished self tormented by conscience.

The existence or non-existence of conscience in Stangl and Speer is not considered as an issue by Sereny because her psychoanalytic approach presumes the existence of conscience. The definition and nature of conscience are in fact issues of continuing controversy, and the references here to conscience relate to Sereny's assumption of its existence and its being active enough in Stangl and Speer to cause them inner anguish and 'turmoil' even though there is no behavioural evidence that would indicate a conscience in either man active enough to exert influence on behaviour or experience. Even if one were to accept the existence of conscience as axiomatic the lack of evidence of it in Stangl's and Speer's wartime and post-war behaviour, and the compelling alternative explanation of their behaviour as having optimised their own outcomes both in the war and after it, is indicative of the distorting effect on Sereny's assessment of Stangl and Speer of her psychoanalytic assumptions regarding conscience. For ultimately the existence of an active and influential conscience can only be inferred from its observed influence on behaviour and on experience inferred from behaviour without the distorting effect of a pre-existing narrative and an approach that is impressionistic and overconfident despite no training even in psychoanalysis.[26]

Sereny's initial disposition towards Speer is indicated by her feeling that 'neither the Nuremberg trial nor his books had really told us how a man of such quality could become not immoral, not amoral but, somehow infinitely worse, morally extinguished.' Sereny continues, 'eventually he had gained knowledge of the abominations and recognized that they originated with Hitler. What then kept this man in place? What had prevented him, whose possibilities for escape were unlimited, from taking himself and his family out of it?'.[27]

Sereny does not consider the possibility that Speer remained in post because his own personal aspirations and status mattered to him more than the fate of the Jews, and she does not explain exactly what 'quality' in Speer she is referring to, though her relationship with Speer does seem to have been informed by her respect for Speer's upper-middle-class background, education and urbanity. Sereny found Speer to have been afflicted by a 'profound malaise with his own conscience', an indication of the influence of her psychoanalytic assumptions and her reliance on her personal impression of Speer. It is worth noting that a psychoanalytical perspective, a reliance on personal intuition and impressions, and a tendency towards sentimentalisation and dramatisation, all characteristics of Sereny, are consonant with each other and result in conjecture without evidence. The consequence was that Sereny did not consider the possibility that Speer engaged in the same sort of presentation of self with her that he had had so much success with in his relationship with Hitler, in the Nuremberg trial, in his books and in his cultivating a public identity as the 'good Nazi' after his release from Spandau.[28]

Sereny's psychoanalytic approach results in her regarding Speer as engaged in a 'battle with truth' and as experiencing anguish over his role in and responsibility for the Holocaust. This is very similar to the view she took of Stangl in its inference of inner turmoil and moral anguish and in its disregard of evidence indicating that Stangl and Speer were not anguished over their role in the Holocaust during the war or after it, and that both conformed to Sereny's expectations in their behaviour with her.

Sereny does acknowledge that Stangl and Speer attempted to evade her questions and to rationalise their records, but sees no inconsistency between such deviousness and the inference that both men experienced inner turmoil over their roles in the war, despite the fact that the sort of personality that tries to evade admission of personal guilt is unlikely to be experiencing moral anguish.

These sources of bias in Sereny, the psychoanalytic orientation that tended to find what it was looking for in inferences that can be neither proved nor disproved, the class attitudes, her impressionistic approach, her overconfidence in her own judgement, and her becoming far too close to her subjects to have remained impartial, influence her assessments of Speer and Stangl.

In a revealing appraisal of Sereny's book on Speer by a noted historian on the Third Reich, Richard Overy notes that Speer 'enjoyed the power and responsibility and was, certainly as Armaments Minister, anything but a political innocent', despite the fact that 'in his memoirs he denied that he was ever involved in anti-semitism or in the slave-labour programme', the latter an extraordinary claim given that Speer directed what labour Sauckel should be providing for armaments production. Speer showed Sereny a document in which he claimed that 'he shared collective responsibility, but that his personal fault was to "turn away" from the fate of the Jews, not to participate in it'.

Overy also notes Speer's apparent lack of awareness of the significance of the immediate context for other people when he visited Vienna not long after the Nazi occupation, for when asked what he remembered all he could recall was his own personal pleasurable experiences. Overy infers that Speer may have been 'capable of shielding himself one way or another – innocence or detachment or overwork', and though he notes Speer's 'guilelessly' recalling his trivial personal experience of being in Vienna four decades later he does not draw the inference that Speer simply did not care what happened to the Jews of Vienna, that he was, like the general German population, 'indifferent' to the Jews, and exclusively concentrated upon his own experience of life, indicating a combination of egocentricity, pursuit of his own interests and disregard for those of anyone else who could not assist him, and absence of conscience.

There does seem to be an inconsistency in Overy's review of Sereny's assessment of Speer. For Overy notes Sereny's having found in Speer's testimony 'endless examples of misrepresentation, distortion and massaging of the record', wonders if 'Speer wasn't in fact manipulating Sereny', characterises Speer as a 'ruthless self-publicist', notes that Speer did not have a 'developed sense of moral discrimination', and that Speer continued to insist that he had not known of the Holocaust for the rest of his life to maintain a 'new post-Spandau career as the Nazi who pleaded guilty' even though he claimed to be not guilty in any personal sense, and quotes a telephone call from Speer to Sereny in which he told her 'he had not done badly: "after all, I was Hitler's architect; I was his Minister of Armaments and Production; I did serve twenty years in Spandau and coming out, did make another good career. Not bad after all, was it?". Even so Overy concludes that 'the truth that Speer wrestled with was simply that he was proud of what he had done', and seems to accept Speer's 'inexpressible sadness', noting that 'the moral torment was real enough.' He also refers to Sereny's commitment of time to Speer and notes her unique access to 'so intimate and so frank a record', despite his own reference to Speer's testimony's being 'suspect on all kinds of grounds'.[29] Given the evidence of Speer's manipulativeness at Nuremberg and even in Overy's estimation one does suspect that the record of Speer to which Overy is referring was neither intimate nor frank.

The alternative explanation, that Speer was exclusively focused on his own outcomes and indifferent to those of other people, is simply not considered even though it would explain the evidence of Speer's behaviour. Questions appear not to have been asked, for instance how would a man afflicted by guilt and inner turmoil be motivated to evade the truth so brazenly over so long a period and have a record of behaviour that was devious and manipulative throughout his life during and after the war and even after his time in Spandau, and how a genuinely contrite man would, inebriated, with drink known to disinhibit, engage in such conceited boasting of his achievements in life without any trace of the guilt he is supposed to have experienced.

Though Overy remains unconvinced by Sereny's book he does seem to endorse Sereny's view of Speer as a tormented individual battling with the truth, despite the evidence to the contrary and the lack of evidence to support such a view. That seems to indicate the influence of premises such as the existence and influence of conscience in Speer.

In a different appraisal of Sereny's book of Speer by another noted historian on the Third Reich, Richard Evans approves of Sereny's exposure of 'Speer's published memoirs' as 'inaccurate or misleading', and applauds Sereny's establishing that Speer was at the Posen meeting where Himmler spoke openly of the extermination of the Jews and her establishing that Speer's affidavits to the contrary were 'false'.

Evans goes on to congratulate Sereny on not accusing Speer of 'deliberate lying', referring to the view that 'Speer deceived others but also deceived himself', yet the instances he cites of Speer's untruths could not be other than deliberate fabrications. And of course cultivation of semantic ambiguity around what it is to 'know' anything would have given Speer the chance to misrepresent himself as not having 'known' what he did not want to 'know' and as having wrestled with his conscience over that avoidance for decades. Another inference is that, like other Nazi war criminals, including Eichmann and Stangl, Speer found himself an object of endless fascination and was quite content to expatiate upon his own inner state and experience over years, not least when introspection and discourse regarding his experience offered opportunities for implicit denial of responsibility or oblique acceptance of indirect responsibility for not 'knowing' what he should have 'known', with its implication of no direct responsibility.

Evans refers to Sereny's inference that Speer's close personal relationship with Hitler resulted in Speer's not being told of the extermination of the Jews because 'Hitler wanted it kept secret', to Speer's having continued in post even after knowledge of the Holocaust from the Posen meeting in October 1943 and Speer's visit to the Dora rocket manufacture site with its terrible slave labour in December of that year because of Hitler's profound influence on him, and to Speer's having deceived himself that he had to continue working for Germany's sake. These arguments seem implausible and reflective of a bias intent on excusing Speer.

Even so, Evans does find it 'difficult to share Sereny's optimism that he finally overcame the great lie he had lived with' and notes that Sereny's reference to Speer's 'tacit acceptance of the persecution and murder of millions of Jews' and her regarding it as 'Speer's final, direct confession of guilt' in the final chapter of her book disregards the fact that Speer 'coupled it with a statement that his "tacit acceptance" meant "looking away, not by knowledge of an order or its execution"', concluding that 'Albert Speer lived his lie to the last'.[30] In the context of Evans' previous comments, referred to above, it would seem that Evans endorses the 'battle with truth' explanation of Speer's behaviour, for which there is no evidence and despite evidence to the contrary. The principle of psychological consistency and circumspection when dealing with claimed experience is missing from these views of Speer.

Sereny spent three years conducting conversations with Speer and many more interviewing people who knew him in various capacities and consulting Speer's books and letters. Sereny found Speer to be rational, calculated and reserved, but does not seem to infer from his success in manipulating the judges at Nuremberg by playing the penitent Nazi that he may have been manipulating her too, not least as Speer, following his initial contact with Sereny in July 1977, wrote to tell her that he had read and had been disconcerted by *Into That Darkness*, Sereny's book on Stangl, and so would have been aware of her psychoanalytic inferences of conscience and inner turmoil, and her therapeutic, sympathetic, impressionistic and intuitive approach.[31] For as with Stangl, Sereny depended upon her intuition with Speer, noting that she had not expected that 'sadness could be an essential part of him. I now believed that it was, and it intrigued me,' an intuitive inference. Far from interrogating it and her own tendencies Sereny takes her intuition as a legitimate starting point, and her intertwining of evidence on Speer with anecdotes from her own experiences is also similar to *Into That Darkness*, not least in their class snobbery and conceit. To take just one instance, she notes that she was 'from the kind of background the Germans were likely to respect'. Her therapeutic orientation seems apparent in her reference to Speer's 'continuing and tormenting awareness of guilt' and to 'out of all this, there came to be another Speer'.[32]

Speer's deviousness in his own cause is apparent in his use of his last letter to Hitler, dated 19 March 1945, to exonerate himself. For in the letter, written when Hitler was facing his last days in Berlin, Speer told Hitler that in 1940, with the German victories, 'we ought to have proved our worthiness to Providence by decency and inner morality.' Speer claims that the letter indicates that 'I saw the mistakes, winced at the abuses, took a critical stand, and was haunted by doubts and skepticism,' and even though he acknowledges that his concern in 1940 was that the German victories would be 'gambled away', Speer's intention to exonerate himself and to distance himself from Hitler when he recognised that the war was lost and defeat was imminent is clear.

The letter seems to be presented as part of Speer's construction of an identity as a non-political individual in a technocratic position in the Third Reich and uninvolved in ideological decisions made by the other leading Nazis. It is an indication of Speer's arrogance that he believed that so transparent an attempt to insulate himself from responsibility was credible.[33] The letter was written on the day of Hitler's 'Nero Decree' that dictated the destruction of German infrastructure and manufacture to deny it to Germany's adversaries, and Speer's defiance of the decree occurred in the certainty of imminent defeat, so Speer may have regarded the risk to himself of such defiance as being minimal and have seen some possible advantage for his future after the war in what he did. It does not bear upon Speer's complicity in the Holocaust.

Kitchen notes that in the 'Spandau Diaries' Speer 'continues adamantly to deny any knowledge of the mass murder of European Jews'. He notes too Speer's 'efforts at reinventing himself' and cites evidence of Speer's antisemitism in his indifference to the welfare of the Jews who were the slave labourers he indicated were needed.[34] It is worth noting the dearth of evidence of Speer's 'battle with the truth' at the level of personal conscience as opposed to stratagems of denial and refutation of complicity in or even knowledge of the destruction of the Jews to protect his reputation and cultivate his post-Spandau career.

The historian Claudia Koonz, in an article entitled 'Blind by Choice', on Sereny's book on Speer in *The New York Times* dated 8 October 1995, refers to Speer's 'detached bearing', 'upper-class manner', 'personal integrity' and intellect, attributes she claims differentiated him from other Nazis. Yet there is no evidence of Speer's 'personal integrity' in her article and she herself regards Speer as a 'slick opportunist' who cultivated a relationship with Hitler, manipulated the Nuremberg judges, and found a new identity as the 'good Nazi' after his release from Spandau.

There is some inconsistency in Koonz's characterisation of Speer. For she describes him as a devious and opportunistic personality who employed a strategy of deflection with Sereny, who had an enduring desire for 'fame' and 'celebrity' and for whom 'truth' 'was an elaborate intellectual game', yet also refers to his 'personal integrity' and to a 'moral rectitude' that 'salved his conscience' as genuine rather than postures by which Speer deceived his intended audiences.

Koonz notes of Speer that 'feelings for Hitler, the trial' and 'his years of solitude in prison' 'pervaded his prison letters and notebooks', and that 'until an editor suggested he add some comment on "his own feelings" on the Nazi extermination of the Jews for the American edition of *Inside the Third Reich*, Speer had written virtually nothing about genocide or even anti-Semitism'. Goda notes that in the first draft of *Inside the Third Reich* there was no reference to Kristallnacht and that mention of it was added at the exhortation of Joachim Fest, a journalist and collaborator.[35]

This is indicative of Speer's indifference to what had happened to the Jews except when it was in his interests to display concern and 'guilt', and any 'inner turmoil' would seem more genuine if it were not part of a narrative of devious denial of what he knew of the Holocaust to maintain his career as the 'good Nazi'. For genuine contrition would have been a private matter, as would personal guilt.

This point, just what Speer knew of the Holocaust, seems central to the issue of Speer's guilt and complicity, and to his veracity as a witness after the war. According to Fischel, 'Speer was adamant' that he knew nothing 'directly pertaining to the murder of European Jewry, although admitting his responsibility for the murderous excesses of the Nazi slave labour system'.[36]

For this vital issue of Speer's knowledge of the Holocaust, the infamous meeting at Posen, where Himmler was open with senior SS officers regarding the SS task of exterminating the Jews of the occupied territories, is central. Sereny refers to Erich Goldhagen's article entitled 'Albert Speer, Himmler and the Secret of the Final Solution', in *Midstream*, in October 1971, and to its claim that 'Himmler's direct address to Speer in his Posen speech was clear proof that he was present when it was given' and that it established Speer's 'complicity and the hypocrisy of his admission of generalized rather than specific guilt at Nuremberg and ever since'. Sereny notes Goldhagen's having included in a note to the article an indication that Himmler had specifically claimed in the speech that Speer endorsed the extermination of Poland's Jews, and refers to her having established that the note was an error. She notes that Speer raised the Goldhagen evidence with her in a state of some agitation and distress in anticipation of being challenged with it, and that he admitted that he had been in Posen on the day of Himmler's speech but claimed he could not remember having heard it. Sereny also recalls her having told Speer that she had challenged Goldhagen over his inference from Himmler's speech that Speer endorsed the extermination of the Jews of Poland, Speer's gratitude, and his claim that he had been distressed by the issue for some time but that he had found witnesses who had told him that he had left the Posen meeting at lunchtime and so had not been present at Himmler's speech in the afternoon.[37] Sereny records the great lengths to which she went to assess the evidence of two affidavits Speer had obtained to the effect that he had left the Posen meeting before Himmler's speech, one of which she found to have been obtained under duress and the other of which was of dubious credibility when set in the context of other evidence. The interaction recorded by Sereny over the Posen evidence does seem another example of Speer's extraordinary capacity for inventive exculpation of himself, for he had not admitted having been present at the Posen meeting until he had become apprehensive that conclusive evidence of his presence there was to be presented to him in public.

An article in the *Smithsonian Magazine* of 8 January 2013, entitled 'The Candor and Lies of Nazi Officer Albert Speer', refers to the Goldhagen evidence of Speer's attendance at the Posen meeting and to Speer's characteristically devious response that he had left before Himmler's speech regarding the annihilation of the Jews, but notes that Speer finally betrayed himself in a letter dated 23 December 1971 to the widow of a Belgian resistance leader, in which Speer said, 'there is no doubt – I was present as Himmler announced on October 6 1943 that all Jews would be killed', adding 'who would believe me that I suppressed this, that it would have been easier to have written all of this in my memoirs?' (See also *The Guardian* dated 13 March 2007.) The letter seems to have been discovered in the UK in 2006 or 2007, some years after the publication of Sereny's book on Speer. Taken in the context of Speer's evasive and innovative defence at his trial at Nuremberg and other evidence indicating a manipulative and devious personality presented above it would seem that the reason for Speer's not revealing that he had attended the Posen meeting and had heard Himmler's speech regarding the policy of exterminating the Jews was that any admission would have risked Speer's 'career' as the 'good Nazi', which he pursued with some avidity and reward in terms of affluence and reputation after his release from Spandau.

Sereny's verdict on Speer is revealing of her biases. She acknowledges that Speer 'manipulated, cajoled, intrigued against and threatened those who interfered with his power and his aims, demanded rather than merely participated in the brutal subjugation of foreign workers for slave labour and unconsciously or consciously blinded himself to licensed murder' even though he had no racial or religious hatred – on the contrary, 'he felt nothing', and 'pity, compassion, sympathy and empathy were not part of his essential vocabulary'. These comments do seem supported by the evidence on Speer, apart from the conjectural inference of his having 'blinded himself to licensed murder',[38] for an alternative explanation of Speer's behaviour is that he was not interested in the human cost of the means by which his plans for armaments production were achieved and was simply indifferent to the welfare of the Jews and other foreign workers because of egocentricity and exclusive attention to his own outcomes in the Nazi elite.

Sereny claims of Speer that 'while he sincerely grasped any opportunity to reiterate his sorrow and pain at having been – the automatic formula he used – "a part of a government that committed such crimes", he was totally incapable of saying that he had known about them at the time', and of Posen Sereny claims that 'the fact is that the more Speer tries to explain away awkward facts, the clearer it is that he is trying desperately to avoid facing the truth. There is simply no way that Speer could have failed to know about Himmler's speech, whether or not he sat through it.'[39] These quotations from Sereny indicate her view that Speer could not face admitting his complicity for psychological reasons rather than for pragmatic ones associated with adverse personal consequences. Sereny does not consider that the explanation of Speer's avoidance of admission of knowledge of the Holocaust is that he was trying to maintain his public persona as the 'good Nazi', his post-Spandau career, and to avert the possibility of exposure and disgrace. Sereny's inference reflects her psychodynamic bias in presuming the existence of conscience in Speer and his battling with it and in not considering the alternative explanation for Speer's behaviour.

Sereny goes on to make more controversial claims regarding Speer. She seems to claim that Speer's illness in 1944 was a consequence of 'Speer's tragedy, a paradox of Greek dimensions' that involved his recognition after Posen and Dora of his 'involvement and thus his guilt', the result of which was that he 'essentially needed and longed to die' but was prevented from doing so by 'his will to live' being more compelling than 'his need to atone'. Sereny claims that Speer experienced 'feelings of personal guilt', a 'wish, almost, for death and yet fear of execution', and 'the shame of being spared', followed by 'his discovery of humility', and that, 'in the monastic peace of Spandau', 'morality and repentance became the ruling factors in his life'.[40]

In these inferences Sereny seems to attach more credibility to Speer's demeanour and discourse with her, and to her own intuitive and impressionistic experience of him (informed as it was by her amateur psychologising and psychoanalytic influence), than to the objective record of Speer's behaviour. For Sereny's inferences are inconsistent with the evidence of Speer's self-exculpating 'Spandau Diaries' and 'Inside the Third Reich' and of his attempts to deceive Sereny herself. There is no evidence of Speer's wish to die, for instance, and a great deal of his desire to survive at the expense of others, Sauckel for instance, and of his optimising his personal outcomes after his release from Spandau through his books, his cultivation of the identity of the 'good Nazi', and his relationship with Sereny, which permitted him to be the object of attention and fascination. And the evidence of Speer's pleasure in the fame he achieved and his boasting of his life in his telephone call with Sereny is hardly indicative of any desire to atone. Even so Sereny concludes that Speer 'elected to spend the rest of his life in confrontation with this past, unforgiving of himself for having so nearly loved a monster'.[41]

Sereny's inferences seem to be entirely conjectural, contrary to the objective evidence, and biased by her psychoanalytic approach, her complacent assurance that her impressions and intuition are valid, her sentimentalisation of Speer and his life, her belief in the possibility of therapeutic transformation and her tendency to dramatise. She does not notice that one commonality between Stangl and Speer was their preparedness to talk endlessly regarding their experience, difficulties and anguish in their narratives of their lives and to spend little time on the experience of their victims. Whereas for Stangl Sereny could claim that her interviews resulted in the therapeutic breakthrough for which she had hoped, albeit only by conjectural inferences that seem invalid, that was not possible with Speer, though she insisted on her portrayal of Speer as tormented despite there being no evidence of it apart from her own inferences and despite evidence to the contrary, of his being all too pleased with himself, of his being a cultured, upper-middle-class, educated, urbane sociopath who assumed identities optimal to his interests at the time.

For Speer's lies and manipulative, devious evasion of admission of knowledge of and complicity in the Holocaust there is abundant objective evidence. For attributions of 'inner turmoil' there is only Sereny's psychoanalytic predisposition to believe in the existence and salience of conscience, her tendency to reliance on her own intuition and impressions and to sentimentalisation and dramatisation of individual experience, her desire for a therapeutic breakthrough, and Speer's own cultivating ambiguity regarding what it is to 'know' and denial of knowledge of the Holocaust to permit him to evade obloquy and continue to be accepted as the 'good Nazi'.

One possible explanation is that Sereny's position is that Speer did have a 'battle with truth' and his conscience, one that he lost, the result of which was that his 'inner turmoil' had no influence on his behaviour. That does of course have the merit for Sereny of attributing to Speer experience that cannot be disproved, for even though the evidence indicates Speer's knowledge of and relative indifference to the Holocaust as not being his concern in an exclusive attention to optimising his own career, Sereny's attribution of private experience from Speer's presentation of self cannot then be refuted by direct objective evidence.

Goda's verdict seems far less impressionistic and more reflective of the evidence on Speer than that of Sereny. He claims that 'Speer was a liar. He lied at Nuremberg, he lied repeatedly to his children, and he lied in his post-Spandau writings about his role in the Nazi state and his consciousness of its anti-Jewish policies.' Goda also claims that Speer attempted to effect an early release from prison by means of 'bribery, arm twisting, and influence peddling' and by trying to convince officials that his 'guilt was very limited'. Goda refers to Speer's reconstruction of Berlin for Hitler and to Speer's use of slave labour to that end, and claims that 'Speer proposed the eviction of Berlin Jews into camps.' He notes Speer's claim not to have known of the effect of Hitler's anti-Jewish policies despite having taken advantage of them to purchase an affluent property for a low price from a Jewish woman, Speer's claim that he had been '"sheltered from (the) harsh reality" of Hitler's antisemitism', and Speer's postured anguish in his 'Spandau Diaries' in passages Goda claims were invented rather than genuine and composed at the time.[42] In addition to Goda's evidence there is of course the evidence of Speer's having witnessed the conditions for slave labourers in armaments production and his having been present at the Posen meeting and having heard Himmler's speech regarding the extermination of the Jews, despite decades of Speer's protestations to the contrary, that he did not know of the Holocaust.

Sereny's books do seem to exemplify the resistance of central attitudes to disconfirming information, which is selectively disattended to or rationalised to maintain the credibility of central attitudes (referred to above as 'confirmation bias'), in this case Sereny's combination of psychoanalytic assumptions, romanticisation of her subject, sentimentalisation and dramatisation and conceit regarding her own intuition and impressions of Stangl and Speer. The explanation may be that Sereny's work optimised her outcomes, in the case of Stangl and Speer her reputation as an intellectual, an astute observer of personality as a consequence of her intuition and use of psychoanalytic concepts, and as adept at achieving therapeutic outcomes. Her arrogance and pursuit of her own interests and reputation do then seem not dissimilar to Speer, for whom interaction with Sereny was optimal to his desire to discuss himself and his own life at great length and to his cultivation of an identity as the 'good Nazi' and the celebrity that accompanied it. Sereny and Speer do then seem to have had a commonality of interest in cultivating and perpetuating the myth of Speer's anguish and 'collaborated' over it.

Notes

[1] See Sereny, Gitta, *Into That Darkness: From Mercy Killing to Mass Murder*, Random House, 2013, p. 10.

[2] See ibid, p. 12. See also p. 10 for Sereny's arrogant reference to her realisation that the task of identifying the causes of Nazi perpetrator behaviour by appreciating perpetrators' backgrounds and personal experience would require 'someone with an exceptional capacity for detachment and objectivity' and that 'only someone equipped with enough professional experience and discipline to avoid the manipulation that would certainly be tried, could risk it'.

[3] See ibid, pp. 53, 54, 80, 81, 102–14, 160, 210, 230 and 234.

[4] See ibid, pp. 133, 163 and 164.

[5] See ibid, p. 201.

[6] See ibid, p. 134, and Hughes, *The Holocaust and the Revival of Psychological History*, op. cit., p. 146.

[7] See Sereny, *Into That Darkness*, op. cit., p. 201, and Hughes, *The Holocaust and the Revival of Psychological History*, op. cit., p. 147. But see Arad, Yitzhak, *Belzec, Sobibor, Treblinka: The Operation Reinhard Death Camps*, Indiana University Press, 1987, p. 80 for reference to Stangl's having directed a subordinate to shoot a woman who had come to enquire as to her husband, who was no longer alive, and to Stangl's contempt for the task's delegation to someone else, indicating Stangl's view that exterminatory callousness and ruthlessness were positive attributes he associated with discipline and courage.

[8] See Kekes, *The Roots of Evil*, Cornell University Press, 2014.

[9] See Sereny, *Into That Darkness*, op. cit., pp. 36, 45 and 131. See Bartrop, Paul R., and Grimm, Eve E., *Perpetrating the Holocaust: Leaders, Enablers, and Collaborators*, ABC-CLIO, 2019, pp. 262 and 263 for reference to Stangl's being regarded as the 'best camp commander' in Poland. And see Klee, Ernst, Dressen, Willi, and Riess, Volker, *"The Good Old Days": The Holocaust as Seen by Its Perpetrators and Bystanders*, Free Press, 1991, p. 232 for Bauer's recollection of the conversation at Sobibor.

[10] See Sereny, *Into That Darkness*, op. cit., p. 22.

[11] See ibid, p. 134.

[12] Ibid, p. 39. See also p. 24 for another reference to the sanctimonious moral rectitude of a member of the younger generation, one who had no experience whatever of the Third Reich.

[13] See Sereny, *Into That Darkness*, op. cit., p. 364, and Hughes, *The Holocaust and the*

Revival of Psychological History, op. cit., p. 150.

[14] See Van Voren, Robert, *The Undigested Truth: The Holocaust in Lithuania*, Rodopi, 2011.

[15] See Eaglestone, Robert, *The Broken Voice: Reading Post-Holocaust Literature*, Oxford University Press, 2017, p. 44.

[16] See Sereny, *Into That Darkness*, op.cit., pp. 22 and 23.

[17] See Eaglestone, *The Broken Voice*, op. cit., p. 44.

[18] See Sereny, *Into That Darkness*, op. cit., p. 22.

[19] See Gitta Sereny's Presentation to the Inner Circle Seminar, 'Into That Darkness 30 Years On: The Psychology of Extermination', 10 October 2004, Regent's College, London.

[20] See Hughes, Judith M., *The Holocaust and the revival of Psychological History*, Cambridge University Press, 2015, p. 151.

[21] See ibid, p. 151.

[22] See Sereny, *Into That Darkness*, op. cit., p. 12.

[23] See ibid, p. 164.

[24] See Goda, Norman J. W., *Tales from Spandau: Nazi Criminals and the Cold War*, Cambridge University Press, 2007, pp. 19 and 177.

[25] See ibid.

[26] See Giubilini, Alberto, 'Conscience', *The Stanford Encyclopedia of Philosophy* (Spring 2021 Edition), Edward N. Zalta (ed.), https://plato.stanford.edu/archives/spr2021/entries/conscience/.

In an exhaustive review of various understandings of 'conscience', there is reference to its being 'moral knowledge' 'shared with oneself' and being related to introspection, and to its having a variety of possible sources, including ones external to the individual, for instance tradition, culture and upbringing. These external causes are not inconsistent with a definition of conscience as representing a 'general sense of moral obligation' to avoid 'a sanction imposed by the self on the self' and as being related to 'moral identity'. There seem to be two implications of these observations. The first is that to the extent that conscience represents socialisation it would be impossible to discern when an individual is conforming to the normative order of society to avoid sanctions for failure to comply with societal norms and when that individual is following his or her conscience – the evidence tends to indicate that norms without sanctions for their violation are not observed, and that means that conscience has little autonomous influence on behaviour. The implication for Nazi war criminals appears to be that they were in committing their atrocities following their 'conscience' or, as the case made here would indicate, optimising their outcomes. The other implication is that even if following 'conscience' is the understanding of something individual in origin rather than societal, the individual would be doing so to avoid the adverse experience of guilt for having transgressed against his or her conscience, that is, optimising psychological outcomes. Sereny's use of the term 'conscience' is in this latter sense, of an individual imperative and restraint. Even so, her definition of 'conscience' is that of a western liberal democrat with primary respect for human rights and is then a reflection of a culture that was entirely antithetical to that of the German interwar right wing and of the Nazi Party and the SS. It is common to find Nazi war criminals sanctimoniously referring to having done their 'duty', a concept related to conscience, when doing their 'duty' was optimal to their personal outcomes at the time, and of course reference to 'duty' after the war was an expedient attribution then as it implicitly exonerated them from responsibility and attributed it to the experiential context of the time.

[27] See Sereny, Gitta, *Albert Speer: His Battle with Truth*, Pan Macmillan, 1996, p. 10.

[28] See ibid, p. 13.

[29] See Overy, Richard, 'Didn't he do well? A review of Gitta Sereny's "Albert Speer: His Battle with Truth"', in *The London Review of Books, Vol.17., No.18*, 21 September 1998.

[30] See Evans, Richard J., *Rereading German History: From Unification to Reunification, 1800–1996*, Routledge, 2015, pp. 210–13. It is worth noting that the book was first published in 1997, before the letter Speer wrote in 1971 admitting having heard Himmler's speech in Posen in October 1943 was made public.

[31] See Hughes, Judith M., *The Holocaust and the Revival of Psychological History*, Cambridge University Press, 2015, p. 153.

[32] See Sereny, Gitta, *Albert Speer: His Battle With Truth*, Pan Macmillan, 1996, pp. 7, 8 and 719.

[33] See Speer, Albert, *Inside the Third Reich*, Hachette UK, 2015. First published in 1969.

[34] See Kitchen, Martin, *Speer: Hitler's Architect*, Yale University Press, 2015, pp. 350 and 359.

[35] See Goda, *Tales from Spandau*, op. cit., pp. 177 and 178.

[36] See Fischel, Jack R., *Historical Dictionary of the Holocaust*, Roman & Littlefield, 2020, p. 299. In fact Speer's awareness of the nature of the slave labour system was impossible to refute given evidence of his having visited the Dora rocket manufacture site and having witnessed the terrible conditions for slave labourers there in December 1943.

[37] See Sereny, *Albert Speer: His Battle with Truth*, Pan Macmillan, 1996, p. 393.

[38] See ibid, p. 719.

[39] See Sereny, Gitta, *Albert Speer: His Battle with Truth*, Knopf, 1995, pp. 340 and 401. And see Costello, Melanie Starr, *Imagination, Illness and Injury: Jungian Psychology and the Somatic Dimensions of Perception*, Routledge, 2013, p. 35 for the claim that Speer lived in a 'twilight state of knowing', an indication of the influence of a psychodynamic perspective on inferences regarding Speer.

[40] See Sereny, *Albert Speer: His Battle with Truth*, Pan Macmillan, 1996, pp. 704 and 719. See also p. 13 for reference to the view of Speer of a French pastor, Casalis, who found Speer the 'most tortured man I had ever met' and 'the most repentant'. How Casalis could have formed such a view of Speer given the latter's refusal to acknowledge his complicity and guilt and atone is difficult to understand. As a minister of course Casalis would have been all too susceptible to Speer's presentation of self because of his creed and its doctrine of forgiveness. It is worth noting that Sereny refers to Casalis as her own 'counsellor', another indication of her influences. There is no attempt by Sereny to consult a behavioural or personality psychologist or a psychiatrist, for instance, to assess Speer's veracity in his representation of his experience.

[41] See Sereny, Gitta, *Albert Speer: His Battle with Truth*, Pan Macmillan, 1996, p. 719,

and see the Knopf edition, 1995, p. 711 for Speer's bragging of his life on the telephone to Sereny, just six pages after her reference to his 'morality and repentance'.
[42] See Goda, *Tales from Spandau*, op. cit., pp. 177, 178 and 179.

Chapter Five
Conclusion

The great majority of Nazi perpetrators (broadly defined) do appear to have evaded prosecution and punishment in West Germany, especially those in the professions or of some social status. This may be attributed to a number of factors. There was the West German public's concentration upon recovery from the post-war devastation of the country consequent upon Allied bombing and their sympathy for the wartime situation and experience of perpetrators and belief that Germans were also victims in the war. The emerging Cold War enhanced the sense of insecurity of the West German state and western endorsement of West German leniency for those Nazi war criminals who were actually apprehended and punished by US military courts. There was also West German public and professional concern that post-war investigation of Germans complicit in the crimes of the Nazi regime could implicate them, given the totalitarian nature of the Nazi state and its involvement of the great majority of its citizens in its central enterprise. In other words, post-war priorities and optimisation of outcomes by ordinary West Germans and the Cold War context dictated the nature of post-war justice, and those who would have been expected to impose post-war justice, the West German judiciary, were in many cases former Nazis concerned not to implicate themselves and in sympathy with the experiential context that had faced fellow Nazis. A change came with a West German generation that had no experience of the war as adults and so no possible complicity in it and no motive for avoidance of the issue of German complicity in war crimes and crimes against humanity, and this younger generation of post-war Germans seems to have attempted to establish its own liberal humanitarian credentials by demanding perseverance with a post-war accounting of those complicit in the criminality of the Third Reich regardless of defendants' experiential context of which they knew nothing and regardless too of the presence or absence of criminal intent or brutal behaviour beyond the requirements of role.

Most of the views taken of the nature of post-war justice referred to above indicate the influence of a modern western liberal democratic humanitarian ethos on western historical and legal judgments. This ethos has, it has been argued, resulted in an expectation that ordinary Germans in the Third Reich should have behaved in a moral manner that either involved great perceived risk to themselves or that did not conform to the attitudes and behaviour of the majority and so risked ridicule and ostracism from their peer groups. This judges German behaviour in the Third Reich, with its totalitarian repression and belief in the likelihood of draconian punishment for failure to conform, by the moral standards of modern liberal democracies in which not conforming is not punished by the state unless it involves criminality and in which the great majority of people do conform to the laws and protocols of their own societies to be accepted and approved of by peer groups. The indignation, occupancy of the moral high ground and posture of moral rectitude of modern liberal democratic historians and lawyers in the west do seem to reflect a number of factors. There is their apparent lack of awareness of the reality that the primary drive in human motivation is to optimise outcomes for the self, and especially to avoid adverse consequences. There is their socialisation in liberal democratic societies with respect for human rights. And there is possibly inadvertent conformity to a norm of condemnation of Nazi perpetrator behaviour and complicity to avoid criticism from peers. The same motive, of conformity to avoid disapproval, ridicule and ostracism, and to optimise reputation and status, appears to have motivated Nazi perpetrator behaviour in both the minimal and the more opportunistic conformity of those complicit in Nazi perpetrator behaviour, but this is not to claim any moral equivalence between the two forms of conformity but rather to indicate that the motives seem to have been similar, though of course the contexts and so the consequences of the resulting behaviours are utterly dissimilar. There is no intention here to impugn the integrity or good intentions of historians or lawyers, just to analyse the motives that explain human behaviour both in the Third Reich and in its assessment by historians and lawyers.

Of the approaches to post-war justice the one that does take account of the experiential context of the Third Reich and so of the psychological reality of Germans complicit in Nazi perpetrator behaviour is that of the German Penal Code that required evidence of individual guilt indicated by perpetrator behaviour beyond the requirements of role and orders and that took a circumspect view of oral testimony compared to documentary evidence. That standard is of course similar to that of liberal democratic legal systems with their presumption of innocence and requirement of proof beyond all reasonable doubt. The consequences of abandonment of that standard have been indicated by a German court's conviction of Demjanjuk, which does not seem to represent justice because of the indeterminacy of his role and behaviour at Sobibor and the experiential context of Soviet POWs, and his trial in Jerusalem is indicative of the sort of justice that emerges when the court and the legal system are used for didactic or therapeutic purposes for victims, with eyewitness testimony mistaken in identifying Demjanjuk as Ivan the Terrible at Treblinka, a camp he was never proved to have been at by documentary evidence.

This view is contrary to that of Fulbrook and her criticism of the West German record on Nazi war criminals. And it does argue that the defences of those tried as Nazi perpetrators, of putative duress and reference to the experiential context of the Third Reich in the form of the effect of ideological indoctrination regarding the need for the extermination of Jews in the east given Nazi association of them with Bolshevism and partisans, and the culture of compliance with orders in the SS and under the Führerprinzip, which meant Hitler's decisions had the force of law in the Third Reich, should not be dismissed just because they served the objective of exoneration of Nazi perpetrator behaviour, for it is possible that both exerted some influence on the behaviour of Nazi perpetrators. 'Putative duress' was a legitimate defence despite the counterargument that there appears to have been no instance of severe reprisals for someone not meeting the requirements of their role in the SS, for example, for 'putative duress' referred to belief that severe repercussions would ensue for failure to meet role requirements, and the lack of evidence of such repercussions could in fact be evidence of the deterrent effect of belief in them. The most plausible decisive causal influences do seem to be unreflective conformity to the majority behaviour, which in the culture of the SS was compliance with orders, avoidance of perceived formal sanctions, for instance dismissal and being sent to combat on the eastern front, and avoidance of being the one to have defied conformity and having to endure ridicule, ostracism and disapproval from the peer group for having failed to participate in unpleasant tasks.

The argument here is not that Nazi perpetrator behaviour should not have been punished, for it is contrary to public policy that such behaviour should not be punished, not least to express popular revulsion and to reaffirm desired standards of behaviour. There is also a comprehensible attempt to deter perpetrator behaviour in the future, a hope for some deterrent value that has not been met because the influence of the immediate situation is far more compelling for individuals than that of some abstract moral principle or apprehension that they might be arraigned before a court and punished should their side lose the war. Recent experience of genocide in the Balkans, Cambodia and Rwanda seems indicative of the lack of deterrent value of human rights courts.

What does seem inappropriate is the implicit presumption that those delivering the judgements in court or elsewhere would not have behaved in the same manner as some Nazi perpetrators had they been in their roles. For a small minority of Nazi perpetrators who exceeded the requirements of their roles in their sadism, revulsion is of course appropriate, and the criticism is that there does not seem, in western liberal humanitarian judgements of those complicit in Nazi perpetrator behaviour, to be any appreciation of the psychology of human motivation and experience or of the commonalities of process between Nazi perpetrators and their conformity and ordinary conformity in all cultures and societies at all times.

The Einsatzgruppen trial indicates the nature of the case for the defence, including reference to the experiential context of the Third Reich and to the perceived need to follow orders of superior officers for fear of punishment, and to the contradiction between the argument of reluctant compliance with orders despite reservations and that which refers to an experiential context that elicited conviction that the perpetrator behaviour was legitimate for Germans in the east. The reference to ideological conviction and so to the experiential context of the Third Reich and the SS in the east was rejected by the court because Jews were exterminated because they were Jews, not just after identification as Bolsheviks, but the experiential context included association of Jews with Bolshevism regardless of evidence. The 'superior orders' defence was also dismissed by the court, indicating the judgement of a US military tribunal rather than that of a German criminal court, but the sentences imposed were in many cases commuted because of West German resentment, as has been seen. The nature of the 'justice' initially meted out at the Einsatzgruppen trial does seem, because of the visceral immediacy of the murders of Jews, to have been difficult to avoid, and as has been seen there has been liberal outrage at the commutation of the sentences for reasons associated with the Cold War, but Einsatzgruppen, Einsatzkommando and Sonderkommando commanders were acting under orders received from Heydrich and Himmler with Hitler's authority and could under the German Penal Code have been acquitted because there was no evidence of volition or barbarism beyond that required by their roles and so no criminal intent.

The interests of justice and deterrence did of course necessitate the imposition of some punishment for murders of Jews in so visceral a manner and in such numbers, even though experience since then has established that there is no apparent deterrent effect because of the immediacy of other dictates. The case does seem to be an indication of the competing requirements of a justice system, between the need for exemplary punishment to reflect moral outrage at the criminal behaviour concerned, for some exhibition of society's repugnance for the criminality concerned (whether or not the society concerned actually feels such outrage and repugnance) and for a deterrent to similar criminal behaviour in the future, and the requirement of any justice system to administer justice to the accused by following a legitimate standard of proof and treatment of evidence.

The case of Höss is indicative of the individual nature of 'guilt' in his acceptance of the rectitude of the task assigned to him without reflection on its nature, an indication of the power of the situation in the form of authority figures for the attitudes and behaviour of individuals susceptible to their influence. In the Soviet sphere, in Warsaw, Höss had no realistic prospect of evading execution because Nazi perpetrators tried in Soviet eastern Europe received harsher sentences because of the ideological antipathy of communism for Nazism and the Soviet experience of the war, but Höss made no attempt to disguise his role or behaviour at Nuremberg or in Warsaw, representing himself as having been a genuine believer in Nazism, an individual who had been deceived and mistaken in trusting the authority figure of Himmler.

Unlike most other Nazi perpetrators he accepted his sentence and execution despite his defence of having followed orders without reflection on them. Here too the German Penal Code could have resulted in acquittal, for Höss was a case of compliance with the directives of an authority figure with no autonomous volition or murderous intent beyond that dictated to him. As with the Einsatzgruppen trial, the objective evidence on Höss also dictated exemplary punishment as a matter of public policy for the Allied powers. And so did that of Eichmann, who argued that he was a functionary who had implemented orders from superiors rather than ever taking initiative on his own. Both men seem to have been susceptible to the influence of authority figures, but unlike Höss, Eichmann did not accept his sentence and appealed for clemency in Israel and was denied it by the Israeli court, as would be expected after his show trial in Jerusalem.

One difference between Höss and Eichmann seems to be that Höss was a genuine believer in what he was told by Himmler as an authority figure, whereas Eichmann seems to have been careerist and opportunistic in enhancing his SS career and embracing Nazi ideology or appearing to as a means of securing the approbation of bosses and peers in the SS and maintaining or enhancing his status and identity as an SS officer of some rank. It is possible to argue that this difference makes Höss less culpable and Eichmann more so, because Eichmann was not deluded in the way Höss was, so there cannot be legitimate reference to influence from Eichmann's ideological or personal experiential context, and because Eichmann seems to have optimised his outcomes in the form of approbation and career and avoidance of disapprobation and demotion in the SS. Such considerations were not reflected in the judgments imposed by the Warsaw and Israeli courts on Höss and Eichmann, for they reflected the agendas of the powers holding the trials.

Whereas the cases of the Einsatzgruppen, Einsatzkommando and Sonderkommando commanders, Speer, Stangl and Eichmann seem to reflect various degrees of aspiration to the privileges of rank and an elite identity in the SS (or, in the case of Speer, in the Nazi elite), the case of Höss may be one of a different form of identification, one less optimising in terms of privilege and an elite identity and more related to an authority figure in the form of Himmler, in whom Höss seems to have believed. Having said that, whether or not Höss would have been as credulous had Himmler not been an authority figure in the Nazi movement is counterfactual and so unknown. What is known is that Höss was influenced by authority figures to commit criminal perpetrator behaviour before the war when the authority figure, Bormann, had no great status and when the behaviour could not be conducted with impunity, when he participated in the murder of a member of another right-wing party on the authority of Bormann and was jailed for his role. Höss does then seem different in motivation to the other cases mentioned above.

The cases of Stangl and Speer are different from each other. Stangl was a notoriously efficient extermination camp commandant who claimed to be under threat against his life from his immediate superior to explain his perpetrator behaviour, whereas Speer was a part of Hitler's elite and the one major Nazi arraigned at Nuremberg who devised a manipulative strategy that permitted him to evade the gallows, accepting collective responsibility for the Holocaust whilst disclaiming individual knowledge and so responsibility in an argument that he should and could have known but did not know, which was later proved to be untrue. These cases also indicate that individuals in the Third Reich as elsewhere reacted to their context to optimise their material, social and psychological outcomes, regardless of the cost to their immediate or more remote victims. The verdicts in their cases were what would be expected given the magnitude of their responsibility and it is worth noting that they claimed not to be responsible, indicating desire to exculpate themselves, in Stangl's case claiming fear that he would have been executed had he not done what he did, and in Speer's case lack of knowledge.

For all the Nazi perpetrators referred to above it could be argued that they could have been less concerned to maximise their 'efficiency' as perpetrators by employing the sort means of evasion some of Browning's 'Ordinary Men' used to evade murdering Jewish elderly people, women and children without risking sanctions against them, but the aspirational and opportunistic nature of many Nazi perpetrators appears to have resulted in their being dominated by desire for enhanced status in the SS (or the Nazi elite for Speer) and for all who engaged in perpetrator behaviour concern that they could be compared to other more ruthless peers and regarded as failures does seem to have been more compelling than moral considerations or ones of regard for the welfare of the Jews.

Sereny's work on Stangl and Speer claims an experience of anguish in both men over their perpetrator behaviour that is not credible given the evidence on them, and does seem to be a consequence of Sereny's psychodynamic, therapeutic and impressionistic approach, but the implication appears to be that she believes that Stangl deserved the sentence to life imprisonment he received despite what she claims to be his final acknowledgment of 'guilt', because of the numbers of Jews over whose extermination he presided at Sobibor and Treblinka and Stangl's role in enhancing the 'efficiency' of the extermination process at Treblinka. There seems to be no indication that Stangl's claimed acknowledgement of 'guilt', such that it was, should lessen the severity of his sentence, for Sereny's post-war moralising liberal democratic perspective and its expectations do seem to be decisive for her judgement of the justice meted out to Stangl and the cause of her failure to appreciate the implications for human behaviour of the primacy of optimisation of personal outcomes regardless of context and consequence for others.

For Speer the case Sereny makes seems to contradict itself, for she claims that Speer was manipulative and devious but also anguished (she appears not to see these attributes as mutually exclusive). Even so, in Speer's case the inference seems to be that his lenient sentence resulted from his manipulation of the court and should have been more severe given his culpability in the form of knowledge of the Holocaust and knowing use of slave labour in his armaments production facilities. It is worth noting that Sereny's objective was not to investigate the lives and personalities of Stangl and Speer to assess their responsibility for their perpetrator behaviour and the extent of their culpability but to obtain from them admissions of guilt and responsibility she attributed to them regardless of their perceived circumstances and motives because of her liberal democratic humanitarian perspective and assumption of individual responsibility for behaviour, a western liberal concept that meant that the post-war justice Stangl received may in fact have been regarded by her as insufficient punishment because of his years on the run between 1945 and his arrest in 1967 and that meant that Sereny could have regarded the sentence received by Speer as inadequate because he had lessened his sentence by his devious dissembling in his own defence. One possible inference from Sereny's claims regarding Stangl's and Speer's 'inner turmoil' is that she regards them as having received a form of 'justice' for their perpetrator behaviour in their post-war unhappiness and guilt, an inference derived from her psychoanalytic perspective and challenged by the evidence presented here.

The views expressed by Fulbrook, Weinschenk, Douglas, Sereny and others referred to above have been seen to reflect varying combinations of disciplinary perspective, political or ideological principle, agenda, and conformity to a current narrative. Fulbrook is an academic historian who writes from a liberal humanitarian perspective, as does Douglas, who claims that the legal system should be used for liberal humanitarian and even therapeutic purposes and that such use would not diminish the accomplishment of the primary role of any justice system, to deliver justice for the accused, whereas Weinschenk appears to have an exclusively legal perspective, and Sereny's agenda is apparent in her liberal humanitarian judgment and her therapeutic and psychodynamic approach to Stangl and Speer. Sereny does contribute to the debate over 'justice' for Nazi war criminals and its legitimacy in investigating the backgrounds and contexts of Stangl's and Speer's perpetrator behaviour and their experience of their respective situations and their possibilities, if with mistaken inferences and conclusions. Even so Sereny judges Stangl and Speer from a moralising liberal humanitarian perspective, explicitly rejected Stangl's compliance-with-orders defence at her first meeting with him, and so endorsed the rejection of the characteristic Nazi war criminal defence of reference to the experiential context of Nazi perpetrators in the war by the US military courts after the war.

The post-war justice meted out to Nazi war criminals or perpetrators and those complicit in Nazi war crimes and crimes against humanity was inadequate if the terms 'perpetrator' and 'complicit' are defined liberally, as Fulbrook does, and if the concept of 'guilt' is defined in such a way as to preclude reference to the experiential context of the Third Reich and the SS with its culture of universal compliance, to a defence that the perpetrator behaviour concerned reflected orders from above, to a defence that there was no autonomous criminal intent, or to the German Penal Code. And the *tu quoque* defence that the victors had also engaged in wartime criminality in their indiscriminate bombing campaigns over German cities and the behaviour of the Red Army was also rejected. In other words post-war justice reflected the power and objectives of the victors and victors' justice. But all conceptualisations of legality reflect the objectives and agendas of those with power and are manipulated to their ends.

Overall Conclusion

The common theme of the books in this trilogy is the primacy of pursuit of personal interest in human behaviour and its being the decisive influence on ordinary Germans' conformity and complicity in the Third Reich, regardless of gender, with Goldhagen's claim that the decisive influence on the Holocaust was a German culture before the Nazis characterised by eliminationist antisemitism and claims of influence from Nazi indoctrination contradicted by the evidence.

The case of Eichmann is indicative of the effect of aspiration and desire for privilege, enhanced status and elite identity on human behaviour in the more maximising part of any population, and of the lack of any psychological abnormality in Eichmann and other Nazi aspirants and careerists. It also indicates the relevance of the evidence of social psychological experiments for inferences regarding normality of behaviour, and the reality that ordinary people may become perpetrators just because a small cost to them, in Eichmann's case possible loss of career prospects or the risk of disapprobation from superiors and peers, matters far more than a colossal cost to others, in Eichmann's case the Jews of the occupied territories. Eichmann's very normality means that it is not inappropriate to point to supportive evidence on his motivation from that on other Nazi perpetrators in its indication of the primacy of optimisation of personal outcomes in human behaviour.

The book on the issue of post-war justice indicates the influence of a liberal humanitarian perspective on judgments regarding the nature and adequacy of post-war justice, and argues that establishing liberal credentials by making adverse judgements regarding Nazi perpetrators whose experiential context was very different to their own in modern western liberal democracies could be seen to be another instance of influence of optimisation of outcomes, this time by liberal humanitarians who are applauded by their peers for their condemnation of the failure to exact justice against Nazi perpetrators.

The argument here is not that the war crimes trials should not have taken place, for the extermination of the Jews by the SS necessitated some indication of revulsion. The argument is that it is not legitimate to claim that the trials did not represent victors' justice, because of the war crimes committed by all the victorious powers, albeit not gratuitous genocide and so not to be compared to the Holocaust and its deliberate attempt to exterminate a people.

There is also the argument that judgement from a position of liberal humanitarian moral rectitude without any personal experience of the circumstances faced by ordinary Germans in the Third Reich assumes that those making the judgement would have behaved differently, despite the evidence of social psychological experiments replicated many times in different cultures and time periods indicating that they would have behaved much as Nazi perpetrators did, that is, that they too would have acted in compliance with the requirements of role.

The insistence of a generation of young Germans with no experience of, or possible responsibility for, the Holocaust on the prosecution of very elderly concentration camp personnel convicted on the basis of merely being present in a camp when Jews were being exterminated does seem another instance of human optimisation of social outcomes, in this case by advertising their liberal humanitarian credentials to liberal audiences. This conformity to perceived norms to optimise social outcomes seems not dissimilar in motive to the conformity these young liberal Germans find contemptible in the defendants they are responsible for imprisoning even without evidence of their having been involved in the extermination process.

What differentiates the cases of young Germans now demanding 'justice' against elderly SS personnel and the cases of those alleged to have been complicit in the Holocaust is the experiential context of liberal democratic Germany now and the very different experiential context of the Nazi regime with its totalitarian repression, and the contrast in outcomes for those disadvantaged by the conformity concerned. For the recent individual court cases against SS personnel have reflected the liberal humanitarianism of modern Germany, but have resulted in relatively short prison sentences, whereas the behaviour of those complicit in the Holocaust in the Third Reich occurred under Nazi totalitarianism in wartime, but resulted in the persecution and extermination of millions of innocent Jews. Context, circumstances and outcomes are then key differentiators. Motive and conformity are however common to both instances.

Given that the human drive to optimise personal outcomes in all circumstances is virtually universal and is the decisive influence on human behaviour, with the only exceptions being a tiny minority of highly principled individuals, the evidence presented here indicates that to preclude genocide or systematic violence perpetrated against any group the concentration should not be on show trials of individuals whose guilt is uncertain but on enhancing the pluralism of liberal democratic politics with their decentralisation of power, not least because democracies have shown themselves vulnerable to populist demagogues whose rhetoric appeals to ethnocentric and xenophobic tendencies rather than to rational consideration of policies and their consequences.

Bibliography

Ordinary Germans

Asch, S. E., 'Opinions and Social Pressure', *Scientific American, 193*, 1955.

Baez, S., Flichtentrei, D., Prats, M. et al, 'Men, Women … who cares? A population-based study on sex differences and gender roles in empathy and moral cognition', PLoS One. 2017: 12/61: e0179336.

Browning, Christopher, *Ordinary Men, Reserve Police Battalion 101 and the Final Solution in Poland*, Penguin, London, 2001.

Browning, Christopher R., 'Ordinary Germans or Ordinary Men? A Reply to the Critics', in Berenbaum, Michael and Peck, Abraham J. (eds.), *The Holocaust and History: The Known, the Unknown, the Disputed, and the Reexamined*, United States Holocaust Memorial Museum, Indiana University Press, 1998.

Chodakiewicz, Marek Jan, *Between Nazis and Soviets: Occupation Politics in Poland, 1939-1947*, Lexington Books, 2004.

Cohen, Philip J., *Serbia's Secret War: Propaganda and the Deceit of History*, Texas A & M University Press, 1996.

Crownshaw, R., *The Afterlife of Holocaust Memory in Contemporary Literature and Culture, Springer*, 2016.

Dallas, Gregor, *1945: The War That Never Ended*, Yale University Press, 2005.

Eagly, Alice H., and Chrvala, Carole, 'Sex Differences in Conformity: Status and Gender Role Interpretations', in *Psychology of Women Quarterly*, September 1, 1986.

Eisenberg, Nancy, and Strayer, Janet (eds.), *Empathy and Its Development*, CUP Archive, 1990.

Eley, Geoff (ed.), *The 'Goldhagen Effect': History, Memory, Nazism – facing the German Past*, University of Michigan Press, 2000.

Evans, Richard J., 'Coercion and Consent in Nazi Germany', Raleigh Lecture on History, 24 May 2006, Proceedings of the British Academy 151, 2007.

Fitzpatrick, Sheila, *The Practice of Denunciation in Stalinist Russia*, The National Council for Soviet and East European Research.

Fulbrook, Mary, *Dissonant Lives: Generations and Violence through the German Dictatorships*, OUP, 2011.

Gellately, Robert, *Backing Hitler: Consent and Coercion in Nazi Germany*, Oxford University Press, 2002.

—, *Hitler's True Believers: How Ordinary Germans Became Nazis*, Oxford University Press, 2020.

Goldhagen, Daniel Jonah, *Hitler's Willing Executioners: Ordinary Germans and the Holocaust*, Knopf Doubleday Publishing Group, 2007.

Gordon, Sarah Ann, *Hitler, Germans and the "Jewish Question"*, Princeton University Press, 1984.

Haslam, S. A., and Reicher, S. D., 'The Psychology of Tyranny', *Scientific American Mind, 16 (7)*.

Haslam, S. Alexander, Reicher, Stephen D., and Van Bavel, Jay J., 'Rethinking the nature of cruelty: The role of identity leadership in the Stanford Prison Experiment', *American Psychologist 2019, Vol. 74, No. 7*.

Herbert, Ulrich, 'Good Times, Bad Times: Memories of the Third Reich', in Bessel, Richard (ed.), *Life in the Third Reich*, Oxford University Press, 2001.

Howarth, Caroline, and Andreouli, Eleni (eds.), *The Social Psychology of Everyday Politics*, Taylor and Francis, 2016.

Kay, Alex J., Rutherford, Jeff, and Stahel, David (eds.), *Nazi Policy on the Eastern Front, 1941: Total War, Genocide and Radicalization*, University of Rochester Press, 2012.

Kaufman, Whitley, Review of Schauer, Frederick, *The Force of Law*, Harvard University Press, 2015, in *Law and Politics Book Vol. 26 No. 5* (September 2016).

Kershaw, Ian, *Hitler, the Germans and the Final Solution*, Yale University Press, 2008.

Kompisch, Kathrin, *Perpetrators: Women under National Socialism*, Bohlau Verlag Cologne Weimar, 2008.

Kruglanski, Arie W., and Higgins, E, Tory (eds.), *Social Psychology: Handbook of Basic Principles*, Guilford Publications, 2013.

Lower, Wendy, *Hitler's Furies, German Women in the Nazi Killing Fields*, Vintage, 2014.

McDonough, Frank, *The Gestapo: The Myth and Reality of Hitler's Secret Police*, Hachette, 2015.

Metin, Irem, and Metin Camgöz, Selin, 'The Advances in the History of Cognitive Dissonance Theory', in the *International Journal of Humanities and Social Science Vol. 1 No. 6*, June 2011.

Milgram, Stanley, *Obedience to Authority: An Experimental View*, Harper & Row, New York, 1974.

Millon, Theodore, Lerner, Melvin J., Weiner, Irving B., *Handbook of Psychology, Volume 5, Personality and Social Psychology*, John Wiley & Sons, 2003.

Ousby, Ian, *Occupation: The Ordeal of France, 1940–1944*, Random House, 1999.

Rector, John M., *The Objectification Spectrum: Understanding and Transcending Our Diminishment and Dehumanization Of Others*, Oxford University Press, 2014.

Sander, David, and Scherer, Klaus, *Oxford Companion to Emotion and the Affective Sciences*, Oxford University Press, 2014.

Schauer, Frederick, *The Force of Law*, Harvard University Press, 2015.

Soutschek, A., Burke, C. J., Raja Beharelle, A. et al, 'The dopaminergic reward system underpins gender differences in social preferences', in *Nature Human Behaviour, Vol 1*, November 2017.

Staub, Ervin, 'The Psychology of Bystanders, Perpetrators and Heroic Helpers', in *The Psychology of Good and Evil: why children, adults and groups help and harm others*, Cambridge, 2003.

Stephenson, Jill, *Women in Nazi Germany*, Pearson Education, 2011.

The Population of Yugoslavia, Demographic Research Center, Institute of Social Sciences, Belgrade, 1974.

Tyler, Tom R., *Why People Obey the Law*, Princeton University Press, 1990 and 2006.

Waller, James, *Becoming Evil, How Ordinary People Commit Genocide and Mass Killing*, Oxford University Press, USA, 2007.

Wieviorka, Olivier, *The French Resistance*, Harvard University Press, 2016.

Perspectives on Eichmann: Explaining Perpetrator Behaviour

Adams, Guy, and Balfour, Danny, *Unmasking Administrative Evil*, M. E. Sharpe, 2015.

Aharoni, Zvi, and Dietl, Wilhelm, *Operation Eichmann: The Truth about the Pursuit, Capture and Trial*, Wiley, 1997.

Alcock, James, and Sadava, Stan, *An Introduction to Social Psychology: Global Perspectives*, Sage, 2014.

Arendt, Hannah, *Eichmann in Jerusalem, A Report on the Banality of Evil*, Penguin, 2006.

Aschheim, Steven E. (ed.), *Hannah Arendt in Jerusalem*, University of California Press, 2001.

See Axelrod, Alan, and Kingston, Jack A., *Encyclopedia of World War Two*, Volume I, H. W. Fowler, 2007.

Bartov, Omer, *The Eastern Front, 1941–45, German Troops and the Barbarisation of Warfare*, Springer, 1986.

Bazyler, Michael E., and Tuerkheimer, Frank M., *Forgotten Trials of the Holocaust*, NYU Press, 2015.

Berghahn, Volker Rolf, and Lassig, Simone, *Biography between Structure and Agency: Central European Lives in International Historiography*, Berghahn Books, 2008.

Blass, Thomas, 'The roots of Stanley Milgram's Obedience Experiments and Their Relevance to the Holocaust', *Analyse und Kritik 20* (1998), 2. 46–53, Westdeutscher Verlag, Opladen.

Braham, R. L., ed., *Contemporary Views on the Holocaust*, Springer Science and Business Media, 2012.

Browning, Christopher R., *Nazi Policy, Jewish Workers, German Killers*, CUP, 2000.

—, *Ordinary Men, Reserve Police Battalion 101 and the Final Solution in Poland*, Penguin, London, 2001.

—, *The Origins of the Final Solution: The Evolution of Nazi Jewish Policy, September 1939 – March 1942*, University of Nebraska Press, 2007.

—, 'Ordinary Germans or Ordinary Men? A Reply to the Critics', in Berenbaum, Michael and Peck, Abraham J. (eds.), *The Holocaust and History: The Known, the Unknown, the Disputed, and the Reexamined*, United States Holocaust Memorial Museum, Indiana University Press, 1998.

Brudholm, Thomas, and Lang, Johannes (eds.), *Emotions and Mass Atrocity: Philosophical and Theoretical Explorations*, Cambridge University Press, 2018.

Brunner, José, 'Eichmann's Mind: Psychological, Philosophical and Legal Perspectives', in *Theoretical Inquiries in Law 1.2* (2000).

Cesarani, David, *Eichmann: His Life and Crimes*, Vintage Books, 2005.

Crozier, W. Ray, *Shyness and Embarrassment: Perspectives from Social Psychology*, Cambridge University Press, 1990.

Dimsdale, Joel, E., *Anatomy of Malice: The Enigma of Nazi War Criminals*, Yale University Press, 2016.

Earl, Hilary, *The Nuremberg SS-Einsatzgruppen Trial, 1945–1958: Atrocity, Law and History*, Cambridge University Press, 2009.

Eley, Geoff (ed.), *The 'Goldhagen Effect': History, Memory, Nazism – facing the German Past*, University of Michigan Press, 2000.

Fischel, Jack R., *Historical Dictionary of the Holocaust*, Rowman and Littlefield, 2020.

Fritz, Stephen G., *Ostkrieg: Hitler's War of Extermination in the East*, The University Press of Kentucky, 2011.

Fulbrook, Mary, *Dissonant Lives: Generations and Violence through the German Dictatorships*, OUP, 2011.

Gellhorn, Martha, 'Eichmann and the Private Conscience', The Atlantic Online, February 1962.

Gibson, Stephen, *Arguing, Obeying and Defying: A Rhetorical Perspective on Stanley Milgram's Obedience Experiments*, Cambridge University Press, 2019.

Goldhagen, Daniel Jonah, *Hitler's Willing Executioners: Ordinary Germans and the Holocaust*, Little, Brown, New York, 1996.

Haslam, S. Alexander, Reicher, Stephen D., and Van Bavel, Jay J., 'Rethinking the nature of cruelty: The role of identity leadership in the Stanford Prison Experiment', *American Psychologist*, 2019, Vol. 74, No. 7.

Haslam, S. Alexander, and Reicher, Stephen D., 'Contesting the "Nature" of Conformity: What Milgram and Zimbardo's Studies Really Show', PLoS Biol 10 (11): e1001426 http://doi.org/10.1371/journal.pbio.1001426, November 2012.

Headland, Ronald, *Messages of Murder: A Study of the Reports of the Einsatzgruppen of the Security Police and the Security Service, 1941–1943*, Fairleigh Dickinson University Press, 1992.

Hollander, Matthew M., and Turowetz, Jason, *British Journal of Social Psychology*, Volume 56, Issue 4, 2017.

Jonas, Klaus, *An Introduction to Social Psychology*, John Wiley and Sons, 2012.

Kershaw, Ian, *Hitler, the Germans and the Final Solution*, Yale University Press, 2008.

—, *The Nazi Dictatorship: Problems and Perspectives of Interpretation*, Bloomsbury Publishing, 2015.

Lawrence, Bruce B., and Karim, Aisha (eds.), *On Violence: A Reader*, Duke University Press, 2007.

Lehrer, Stephan, *Wannsee House and the Holocaust*, McFarland, 2015.

Le Texier, Thibault, 'Debunking the Stanford Prison Experiment', *American Psychologist 74 (7)*, 2019.

H. Skipton Leonard, Rachel Lewis, Arthur M. Freedman and Jonathan Passmore (eds.), *The Wiley-Blackwell Handbook of the Psychology of Leadership, Change, and Organizational Development*, John Wiley & Sons, 2013.

Lidegaard, Bo, *Countrymen: The Untold Story of How Denmark's Jews Escaped the Nazis*, Atlantic Books, 2014.

Longerich, Peter, *Goebbels*, Random House, 2015.

—, *Heinrich Himmler: A Life*, Oxford University Press, 2012.

—, *Holocaust: The Nazi Persecution and Murder of the Jews*, Oxford University Press, 2010.

Lunt, Peter, Stanley *Milgram: Understanding Obedience and Its Implications*, Macmillan International Higher Education, 2009.

MacLean, French L., *The Field Men: The SS Officers Who Led the Einsatzkommandos – The Nazi Mobile Killing Units*, Schiffer Military History, 1999.

McKale, Donald M., *Nazis After Hitler: How Perpetrators of the Holocaust Cheated Justice and Truth*, Rowman & Littlefield, 2012.

Milgram, Stanley, 'Behavioral Study of Obedience', *Journal of Abnormal and Social Psychology, 67 (4)*, 1963.

—, 'Some Conditions of Obedience and Disobedience to Authority', *Human Relations 18 (1)*, 1965.

—, *Obedience to Authority: An Experimental View*, Harper & Row, New York, 1974.

—, *Obedience to Authority: An Experimental View*, HarperCollins, New York, 1975.

Miller, Arthur G. (ed.), *The Social Psychology of Good and Evil*, Second Edition, Guilford Publications, 2016.

Minerbi, Sergio, *The Eichmann Trial Diary: A Chronicle of the Holocaust*, Enigma Books, 2011.

Mulisch, Harry, *Criminal Case 40/61, The Trial of Adolf Eichmann: An Eyewitness Account*, University of Pennsylvania Press, 2009.

Nazi Conspiracy and Aggression, Volume VIII, Office of United States Chief of Counsel for Prosecution of Axis Criminality, United States Government Printing Office, Washington, 1946.

Perry, Gina, *Behind the Shock Machine: the untold story of the notorious Milgram experiments*, Scribe Publications, 2013.

Powers, Roger S., and Vogele, William B., *Protest, Power and Change: An Encyclopedia of Nonviolent Action from ACT-UP to Women's Suffrage*, Routledge, 2012.

Rattansi, Ali, *Bauman and Contemporary Sociology: A Critical Analysis*, Oxford University Press.

Reicher, Stephen, and Haslam, S. Alexander, 'Rethinking the Psychology of Tyranny: the BBC Prison Study', in *British Journal of Social Psychology*, 2006, 45.

Rubenstein, Richard L. and Roth, John K., *Approaches to Auschwitz: The Holocaust and Its Legacy*, Westminster Knox Press, 2003.

Russell, Nestar, 'Stanley Milgram's Obedience to Authority "Relationship" Condition: Some Methodological and Theoretical Considerations', in *Social Sciences*, 2014, 3.

Searls, Damion, *The Inkblots*, Simon and Schuster, 2017.

Sevaldsen, Jørgen, Bjorke, Bo, Bjorn, Claus, *Britain and Denmark: Political, Economic and Cultural Relations in the 19th and 20th Centuries*, Museum Tusculanum Press, 2003.

Shaked, Michal, *The Unknown Eichmann Trial: The Story of the Judge, Holocaust and Genocide Studies*, Volume 29, Issue 1, Spring 2015.

Stackelberg, Roderick, and Winkle, Sally A., *The Nazi Germany Sourcebook: An Anthology of Texts*, Routledge, 2013.

Stangneth, Bettina, *Eichmann before Jerusalem: The Unexamined Life of a Mass Murderer*, The Bodley Head, 2014.

Szasz, Thomas Stephen, *Ideology and Insanity: Essays on the Psychiatric Dehumanization of Man*, Syracuse University Press, 1991.

Taylor, Shelley E., Peplau, Letitia Anne, and Sears, David O., *Social Psychology*, Prentice Hall, 2000.

Von Lang, Jochen (ed.), *Eichmann Interrogated: Transcripts from the Archives of the Israeli Police*, The Bodley Head, 1983.

Waller, James, *Becoming Evil, How Ordinary People Commit Genocide and Mass Killing*, Oxford University Press, USA, 2007.

Westermann, Edward B., "'Ordinary Drinkers" and Ordinary "Males"? Alcohol, Masculinity, and Atrocity in the Holocaust', in Kaplan, Thomas Pegelow, Matthäus, Jürgen, and Homburg, Mark W. (eds.), *Beyond Ordinary Men: Christopher R. Browning and Holocaust Historiography*, Ferdinand Schöningh, 2019.

Wojak, Irmtrud, *Eichmanns Memoiren: Ein Kritischer Essay*, Zuerst, 2001, Frankfurt: Fischer TB, 2004.

Zanna, Mark P. (ed.), *Advances in Experimental Social Psychology*, Volume 25, Elsevier, 1992.

Zillmer, Eric A., Harrower, Molly, Ritzler, Barry A., and Archer, Robert P., *The Quest for the Nazi Personality, A Psychological Investigation of Nazi War Criminals*, Lawrence Erlbaum Associates, Publishers, New Jersey, 1995.

Zimbardo, Philip G., The Stanford Prison Experiment: A Simulation Study of the Psychology of Imprisonment, on http://web.stanford.edu.

Post-War Justice For Nazi War Criminals: Context, Culpability and Legitimacy

Arad, Yitzhak, *Belzec, Sobibor, Treblinka: The Operation Reinhard Death Camps*, Indiana University Press, 1987.

Arendt, Hannah, *Eichmann in Jerusalem: A Report on the Banality of Evil*, Penguin, 2006.

Barnes, Thomas Garden, and Feldman, Gerald D. (Eds.), *Breakdown and Rebirth, 1914 to the present: A Documentary History of Modern Europe, Volume IV*, University Press of America, 1972.

Bartrop, Paul R., and Grimm, Eve E., *Perpetrating the Holocaust: Leaders, Enablers, and Collaborators*, ABC-CLIO, 2019.

Bassiouni, M. Cherif, 'The '"Nuremberg Legacy"', in Mettraux, Guénaël (ed.), *Perspectives on the Nuremberg Trial*, Oxford University Press, 2008.

Bazyler, Michael E., and Tuerkheimer, Frank M., *Forgotten Trials of the Holocaust*, NYU Press, 2015.

Browning, Christopher, *Ordinary Men, Reserve Police Battalion 101 and the Final Solution in Poland*, Penguin, London, 2001.

Cesarani, David, *Eichmann: His Life and Crimes*, Vintage Books, 2005.

Costello, Melanie Starr, *Imagination, Illness and Injury: Jungian Psychology and the Somatic Dimensions of Perception*, Routledge, 2013.

Douglas, Lawrence, *The Memory of Judgment: Making Law and History in the Trials of the Holocaust*, Yale University Press, 2001.

—, *The Right Wrong Man: John Demjanjuk and the Last Great Nazi War Crimes Trial*, Princeton University Press, 2018.

Eaglestone, Robert, *The Broken Voice: Reading Post-Holocaust Literature*, Oxford University Press, 2017.

Earl, Hilary, 'A Judge, A Prosecutor, and a Mass Murderer, Courtroom Dynamics in the SS-Einsatzgruppen Trial', in Priemel, Kim C., and Stiller, Alexa, *Reassessing the Nuremberg Military Tribunals: Transitional Justice, Trial Narratives, and Historiography*, Berghahn Books, 2012.

—, *The Nuremberg SS-Einsatzgruppen Trial, 1945–1958: Atrocity, Law and History*, Cambridge University Press, 2009.

Earl, Hilary C., 'Legacies of the Nuremberg SS-Einsatzgruppen Trial after 70 years', 39 Loy. L.A. Int'l. and Comp. L. Review 95 (2017).

Evans, Richard J., *Rereading German History: From Unification to Reunification, 1800–1996*, Routledge, 2015.

Fischel, Jack R., *Historical Dictionary of the Holocaust*, Roman & Littlefield, 2020.

Frei, Norbert, *Adenauer's Germany and the Nazi Past: The Politics of Amnesty and Integration*, Columbia University Press, 2002.

Fulbrook, Mary, *Reckonings: Legacies of Nazi Persecution and the Quest for Justice*, Oxford University Press, 2018.

Gilbert, Martin, *Winston S. Churchill, Never Despair*, 1945–1965, Rosetta Books, 2015.

Gitta Sereny's Presentation to the Inner Circle Seminar, 'Into That Darkness 30 Years On: The Psychology of Extermination', 10 October 2004, Regent's College, London.

Giubilini, Alberto, 'Conscience', *The Stanford Encyclopedia of Philosophy* (Spring 2021 Edition), Edward N. Zalta (ed.), https://plato.stanford.edu/archives/spr2021/entries/conscience/.

Goda, Norman J. W., *Tales from Spandau: Nazi Criminals and the Cold War*, Cambridge University Press, 2007.

Goldensohn, Leon, *The Nuremberg Interviews: Conversations with the Defendants and Witnesses*, Random House, 2010.

Gutman, Israel, and Berenbaum, Michael, *Anatomy of the Auschwitz Death Camp*, Indiana University Press, 1998.

Hilton, Laura, and Pratt, Avinoam (eds.), *Understanding and Teaching the Holocaust*, University of Wisconsin Press, 2020.

Hoess, Rudolf, *Commandant of Auschwitz: The Autobiography of Rudolf Hoess*, Pan Books Limited, 1974.

Housden, M., *Hans Frank: Lebensraum and the Holocaust*, Springer, 2003.

Hughes, Judith M., *The Holocaust and the revival of Psychological History*, Cambridge University Press, 2015.

Kay, Alex J., Review of Earl, Hilary, *The SS-Einsatzgruppen Trial*, in *Journal of Contemporary History, Volume 46, No 2*, April 2011.

Kekes, *The Roots of Evil*, Cornell University Press, 2014.

Kershaw, Ian, *Hitler, the Germans and the Final Solution*, Yale University Press, 2008.

Kitchen, Martin, *Speer: Hitler's Architect*, Yale University Press, 2015.

Klee, Ernst, Dressen, Willi, and Riess, Volker, *"The Good Old Days": The Holocaust as Seen by Its Perpetrators and Bystanders*, Free Press, 1991.

Koop, Volker, *The Commandant of Auschwitz: Rudolf Höss*, Frontline Books, 2021.

Lipstadt, Deborah E., *The Eichmann Trial*, Knopf Doubleday Publishing Group, 2011.

Longerich, Peter, *Holocaust: The Nazi Persecution and Murder of the Jews*, OUP, 2010.

McGuinness, Peggy, 'Churchill on War Crimes Trials', opinio.juris.org, 23 January 2006.

McKale, Donald M., *Nazis After Hitler: How Perpetrators of the Holocaust Cheated Justice and Truth*, Rowman & Littlefield, 2012.

Milgram, Stanley, 'Behavioral Study of Obedience', *Journal of Abnormal and Social Psychology*, 67 (4), 1963, pp. 371–78.

Overy, Richard, 'Didn't he do well?' A review of Gitta Sereny's 'Albert Speer: His Battle with Truth', in *The London Review of Books*, Vol.17., No.18, 21 September 1998.

Pendas, Devin O., *Democracy, Nazi Trials, and Transitional Justice in Germany, 1945–1950*, Cambridge University Press, 2020.

Priemel, Kim Christian, *The Betrayal: The Nuremberg Trials and German Divergence*, Oxford University Press, 2016.

Primomo, John W., *Architect of Death at Auschwitz: A Biography of Rudolf Höss*, McFarland , 2020.

Review by Christopher R. Browning of *The Nuremberg SS-Einsatzgruppen Trial, 1945–1958: Atrocity, Law, and History*, by Hilary Earl, in the *Canadian Journal of History*, Vol. 45, No. 2.

Sereny, Gitta, *Albert Speer: His Battle With Truth*, Knopf, 1995.

—, *Albert Speer: His Battle With Truth*, Pan Macmillan, 1996.

—, *Into That Darkness: From Mercy Killing to Mass Murder*, Random House, 2013.

Speer, Albert, *Inside the Third Reich*, Hachette UK, 2015.

Taylor, Frederick, *Exorcising Hitler: The Occupation and Denazification of Germany*, Bloomsbury Publishing, 2012.

Trials of War Criminals Before The Nuernberg Military Tribunals under Control Council Law No.10, Volume IV, 'The Einsatzgruppen Case', Nuernberg, October 1946–April 1949, U.S. Government Printing Office, Washington D.C.

Van Voren, Robert, *Undigested Truth: The Holocaust in Lithuania*, Rodopi, 2011.

Weinschenk, Fritz, 'Nazis Before German Courts: The West German War Crimes Trials', in *International Lawyer*, Vol.10, No.3, Summer 1976.

Winkler, Heinrich August, *Germany: The Long Road West: Volume 2: 1933–1990*, OUP, 2007.

Index